D1461621

THE
LITTLE
BOOK
OF
STILLORGAN

HUGH ORAM

The History Press Ireland

First published 2017

The History Press Ireland
50 City Quay
Dublin 2
Ireland
www.thehistorypress.ie

The History Press Ireland is a member of Publishing Ireland,
the Irish book publishers' association.

British Library Cataloguing in Publication Data.
A catalogue record for this book is available from the British Library.

ISBN 978 0 7509 8353 2

Typesetting by Geethik Technologies, origination by The History Press

Printed and bound by TJ International

Front cover image: 'The Fiddler of Dooney' statue by Imogen Stuart has
been a highlight of Stillorgan's shopping centre since it opened in 1966.
(Author's collection)

CONTENTS

ACKNOWLEDGEMENTS

I should first of all like to thank my dear wife Bernadette for all her loving support during the nearly forty years I have been writing books, as well as six true and steadfast friends, for all their encouragement during the production of this book: Aisling Curley, Dublin; Maria Gillen, Athlone; Caroline Henry, Dublin; Ellen Monnelly, Dublin, Thelma Byrne, Dublin and Mary J. Murphy, Caherlistrane, Co. Galway.

I'd also like to give special thanks to Bryan MacMahon of the Kilmacud Stillorgan Local History Society, for all his and their help. The Pembroke Library in Dublin 4, Stillorgan Library, the Dún Laoghaire–Rathdown County Library Service (Geraldine McHugh) and the National Library of Ireland, Dublin, also gave me much assistance. Hacketts of Lower Baggot Street, Dublin, gave me lots of help, very courteously and efficiently, with reprographics for the book. I much appreciate the technical assistance given by Dean Lochner of the Bondi Group, Ballsbridge, Dublin.

A significant contribution to the book comes from artist Nick Fegan who has done the line drawings. I should also like to thank Olivia Hayes for her permission to reproduce two watercolours of Stillorgan.

The following people and firms are also thanked for all their help, in alphabetical order: Baumanns, Stillorgan; Sarah Bell (The Childrens' House School); Rachel Bewley-Bateman; Éamonn de Búrca (de Búrca Rare Books); Sinead Butler (Irish League of Credit Unions); Ray Byrne (Byrne's pub, Galloping

Green); Aoife Clarke (Lidl Ireland); Ray Coary (Stillorgan Village Shopping Centre); Rev. Patrick Comerford; Julie Cox (Beaufield Mews); Communications Office, Dún Laoghaire–Rathdown County Council; Desmond Croasdell; Alan Crowley (cellar master); Gillian Daly (Licensed Vintners Association); DID Electrical; independent councillor Deirdre Donnelly; Dave Downes (Dublin Book Browsers); Jennifer Finegan (South Dublin Credit Union); Gunn's Cameras, Wexford Street, Dublin; Emer Halpenny (Emer Halpenny School of Drama); Olivia Hayes, artist; Richard Holfeld, (H.R. Holfeld Group); John Holohan (Ballsbridge, Donnybrook and Sandymount Local History Society); Isaac Jackman; Joan Kavanagh (hon. sec., Dublin Painting and Sketching Club); Ossie Kilkenny; Dominic Lee (photographer); John Lowe (the 'Money Doctor'); Kate McCallion (St John of God Hospital, Stillorgan); Peter McCann; Catherine McDonald (Anne Sullivan Centre); Philip Mulligan (Glenalbyn tennis club); Anne O' Connor; Clive O'Connor (Kilmacud Stillorgan Local History Society); Conor O' Dwyer (Stillorgan Orchard pub); Peter Pearson, Co. Wexford (*Between the Mountains and the Sea*); Karen D'Alton; Sorcha Ní Riada (RTÉ); Peadar Ó Riada; St Brigid's National School; Katherine Staunton (Nimble Fingers) and Pat Staunton.

INTRODUCTION

In the eighteenth and nineteenth centuries, Stillorgan was little more than a small, rustic village, the proud possessor of several village pumps, with one main street, which is today The Hill in Stillorgan. The oldest building is St Brigid's church (Church of Ireland), which was built over 300 years ago. Especially in the nineteenth century, many fine mansions were constructed close to the village of Stillorgan, as it became a desirable place to live for wealthier people. Many of those mansions were subsequently demolished to make way for housing estates; those that survived were taken over by various institutions. Stillorgan Castle, also known as Mount Eagle, was taken over in 1882 by St John of God and has been a hospital ever since. Such was the scale of land ownership in those far-off days that in 1870, one man living in Stillorgan, the Hon. George F. Colley, owned no less than 4,216 acres (280ha) of land around the country.

However, one remarkable early eighteenth-century construction still survives, the Obelisk, which these days is surrounded by housing estates.

Even by the late 1930s, Stillorgan's population was remarkably static, at around 2,000 residents. By the early 1960s, places on the fringes of Stillorgan, like Galloping Green, were still in open country, essentially rural in character.

The first development in Stillorgan came in 1963 when the Stillorgan Bowl was opened; it too has long gone, superseded by the Leisureplex complex. The next major change came in 1966, when Ireland's first shopping centre was opened at Stillorgan. It started a wave of shopping-centre construction across the country that only ended when the great economic collapse began in 2008. In recent years, the shopping centre in Stillorgan has got new owners, who are completing a major refurbishment and upgrade of what is now the Stillorgan Village shopping centre, harking back to the times when Stillorgan really was a delightfully rural country village.

Kilmacud Stillorgan Local History Society

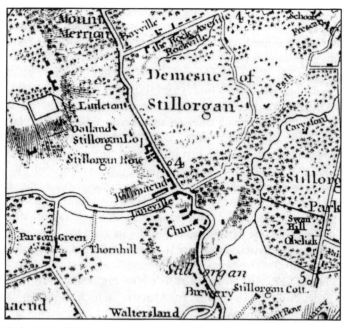

Taylor's Map 1816

Some businesses in the vicinity of the shopping centre have had remarkable longevity, such as the Beaufield Mews Restaurant, started in 1950, making it the oldest restaurant in the Dublin area. Baumanns, on the old Dublin Road, began in 1947 and for many years was primarily a hardware store, although it has since diversified into other areas of retailing. Nimble Fingers, going back to the 1960s, has a fine reputation for educational toys for children. John Lowe, known nationwide as the 'Money Doctor', has been trading as a financial adviser in Stillorgan for close on twenty years. Éamonn de Búrca has been running his rare-books business in Stillorgan for thirty years, while Dave Downes, another long-time purveyor of books, lives and works in Stillorgan.

Besides being a substantial residential suburb, present-day Stillorgan is also noted for its many first-class educational establishments. Moreover, Stillorgan has fine sporting traditions, most notably that of Kilmacud Crokes GAA Club, but also that of others clubs, such as Glenalbyn's swimming club and its tennis club. But the redevelopment of a local swimming pool is still awaited, as is construction on sites that have lain derelict for years, such as the old Blake's restaurant/Ping's restaurant location and the site of the old Esmonde Motors.

Stillorgan is also noted for its various health institutions, the most notable of which is St John of God, which has been treating people since it was first established in Stillorgan in 1882, 135 years ago.

Residents of note in the Stillorgan area have included Sir William Orpen, the distinguished society portrait painter, who is destined to get his own statue in Stillorgan; Dr T.K. Whitaker, who died in early 2017 at the age of 100, and who was responsible for planning Ireland's transition into a modern consumer society in the 1960s, and T.P. Hardiman, a former director-general of RTÉ. Jarlath Hayes, long regarded as one of Ireland's finest book designers, lived and worked in Stillorgan, while German-born Peter Jankowsky, the owner of the most distinctive voice ever to broadcast on *Sunday Miscellany*, also lived in Stillorgan for many years.

It's hardly surprising, given Stillorgan's strong historical provenance, that the Kilmacud Stillorgan Local History Society attracts such vital support. One of its achievements, for over ten years now, has been the production of *Obelisk*, its annual publication. Some industries in Stillorgan have long since vanished, such as Darley's Brewery, in which the Guinness family was closely involved, but all these bygone aspects of Stillorgan's history are lovingly documented by Stillorgan's historians.

1

TIMELINE

900 The area of Stillorgan is given the name *Tig Lorcáin*; the present name is an anglicisation

1649 Stillorgan Village has eighteen houses, with twenty-five Irish inhabitants and thirteen English

1695 The Allen family builds Stillorgan Park Castle, which is where Stillorgan House (Rehab Ireland) is today. The arrival of the Allens is considered to be the starting point of Stillorgan Village proper

1727 The Stillorgan Obelisk is built

1805 Stillorgan has much small industry, brewing as well as cloth mills and cotton mills

1810 The penny post comes to Stillorgan

1834 Stillorgan's first post office opens, with Mrs Anne Carty as postmistress

1859 The Harcourt Street to Bray railway line is opened, including the station at Stillorgan

1863 Death of Archbishop Whately

1869 Twenty-four charitable homes are built by Charles Shiels

1878 Sir William Orpen, distinguished society portrait painter, is born in Stillorgan

1882 St John of God Order moves to Mount Eagle (Stillorgan Castle)

1886 The population of Stillorgan is 1,558, of whom 562 live in the village

1901 The death of Queen Victoria is marked by a service in St Brigid's church

1902 St Brigid's church commemorates the coronation of King Edward VII

1903 Redesdale becomes St Kevin's Park

1908 A major fire destroys Stillorgan Castle, belonging to St John of God, as well as the church

1915 Major flooding in the village, including at St Brigid's

1916 The house at St Kevin's Park becomes St Kevin's Training School of Domestic Economy

1918 William Orpen, the Stillorgan-born portrait painter, is knighted

1920 Population of Stillorgan area still 1,558

1922 Michael Collins escapes an ambush at Pim's Gate, Stillorgan; five men attacked his car, firing up to thirty shots and throwing a bomb at it

1923 Canon E.H. Lewis-Crosby becomes the rector of St Brigid's

1924 The Sunshine Home is built, across the road from its present site

1927 The parish school becomes St Brigid's National School

1938 Population of Stillorgan: 2,000; Beaufield Park is completed

1945 St Kevin's is renamed St Anne's Industrial School

1946 There are 350 houses in Stillorgan

1949 Kilmacud House and its lands are sold by Col. Dwyer to the Sisters of Our Lady of Charity; eventually, St Lawrence's church is built here

1950 Beaufield Mews, the oldest restaurant in Dublin, opens in Stillorgan, which still has a population of 2,000

1951 Dale Drive is completed

1954 The Ormonde opens as a single-screen cinema; today, the Odeon is on the site. Highridge Green and St Laurence's Park are completed

1954 More heavy flooding; the main road, now the N11, is impassable

1955 Oatlands College opens

1957 There are 1,200 houses in Stillorgan

1959 Stillorgan railway station, on the Harcourt Street to Bray line, closes down

1960 Tigh Lorcáin Hall is sold to the developers of the Bowling Alley, which opens at the end of 1963
1965 Hazel Villas completed

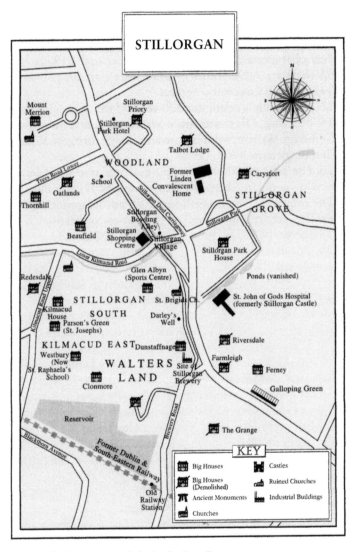

Between the Mountains and the Sea by Peter Pearson.

1966 Stillorgan shopping centre opens

1967 Stillorgan Credit Union opens

1969 By this date, virtually all the agricultural land in the Kilmacud and Stillorgan area has been used for housing development

1973 Stillorgan swimming pool is built

1979 Stillorgan dual-carriageway bypass opens; it replaces the dual carriageway built at Galloping Green in the 1950s

1982 There are 3,000 houses in Stillorgan

2004 Stillorgan Luas station opens

2012/13 St Brigid's celebrates 300 years of the church building

2016 Bowling Alley site, by now Leisureplex, is sold to Kennedy Wilson, who also owns the Stillorgan Village shopping centre

2016 The revamp of the shopping centre is started by its new owners, an American firm, Kennedy Wilson Europe. The centre is renamed Stillorgan Village shopping centre. By 2017, the revamp is well on the way to completion

2

BUILDINGS

BURTON HALL

Today commemorated by a road on the Sandyford Industrial Estate, this big house was built by Samuel Burton in about 1730. The great house had many distinguished owners, including the Guinness family. One of them, Henry Guinness, who played a prominent role in running the family's Dublin brewery, was born at Burton Hall in 1829 and continued to live there for many more years. He died in 1893, aged 64, his wife Emelina died in 1906, aged 77, and their eldest son, Henry Seymore Guinness, died in 1945, aged 86.

During the Civil War, in March 1923, republican anti-Treaty elements tried to burn down Burton Hall, fortunately without success. Then in 1939, Agnes Ryan bought the house. She and her husband Séamus, who had died young, in 1933, had started the Monument Creamery chain of shops in 1919. The first outlet was in Parnell Street and the company was named after the nearby Parnell monument on Upper O' Connell Street. Soon, their shops were well known in many parts of Dublin for their fresh food, including dairy and bakery products. Agnes herself died comparatively young, at the age of 63, in 1985.

Subsequently, Burton Hall was taken over by the St John of God Hospitaller group.

ESSO IRELAND

One of Stillorgan's old mansions, called The Grange, was demolished to make way for the new headquarters of Esso Ireland in the early 1960s. These new offices were close to where Brewery Road joins the main N11 road. The Esso company was one of the first in the country to install a computer, in 1962, as part of its new office development. Esso Ireland's headquarters stood on 5 acres (2 hectares) of land and the firm, which is now part of Topaz, lasted in Stillorgan for the best part of forty years, before vacating the premises in 2001. The whole site was sold in 2000 to developers for IR£25 million. Before long, planning permission was given for 168 two- and three-bedroom apartments, 19 houses and extensive office spaces. The apartments were to be built in nine blocks. Local residents' associations were strongly opposed to the development, but today what was once home to Esso Ireland has a vast array of apartment blocks.

FERNEY

This house, off the Stillorgan Road and close to the St John of God Hospital and Granada, has long been known as 'the deaf boys' school'. The original house was built at the end of the eighteenth century and nearly a century later, in 1880, the house was sold to John Darley, of the family that owned Darley's brewery, which once stood at the end of Brewery Road, close to the present-day dual carriageway.

The house itself is unusual, despite its small size, with cylindrical walls rising to conical roofs. John Darley died in 1935, but his wife continued to live in the house for two years, until it was sold to the Cullen family in 1937. They renamed it Beechpark. In 1956, the house was sold to the Daughters of the Cross, who opened the Mary Immaculate School for the Hearing Impaired there.

GRANADA

This fine house, part of St John of God, can be easily seen from the main N11 road. The house was built in around 1778 and, for many years subsequently, was known as Ravensdale. In the early twentieth century, it was occupied by one of the Bewley family, Mrs Harriet Bewley, who bought it in 1926 and lived there until 1948. It was then bought by William Ahern from Ballsbridge, who, six years later, sold it to the St John of God Brothers. They were keen to acquire the property, as it was so near to their own establishment.

The renovation of the house was entrusted to Brother Stanislaus Phillips, who completely changed the architectural style of the property, making it very Spanish in appearance. It was also renamed Granada, in homage to the origins of the St John of God Order in Spain in the sixteenth century. The interior of the house has exquisitely designed rooms, staircases, flooring and and stained glass and it is still in use as part of the St John of God facility.

LEISUREPLEX

This sports complex replaced the old Stillorgan Bowl and, in recent years, various plans have been put forward for its redevelopment. Back in 2005, the then owners of Leisureplex, developers Ciarán and Colum Butler, wanted to replace the bowling and games complex with 314 apartments, a library, a gym, commercial and retail space and a new Leisureplex in fifteen blocks, incorporating a fifteen-storey tower. These plans were approved by Dún Laoghaire–Rathdown County Council but rejected by An Bord Pleanála. Then, the following year, the Leisureplex site was sold for €65 million.

Leisureplex came up for sale again in 2016, having been owned by Treasury Holdings, and was bought for €15 million by Kennedy Wilson, owners of the Stillorgan Village shopping centre. At the time of writing, the Leisureplex buildings, constructed in the 1960s, are still standing. Kennedy Wilson is discussing with Dún Laoghaire–Rathdown County Council the redevelopment of the site and how it can be linked to the shopping centre across the road. It's understood that part of those plans may involve moving the Stillorgan Library from its present site in the St Laurence's Park area, adjacent to Leisureplex.

LINDEN CASTLE

This once fine mansion dated back to the earlier nineteenth century but, by the end of the 1850s, it had been unoccupied for a number of years. In 1862, Francis Kiernan, from Westmoreland Street in Dublin city centre, bought the unexpired term of the 150-year lease for £1,210. Two years later, the castle was put to good use. St Vincent's Hospital, then at St Stephen's Green, wanted to create a convalescent home for recovering patients. The Sisters of Charity, who ran the hospital, had been given a large sum of money by a benefactor for this very purpose and, in 1864, they bought Linden Castle for £2,000. In time, the facility was developed into the Linden Convalescent Home and was run as such for many years subsequently. The grounds were renowned for their linden trees.

It was at Linden that former Taoiseach and President Éamon de Valera died on 29 August 1975, aged 92. The building no longer exists; the Sisters of Charity sold the house and its 3.5ha of land in 1997 for IR£8 million. The old castle was demolished and the first apartments on the site were offered for sale in 1999.

MOUNT MERRION HOUSE

This fine stately home was built on land where the present Talbot Hotel stands on the main N11 road in Stillorgan. The original house was built in the early nineteenth century, and later that century it was improved with the addition of gabled wings and a fine portico in granite. The end result was a stately Victorian mansion with magnificent gardens. The interior of the house had gilded plasterwork, fine woodwork and stained-glass windows, as well as a private oratory and a library.

By the 1970s, close to the old house, there were a number of businesses familiar to people in the Stillorgan area, including the Texaco petrol station and garage owned by the O'Gorman family, O'Shea's chemists, a sweet shop run by the Bull family, Lennon's shoe-repairing shop and a drapery shop run by a Mrs Tew.

After Mount Merrion House was demolished in 1986, big changes came to this part of Stillorgan. A new hotel called the South County was built on part of the Mount Merrion site. Opening in 1961, the South County comprised twenty-six bedrooms. It was built by a well-known hotelier P.V. Doyle, who modelled it on his Montrose Hotel, close to Stillorgan, which has now been converted into student accommodation. In time, the South County was renamed as the Stillorgan Park Hotel. In 2015, €10 million was put into the expansion of facilities and accommodation at this hotel. Today, the hotel is known as the Talbot Hotel, one of six in the Wexford-based Talbot Hotel group.

OATLANDS HOUSE

This extensive mansion dated from the eighteenth century and stood on 5ha of land. It was a spacious Georgian house with ten rooms and its own observatory, complete with a powerful telescope. Part of the land at the back of the house formed a kitchen garden, which provided plenty of fruit and vegetables.

The house was owned by the Pollock family from 1840 until 1910, when it came into the possession of the Darley family of Stillorgan brewery fame. After the then owner, Lady Jane O'Connell, died in 1949, the fine telescope was acquired by Dunsink Observatory, but in a disastrous fire at Dunsink in 1977 it was destroyed. In May 1950, the house was acquired by the Christian Brothers, who turned it into a secondary school, which opened in September 1951. The house lasted until 1968, when it was demolished to make way for the present Oatlands College buildings.

OBELISK

In many ways, this is the symbol of Stillorgan and it's also the oldest constructed edifice in the area, together with St Brigid's church. The Obelisk was built in 1727 for Lord Allen, to help create employment in the district, and it's also thought that he had it built to commemorate his wife, Lady Allen, although she wasn't buried there. The monument, made from granite, stands over 30m tall.

The architect was Edward Lovett Pearce (1699–1733), who lived at a house in Stillorgan called The Grove. Subsequently, this became known as Tigh Lorcáin Hall, which was demolished to make way for the bowling alley. Today, Leisureplex stands on the site. Pearce, who had a promising career as an architect, died young, but not before he had designed the Obelisk, based on an obelisk in Rome that had been designed by Bernini.

Legend has it that the 2nd Viscount of Stillorgan, Joshua Allen, had his favourite horse buried beneath the Obelisk. In

time, the Allen family sold on their house and estate and after a succession of owners, the property passed to a man called Marcus Goodbody. He had become friendly with members of St John of God in Stillorgan and in 1923 he sold what had become Obelisk Park and its house to the order, for the grand sum of £4,500. The house reopened in 1924 as a residential geriatric facility and in 1931 it became a home for patients with learning difficulties. By the early 1950s, it had yet another conversion, when the house became a school providing vocational and other forms of training.

In its early days, the Obelisk overlooked open countryside, but these days, the view is of housing estates. Pearce also created a brick grotto on the estate, which today stands in the back garden of a house in Stillorgan Park Avenue.

OBELISK PARK

This large, rambling house in Stillorgan was built about 1790 for Richard Sinclair. In 1829, it was bought by two Quaker businessmen brothers, James and Henry Perry, who enlarged the house so that their respective families could each live in a half of it. The Perry brothers owned a large ironworks at Ringsend and had many other financial and property interests; they were among the first people to invest in the coal mines of the Ruhr valley in Germany.

Despite their considerable wealth, the Perrys joined other Quakers, such as the Bewley family, in giving much-needed practical help and assistance to those in need during the great mid-nineteenth-century famine.

In the 1890s, the house had come to be owned by Marcus Goodbody, also a Quaker and an in-law of the Perrys. He built an attractive gate lodge in 1896. The Goodbodys lived at Obelisk Park until 1923, when the house was sold to the Brothers of the Order of St John of God. In the 1990s, by which time most of the land surrounding the house had been built upon, the house itself was sold and converted into apartments.

PARK HOUSE

One of the smaller stately homes in the Stillorgan area, Stillorgan Park House was built with stones from the most elegant house ever built in the area, Stillorgan House. Stillorgan Park House was erected in 1695 by the Allen family, who were lords of Stillorgan in the seventeenth century, but whose male line died out in 1745. The Allens had many festive gatherings in the house, where beauty, wit and fashion were to the fore. One of the guests of the Allens was Dean Swift, Dean of St Patrick's Cathedral.

The two-storey house was over a basement and it also had an attic floor, as well as two connecting wings on the north side while, on the south side, the facade was made up of twenty-one windows. The house was always noted for its gardens, which in the early days of the house were in the Dutch style, very square, with lots of clipped hedges and topiary work. The garden was also renowned for its three fish ponds, its walkways and its carriageways. The gardens and conservatories were famous for their rare plants and flowers.

Arthur Lee Guinness, of brewing family fame, was the last occupant in Stillorgan House, which he bought in 1839 and abandoned in 1860. When he owned the house, the fantastic interior décor included embroidered silks, ivories, carved teak and bronze artefacts.

Guinness had a blind harper, who had flowing white hair and a beard and played his harp every afternoon; it's said that Arthur Lee Guinness and his fondness for the harp led the Guinness firm to use the harp in its logo.

Arthur Lee Guinness never married, so a cousin, Eliza O'Grady, lived at the house and acted as hostess at the many parties there, whose guest lists were mostly aristocratic.

Soon afterwards, the contents were sold off. The house itself soon fell intro disrepair and then into ruin, before being demolished, not much more than twenty years after Arthur Lee Guinness had left. Park House was then built on the site in the late 1880s by one of the Carysfort family. In the early years of the twentieth century, part of the grounds became a short-lived golf course.

In time, Park House was bought in 1948 by the Hendrons, a family who had a flourishing hardware and machinery business in Dublin. Thomas Hendron, who was a great horse lover, had a magnificent gateway created in his foundry. The design was made entirely from horseshoes, stirrups and riding crops and it was erected as the gateway leading to Park House from the grove side. Beside it was a smaller horseshoe gate leading into the garden.

The Hendrons stayed at Park House until 1961 and they subsequently let part of the house for a short period to an up-and-coming Dublin businessman, Dermot Ryan, well known in the taxi business. In 1963, the house, with its classic windows and well-spaced rooms, was sold to the trustees of the Polio Fellowship of Ireland. In 1986, this organisation merged with Rehab, but Park House continued to be a place of rehabilitation for people with disabilities.

REDESDALE HOUSE

This stately house was built in the early eighteenth century and over a century later, in the mid-nineteenth century, it was known as one of four principal houses in the Stillorgan area. But like so many big houses in the area, it was taken over by a religious group and put to use for social purposes. In 1903, a Catholic organisation made it into a place of rest for Catholic working women. Many of them were worn out working long hours in workrooms, shops and offices. The name of the house was changed to St Kevin's.

In 1916, the house became St Kevin's Training School of Domestic Economy, then in 1945, after much refurbishment, it was reopened in a completely different guise, run by the Sisters of Our Lady of Charity. It was known as St Anne's Industrial School, and subsequently as 'Girlsville', designed to cater for homeless and 'recalcitrant' young women. The old house remained in use until 1975, when a new 'Girlsville' was built nearby. Finally, in 1976, the St Michael's House group bought the old house as a day-care centre for mentally and physically disabled children.

SHEILS' HOUSES

A total of twenty-four houses were built in 1869 at the top of Brewery Road, close to Leopardstown Racecourse and Leopardstown Hospital. They were erected by a rich merchant from Killough, Co. Down: Charles Sheils, who was widowed early in his marriage and never remarried. He had no family, so after his wife's death, he concentrated on his philanthropic works, building rent-free accommodation for elderly residents. Sheils' houses were built at four locations in Northern Ireland; those in Stillorgan were the only ones in this part of Ireland.

They were constructed around a courtyard and the development had a Gothic clock tower, as well as a giant Sequoia tree at the entrance. In 1986, the site was sold to developers, who refurbished the twenty-four houses to modern standards, as well as building adjacent apartments in what is now Arkle Square.

ST HELEN'S

This magnificent house, just off the main N11 road, dates back to 1750, when it was built as a red-brick mansion by Thomas Cooley, a barrister and a member of parliament for Duleek, Co. Meath. At first, the house was called Seamount, but it was subsequently renamed St Helen's. During the latter part of the nineteenth century, it was occupied by the Right Hon. Hugh Gough, who came from Co. Limerick and who had a distinguished career in the British Army. He and his wife Frances, Lady Gough, had a long marriage, fifty-six years. Lady Gough died in 1863 and her husband died in 1869, aged 90. He died at St Helen's, which had been the family home for many years.

After his death, a statue in his honour was erected in the Phoenix Park in 1890. In 1944, it was defaced by vandals and what remained was blown up in 1957.

As for St Helen's, after the death of Gough, it was occupied by his son, until 1895. In 1899, the property was acquired by Sir John Nutting, a prominent director of the Great Southern

Railway. He carried out extensive refurbishments to the house, making it highly ornamented. From the mid-1920s until 1988, the great house was owned by the Christian Brothers. But in 1988, the 29ha site was sold to a property developer. A preservation order was placed on the house, but in the adjacent parkland, new apartment blocks were built. The house itself became one of Dublin's most luxurious hotels, run by the Radisson Blu group.

STILLORGAN CASTLE

Stillorgan Castle, now the site of the St John of God Hospital, has origins going back further than any other stately home in the area. It is said that the castle was built on the site of Wolverston House, the original home of the Anglo-Norman knight Desmond Carew, who in the twelfth century owned the whole of the Stillorgan area. After Carew, the once-fortified manor house passed through many hands, including those of the Hackets and the Cruises and, finally, the Wolverstons. The great house, Stillorgan Castle, also known as Mount Eagle, was built in the mid-eighteenth century and its rooms were the scenes of many aristocratic social occasions.

Then, in 1882, the St John of God Order, already established in Dublin, paid £4,000 for the castle and converted it into their hospital, which it is to this day. The hospital in the old castle was soon expanded to cater for a

rapidly growing demand, but in 1908 fire swept through the building and destroyed what had been the old Stillorgan Castle. Within three years, a brand-new hospital was built on the site, and in March 1913 the foundation stone for the new chapel was laid. However, new buildings weren't to be added for another sixty years.

STILLORGAN CONVALESCENT HOME

This fine mid-Victorian building, at the top of Brewery Road, is close to the Sheils' houses, but differs from them in that it is built of red brick. It was never a home as such, since it was meant as a convalescent institution for poor, deprived people from Dublin. In 1864, a parcel of land, about 3ha in all, was leased to a group of wealthy benefactors so that they could build this convalescent home. It was created so that poor people, when discharged from hospital, didn't have to return to their hovels and tenements. It served this purpose for many years, until 1964, when it was taken over by the Catholic Institute for the Deaf, who changed its name to St Joseph's House for Adult Deaf and Deaf Blind.

STILLORGAN'S OLD NIGHT CLUB

In 2008, Treasury Holdings, which then owned what had been the Bondi Beach night club, made a major reduction in the rent on the property. The rent was reduced from €350,000 a year to €180,000 a year for a lease of at least three years and the hope was that the building could be used as a showroom development for a bulk-goods business, which never happened. The property shared a large car-park space with Pappa Gallas restaurant, which had closed by 2008, and Ping's restaurant, which was still in operation in 2008.

At that stage, Treasury Holdings had received planning permission for the whole complex, but redevelopment has not yet come to pass.

Author   Cram Hugh 1943-author
Title   The little book of Stillorgan / Hugh
Item barcode   DCPL0001012664

Surname   First name   Until

O'Brien   M   Mon 13 Sep

Patron barcode   010878484
Notice type   Email
Email   no
Hold note

STILLORGAN RESERVOIR

Although not a building in the strict sense of the word, Stillorgan reservoir is undoubtedly the largest construction in the area.

The Vartry water scheme was started in 1862 with the creation of a reservoir at Roundwood in Co. Wicklow; the idea behind the scheme was to supply the fast-growing city of Dublin with adequate water supplies. A 84cm cast-iron main brought the water from Roundwood to the new reservoir at Stillorgan, a distance of 28km. From Stillorgan, two 68cm-diameter mains were laid to bring the water to the city mains, just over 7km away. The new reservoir was built on lands belonging to an eighteenth-century house called Rockland, later known as Clonmore.

Since the 1950s, it has also been taking water from the treatment plant at Ballymore Eustace, Co. Kildare. Today, the Stillorgan reservoir still supplies 15 per cent of Dublin's drinking water.

The reservoir nearly played a part in the 1916 Easter Rising. Along with the Howth gun running in 1914, a large shipment of arms and ammunition from Germany was landed

at Kilcoole beach in north Co. Wicklow. The plan was to transport them from Kilcoole to Stillorgan reservoir by charabanc, but at the last minute it had to be called off because armed guards had been posted to the reservoir. Instead, the shipment was transferred to Pádraig Pearse's school, St Enda's, at Rathfarnham.

In recent times, there have been three reservoirs at Stillorgan, nicknamed the 'ponds' by the people who work there. At the end of 2016, Irish Water applied for planning permission to build a giant new reservoir at Stillorgan, at a cost of €80 million. This new reservoir will be covered, whereas the three that it will replace are all open. Once the new reservoir is built, the two smaller, older reservoirs will be closed down.

STILLORGAN SHOPPING CENTRE

This was the first shopping centre to be built in Ireland; it was the idea of Kennedy Kisch, an English property developer who had long lived in Ireland with his family at a fine mansion in Newtownmountkennedy, Co. Wicklow. It's said that the idea of the shopping centre had been put forward in 1962 by David Philips, who developed the Ballyfree egg company in Co. Wicklow. The shopping centre, on a 3.5ha site, was developed by a British company, Metropolitan Estates and Property Corporation, and was designed by a local architect called John Costello of Costello Murray Beaumont.

To clear the land for the centre, Moores Cottages, one- and two-storey dwellings which fronted the old Dublin Road in Stillorgan, were demolished. The cottages extended from close to Oatlands right round to the Lower Kilmacud Road. One of the buildings demolished to make way for the centre was St Laurence's Hall, opposite the present-day St Laurence's Park. The rubble from the demolition was used to create the sports ground now occupied by the Glenalbyn GAA Club.

Many of the old people who had lived in the cottages for years were disgruntled at being evicted to make way for the shopping centre. They found themselves living in newly erected accommodation, such as Patrician Villas and Patrician Grove, on the other side of the main road. The facilities were much better, but the new residences lacked the neighbourly atmosphere of the old cottages. It had taken three days to demolish all the cottages, along Lower Kilmacud Road and the Old Dublin Road, and it was said that not a vestige of them was left. Some of the longest-established residents wept to see the sudden disappearance of their community, which hadn't looked affluent, but which had grown naturally and had a native character.

The centre was designed along simple lines, with a small central square, and it also featured Imogen Stuart's sculpture, *The Fiddler of Dooney*, which still has pride of place. Imogen Stuart, one of Ireland's most renowned sculptors, was born in Berlin in 1927.

One of Ireland's best-known building contractors, Cramptons, built the centre. In a major technical advance, computers were used for programming the structural portion of the contract. But work on the new centre was badly delayed by wet weather, which lasted from November 1965 until April 1966. The 400 men employed on the site then worked at top speed to get the centre finished for its opening that summer.

The centre was described as setting the style for the future of shopping in Ireland, with plenty of car-parking space and covered pedestrian malls. Other features included a free nursery for children. The centre had four supermarkets, only one of which, Quinnsworth, is still trading, as Tesco. Other shops included fashion boutiques, men's wear shops, and that now-rare phenomenon, a travel agency. Within the past two years, the shopping centre has been transformed by its new owners, Kennedy Wilson Europe, who were doing a complete makeover, although the basic layout remains the same.

Planning permission to upgrade the shopping centre had been given by An Bord Pleanála back in 2007. The approved plan allowed for two-thirds of the existing sixty-two shops to be retained, with the overall number of shop units being brought up to seventy-nine and the addition of new facilities such as a crèche, a gym and a rooftop restaurant.

The shopping centre was then owned by Real Estate Opportunities, in which Treasury Holdings held the majority stake. Treasury Holdings planned to invest €40 million in the centre, but the expansion plans never materialised. After planning permission was given for this, many local residents objected strongly to the plans.

Strong competition came from the Dundrum Town Centre, whose opening in 2005 had a drastic effect on the Stillorgan Centre. Then in 2008 came Ireland's great economic crash.

The lowest point of the Stillorgan Centre's fortunes came in 2009, when twenty shops closed. Many of the retailers who remained got into severe difficulties and the rents received from retailers fell by 20 per cent. But by 2013, the centre had just two vacant shops.

In 2013, the Stillorgan shopping centre was bought by a London-listed property firm, Kennedy Wilson Europe, whose headquarters are in Los Angeles. Soon afterwards, the company's chief executive, Mary Ricks, said that the firm was planning a major refurbishment. She said at the time, 'Although it's a great centre, and is 100 per cent occupied, it needs a lot of tender, loving care, as there has been very little capital expenditure in recent years'.

The amount spent on buying the centre wasn't disclosed, but Kennedy Wilson paid €306 million for the so-called Opera portfolio of sixteen developments, including the Stillorgan shopping centre, which averaged out at €19 million per development. The Opera portfolio had belonged to Treasury Holdings, the previous owners of the shopping centre, and this deal was struck by Kennedy Wilson with the National Asset Management Agency (NAMA). Altogether, Kennedy Wilson now has €1.2 billion in Irish assets.

The firm said then that they planned to spend €15 million on refurbishing the centre to make it the best neighbourhood centre in Ireland. They said that the low canopies were to become a thing of the past and that a big canopy was going to be put over the centre, to weatherproof it. The facade, too, was going to be changed.

That major upgrade has now been largely completed and the basic layout remains the same, although significant extra space is being added to the Tesco supermarket, in 2017. This is on the Lower Kilmacud Road side of the centre, which has now been rebranded as the Stillorgan Village Centre.

STILLORGAN'S STATELY HOMES IN 1837

Samuel Lewis's Topographical Directory of Ireland in 1837 stated that Stillorgan Village had 650 inhabitants. The parish itself consisted of 648 statute acres, of which 75 per cent were meadows and pastures, with most of the rest accounted for by gardens. Lewis said that the district had numerous handsome seats and pleasing villas commanding fine sea views over Dublin Bay and vistas of the Dublin Mountains.

Among the great houses named were Stillorgan House, formerly the property of the Allen family, and Stillorgan Abbey, built in 1833 in the Elizabethan style, near the site of the old abbey. Mount Eagle (Stillorgan Castle) was listed, together with Obelisk Park, Beaufield and Oatlands. Talbot Lodge, owned by Captain Newenham, was also mentioned. Altogether, Samuel Lewis listed Stillorgan as having a grand total of twenty-two fine mansions.

TALBOT LODGE

Close to Linden and built at around the same time, in the early nineteenth century, was Talbot Lodge, which also stood alongside the grove of lime trees at Linden. Talbot Lodge was eventually acquired by the Sisters of Charity and became part of the Linden convalescent home. The house itself was enlarged in late Victorian times, which altered its original form. Sadly, the fine house came to a tragic end, like so many others of its kind in Stillorgan. In 1989, the nuns sold Talbot Lodge to a property developer, who promptly demolished it and redeveloped the 1.6ha site with houses.

TIGH LORCÁIN HALL

This old mansion existed for many years where the present-day Leisureplex is situated. It had previously been called The Grove. In the early twentieth century, Tigh Lorcáin Hall was a substantial building, complete with upper and lower yard, a hen run, tennis courts and a large garden where an abundance of fruit and vegetables grew. In 1928, the house was bought for £2,400 and turned into a 12ha dairy farm that supplied milk to the growing suburbs of Blackrock and Mount Merrion.

The house itself was renovated in 1938. A decade later, in 1948, building started on the Priory lands to the north of Tigh Lorcáin Hall, one of the first indications that great changes were afoot, transforming Stillorgan from a semi-rural village to a built-up suburban area. After 1950, when Dublin County Council widened the main road to bypass Stillorgan Village, the new road split the farm in two and part of it was then used to build council housing. In 1952, the farm was sold to the county council for £5,500 and the dairy farm was closed down. Eventually, the house was demolished to make way for the bowling alley. Today all that remains of Tigh Lorcáin Hall and the farm is part of the garden wall, smothered in ivy, and a group of pine trees at the junction with the N11.

3

CHURCHES AND RELIGIOUS PLACES

CARMELITE SISTERS

A new development in the parish life of the Stillorgan area came in 1881, when the Carmelite Sisters bought Kilmacud Manor on the Upper Kilmacud Road, and converted it into the Monastery of St Joseph.

KILMACUD PARISH

In 1948, the chapels of ease at Kilmacud and Mount Merrion were amalgamated into a single parish and in 1964 Kilmacud became a parish in its own right, with Canon Harley as the parish priest. By this stage, the chapel in Kilmacud was becoming much too small for the parish, so the Sisters of Our Lady of Charity donated a site, on which the church of St Laurence O' Toole was built. It was opened on 14 December

1969, by the then Archbishop of Dublin, Most Rev. John Charles McQuaid. The church had been designed by a renowned Dublin architectural practice, Stephenson Gibney.

Canon Harley died in 1981 and Monsignor Val Rogers was appointed parish priest the same year, a position he held with great distinction until he retired, aged 75, in 1995. He was succeeded by Fr Michael Loftus, who died in 2007. Fr Liam Lacey was appointed parish priest that same year and Fr Tony Coote became administrator of Kilmacud in 2010.

While the original church was designed for a congregation of 1,500, in recent years numbers attending have shrunk significantly, thus GKMP Architects were commissioned to make the church more intimate and functional for a much smaller congregation. Despite the many changes to the interior, the facade of the church remained untouched. This project was completed in December 2015.

ST BRIGID'S

St Brigid's Church of Ireland is by far the oldest building in present-day Stillorgan, dating back just over 300 years.

But the history of Stillorgan having a church goes back far earlier than that. Karen D'Alton, who has done a lot of research on the history of Stillorgan, says, on the website of St Brigid's parish, that the name of Stillorgan comes from *Tig Lorcáin*, or the House of Lorcan, and dates from about AD 900. Long before that, however, the first name for Stillorgan was '*Acrankill*' or '*Atnakill*', meaning 'the place of the church'.

Missionaries also played their part. St Brigid had founded her monastery in Co. Kildare in the fifth or sixth century and it became one of the 'big three' monasteries, joining Armagh and Iona in Scotland. St Brigid also gave her name to the Stillorgan church.

These missionaries came from Co. Kildare to Stillorgan, probably in the ninth century, and founded a monastery where St Brigid's church now stands. The monastery was surrounded by a wall or ditch; it had a small wooden church with a thatched roof, cells for the monks, a refectory and a school. In those far-off days, the area embraced by Stillorgan was far wider than it is today, going as far as present-day Blackrock and Seapoint and taking in Mount Merrion, too.

In 1181, the lands of Stillorgan and Dundrum were granted to Christchurch Cathedral as part of the Manor of Kill o' the Grange. The convent at Kilmacud was held by a convent at Graney, Co. Kildare, from about 1200 until the dissolution of the monasteries in the sixteenth-century Reformation. But in 1216, Raymond Carew of Stillorgan granted St Brigid's church to Christ Church Cathedral in Dublin. St Brigid's in Stillorgan was attached to the church at Kill o' the Grange until the Reformation, although, by 1500, it was in ruins. In the seventeenth century, St Brigid's was rebuilt; in 1660, it was described as a 'church surrounded by trees'. The parish of Stillorgan and Kilmacud was united with that of Monkstown.

Stillorgan began to develop as a village after Captain John Allen (1660–1726), later the 1st Viscount Allen, built Stillorgan House, in 1695, complete with demesne and deer park. In all probability, Stillorgan House and its surrounding lands stood on the site of the present-day Stillorgan House, occupied by Rehab Ireland.

Allen held high positions, including that of high sheriff of Dublin and MP for Co. Dublin, but he was also assiduously involved in the rebuilding of St Brigid's church between 1706 and 1712. However, that church was comparatively short-lived; by 1760, it was in such a bad state of repair that it needed to be rebuilt. In 1762, Stillorgan became a separate parish and the Dean and Chapter of Christ Church Cathedral transferred the tithes to the incumbent rector.

In 1812, the church underwent extensive restoration and the north aisle and the tower were added. Further progress came when two schoolrooms, a schoolhouse and a residence for a schoolmaster and a schoolmistress were built in 1820.

The mid-nineteenth century saw the end of the Allen family's involvement with Stillorgan; the last of their land was sold off in 1851 and Stillorgan House, which had been their home, was demolished in the 1880s.

After the notorious Archbishop Whately died in 1863, a memorial window was erected at St Brigid's. In 1874, plans were announced to remove the tower, the galleries and the vestibule in St Brigid's, but they came to nothing. The rectory at St Brigid's was built in 1881.

One of the most famous rectors of St Brigid's was Canon Ernest Lewis-Crosby (1864–1961), the last chaplain to a lord lieutenant of Ireland. He became the rector of St Brigid's in 1923 and remained in the parish for fifteen years, until 1938, when he was appointed Dean of Christ Church Cathedral, a position he held until his death. He was renowned as a scholar and historian and one of the books he produced in the 1930s was *A Short History of Stillorgan*.

Much more recently, in 1978, All Saints in Blackrock was united with St Brigid's; the present rector is Rev. Ian Gallagher, who was appointed in 2001. A new parish centre beside St Brigid's was opened in 1994. The graveyard of the church is particularly interesting; since the church predates the disestablishment of the Church of Ireland in 1869, it was open for burial for all who lived in the parish of Stillorgan, regardless of their denomination.

The entrance to St Brigid's church. (Olivia Hayes)

SISTERS OF OUR LADY OF CHARITY

This order still has a convent in the Stillorgan area, St Ann's in Kilmacud. The order was once very involved in the running of convent laundries and industrial schools.

SOUTH CITY CHURCH

One of the newer religious places in the Stillorgan area, it's based at the Glenalbyn Sports Club and Conference Centre and is a Bible-based church of believers, with a strong emphasis on Bible preaching and teaching. It also has a Sunday school. Many people who have attended services there have spoken highly on Facebook of the new church.

STILLORGAN GROTTO

This small but well-kept grotto was opened on the opposite side of the Old Dublin Road to the Stillorgan Village shopping centre, in 1986. It's at the entrance to St Laurence's Park, is railed in and has a very simple inscription: 'Erected by the people of Stillorgan, 1986'.

TWELVE APOSTLES' WELL

This famous well has existed for hundreds of years and in 1930, *The Irish Times* described it as being in the Belfield estate of Captain F.C. Bernard at Stillorgan; three years later, he sold the estate to University College Dublin, for a new campus, although building work didn't begin until the 1960s.

Around the well stood twelve tall trees and it was these trees that gave rise to its name, the Twelve Apostles. The waters in the well were renowned for their curative properties and pilgrims came from all over Ireland to the Belfield estate to imbibe the waters. The well was never known to run dry. But with the development of Belfield by UCD and the creation of the dual carriageway on the N11, the well was buried under the new road. It lies far beneath the central reservation on the dual carriageway, opposite the new student accommodation built on the site of the old Montrose Hotel.

4

CRIME AND MAYHEM

1928

On 19 August 1928, one of the worst traffic accidents in the history of the area happened right in the centre of Stillorgan Village. It involved a car driven by a young Oxford University student, James McCann, which had one passenger, Mary Philomena Smith, a nurse working for the McCann family. The car was returning from the house the McCanns, from Donnybrook, had rented for the summer in Ballybrack; James was taking Mary Philomena back to her home in Harold's Cross.

When the car arrived in Stillorgan, the driver was unsure which direction to take and he suddenly lost control of the vehicle, which crashed into the wall of Tigh Lorcáin Hall (where Leisureplex is now located). The two people in the car were killed instantly, while a 33-year-old Garda, William Nolan, who lived nearby with his wife, at Grove View, was critically injured. The first person to arrive at the scene of the accident was Garda Nolan's pregnant wife. Garda Nolan died later from his injuries. Born at Coolcullen, Co. Kilkenny, in 1895, he had joined the DMP in 1916 and became a Garda when the Gardaí were merged with the DMP in 1925. He was one of five brothers in the force.

1940S

In the 1940s, farmer militancy was as commonplace as it was in a later decade, the 1960s. The group responsible for much of the farmers' militancy in the 1940s was the Irish Farmers' Federation, formed in 1937, which had close connections with Stillorgan, then a remote and largely rural village with lots of farms. When what became the Irish Farmers' Association was formed in 1955, one of the groups it absorbed was the Irish Farmers' Federation, thus ending the farming community's organisational links with Stillorgan. The disconnect between Stillorgan and rural Ireland has continued over the past fifty years, as the many farms in the area have long since been turned into housing estates.

1976

On 21 July 1976, as the then newly arrived British ambassador, Christopher Ewart-Biggs, was driving out of his official residence, Glencairn, a culvert bomb planted by the Provisional IRA exploded. The new ambassador had arrived in Dublin just two weeks previously. On the day of the explosion, the driver of his official car left Glencairn, which is 3km from the centre of Stillorgan, and, inexplicably, turned right instead of left. He had only driven about 300m down Murphystown Road, which was then little more than a country lane, when the bomb went off, killing the ambassador and a 26-year-old civil servant called Judith Cooke. The ambassador had been on his way to Iveagh House to meet, for the first time, the then minister for foreign affairs, Dr Garret FitzGerald.

Today, Murphystown Road, the scene of the assassination, is a busy suburban thoroughfare close to the Luas line.

1981

On 30 December 1981, a major bank raid was staged at the Stillorgan shopping centre. A gang smashed the front windows of the Bank of Ireland branch to gain entry, and then held up staff at gunpoint. The raiders stole about £105,000 in cash. An off-duty Garda who was in the vicinity gave chase. The robbers got as far as Carrickmines, where they fired 200 shots at a garda car, badly injuring the two detectives inside. Then the gang managed to flee to the Dublin Mountains, where they were eventually surrounded by Gardaí. Only one of the Gardaí was actually armed, but others cupped their hands to make it look as if they had guns, and by means of this ruse, the robbers were persuaded to surrender.

2002

In April 2002, two Gardaí were killed in a collision with a stolen car in Stillorgan. The two Gardaí were Anthony Tighe (53), married with four children, and Michael Padden (27). Both were stationed at Donnybrook Garda Station. Their patrol car was in the middle of turning at the junction of the N11 and Foster's Avenue when it was struck at high speed by a stolen Mazda.

2011

In January 2011, a fire started in an empty retail unit which had previously been occupied by Chartbusters, on the Lower Kilmacud Road. The fire spread quickly to an adjoining Indian restaurant and a dry cleaners as well as to the Mill House pub. All the buildings involved, as well as a number of nearby apartments, were evacuated as a precaution, but no injuries were reported.

2014

In April 2014, posters on trees and lamp posts in the Stillorgan area urged residents to clobber burglars with hurleys and golf clubs, in response to the wave of petty crime in the district, which particularly targeted elderly people. The posters urged people to hit the 'sewer-crawling rats' of the district, saying it was time they were exterminated.

2015

In September 2015, a massive fire broke out at the derelict complex of the long-closed Ping's restaurant. At one time this complex housed Blake's restaurant. Although the fire was extensive, it was eventually extinguished.

2016

In October 2016, a teenage girl was held up at gunpoint in Markethill, Co. Armagh, and forced to hand over the keys to her car. The car was subsequently recovered by Gardaí in Stillorgan and two teenagers were arrested.

5

MODERN HOUSES

HOUSING ESTATES

The first housing estate to be built in Stillorgan was Beaufield Park, whose sixty houses were completed in 1938. The two-up, two-down council cottages for labourers and their families had open fires, in the bedrooms as well, big range cookers in the kitchens, gas lighting and, a real novelty for the time, indoor toilets and running water.

These modest dwellings cost 5/4*d* a week to rent and 2/9*d* a week to purchase over twenty-five years. Nearly eighty years later, Beaufield Park has close on eighty houses, but many once well-known landmarks, such as Jolly's Lane and Moore's Lane, no longer exist.

After the Second World War, or the Emergency, as it was known in Ireland, the next estate to be completed was Dale Drive. At that stage, Stillorgan had a little over 300 houses. Merville was developed in the 1950s, while that decade also saw Highridge Green and St Laurence's Park completed in 1954. The Lakelands estate was finished in the 1960s, while 1965 saw Hazel Villas completed.

INFILL DEVELOPMENTS

In addition to the large-scale housing developments that have been built in Stillorgan over the past fifty years, some smaller infill developments have also been carried out, such as that in 2015 at Aberdour on the Stillorgan Road. The site extends to 0.64ha, where the former Aberdour House was located. In the 1950s, Aberdour was owned by David Vard of the well-known furrier-shop-owning family, the Vards. Although in 2015 the Aberdour site was listed as an unfinished development, in October of that year the incomplete house was sold for €2.7 million.

LAKELANDS

This is a tree-lined estate of large semi-detached houses, close to St Benildus School. By the end of the 1990s, prices had risen significantly, with one of the houses there being sold in 1999 for IR£260,000. Just across the road from Lakelands is a smaller estate of three-bedroomed semi-detached houses, Marsham Court.

LINDEN APARTMENTS

One of the first modern developments in Stillorgan was on the site of the old Linden convalescent home, located on 3.5ha of land at Grove Avenue. The house and site were sold by the Sisters of Charity in 1997 for IR£8 million, to a property developer. Two years later, in 1999, the first phase of the major new development came to market – fifty-three luxurious apartments. The prices quoted ranged from IR£270,000 for a two-bedroom apartment to IR£485,000 for a penthouse. The apartments were the first housing development in Dublin to have invisible heating, since the electric heating units were placed beneath the floors and in the ceilings.

MERVILLE ESTATE

This estate, close to St Brigid's church, was once a large farm that covered over 80ha. In the mid-twentieth century, this was a substantial dairy farm run by the Jolly family. The farm was sold to developers and the Merville estate built there in the 1950s.

OLD STILLORGAN RAILWAY STATION

After the old Harcourt Street to Bray railway line was closed down at the end of 1959, the station at Stillorgan, standing at the top of Brewery Road, was converted into a private house, now known as Leopardstown Station House. Architectural features of the old station still survive, such as the window surrounds and the wooden roof edgings. These days, the house faces the Luas depot at Sandyford.

OLD STILLORGAN ROAD

Houses off the old Stillorgan Road, near the Glenalbyn sports centre, still rarely come on the market. On the far side of the dual carriageway, prices are normally higher. Close by here, the Orpen estate, named after Stillorgan's most famous painter, has an open green and a tennis court.

PATRICIAN VILLAS AND PATRICIAN GROVE

These two roads are on the far side of the N11 from Stillorgan Village and were built in the mid-1960s, at the same time when the shopping centre was being constructed. Beyond the Stillorgan telephone exchange, a turn left from the main road, into Stillorgan Park, leads immediately to Patrician Villas and Patrician Grove.

After the row of cottages along the Old Dublin Road was demolished to make way for the new shopping centre, many people who had lived in the cottages transferred to the new houses in these two roads, houses which had much better facilities.

These days, Patrician Villas is known as such by all and sundry and the latest edition of the Ordnance Survey map of Dublin shows 'Patrician Villas'.

Back in 2008, a big name change came to nothing. The name of the road was changed to Patrician Park by Dún Laoghaire–Rathdown County Council, but the residents were told nothing of this and, when they contacted the local authority, no one there knew anything about the change. In 2007, the residents had voted for the name change, but the required quota for it to happen hadn't been reached. The name change was short-lived. So today, after all the fuss, Patrician Villas is still Patrician Villas!

In recent years, the houses in Patrician Villas and Patrician Grove have been considerably improved and there's the added bonus of the underpass beneath the N11 leading directly to Stillorgan Village.

THE PRESENT-DAY COST OF HOUSING

The cost of housing in Stillorgan has rocketed since the 1990s and, today, the average price of a house in Stillorgan is put at close to €0.5 million. In 2015, a three-bedroom semi-detached house at Marsham Court cost €415,000, while a one-bedroom apartment at Thornwood was €225,000. A new two-bedroom apartment at the Whately Place development on the Upper Kilmacud Road cost over €300,000. That same year, 2015, the cheapest house on offer in Stillorgan was a two-bedroom end-of-terrace house at Patrician Villas for a mere €325,000.

REDESDALE GARDEN ESTATE

In 1967, questions were asked in the Dáil about the condition of Dale Park in Stillorgan, otherwise known as Redesdale Garden estate. It was stated by the minister in charge of local government, Kevin Boland, that the houses in the estate had been taken in charge, earlier in the 1960s, by what was then Dublin County Council, but that some of the laneways on the estate had not been taken over by the county council, leading to problems of littering and dumping.

NORMA SMURFIT'S HOUSE

Norma Smurfit, once married to packaging tycoon Michael Smurfit, lived for a time in Stillorgan, at Tyne Villa, on the Old Dublin Road, close to Oatlands College. In 2002, she paid €2,275,000 for a five-bedroom detached house at St Thomas Road in nearby Mount Merrion, but, at the time, sources close to the Smurfit family said she was unlikely to sell Tyne Villa, a bungalow in extensive grounds with a separate residence for a security guard. In 2005, she was still listed as owning Tyne Villa. The large house, complete with swimming pool, a very large fridge and plush carpets, had been built in the late 1950s for Michael Smurfit's father, Jefferson Smurfit. At the time it was constructed, the arrival of such a lavish and palatial new house in Stillorgan caused great excitement in the area.

REDESDALE

In 1998, Redesdale House, a late-eighteenth-century house, once used by St Anne's Industrial School, was demolished, and smart new townhouses were built on the site. When the new estate was being marketed, in 1999, the price of the smallest units, two-bedroom houses, was IR£320,000.

STILLORGAN GATE

One of the most recent developments in the area, these apartments and duplexes came to market in 2016. All apartments and duplexes have independent entranceways and south-facing gardens, while the facades of the complex are faced in red brick. The two- and three-bedroom apartments and the largest terraced houses, with four bedrooms, were priced at €400,000 to €795,000.

STILLORGAN RENTS

Data released by the Residential Tenancies Board in April 2017 shows that Stillorgan is the dearest place in the country to rent a house or an apartment. The average monthly rent of such a property was put at €2,062.

ST LAURENCE'S PARK

Over the past two years, much concern has been voiced over the sixteen social-housing units at St Laurence's Park, close to Stillorgan Library, which are boarded up. The local authority, Dún Laoghaire–Rathdown County Council, has been considering developing a new swimming pool, to replace the closed facility at Glenalbyn, and has two sites in mind, one of them at St Laurence's Park. One local councillor, independent councillor Deirdre Donnelly, has condemned the state of the houses and has said that the council should revamp them and use them to house some of the homeless families living in the area.

THE GRANGE

Just facing the main N11, the apartments here came to market in 2005; then, one-bedroom apartments started at €435,000, while two-bedroom apartments were priced at €575,000. The name of the development, The Grange, comes from the grand old house that stood here before it was demolished to make way for the headquarters of Esso Ireland. Those premises were also subsequently demolished to make way for the apartments, which were marketed as the last word in luxury living. Many of the people who had bought there had a nasty shock in 2008 when the developers, Glenkerrin Homes, agreed to sell seventy-five apartments to Dún Laoghaire–Rathdown County Council, so that they could accommodate people on the social-housing list.

WESBURY ESTATE

This small upmarket estate, with its cul-de-sacs, is off the Upper Kilmacud Road. The houses were built on part of the grounds of the Carmelite Monastery, which had been sold off in the 1970s.

WOODLEY PARK ESTATE

This estate, close to the top end of the Lower Kilmacud Road, in the Dundrum direction, was built on the old Woodley estate, which had been sold off in the 1960s to property developers by relatives of the MacNeill family, owners of the estate. The old house here had been designed in the Georgian style and was complemented by a large farm and a walled garden.

6

HEALTH

ANNE SULLIVAN FOUNDATION
FOR DEAF BLIND PEOPLE

In 1989, the Anne Sullivan Foundation for Deaf Blind People was established by a group of concerned parents whose children had been diagnosed with congenital rubella syndrome. It was named after an Irish emigrant to the US in the late nineteenth century, who became a prominent deaf-blind teacher there. The foundation is located in the grounds of St Joseph's House for Adult Deaf and Deafblind.

In 1996, the Anne Sullivan Foundation's residential service was opened. Since 1997, four houses have been bought and the main centre has been renovated. In the spring of 2017, the foundation had eleven adults resident in the Stillorgan centre and one other adult availing of day and respite-care services. In 2010, the Anne Sullivan centre set up an outreach service to support deaf -lind people in their schools, homes and communities.

BEECHWOOD CHILDCARE AND
MONTESSORI SCHOOL

This establishment, just off the Stillorgan Road at Galloping Green, is purpose built and has been going strong for over twenty years, providing childcare and early childhood education. It has a wide range of facilities, including a baby room, a pre-school room and a pre-wobbler room.

BELMONT NURSING HOME

One of the best-known nursing homes for elderly residents in south Dublin is the Belmont Nursing Home at Galloping Green, which was established in 1996. It even has a stone church in its grounds. The home provides luxurious accommodation for elderly people, ranging from independent living to high-dependency care. It provides both short- and long-term care.

Another company providing care for elderly people, this time in their homes, is also based in Stillorgan: Home Care Plus, in the Priory Office Park. Between 2012 and 2015, a 'living well with dementia' programme ran in Stillorgan and Blackrock, designed to help people suffering from dementia to live in their own homes for as long as possible.

ST ANNE'S INDUSTRIAL SCHOOL

This institution was started in the Stillorgan area in 1945 by the Sisters of Our Lady of Charity, in Redesdale House, and lasted for thirty years, until 1975. It accommodated boys and girls from deprived backgrounds, who were too old for nursery school and too young for other industrial schools. When they were 7 or 8, the girls were sent on to Lakelands Industrial School in Sandymount, while the boys went to the notorious Artane Industrial School on Dublin's north side. Few of the children were ever adopted.

The Stillorgan area had two other industrial schools, St Philomena's, where the nuns were regarded as being harsh, and the Stillorgan Industrial School. The latter was run by the Church of Ireland and, when it closed down in 1917, it was the end of that church's involvement in the running of industrial schools.

ST JOHN OF GOD

For the past 135 years, the St John of God Order is the biggest healthcare provider in the Stillorgan area. In Ireland, the order provides services for older people, as well as in the areas of intellectual disability and mental health.

The St John of God services are grouped into a number of limited companies. A development company was set up in 1960 to raise funds and donations for the order. For many years, the order ran a company called OH Pools Ltd, which operated a lottery called the OH Pools, but these were discontinued in 1978, when the St John of God Development Company was set up. In more recent times, most of the fundraising has been done on a door-to-door basis, with people being encouraged to donate through standing orders at their bank. Major appeals are also made twice a year and these raise substantial funds. Other appeals are made from time to time and the company has also expanded into different areas of fundraising, such as events. The company says that its staff strive to maintain the values inherent in the life of St John of God.

The founder of the order was John Ciudad, a little-known bookbinder in Granada in southern Spain. He was struggling to get his life together, after becoming mentally ill and suffering homelessness. A friend of his, Don Miguel Venegas, allowed John to sleep in his porch, thus beginning the Hospital Order of St John of God. John, who became St John of God, died in 1570. Much later, in the 1860s, Irish priests in the order helped it expand in England and from there it spread to Ireland. In 1882, the order bought Stillorgan Castle, using it at first to cater for 'demented' men.

From that day to this, the order has had thirty directors of its acute psychiatric teaching hospital in Stillorgan, which has close to 200 beds. During its many years in Stillorgan, the order has seen dramatic events, such as the great fire in 1908 that virtually destroyed the old castle, which had to be rebuilt. But from the time when the chapel was opened in 1913 until 1973, no major construction work was carried out at the hospital. That year saw the Brothers' Community

House being built and the areas previously used as community rooms being converted into patients' rooms. In 1979, an IR£1.75 million renovation and extension of the hospital was carried out. In the early 1980s, a new inpatient block on two floors was added to the hospital. It was constructed around a quadrangle, with a Korean garden, featuring a flowing riverlet and a tea house. Further major renovations and refurbishments were carried out in 1996. In recent years, new additions have included a gym in 2009 and a prayer room in 2010.

In June 2017, it was revealed that senior managers had received top-up payments of £6.24 million and that the Order had ignored public service pay guidelines for over thirty years. The Minister for Health, Simon Harris, said that the top-ups would have to be returned. Earlier that year, Brother Fintan Brennan-Whitmore, the charity's acting chief executive, had revealed, after a meeting with the Health Information and Quality Authority, the charity's failings in relation to compliance and patient safety, stating that, if the charity didn't radically address these during 2017, units could close or be handed over to the Health Service Executive. Apart from its services in Stillorgan, the charity also operates in counties Kerry, Kildare and Louth. Also close to Stillorgan, it operates Burton Hall, in Sandyford. Brother Brennan-Whitmore died in June 2017.

ST JOSEPH'S HOME

This residential facility located on the Brewery Road, Stillorgan, looks after deaf-blind people and has been operating for over fifty years. It was established in 1965 by Sister Ursula, who was also the principal of St Mary's School for the Deaf in Cabra, Dublin. She and the then Catholic Archbishop of Dublin, Dr John Charles McQuaid, decided to open St Joseph's in Stillorgan as a place of safety for deaf-blind people, where they could communicate through Irish sign language. The grounds of St Joseph's are extensive and the buildings are listed.

SLIEVEMORE CLINIC

Located on the Old Dublin Road, opposite Oatlands College, the clinic was started in 1997 by Dr Conor O'Toole and Dr Paul Carson. It was expanded in 2007, and today it provides a general practice, a dental practice and a wide range of clinics, covering such areas as women's health and men's screening.

Nearby is the smaller Gleneagle medical clinic, at Greygates on the main Stillorgan Road (N11).

7

NATURAL HISTORY

BATS

Bats can often be observed in older buildings in Stillorgan and it's no surprise to find that UCD has plenty of bats in the belfry. The two species of pipistrelle bat are the most commonly found in Ireland and can often be seen in summer, both on the UCD campus and elsewhere in Stillorgan, foraging around trees, hedgerows and ponds, and feeding on many small insects. The Leisler's bat is the third most common in Ireland and it too can sometimes be seen flying very high and over open environments such as the UCD campus. Also to be seen there, from time to time, is the Daubenton's bat, which feeds over water, catching insects off the surface with its large feet.

FOXES

Since Stillorgan is now such a built-up area, most animals resident there are of the domesticated variety, such as cats and dogs, but foxes are seen on the prowl quite frequently and as they search for food in an urban setting, with many bins blocked off from their depredations, they are increasingly audacious. Six years ago, a man resident in Stillorgan reported on social media that a starving fox had come up to him, in Stillorgan, looking for food. This incident inspired a Ukrainian artist, Liubov Kadyrova, who has been living in Dublin since

2001 and who graduated from the National College of Art and Design in 2007, to create a series of paintings of the Fox of Stillorgan.

SCHOOL GARDENS

One of the most impressive school gardens in Stillorgan is the one at St Brigid's National School. That garden was once part of the rectory garden at St Brigid's and, as a previous rector had kept a couple of donkeys there, the long-term benefit of their droppings has been excellent soil fertility. Good soil fertility and soil structure is maintained by a three-bay composting system, which decomposes a diverse mixture of plant matter and poultry manure. In recent years, a honeybee brood box was set up in the garden and the children also help rear hens, but it is a big responsibility for everyone involved to protect the hens from the increasingly brazen urban foxes that roam Stillorgan.

UCD CAMPUS

The best area for natural habitat and flora and fauna close to Stillorgan is the UCD campus, which is noted for its parkland setting and mature landscapes. A series of five walks have been developed on the 133ha campus, giving walkers paths of different lengths, each with its own natural characteristics. These woodland paths extend to 8km and, altogether, the campus has some 50,000 trees in seventy-five different species.

In the late eighteenth century, ornamental conifers were widely planted on the estates that make up the UCD campus and many of them remain, as well as mature lime trees. During the 1960s and 1970s, much more tree-planting was done on the campus, while as a millennium project, a large area was planted with London plane trees, in front of the restaurant and Oak Walk. In recent years, large parts of the woodland in the boundary areas of the campus have been augmented with native species such as alder, birch, oak and willow.

On the campus, the woodlands, wetlands, wildflower meadows and mowed-grass areas provide habitats for many birds, mammals, insects and other wildlife. Most of the common woodland birds breed on the campus. The boundary walk gives views of some birds, such as the long-tailed tit and the willow warbler, which are hard to spot in conventional gardens.

Many species of butterfly, such as the orange-tip and tortoiseshell, are found in the woodlands and meadows of UCD, along with many wild bees.

WOOD PIGEONS

These birds are frequently seen in Stillorgan. They've also been spotted on the menu from time to time at The Talbot Hotel in Stillorgan. Wood pigeons thrive in the woodlands of the UCD campus, along with finches, greenfinches and linnets. Stillorgan is also home to one of Ireland's best-known pigeon fanciers, Peter Kennedy.

The lakes and wetlands of the UCD campus also provide habitats for many bird species, including mallards, mute swans and tufted ducks. In winter, species such as the grey heron and the kingfisher can often be seen. Also in winter, the playing pitches attract coastal wading birds, such as the curlew and the oystercatcher, which is hardly surprising since the coast at Sandymount and Booterstown is only about 2km away. Fieldfares and redwings can also be seen. Then, in spring, these birds are replaced by breeding blackbirds, mistle and song thrushes, collecting worms to feed their chicks.

8

PUBS, RESTAURANTS AND LEISURE

APRILE RESTAURANT

This restaurant, on the Lower Kilmacud Road, is described by Lucinda O' Sullivan, a famous restaurant critic, as a wonderful asset to the Stillorgan eating-out scene. She says it has a cool, contemporary look with a *dolce vita* feel about it, which makes it a buzzy and stylish venue. Aprile's has been a well-known Irish/Italian family-owned restaurant for over fifty years in Stillorgan, much upgraded in recent times.

AROMA NOODLE BAR

This popular noodle bar is located at 72 St Laurence's Park, directly across from the Stillorgan Village shopping centre. Another popular takeaway in the Stillorgan area is Indus Spice on the Lower Kilmacud Road, which has a pan-Indian menu and Bollywood-style artwork decorating its premises. Loco's Mexican takeaway is on The Hill.

BEAUFIELD MEWS

Beaufield Mews started with Doreen, nicknamed Go-Go, who was married to solicitor Eddie (Valentine) Kirwan. Doreen got her two daughters to work, baking cookies and serving tea to her customers who were buying antiques from her. Her dynamic approach to business was well reflected in her nickname. Doreen eventually turned the coach house into a restaurant. When it started, the table d'hôte menu cost was a mere 3/6d. But in 1988, it was among the first restaurants to be awarded a special restaurant licence, which allowed it to sell all alcoholic drinks. The previous year, vandals broke into the derelict Beaufield House and set it on fire. It was demolished and Beaufield Manor developed on the site.

Despite all this, the restaurant has continued to do well, always known for its individualistic approach. In the 1970s, Jill Cox had two cats in the restaurant, one called Paisley, after Ian Paisley, the other called Bernadette, after Bernadette Devlin.

The field at the back of the restaurant was converted into a wonderful garden, with large rose bushes and plenty of herbs. Then in the 1990s, the famous architect Alfred Cochrane designed an iron pavilion that has withstood the test of time and is still often used for weddings and other ceremonies. The restaurant retains many of its original artefacts, including the old water troughs for horses, the original arch entrances for coaches and many items bought by Doreen and her daughter Jill. These days, the restaurant is still thriving, run by Jill's daughter Julie and a wonderful team. Facilities now include the Loft Brasserie, upstairs, for evening meals.

BEWLEY'S CAFÉ

For many years, Bewley's first-floor café was a prime meeting place in the Stillorgan shopping centre; the space is now occupied by Brambles café.

The firm had opened a shop in the shopping centre in 1970 and, a couple of years later, the café was opened. For many years, Michael Dempsey and Lena D'Alton managed the shop and the café. From 1989 until 1994, the shop was run as a franchise by Eddie and Sylvia Kinlan and in 1989, the franchise for the café was given to Liam and Anne Kelly, who also had the Bewley's franchises in Dundrum, Nutgrove, Santry and Tallaght. The Bewley's name lasted in the Stillorgan shopping centre until 1996, when the shop unit was taken over by An Post. Today, the café tradition in the centre is carried on by Brambles and other catering establishments.

People connected with the old Bewley's in the Stillorgan shopping centre remember that the day after the Dublin city centre bombings in 1974, the Bewley's café and shop were jam-packed with customers, as people were so reluctant to go into town. Staff had the greatest difficulty coping with the long queues of people.

On Christmas Eve in years gone past, while city cafés went quiet, the Bewley's café and shop in Stillorgan were packed with late shoppers.

BLAKE'S RESTAURANT

When Blake's restaurant, just off The Hill in Stillorgan, was opened on 22 November 1983, it was described as the largest restaurant in Ireland. The opening was performed by Dublin's lord mayor of the time, Michael Keating, TD. The restaurant itself had been extensively refurbished and a separate pizzeria, as well as an ice-cream parlour and a wine bar, had been added. At the time, Gerry Stevenson was the managing director of Blake's; he had been the general manager of Thomas Lydon's bakery and restaurant group in Galway. Blake's had been started by John O'Sullivan, who owned a couple of restaurants in the city centre. Later, Paddy Shovlin and Paddy Gallagher took over Blake's and revamped it.

John and Angela O'Sullivan went on to found Roly's restaurant in Ballsbridge, together with chef Cathal O'Daly, who had owned the Park restaurant in Blackrock. Blake's is long gone, but Roly's is still thriving.

BOLAND'S PUB

Boland's pub, at the top of The Hill in Stillorgan, has been trading in the village since the mid-nineteenth century, which makes it the oldest continuously trading pub in the Stillorgan area. It was owned for many years by the Bolands, one of whom married into the Cullen family, who had owned the land here since 1764 and who an earlier pub and grocery shop on the site. Then it became Cassidy's pub. The pub and grocery shop continued to trade until the middle of the twentieth century.

Even in the late 1960s, when John Burke was the manager of the pub, that part of Stillorgan had remained relatively unchanged since Victorian times. A newspaper photograph taken in the late 1960s shows the last of the three public water pumps in Stillorgan Village being dismantled. It was close to Boland's pub.

New management took over at the pub in 2009 and renamed it McGowan's, but the name never caught on. To this day, most people in the district still refer to it as Boland's. In April 2017, the pub was on the market again and sold for over €1.4 million. It was described as having a lounge bar and outdoor smoking area on the ground floor and another lounge bar, as well as a catering kitchen, on the first floor. It has long been a popular venue for people in the Stillorgan area and two of the most famous regulars there were writers Brian Ó Nualláin and Maurice Walsh. In the 1940s, two top celebrities in Dublin were Jack Doyle (1913–1978), a boxer known as the Gorgeous Gael, and his Mexican film-star wife, Movita. In those days, Doyle often drank at Boland's. Slightly later, another rumbustious character in Dublin did the same, writer Brendan Behan (1923–64).

BYRNE'S PUB, GALLOPING GREEN

Byrne's, in the townland of Galloping Green, beside the N11, was established in 1879 by Philip Byrne, great-grandfather of the present owner, Ray Byrne. It's unusual for a pub to be so long in the ownership of one family and, today, the sixth generation of the Byrne family lives over the pub.

Over the years, some changes have been made to the pub. In the 1940s, the family sitting room was converted into a lounge, but the last major changes were made in the early 1960s. Today, Byrne's, with a delightfully cosy atmosphere, is one of the last traditional pubs left in the Dublin area.

Philip Byrne, who built the pub, also built the adjacent cottages. Most of the trade for the pub remains local and it's less dependent on passing trade than it used to be. Ray Byrne recalls that when the new dual carriageway was opened, with two lanes in each direction, one lane in the southbound direction used to have so many cars belonging to people who were drinking in the pub that southward-bound traffic was effectively restricted to one lane.

Back around 1900, the area around Galloping Green was home to 200 people, Ray Byrne says, and even into the 1960s, the district was still open countryside. Over the years, the pub's most famous customer was Séan Ó Riada, the musician and composer. In 1958, he rented a house close to Byrne's pub from Ray Byrne's grandfather; the family lived there for five years, until 1963. While Ó Riada had a reputation for being a heavy drinker, Ray Byrne says that he has never heard of any stories of the great composer overdoing it in his family pub. He often brought fellow musicians to his house for rehearsals at the weekend, and after each session they would all duly retire to Byrne's for refreshments.

CHINA SICHUAN RESTAURANT

This highly regarded Chinese restaurant used to be located on the Lower Kilmacud Road at Stillorgan, but is now based on the Sandyford Industrial Estate. It is run by Kevin Hui, whose parents ran the original restaurant in Stillorgan.

GOTHAM SOUTH RESTAURANT AND CAFÉ

This popular establishment on the Lower Kilmacud Road, in close proximity to RIBA, is a contemporary spot that's very popular for its brunch, its wood-fired pizzas and its grilled mains. It opened in May 2010, in premises that had previously been the China Sichuan restaurant, which relocated to its present site based in the Sandyford Industrial Estate.

KILMACUD STILLORGAN
LOCAL HISTORY SOCIETY

The idea of this dynamic local history society germinated among a group of friends in the Kilmacud and Stillorgan area at the start of the twenty-first century. Their aims were to discover and promote information about the history of the area, to preserve artefacts, documents and memories that might otherwise disappear, to encourage research into local and family history and to help sustain an interest in the culture, heritage and history of the area.

In September 2001, the first committee meeting was held, with Peter Sobolewski as chair, Julia Barrett as secretary and Clive O'Connor as treasurer. The other committee members were Bryan MacMahon, Anne O'Connor and Pat Sheridan. The president was Bonnie Flanagan, the 'first lady' of local history in Stillorgan.

The first talk, given by Bonnie Flanagan on 'Old Stillorgan', was held in the parish hall in November 2001. As the workload increased, Lyn Lynch and Margaret Smith joined the committee, which continues to run the society up to the present day. The honorary chairman is Paddy Rochford.

Since it started, the society has staged 126 talks. Its monthly talks and presentations take place in Glenalbyn on the second Thursday of the month, between September and April. These events are always well supported, with an average attendance of sixty-five, sometimes going up to 100.

The society has had an annual outing every year since 2003 and venues visited have included Armagh city, Belvedere House in Co. Westmeath, Birr Castle in Co. Offaly, Castlepollard in Co. Westmeath, Carlingford in Co. Louth, Clonmacnoise and Waterford city. The first tour abroad was to the First World War battlefields in France and Belgium, in September 2015, and proved to be a very successful trip.

A celebration by the society of the life and work of Sir Edward Lovett Pearce, the architect who designed the Obelisk and lived in Stillorgan, began in March 2013 and continued until the end of 2014. It began with a talk by Pat Sheridan, a seminar in the

Stillorgan Park Hotel and a heritage walk in Stillorgan, visiting the places associated with Pearce.

The society has also published a number of books. Its first venture into publishing came in March 2005, when Bryan MacMahon's book *Eccentric Archbishop: Richard Whately of Redesdale* was very successful. In March 2014, the society published another book by Bryan MacMahon, *Robert Tressell, Dubliner: author of The Ragged Trousered Philanthropists*, which was also highly regarded.

In December 2006, the society published the first issue of its annual journal *Obelisk*. It includes memories and stories of local people and places, articles about family members in the past, the history of local places and reports of society activities. The journal has gone from strength to strength; 2017 is the twelfth year of publication, with 1,000 copies produced of each issue.

Then in 2014, the society launched its new website, www. kilmacudstillorganhistory.ie. The site has information on the society, details of forthcoming talks and events, other material relevant to the area and links to other societies.

As of 2017, the society has close to seventy members and organises a wide range of activities. These include talks on matters of local and national historical interest, annual outings to historical places, publishing its annual journal, *Obelisk*, hosting events in Stillorgan for Heritage Week, organising occasional walks with historical themes, collecting old photographs and memorabilia of the local area, encouraging research into family history, supporting local schools with information and talks on local history and heritage walks of the area and liaising with other local history groups.

LEOPARDSTOWN INN

This pub/bistro has long been a feature of Brewery Road; in 2014, an interim examiner was appointed but the pub continued to trade. It had been owned by Brian and Desmond Reddy, whose family connections in the licensed trade dated back to the 1750s. In 2015, Brian O'Malley and Stephen Cooney bought the Leopardstown Inn for €4.5 million.

MILL HOUSE PUB

This modern bar and lounge on Lower Kilmacud Road, Stillorgan, is popular for its pub grub, including Sunday lunch. It's frequented as much for its food as for its drink. The pub is named after the Kilmacud Stream, which is now culverted for its entire length, totally obscured from human view. The stream flows deep underground beneath Stillorgan Village, goes under the Old Dublin Road and merges with the Carysfort-Maretimo Stream in the grounds of Stillorgan Park House.

O'DWYER'S PUB

O'Dwyer's pub on the Lower Kilmacud Road has had an extensive makeover in recent times and additions include Restaurant 118. The O'Dwyer brothers owned both the Stillorgan Orchard and O'Dwyer's on the Lower Kilmacud Road; their mother ran the pubs before them.

In January 2017, Stephen Collins of *The Irish Times*, who has close connections with Stillorgan, wrote 'An Irishman's Diary' in that newspaper on Eamon Huff, a barman with forty-three years' service at O'Dwyer's, who was then on the point of retirement. Eamon's family have lived in the area for generations and he was brought up in Moore's Cottages, demolished to make way for the Stillorgan shopping centre. He and his family moved to the newly built Patrician Villas. A bachelor, he still lives in the family home.

Stephen Collins said that Eamon, during his years at the pub, kept customers up to date with all the important news in the area. Eamon never had any inclination to use social media or a laptop; he always preferred to talk with people in the pub. He has also been for many years a noted guest at funerals, not just in Kilmacud parish church, but in the wider south Dublin community. He has always liked to pay his respects to those who have passed on, for many of whom he pulled pints for years in O'Dwyer's.

ORMONDE CINEMA

The first Ormonde cinema opened with a single screen on 24 August 1954. It could seat 1,000 patrons. The Ormonde was also one of the last suburban cinemas built in the Dublin area in the early 1950s; in 1962, with the arrival of the Irish television service, now RTÉ, suburban cinemas went into permanent decline. At the time the Ormonde opened, it was one of fifty-six cinemas in Dublin city centre and suburbs, a number that dwindled rapidly.

The Ormonde was built facing the Lower Kilmacud Road, which then ended in a T-junction with the Old Dublin Road. The same year as the Ormonde opened, another cinema, the Stella, opened in Mount Merrion, less than a mile away. Despite the competition, the Ormonde survived for twenty-five years. It was owned by an entrepreneur based in Arklow, Co. Wicklow, called J.J. Kavanagh, who operated twelve cinemas throughout the state. Being part of a chain gave the Ormonde a lead when it came to showing new releases.

The cinema was very modern for its day and it also led the way with its stadium-style seating. But eventually it closed, in 1978, because of declining audiences. It was sold to a property developer who demolished it and turned the site into a shopping centre that included a new three-screen cinema, which retained the name Ormonde.

This new cinema opened its doors for the first time on 5 February 1983. Surprisingly, the single-storey shopping centre, the Stillorgan Plaza, failed after a few years, but the cinema did well. When the retail section of the cinema closed, it enabled the Ormonde to expand into a two-storey, seven-screen multiplex, which reopened in 1997. The Ormonde became the first and only purpose-built multiplex cinema in Dublin, although its position in the shopping centre meant that it didn't have a recognisable facade.

In 2011, the Ormonde was fully refurbished and reopened as a UCI cinema, subsequently becoming an Odeon. Then in 2014, the cinema was put on the market with an asking price of €3.5 million. Today, the Odeon cinema is still going strong.

PING'S RESTAURANT

Ping's Chinese restaurant, closed down and derelict for well over five years, is on a site that had previously hosted many other restaurants, starting with the Swiss Chalet, then Blake's, then the Bondi Beach night club, where the party was said never to end, and then Pappa Gallos pizzas.

It's said by many people in Stillorgan that Ping's never recovered from a high-profile court case nearly twenty years ago, although it had an excellent reputation as a high-class restaurant.

In February 1998, a noted racehorse owner, Tom Doran, won £67,000 at Leopardstown racecourse after one of his horses had an unexpected victory. He then took a party of fifty-two to Ping's to celebrate. One of his party didn't drink at all during the dinner and took careful note of the food and wine served; photographs were taken also. Tom Doran said that Ping's had charged him for a full dinner menu for seventy-six people and also for thirty-five bottles of Chablis Premier Cru, none of which he believed to have been served. He eventually offered to pay £1,800 in cash for the dinner, which was rejected. Ping's ended up by being given a decree for £1,500 for food and wine, but the substantial costs were awarded against them.

RIBA RESTAURANT

This quality neighbourhood restaurant on Lower Kilmacud Road in Stillorgan offers modern-style cuisine with a strong Italian influence; hardly surprising, since it's a third-generation Borza/Vozza family business, operating on the site since 1962. One of its specialities is weekend brunch, which has long been popular with southsiders. The restaurant is also open for dinner every night from 5 p.m.

STILLORGAN LIBRARY

The present Stillorgan Library, in the St Laurence Park area, between the Old Dublin Road and the main road, is one of eight public libraries run by Dún Laoghaire–Rathdown County Council Library Service. This library was opened in 1975 and extensively refurbished six years ago, in 2011. These improvements provided better access and public facilities. The senior librarian in Stillorgan is Carmel Kelly. When the new Stillorgan Library opened, it replaced the former library, which had been in the parochial hall in St Brigid's.

STILLORGAN ORCHARD

This single-storey pub at the foot of The Hill in Stillorgan is comparatively new, but there has been a pub on this site for over 200 years. One illustration from 1810 shows the main street in the then tiny village of Stillorgan, complete with Cullen's pub and grocery store. This stood where the Orchard, previously known as Stillorgan Inn, is now located.

When the pub was run by the Cullens, the woman who became known as the Widow Cullen was a formidable character. Mary

Anne Cullen married James Boland, from the neighbouring pub family, on 17 January 1893. Her reputation lived on long after her. Around fifteen years ago, when there were plans to call a new bar in the Stillorgan Orchard the 'Widow Cullen's', her daughter, living in Canada, objected, so nothing came of the plan.

In the mid-1980s, the pub, which dates back to the late nineteenth century, had its roof thatched. A thatcher called Kryan O'Grady spent four months on this enormous task, which required 6,500 bundles of reeds. At the time, it was said to have been the largest thatched roof in Europe.

The Hill, Stillorgan, and the Orchard pub. (Olivia Hayes)

Today, the Stillorgan Orchard still has its famous thatched roof, probably the largest on any pub in Ireland. The front part of the pub, facing onto The Hill, is the oldest part.

Inside the very classy pub, the bars have a traditional/contemporary feel. The pub is renowned for its all-day food and for its live music acts. Conor and Tony O'Dwyer have done many refurbishments and improvements to it. Before the O'Dwyers owned it, it had had been owned by the Lavin brothers, who were responsible for getting the roof thatched. Other pubs in the village have long gone, like Lynch's and the one run by the Widow Baumann, but the Stillorgan Orchard and its near neighbour, Boland's, still soldier on. In summer 2017 a sale was agreed for the Orchard.

STILLORGAN PLAYERS

The local amateur drama group, the Stillorgan Players, have been an integral part of the leisure scene in the area since 1969.

It all began after the then rector of St Brigid's, Marcus Taylor, decided to have a parish hall built in the school grounds in 1967. This prefab structure was primitive, with heating supplied by a single-bar wall heater that had to be fed with two shilling pieces. Then, a couple of years later, the curate, Rev. Kevin Dalton, decided to start a drama group in the hall. The first people approached were Arthur Rhys Thomas, usually known as 'Tommy' Thomas, and Geoff Lovegrove, both of whom had lots of theatrical experience.

The first production was of a play called *Killer Dies Twice*, by Lynn Reid Banks, which opened on 9 April 1969. For the next twenty years, the Players put on two shows a year, every March and October. After the death of 'Tommy' Thomas in 1978, Geoff Lovegrove and others, including his brother Jim, and Barbara Kirk, kept the show on the road.

But by the end of the 1980s, the parish hall was showing plenty of symptoms of old age; it was demolished in August 1993 and, by the following year, a brand-new parish hall had been built. It was opened by then president, Mary Robinson, on 12 June 1994.

Despite some subsequent blips and personality clashes, the Players managed to keep going and, to the present day, have staged well over sixty plays and a dozen pantomimes.

STILLORGAN VILLAGE CENTRE EATERIES

The revamped shopping centre has a number of restaurants and cafés. These include Base Pizza, Brambles café, which serves a wide selection of artisan food all day, and Eddie Rocket's Diner. Complementing these outlets are Mao, a renowned Asian takeaway, which also has a sit-down restaurant in the centre, McDonalds, O'Brien's, for handcrafted sandwiches and coffee, and Starbucks. At one stage, the shopping centre even had a pub called The Oyster, owned and run by the Madison pub group.

THE TALBOT HOTEL

The Talbot Hotel, on the main N11 road at Stillorgan, is a four-star establishment providing a wide range of top-class dining, accommodation, wedding and conference facilities. Among its amenities are the Purple Sage restaurant and the Brass bar and grill. Among the many community and business groups that have used the hotel in recent years is the RTÉ Benevolent Society.

In the spring of 2017, the owners of the hotel applied for planning permission to build a four-storey extension at the back of the hotel, which will create an extra 3,555m^2 of space and add 61 bedrooms to the existing 150.

TIDY TOWNS COMPETITION, 2007

In the 2007 Tidy Towns Competition, Stillorgan did quite well, with 174 marks. However, the adjudicators said that while the key focus of Stillorgan was the area of the shopping centre and the junction of the Lower Kilmacud Road and the Old Dublin Road, work needed to be done on researching the boundaries of Stillorgan.

They also said that much of the signage in the centre was quite poor and out of scale with the individual buildings. It was also noted that the cottages below Boland's pub probably represented some of the early houses in Stillorgan; poor signage had taken over and the overall visual impact was rather mediocre. On the other hand, the Stillorgan Decor Centre was commended for its crisp and clear presentation. The credit union building, originally one of a terrace of six houses, was well presented. The Mill House bar used modern lettering that complemented the attractive front elevation.

In some respects, Stiillorgan did poorly, especially in areas of litter control, waste minimisation, weed control and graffiti. It was recommended that the Tidy Towns Committee in Stillorgan look at the idea of starting a Tidy Estates Competition, to improve the visual appearances of the housing estates in the area.

9

REMARKABLE PEOPLE

DR THEKLA BEERE

Thekla Beere, who played a pioneering role in women's advancement in the higher levels of the public service, lived in Stillorgan for many years.

She was born at Streete, Co. Westmeath, in 1901; her father was the Church of Ireland rector there. Although she had no formal primary education, she was one of the first generation of women to graduate from Trinity College Dublin. She then spent two years in the US on an international scholarship and, when she returned home, she got a junior job in the Central Statistics Office. To complement her income, she became the first female lecturer on statistics in Ireland.

From there, she went to the public service and in November 1953 she became assistant secretary at the old Department of Industry and Commerce. In August 1959, she was appointed secretary of the then new Department of Transport and Power, where her expertise on transport and labour issues proved invaluable. The appointment was a milestone for her and for women generally in the higher levels of the public service; she was the first woman appointed to head a government department.

Outside work, she had many other interests and was one of the founding members of An Óige, the Irish Youth Hostelling Association, in 1931. Among her close friends were many leading playwrights, actors and artists. But she kept her personal life a closely guarded secret; for many years, she had a partner, but they never married, because this would have had an adverse effect on her government work. In those far-off days, if a woman working in the public service got married, she had to retire; this antiquated legislation wasn't repealed until 1973.

When Thekla retired from the public service, she had ambitions to do a lot of travelling around the world, but such was the demand for her services that she never fulfilled that post-retirement ambition. She became chair of the Commission on the Status of Women, which did important work in creating equality. She also served on a wide variety of boards of organisations in artistic, charitable and religious spheres.

For many years, Thekla Beere lived at Moyvalley, in Glenalbyn Road in Stillorgan. After she died in 1991, her funeral was held, appropriately, at St Brigid's church.

ÉAMONN DE BÚRCA

Éamonn is an antiquarian bookseller and publisher, who has lived and worked in Stillorgan for many years.

He bought his first antiquarian book in Castlebar in 1966, when he was a 16-year-old student at St Gerald's College. When he was 18, he moved to England and worked there until 1980, when he moved back to Ireland. He set up his bookselling business in Castlebar, then moved to Dublin a few years later. He has been at Priory Drive just off the N11 since 1987 and sells rare books to collectors from all over the world. He is now considered the largest stockist in the world of Irish antiquarian books.

He runs the book business with his son William. Éamonn says that he is a collector at heart and that there are some books that he wouldn't sell unless he had a duplicate. He is especially passionate about the history and antiquities of his native county, Mayo. He also deals in other items, like memorabilia and signed documents, and De Búrca Rare Books also publish limited editions of historical, topographical and biographical books. One of their earliest publications was the book on the Maamtrasna Murders, which they published in 1992.

Éamonn and his son are also noted for their remarkable catalogues, which are published four times a year, both online and in print format. They are so beautifully designed that they are considered works of art in their own right.

JILL COX

Jill, who died in October 2010, was long noted in the Stillorgan area for being the woman who ran the Beaufield Mews restaurant for many years and for being an expert on antiques.

In September 2011, Adams on the Green auctioned more than 800 items from her collection of antiques, from the Beaufield Mews restaurant and from her home in Sandycove.

Jill's parents were Eddie (Valentine) Kirwan, a solicitor, and Doreen, known to all in Stillorgan as Go-Go. In the late 1930s, they bought the then derelict Beaufield House in Stillorgan with the aim of converting it into flats. The house had certain historical connections. During the 1922–23 Civil War, it was a safe house for Éamon de Valera and his secretary Kathleen O'Connell, when it was owned by the Comyn family. Sir James Comyn (1921–1997), one of the few Irish lawyers to have reached senior judicial status in Britain, had been born in the house.

Go-Go bought too much furniture for the house conversion and ended up having to store it in the converted coal shed. She started selling antiques and serving tea and biscuits to her customers: this was the start of Beaufield Mews restaurant, which got going in 1950. Today, it is the oldest standalone restaurant in Dublin, if not the country. Go-Go became a famous figure in Stillorgan, driving round in her open-top Morris Minor, with her latest purchases of antiques on the back seat.

Jill went with her mother to auctions and, in time, she too became an expert on the subject, specialising in Irish furniture, glass, paintings and silver, as well as Staffordshire pottery figures. For many years, she appeared on RTÉ television as an antiques expert.

HENRY DARLEY

During the nineteenth century, Henry Darley (about 1801–1883) was the largest employer in Stillorgan, as the owner of Darley's brewery.

He was the son of Frederick Darley (1763–1841), who was lord mayor of Dublin in 1808/09, and Elizabeth Guinness. Henry Darley started in the legal profession, becoming one of six clerks of Chancery in Ireland in 1829 and then a barrister in 1833.

Henry Darley lived at Beaufield House, Stillorgan, between 1834 and 1841, and then went to live at Grange House, where the present Grange apartment blocks are now located, beside the famous brewery. The Darleys also had a second residence, Wingfield House in Enniskerry. Henry Darley was married to Maria Louisa West (1808–1873) and they had three children. Frederick became chief justice and lieutenant-governor of New South Wales in Australia, Cecil became chief engineer of New South Wales and Henry became a medical doctor, marrying Sarah Guinness, thus continuing the long connection between the Darley and Guinness families. Memorial inscriptions in St Brigid's churchyard bear testimony to the many links between them.

Both the Darley and the Guinness families were generous benefactors of both the church and its school during the nineteenth century. However, Henry Darley wasn't buried at St Brigid's, but at Mount Jerome.

Besides his interest in the brewery, and another in Bray, Henry Darley also held the ground rents of many properties in Stillorgan and his rent ledger for the years between 1822 and 1854 is in the National Library of Ireland. A typical rent for that period, for one of the brewery cottages, was 2 shillings a week.

DENIS DEVLIN

Born in Greenock, Scotland, in 1908, to Irish parents, Denis Devlin returned home to Ireland with his family in 1918. He went on to study at UCD, in Munich and at the Sorbonne in Paris. For a short while, he worked at UCD as a lecturer, before joining what was then the Department of External Affairs (now Foreign Affairs and Trade) in Dublin. From 1940 until 1947, he was a secretary at the Irish Embassy in Washington, then, in 1947, he was made Irish high commissioner in London. In 1950, he was made Irish ambassador to Italy, then, in 1951, he became Irish ambassador to Turkey.

Despite having such a high-flying career in the Irish foreign service, he also found time to write much poetry of great distinction, producing such works as 'Lough Derg', first published in 1930. For many years, he and his family lived in Stillorgan. But, tragically, his life was cut short by leukaemia. He died in Dublin on 21 August 1959. Among personal friends who mourned his loss at such a young age was Éamon de Valera, who was Taoiseach at the time and subsequently became President of Ireland.

DAVE DOWNES

Dave Downes, long known for his work in Dublin Bookbrowsers, has lived for years in Stillorgan and now runs his business from his home in Weir View Drive. He buys and sells old, rare and antiquarian and out-of-print books, old sports programmes, old postcards, old documents and manuscripts, letters and posters – in short, old material on paper of Irish and general interest. Most of his business is with collectors, libraries and institutions both in Ireland and abroad.

He will buy one book at a time or whole collections and he has cleared many institutions. House clearance of books is one of his specialities. Originally from Clontarf, he and his family moved to Stillorgan in 1983. In his career, he has had many different jobs, including managing the old bottle recycling centre at the Merrion Gates, in the 1970s, and working in the probation service. For many years, he ran the Irish Youth Foundation, which he had been instrumental in setting up. After being an avid book collector for many years, he started as a full-time book dealer in 1996.

Dave is a great supporter of the Stillorgan area. He says that it's a wonderful area and that it's a privilege to live there. 'It has so much going for it, wonderful people, fantastic services, lots of open spaces, facilities and amenities'.

SIR THOMAS FARRELL

Sir Thomas Farrell (1827–1900) was born in Mecklenbergh Street, now Railway Street in central Dublin. He was one of six sons of Terence Farrell, a sculptor, and the young Thomas trained in his father's workshop. During a very long career, Thomas Farrell created many statues in Dublin, including the one of Sir John Gray in O'Connell Street, Dublin, and one of Archbishop Whately for St Patrick's Cathedral.

Although he had a very lucrative practice for a long time, towards the end of his life there was a dramatic falling-off in church commissions, which left him in straightened circumstances. But he was the first sculptor to be elected president of the Royal Irish Academy and, in 1894, he was knighted. In 1895, he moved into Redesdale House and spent the last five years of his life there. This is where Whately Place is now situated, on the hill connecting the lower and the upper Kilmacud Road.

MAEVE FLANAGAN

Another writer with close connections with Stillorgan, Maeve wrote a book called *Dev, Lady Chatterley and Me*, published in 1998 by Marino Books. The book told her story of growing up in Stillorgan in the 1960s.

EMER HALPENNY

Emer has long been involved in drama teaching in Stillorgan. Back in 1990, when she was working for a television production company, she suddenly had a ' lightbulb' moment when she realised she would rather be involved in drama teaching and musicals. She then set up her own drama school, that same year, on foot of her involvement with the Stillorgan Youth Musical Company. From its early days in Glenalbyn House to its present home in St Laurence's Parish Centre, her school has been building confidence in people of all ages for the past twenty-seven years.

Somewhere between speech, drama and performing arts in teaching style, Emer and her teachers aim to help students develop through drama, discovering their creative potential while having fun. Emer no longer takes part in exams or competitions, preferring to encourage students to participate in all aspects of a production, from the conception of an idea through writing to backstage management and even budgeting and advertising. She and her teachers are helping students to create life skills, to cope with everyday challenges, without overburdening any one individual. Classes take place on Tuesdays and Saturdays, with two performances a year, and, as Emer says herself, 'happy, confident students are guaranteed'. She has her own website, www.emerhalpenny.com.

T.P. HARDIMAN

For many years, T.P. Hardiman has lived on the Stillorgan Road; born in 1929, he is an engineering and science graduate of UCD. Between 1968 and 1975, he was the director-general of RTÉ, whose independence he studiously maintained.

Shortly after his appointment, he got word that Charlie Haughey, then minister for finance, wanted to meet him, but he refused. A few days later, the two met at a reception in Dublin Castle. Haughey told him that what people wanted from RTÉ was entertainment and that the current affairs people in the station didn't know what they were talking about. In front of an astonished audience, Hardiman then grabbed Haughey by the lapels and said to him: 'Now listen to me, I'm a Christian Brothers boy like yourself. There's a Broadcasting Act and an RTÉ Authority and as far as I'm concerned, I've a job to do, under the Act and the Authority'. He later apologised to Haughey for his behaviour.

Hardiman, who has had a lifelong interest in everything Japanese, went on to become chairman of IBM Ireland and he was also made chancellor of Dublin City University in 1998.

JARLATH HAYES

Jarlath Hayes, who lived at Stillorgan Grove for many years, was considered one of the best Irish book designers of the late twentieth century.

He was born in Dublin in 1924 and began a career in advertising in 1945. Among the ad agencies he worked for was the old O'Keeffe's agency in Fitzwilliam Square. He was also a part-time lecturer in advertising design at Rathmines Technical Institute. In 1958, he was a founder member of the Institute of Creative Advertising and Design.

But his first love was always book and type design. He worked for many leading Irish book publishers, such as the Dolmen Press and Lilliput Press, and he designed magazines like *Books Ireland*. In 1970, he went freelance; initially, his studio was in Percy Place, off Baggot Street Bridge, but in 1979 he transferred it to his home in Stillorgan.

He also designed the typeface used for the credits on the RTÉ television series *Glenroe*. Apart from his work, Jarlath was someone with a great sense of humour and an iconoclastic view of current events. He was also noted for the various dogs he had in succession at his Stillorgan home; they were all called Murphy.

Jarlath was married to Oonagh and they had one son and four daughters. One of their daughters, Susan, worked with her father for many years and, in more recent years, has been very involved with the Ashfield Press in Blackrock. She has done much design work for *Obelisk*, the annual publication of the Kilmacud Stillorgan Local History Society.

Jarlath Hayes died in May 2001 and his wife Oonagh died eleven years later, in 2012.

PETER JANKOWSKY

Peter Jankowsky was a man of many artistic parts, born in Berlin in 1939. He started travelling in Ireland in the 1950s and, in 1971, settled in Dublin. For many years, the family home, with his wife, Veronica Bolay, an artist, and their son, Aengus, was at Linden Lea Park in Stillorgan.

Between 1959 and 1962, Peter had studied at the Max Reinhardt School of Acting in Berlin, and through the 1960s he worked with a number of theatre companies in Germany. After he came to Dublin, he joined the staff of the Goethe Institute as a lecturer on German, a job he held for over thirty years. But Peter was much more than an actor and a teacher; he was a writer, a broadcaster, a translator and a photographer. For many years, he contributed to the *Sunday Miscellany* programme on RTÉ Radio 1.

He was considered to have the most distinctive voice of any contributor to the programme since it started in the late 1960s. When he was working for it, the long-serving producer of the time was Martha McCarron and she often says that when a new script came in from Peter, her face lit up with joy, because it was inevitably so brilliant. Peter also did many poetry translations, for Irish and German publishers, and wrote his memoirs.

Peter was very opposed to modern technology; he always refused to have a car, never used the Internet or a mobile phone and refused to have a television set in the house. Yet he lived an outwardly conformist life in a suburban bungalow in Stillorgan. He died in St Vincent's Hospital on 17 September 2014. The many outstanding characters connected with Stillorgan over the years, Peter Jankowsky was undoubtedly one of the most original.

MAXINE JONES

Maxine Jones is a journalist from London who has long had connections with Stillorgan. She came to Dublin in 1990 to work for the old *Sunday Tribune* newspaper and from there, she moved to *The Irish Times*. Nearly twenty years ago, she started her own publication for the Stillorgan area, called *Suburb*, which lasted for nine issues. The first issue of the fifty-four-page glossy had a 5,000 print run. She started by doing all the production herself, including designing and laying out the pages, taking most of the photographs and doing the distribution.

She hired an ad manager to sell ads from the first issue, paid him commission upfront, as well as giving him expenses and providing him with a mobile phone. It turned out that all the ads he had allegedly sold for the first issue hadn't been sold at all and Maxine had to deal with some irate retailers after she had billed them. Maxine then started selling the advertising herself, a chore she hated, but after ten issues, *Suburb* had become so hard to produce that she killed it off.

She also wrote a book about her life, entitled *Why are you here? An Englishwoman in Ireland*. After divorce became legal in Ireland, Maxine was Ireland's first divorcée, in 1996.

But in 2011, she found a completely new vocation in life when she did her first gig as a stand-up comedian in a Dublin pub. She says that her newspaper background gave her a lot of material and her new career has proved very successful.

OSSIE KILKENNY

Born in Stillorgan in the late 1940s, Ossie Kilkenny became known as the accountant to the stars. He was financial adviser to U2 for twenty years and his many other roles have included chairing the Irish Film Board and being a director of TV3. In late 2016, he and Paul McGuinness, best known as U2's long-time former manager, planned to sell the Ardmore Studios in Bray.

However, Ossie's connection with Stillorgan was comparatively short. He was born in an old house on the Lower Kilmacud Road, where the Decor Centre now stands, but he and the rest of the family moved to Dundrum when Ossie was 6 years of age.

AUGUSTUS KENNEDY-KISCH

Augustus Kennedy-Kisch was the man who developed the Stillorgan shopping centre. Born in Middlesex, England, in 1914, he became a barrister, then became a property developer. He and his wife Joan were married in Northumberland in 1943 and went on to spend much of their married life in Ireland. They had a fine period house, built around 1800, just outside Newtownmountkennedy, Co. Wicklow.

Augustus died in 1977, aged 63, and his wife Joan died in 2000. He once said that he liked his wife to have 'pretty things' and the house was filled with a huge amount of Georgian and

Victorian furniture, silver and paintings. At the end of 2000, the contents of the house were sold, with 343 lots making a total of IR£0.5 million. In total, Joan left an estate valued at over IR£4 million. Tragically, their only daughter, Diana, died in 1973, aged 23; she was buried at Newcastle parish church, Co. Wicklow.

JOHN LOWE

John Lowe, known as 'the Money Doctor', has been an integral part of the Stillorgan retailing scene for many years.

He started as a junior in the Bank of Ireland in 1972. When the Stillorgan shopping centre opened in 1966, the Bank of Ireland opened a branch there and installed Ireland's first ATM machine. When John was working in the Bank of Ireland at Stillorgan, the manager was a man called Eric Henderson, whom he describes as a strange fellow, Church of Ireland, who often handed out edicts to the staff. Female staff, for instance, always had to wear tights, even in the middle of summer. Eric Henderson had been appointed manager of the branch when the centre opened; he retired in 1981.

John joined the old First National Building Society in 1983 and stayed with them until 1999, when he set up his own business on the Lower Kilmacud Road in Stillorgan, Providence Finance Services, trading as the Money Doctor.

Ever since then, he has been an indispensable purveyor of financial information for his customers, while he has also reached a much wider audience through his money-advice work in the media, newspapers, radio and television. In his spare time, he also runs a band, the Heartbeats, which often performs at charitable events. John has had this band, which has six players, for many years.

His office manager in Stillorgan is Stephanie Cahill, who has worked with John for the past seventeen years.

SÉAMUS P. MACEOIN

Séamus MacEoin is revered as one of the founding fathers of the credit union movement in Ireland and he had a close connection with Stillorgan.

Born in Kilkenny in 1920, he served in the army during the Second World War Emergency and, after the war, worked in a number of government departments, including the Land Commission. At the time of his retirement, he was manager of the employment exchange in Dún Laoghaire. Throughout the 1950s, he was very active in promoting the idea of a national credit union movement, and when the first credit union in Ireland was started in Dún Laoghaire, he was one of the founding members. He was also instrumental in setting up the Stillorgan Credit Union in 1967.

He was a gentle and considerate man, a fluent Irish speaker, totally dedicated to the credit union movement. He died in 1993.

MARITA CONLON-MCKENNA

Marita, who lives in Stillorgan with her husband and four children, is a well-known author of children's books, published by the O'Brien Press. Born in Goatstown in 1956, she went to school at Mount Anville. Her work experiences included the family business, a bank and a travel agency. She was always fascinated with the great mid-nineteenth-century famine, and her first book, published in 1990, was based on that period of Irish history. *Under the Hawthorn Tree* was a big success, translated into over a dozen languages. Since then, she has written many other books for children and has won several literary awards.

FRANCIS J. MACMANUS

Francis MacManus had a reputation both as a novelist and as director of talks and features at Radio Éireann, which he joined in 1948. He was always careful about what he wrote, as he didn't want to fall foul of Ireland's then strict censorship laws and get into trouble with his employers at the radio station. The family lived in Stillorgan.

MacManus had a formidable reputation in radio and since 1993 RTÉ Radio 1 has been running an annual short story competition in his honour.

JOHN MURPHY

For years, United Travel was a noted travel agency in Stillorgan, but in 2016, John or Con Murphy, then 66, was found guilty of writing cheques on the account of the Children to Lapland appeal and then lodging them into his personal account. He was given a three-year suspended sentence, because of his age and poor health. He had been diagnosed with bladder cancer in 2010. Murphy had operated United Travel, on the Old Dublin Road in Stillorgan, for many years and one of the services it offered was flights to Lapland, in time for Christmas.

In 1987, he devoted one of those flights to sending terminally ill children to Lapland; they came from hospitals all over the country. These flights became a regular occurrence and from them started the Children of Lapland appeal, with which Murphy was closely associated. United Travel operated until 2007, when it lost its trading licence from the Civil Aviation Authority, because it had incurred losses of €630,105. The directors of United Travel, including Murphy, loaned the company over €0.5 million, but the travel agency never regained its licence.

DISTRICT JUDGE DONNCHADH Ó BUACHALLA

This former judge on the District Court circuit was well known in Stillorgan, where the family home has been for many years. He died in April 2017.

He had been a solicitor in Dublin, having qualified in 1968. A strong supporter of Fianna Fáil, he was made a District Court judge by the then government of Charlie Haughey in 1989. In 1993, he was assigned to District Court area number 23, covering counties Wicklow and Wexford.

The judge became well known for having court sitting continuing through the lunch break and, on one occasion, when he was presiding at Arklow Court, he tucked the bottoms of his trousers into his socks when it was revealed that the court was overrun with mice. He commented: 'We have residents in court'. In his later years, the judge suffered from skin cancer. He retired from the bench in September 2011.

FERGUS O'KELLY

Stillorgan had a direct connection with the world's first radio broadcast, which announced the start of the Easter Rising in O'Connell Street in 1916. The telegraphy school at the corner of Lower Abbey Street and what is now O'Connell Street had been shut down by the British authorities, but a 20-year-old engineering student, Fergus O'Kelly, and his band of six compatriots got the equipment working again and erected an aerial on the roof.

They sent out a message in Morse code: 'Irish Republic declared in Dublin today, Irish troops have captured the city and are in full possession. Enemy cannot move in the city. The whole country rising.' This and other messages were tapped out for two days, after which the building had to be abandoned as it came under intense fire. Their messages were picked up in the US and published in newspapers there.

After the Rising, Fergus was sent to jail in England, then taken to Frongoch Camp in north Wales before being taken to Wormwood Scrubs prison in London and released at the end of July 1916. He then returned to the family home at Stillorgan, a bearded and emaciated figure. After he qualified in electrical and mechanical engineering with his Bachelor of Science degree, he went to work on the Shannon electrification scheme.

SIR WILLIAM ORPEN

Orpen, who was born at Grove Avenue, Stillorgan, in 1878, became one of Ireland's leading portrait painters, portraying the great and the good in Irish society. He died in 1931. A noted contemporary sculptor, Rowan Gillespie, has completed a magnificent bronze sculpture of Orpen, which is due to be unveiled in Stillorgan Village shopping centre during the latter part of 2017. The sculpture stands 3.35m high and once the extensions to Tesco, on the Lower Kilmacud Road side of the shopping centre, have been completed, the sculpture will be placed at the nearby street entrance.

The Stillorgan Chamber of Commerce, the Stillorgan Village Centre, the Smurfit Foundation and Baumanns are among the many organisations that have contributed to the funding for the statue. The unveiling is due to coincide with an exhibition of letters, memorabilia and watercolours by Orpen's father. The unveiling of the sculpture promises to be a big occasion in Stillorgan, as Ronnie Wood, a member of the renowned Rolling Stones, is due to do the needful; he's a long-time admirer and collector of Orpen's work.

BRIAN O'NOLAN

Better known as Myles na Gopaleen, Brian O'Nolan was born in Strabane, Co. Tyrone in 1911 but was educated at UCD. He spent his career in the civil service, but on the side developed as a masterful comic writer with such novels as *At Swim Two Birds*. He also wrote a column for *The Irish Times* called 'Cruiskeen Lawn', which mocked the follies and the characters of the day.

He married Evelyn McDonnell in 1948 and moved out of the family home in Avoca Terrace, Blackrock. Subsequently, O'Nolan lived at various addresses in south Dublin, including Belmont Avenue, Donnybrook. His final address, in the years immediately before he died in 1966, was in Stillorgan. One of the many pubs he frequented was Boland's in Stillorgan, but

O'Nolan had a fearsome reputation as the man who never stood his round.

GLEN POWER

Glen Power has been a well-known session musician since his early teens; he comes from Stillorgan. In the past few years, he's been the drummer in the Dublin-based group *The Script*, which has enjoyed runaway success.

In 2008, he had a bad accident when he fell in a pub toilet and broke his skull, even though he was sober at the time. He said later that if his dad hadn't brought him to hospital, he wouldn't have survived. But Glen made a near-miraculous recovery and left hospital nine days later. He attributed his quick recovery to his faith in God and the support of his band mates.

SÉAN Ó RIADA

Séan Ó Riada was the composer who changed the sound of traditional Irish music in the 1960s. He was from Cork, where he met his future wife, Ruth Coughlan, and his first job was as assistant director of music in Radio Éireann, but he found it so frustrating that he went to Paris and did some work on a French state-owned radio station. He became so down and out in Paris that his wife, Ruth, went there to rescue him from poverty and ill health. On his return to Ireland, he became musical director at the Abbey Theatre.

In 1958, he and Ruth rented a large house at Galloping Green which was owned by the Byrne family, who still own Byrne's pub close by. When Ó Riada was assembling the players for his Ceoltóirí Chualann group, they came to the house at Galloping Green to practise once a week. He also organised impromptu traditional dancing sessions on the bare boards of the main living room. Often, after these musical sessions, he and his friends adjourned to Byrne's pub, although Ray Byrne, who now owns the pub, said there was no evidence then that the great musician and composer was overindulging.

Ó Riada often acted on impulse and Ray Byrne remembers the day that the composer came home and simply announced that from then onwards, Irish was going to be the only language spoken in the house.

One of Ó Riada's seven children, Peadar, is a distinguished composer and musician in his own right and he remembers living at Galloping Green well, when the whole place was open country, with ne'er a housing estate or development in sight. The bus stop was outside the house and Peadar also remembers that since Byrne's pub was so far out of the city, it could stay open all afternoon.

The Ó Riada family lived in the house at Galloping Green for five years, until 1963, and eventually they moved to Cuil Aodha in the West Cork Gaeltacht. But in later years, Seán Ó Riada did begin to drink heavily and he also had a chronic liver condition. He died in hospital in London in 1971, aged just 40, having led a tumultuous life and having left behind a fine musical legacy, including the scores for such films as *Mise Éire*.

EDWARD LOVETT PEARCE

Pearce, who was born in Co. Meath in 1699, was one of the outstanding architects of early eighteenth-century Ireland. He had a close connection with Stillorgan, since he lived there, and he also designed the remarkable Obelisk for Lord Allen's estate, as well as a brick-built grotto on that same estate.

He was the only child of General Edward Pearce, who was a first cousin of a famous architect of the time, Sir John Vanburgh. In 1715, after his father's death, Edward Pearce became a pupil of Vanburgh. Pearce also went to Italy, the only Irish architect of his time to have done so, and studied Palladian architecture there.

Returning to Ireland in 1724, Pearce started his own practice and soon won some important commissions, including the design for the Houses of Parliament in College Green,

Castletown House in Co. Kildare and Cashel Palace in Cashel, Co. Tipperary. In 1725, he married his first cousin, Ann, then in 1727 became the MP for Ratoath in Co. Meath.

He and his family lived at The Grove, just off the Old Dublin Road in Stillorgan. It later became Tigh Lorcáin Hall, which was demolished to make way for the bowling alley opened in 1963 and now occupied by the Leisureplex complex. But Pearce's glittering architectural career was brief; he died in 1733, aged just 34.

PAT QUINN

Pat Quinn was the man who launched a national retail revolution with his first supermarket in Stillorgan. From Cloone, Co. Leitrim, he emigrated to Canada in the mid-1950s and gained invaluable experience there in retailing and in running pubs and restaurants. After five years in Canada, he came back to Ireland in 1961, full of new ideas for retailing here. He opened his first Quinnsworth supermarket in the Stillorgan shopping centre in December 1966 and eventually owned seven such supermarkets. He was a great promoter of his own supermarkets, frequently appearing in TV commercials wearing the white polo-neck sweater that became his personal trademark.

When he opened his new supermarket in the Stillorgan shopping centre on 1 December 1966, curious shoppers saw something many of them had never seen before: a shiny new escalator. Standing at the top of it was a small, bald, smiling man wearing a white polo-neck sweater, Pat Quinn.

In the early 1970s, Quinnsworth was sold to Power Supermarkets, who in turn sold out to Associated British Foods (ABF), controlled by the Galen family, another big business name in Canada. In 1997, the supermarket chain of Quinnsworth was sold on again, this time to Tesco, which bought Quinnsworth and its opposite number in the North of Ireland, Stewarts Supermarkets, from ABF. One retailing idea developed at Quinnsworth became notorious, the Yellow Pack own-label products. These soon became synonymous with low prices and poor quality, so that any product or service that delivered below-standard quality became known as a 'Yellow Pack'.

Nearly fifty years after the invention of the Yellow Pack concept at the old Quinnsworth, the phrase is still widely used today to denote something that's cheap or inferior.

Pat Quinn eventually returned to Canada, where he died in 2009.

NEVIL SHUTE

One of the world's best-selling novelists in the 1950s, Nevil Shute, had a close connection with the Stillorgan district when he was a young man.

He was born in London on 17 January 1899. Before the First World War, his father, Arthur Hamilton Norway, was appointed head of the Post Office in Ireland, based at the GPO in Dublin. Norway was there when the Easter Rising started in 1916. In its immediate aftermath, the young Nevil Shute acted as a stretcher bearer for the St John's Ambulance Brigade.

When the family came to Ireland, they bought a house at South Hill, off Mount Merrion Avenue and very close to Stillorgan Village. Eventually, Nevil Shute returned to England and completed his studies at Oxford University. Between the two world wars, he worked in England as an aeronautical engineer, but by 1939 his fame as a novelist was already on the rise. Of all the best-selling books he wrote, the one he is most remembered for is probably *A Town Called Alice*, published in 1956. Nevil Shute spent the last few years of his life in Australia and died in Melbourne in 1960.

FRANK TRACEY

Born in the Liberties in Dublin in 1943, Frank Tracey graduated from what was then UCG in 1967 with a BA in Celtic Archaeology. He went on to spend most of his career in the public service. But he has also had a lifelong interest in scouting and in hillwalking and in 2008, South Dublin Library Service published his book, *South Dublin Rambles*. He and his wife Bernie live in Stillorgan; they have five adult children.

DESSIE TURNER

Dessie was one of the all-time great 'characters' around Stillorgan Village in recent decades. Born and brought up in Stillorgan, he lived there all his life. For many years, he worked as a porter in what had been the old Munster and Leinster Bank (later to form part of AIB) next door to Baumanns, but retired twenty years ago. He died last year, 2016, aged 84. Another great Stillorgan character, Des Croasdell, remembers Dessie Turner as being a very genial and friendly type of person, always willing to stop for a chat. He remembers Dessie talking of a horrific incident when he was at school in Stillorgan. Dessie had received a ferocious beating across the hands for a minor misdemeanour and the effects of that beating stayed with him all his life.

HILDA TWEEDY

Hilda Tweedy, who was born Hilda Anderson in Clones, Co. Monaghan, in 1911, was the daughter of the local Church of Ireland rector. In 1929, she joined her parents in Egypt, where her father had been made rector of St Mark's Anglican church in Alexandria. While there, Hilda started studying for an external degree in maths from the University of London, although she never completed that course. She and her sister also started a small school in Alexandria for English-speaking children.

In 1936, after her marriage to Robert Massy Tweedy, she returned home to Ireland. She applied for a teaching post but was turned down because she was married. Then in 1941, with a group of other women, she started what became the Irish Housewives Association. The organisation lasted until 1992.

She played a key role in the advance of women's rights in Ireland, such as the implementation of equal pay and the abolition of the marriage bar in the public service. Hilda also taught maths in the secretarial department at Alexandra College, from 1962 to 1982. Her husband was the manager of the Court Laundry for many years.

After he retired in 1962, he and Hilda started Nimble Fingers in Stillorgan to sell educational toys for children and they ran the shop until 1982. It's still going strong, under the ownership of the Staunton family.

For many years, Hilda and Robert lived in a secluded bungalow, Hillcrest, on Church Road, near St Brigid's church. In the last few years of their lives, their existence was cruelly punctuated by break-ins and robberies, while in his old age, Robert was both deaf and blind. He and Hilda died in the same year, 2005.

MAURICE WALSH

Maurice Walsh, born in Co. Kerry in 1879, made a great name for himself as a writer. He spent his career in the excise service and for many years was stationed in Scotland, where he met his wife Caroline, always known by her nickname 'Toshon'. He retired from the excise service in 1933 and the following year bought a fine house on the Stillorgan Road called Árd na Glaise. The house was set on 1.2ha. His wife particularly liked the house, whereas Walsh had initially been reluctant to buy it. But he did and they settled in to a very convivial lifestyle. One of Walsh's favourite occupations was walking down to Boland's pub in Stillorgan Village, for an an evening's drinking in good company.

During the 1930s, Maurice Walsh was a best-selling author in Ireland. He was best known for his short story, 'The Quiet Man', later made into a film of the same name starring Maureen O'Hara and released in 1952. After his wife Caroline died in 1940, Maurice found the house in Stillorgan too big to live in, so he moved a short distance, to Avoca Road in Blackrock, although his son continued to live in Árd na Glaise. Maurice Walsh, legendary storyteller, died in February 1964.

ARCHBISHOP WHATELY

The most eccentric archbishop ever appointed in Ireland, Richard Whately was made Church of Ireland Archbishop of Dublin in 1831 and remained in office until 1863.

Born in London in 1787, he was educated at Oxford and took holy orders in 1814. Eventually, he was made professor of political economy at Oxford in 1829, but his tenure of office was cut short by his unexpected appointment in Dublin. He had had no previous experience of living in Ireland, and soon after he came to Dublin he started to offend fellow clergymen by his blunt manner and lack of a conciliatory spirit. He also gave offence right from the start in Dublin by proposing state endowment of the Catholic clergy. His gruff and uncouth manners were notorious. At the dinner table, he often contorted his legs so much that his foot landed in the lap of whoever was unfortunate enough to be sitting beside him.

Some of his reform efforts, whilst well intentioned, failed. Almost as soon as he had arrived in Dublin, he attempted to establish a national and non-sectarian system of education, but the scheme broke down because of Catholic opposition. Whately was also a prolific writer on theological subjects and his three daughters and his son also became published authors. Many Protestants regarded him as the enemy within, while Catholics saw him as a devious proselytiser. Catholic Archbishop Paul Cullen carried out a sustained campaign against Whately, all of whose grandiose schemes eventually failed.

His personal behaviour was often eccentric and he often compounded the popular view of him by talking at great length, frequently introducing puns into his conversation. In 1856, his medical decline began, but this didn't deter him from carrying out his duties as archbishop. He died in 1863.

Whately also had a long connection with Stillorgan, since he refused to live in the archbishop's palace at St Stephen's Green and instead lived at Redesdale House in Kilmacud for almost thirty years. He loved walking in the gardens there and

liked experimenting with grafting plants. Bryan MacMahon of the Kilmacud Stillorgan Local History Society has written a biography of this most eccentric of archbishops.

T.K. WHITAKER

Dr T.K. Whitaker, widely known as Ken, had a close connection with Stillorgan for many years, through his family home at 148 Stillorgan Road, close to the Belfield fly-over. Born in Rostrevor, Co. Down, he grew up in Drogheda and joined the civil service in Dublin in 1934. In 1956, he was made secretary of the Department of Finance, one of the youngest people ever to hold that position. At the end of the 1950s, he started writing his paper on Ireland's future economic development. He advocated the ending of tariffs on imports and the development of a free-trade economy.

This report was seen as laying the foundation of the new economic model for Ireland which started to flourish in the 1960s; he had played a pivotal role in the transformation of the Irish economy, indeed Irish society generally. In 1969, he became the governor of the Central Bank, a position he held until 1976. With his close Northern connections, he also advised Taoisigh such as Séan Lemass and Jack Lynch on growing cross-border co-operation that had begun in the mid-1960s. In the summer of 2017, Whitaker's house on the Stillorgan Road was up for sale.

Ken Whitaker was married twice. Apart from his official duties, he always had a keen regard for the west of Ireland,

where he frequently went on fishing holidays. A remarkable man, who was always a committed lover of Irish people and of everything Irish, he celebrated his 100th birthday in December 2016 and died the following month, having lived in Stillorgan for the best part of fifty years.

10

SCHOOLS

BUSY BEES CHILDCARE

This childcare establishment was founded in Stillorgan in 1990 to provide exceptional childcare in a loving environment.

GLENALBYN MONTESSORI PRESCHOOL

This preschool was founded in 2003 to provide Montessori-style education for children aged between 2 years and 9 months and 6 years. All the teachers are fully trained in the Montessori method. The preschool is located at Woodview House on Glenalbyn Road in Stillorgan.

LITTLE DALE ACADEMY

Located in Dale Road, close to Stillorgan, Little Dale Academy is affiliated with Little Willows Academy in Dundrum and Room to Grow in Killiney. It's run by the Kelly family and a dedicated team of Montessori teachers and childcare practitioners; it's been in operation for over twenty years, catering for children from 3 months 12 years old. One of the features of the Dale Road establishment is its large garden, with many play facilities.

NEW GAELSCOIL

A new Gaelscoil na Fuinseoige was opened in the Clonskeagh area in 2016 to serve a wide area of south Dublin, including Stillorgan. A permanent building for the new school is on the Department of Education's build list for 2018. The name for the new school was chosen by parents because many of the roads in the Clonskeagh area are named after trees and *an fuinseog*, the ash tree, is a native Irish tree from which hurleys are made. The uniform for the new school is available from O'Farrell's in Stillorgan Village Centre.

The principal of the new school is Aisling Uí Fhéich, who has been a primary teacher for over twenty years and before her appointment to the new school was deputy principal of a Gaelscoil in Maynooth, Co. Kildare.

OATLANDS COLLEGE

Just off the main N11 road, close to Stillorgan Village, Oatlands College, whose present building dates back to the late 1960s, has long been a familiar part of the educational landscape in the area.

The college is a voluntary Christian Brothers secondary school for boys aged between 10 and 18, preparing them for their junior cert and leaving cert exams. It currently has about 550 students. The Christian Brothers first established a community here in 1951, starting a school in 1955. The college is now under the trusteeship of the Edmund Rice Schools Trust.

Over the years, many extensions have been made to the school, such as the new rooms for computer studies, drawing, music and technology, as well as two new science labs, all of which were opened in 2010. In 2012, a new sport hall with a canteen and a new classroom were opened by the President of Ireland, Michael D. Higgins.

Oatlands College has many distinguished past pupils, such as Kenny Carroll, cricketer, Don Conroy, wildlife artist, Paul Griffith, GAA footballer, Dermot Moran, professor of philosophy, the late Dermot Morgan, Father Ted of TV comedy fame, Éamon Ó Cuiv, a grandson of Éamon de Valera and a prominent member of Fianna Fáil, Stephen Power, amateur swimmer, and Stephen Collins, of *The Irish Times*.

Oatlands College had another unusual distinction for the district. The FCA is the army reserve and B Company of the 21st Infantry Battalion was centred on south Dublin. After the college had been established in the 1950s, this company was enhanced by the opening of a new centre at Oatlands College. Army reservists connected to Oatlands College included Commandant Michael Nestor, who died on UN assignment, and Lieutenant Dermot Bradley, who went on to a very successful career as a historian of German military history.

OATLANDS PRIMARY SCHOOL

Located in the grounds of Oatlands College, this is a Catholic school based on the traditions of Edmund Rice, but it accepts children of all religions and none. The primary school opened in 1954, as an all-boys Christian Brothers' school, taking boys from second to sixth class. In 1995, the first infants came to the school and, in 2004, it became co-educational. The school has around 420 pupils.

ST BENILDUS COLLEGE

This college is located in Kilmacud, but serves a wider area, including Stillorgan; it's a Catholic boys' secondary school. It dates back to 1966, when free secondary education was introduced in Ireland. The college was named after the De La Salle saint, Brother Benildus, a French priest.

The college is located on a 10ha site, adjacent to the Luas Green Line. Until the 1960s, the area in which the school is located was farmland, subsequently developed for housing estates. St Benildus, whose principal is Martin Johnson, now has around 750 students with a higher-than-average number going on to third-level education. Most years, there is a 100 per cent progression rate to third-level studies.

St Benildus also has a fine sporting record in such sports as hurling, soccer and basketball and four of its past pupils are David Gillick, twice European indoor athletics gold medallist, Derek Daly, racing driver, Ray Cosgrove, Dublin GAA footballer and former All-Star, and Richard Sadlier, former Ireland international soccer player.

Diarmaid Ferriter, a well-known historian, is also a past pupil, as is Joe Lynam, a BBC presenter and Paul Cunningham, an RTÉ presenter.

ST BRIGID'S PAROCHIAL SCHOOLS

There has been a school connected with the Church of Ireland parish of St Brigid's since at least the beginning of the nineteenth century, and earlier, too, in the seventeenth and eighteenth centuries. The earliest recorded schoolmaster was Thomas Hickes, during the 1650s, when he was being paid £120 a year, a very considerable salary indeed.

During the later eighteenth century, it seems that the school was re-established about 1764, and during the nineteenth century many changes and additions were made to the school and its organisation.

No records survive, because most of the parish records, including those of the school, were destroyed in 1922 when the Four Courts were set alight. But fortunately, the history of St Brigid's parochial schools in Stillorgan, for boys, girls and infants, has been thoroughly researched in recent years. The history of the school from 1862 to 1985 was researched and written by Jessica Classon; Hilda de Nais, then principal of St Brigid's School; Michael Classon, then principal of Newpark School, Blackrock, and Canon M.B. Taylor, then rector of the grouped parishes of St Brigid's and All Saints, Blackrock.

Stillorgan people long believed that the notorious Oliver Cromwell held a prayer meeting for his soldiers at the schoolhouse in Stillorgan during the 1650s. In the late nineteenth century, the parochial schools provided not just education but clothing as well for the pupils, while children in the infants' school got bread every day. The lowest ebb in the school's fortunes came just after the Second World War, in 1949, when it had just eight pupils.

In more recent times, in the early 1950s, the Church of Ireland population of the parish increased from 242 to 654, and by 1957 the school had forty-one pupils. By 1971, it had seventy pupils. By 1980, numbers had gone up again, to over 100. But by that time, the facilities at the school were very unsatisfactory; even the ground floor of the nearby rectory had to be turned over to school use. However, by 1984, the funds to build a new school had been secured: around £360,000 with 90 per cent of the cost paid by the Department of Education. By the end of the 1980s, St Brigid's had an entirely new school building.

ST RAPHAELA'S SECONDARY SCHOOL

This secondary school is a voluntary one for girls, under the trusteeship of the Handmaids of the Sacred Heart of Jesus. The Sisters had come from London to open a retreat centre in Finglas in Dublin in 1942 and from there moved to Blackrock. In 1971, the school moved to its present site in Stillorgan.

The foundation of the school in the Stillorgan area can be traced back to the Pilkington family of glass-making fame, who were the first owners of Wesbury House, built in 1750. The Daughters of Charity had opened an orphanage for boys and a primary school on the site and the original entrance was at the present-day entrance to the Stillorgan Wood housing estate on the Upper Kilmacud Road. The Handmaids of the Sacred Heart of Jesus took up residence on the site in 1971 and they developed the school. The new secondary-school building was opened in 1986.

A new wing was added in the 1990s and the AstroTurf sports complex was completed in 2008. In 2011, the road which goes through the old Wesbury House entrance was renamed St Raphaela's Road. Further classrooms were added in 2015. In October of that same year, the school celebrated its golden jubilee, and today it is a thriving centre of second-level educational excellence, a long way from the original two classrooms in the old convent.

SCOIL LORCÁIN NAOFA (ST LAURENCE'S SCHOOL)

This school can trace its origins back to the founding of the first boys' national school in Stillorgan, opposite the present-day shopping centre, on 25 May 1840. The school moved to its present site in 1931 and since then major extensions and renovations have been carried out, firstly in 1931, to coincide with the move, then in 1986 and 2007. All its classrooms are now networked for Internet access.

When the school started in 1840, it had 56 pupils. The high point was in the 1970s when it had over 750 pupils; the current enrolment is about 450. Michael Garry retired as principal in 2016 and was succeeded by the current principal, Damian Moran.

SETANTA SCHOOL

The school was founded in 1965 by the health authorities and was called St Loman's Special School, next door to St Loman's Hospital. It was intended for pupils with all kinds of special needs, not just autism. In 1990, it was moved to Blanchardstown, then, five years later, to its present site in Stillorgan. Its sister school, Ballyowen Meadows, catering for pre-teens on the ASD spectrum, had been located nearby the previous year, 1994.

For the first year of its existence in Stillorgan, Setanta School, as it had been renamed, shared facilities with the Mary Immaculate School for the Deaf, but Setanta School then had full use of the building. Since then, the scope of the school has been extended significantly. According to the principal, Loman Ó Loinsigh, in the academic year 2016/17, it catered for nearly sixty students, with twelve teachers and twenty-eight special-needs assistants.

The school now also makes use of the buildings vacated by Ballyowen Meadows School, which has temporarily relocated to Loughlinstown.

STILLORGAN COLLEGE OF FURTHER EDUCATION

Based on the Old Dublin Road in Stillorgan, this college has been a specialist centre for post-leaving certificate and further-education studies since 1986. Over the past thirty-one years, it has developed a considerable reputation for its further-education and adult-education courses. The college has state-of-the-art facilities, including computer rooms. It has a very high ratio of computers to students, and up-to-date equipment and industry-standard software are used.

Before it was given its present name, it was known simply as Stillorgan Tech, and one of its teachers, Dermot Morgan, went on to television fame when he became a comedian.

When the original school here opened on 6 September 1965, the first intake had sixty students. There were forty-eight boys in two classes, and one class of twelve girls. One of the first boys to attend was a young lad called Pat Eddery.

He had been born in Newbridge, Co. Kildare, but his family later moved to Blackrock. He enrolled in the new Stillorgan school as soon as it had opened, graduating there from Oatlands primary school. He left the new school at Stillorgan on his fourteenth birthday, in 1966, and signed up as an apprentice jockey at Seamus McGrath's stables near Leopardstown. Pat Eddery went on to become one of the greatest flat jockeys in racing history. Sadly, he died just ten days before the fiftieth anniversary celebrations of the Stillorgan college.

Just five days before that event, the college's widely admired former chair of the board of management, Mary Elliott, also died. One of the guests at the anniversary celebrations, a local TD called Peter Mathews, died in 2017.

As part of those celebrations, a special meal was organised at Eddie Rocket's Diner in the shopping centre and the 1960s horror movie, *Psycho*, was screened in the college. Everyone enjoyed a specially themed fiftieth birthday cake, 'Jive back to '65'. A super raffle was also organised, raising €1,306 for Temple Street children's hospital.

THE CHILDREN'S HOUSE MONTESSORI PRIMARY SCHOOL

This outstanding school for young pupils was founded in 1952 by Veronica Ryan at Thornhill on the Lower Killmacud Road; she had started a class in her home with six pupils two years earlier.

Veronica had trained as a Montessori teacher at Sion Hill in nearby Blackrock and, as interest in the Montessori method of teaching spread, she decided to build her own school. She travelled to the Netherlands to study existing Montessori schools there and then a noted architect, Arthur Douglas, designed the Children's House in the grounds of Veronica's home. It was the first purpose-built Montessori school in Ireland, set in a garden full of trees, with plenty of suitable play areas and equipment for children. The school still remains an outstanding building of its type.

Sadly, Veronica died at a young age; she was 45 when she succumbed to pneumonia in 1966, but the Ryan family was determined to continue her work. Beth Ann Doyle was the principal until 1968, when Madeleine Coen and Elizabeth Carbery took over as joint principals. When Madeleine retired in 2006, Micaela Kuh, the present principal, took over. She has overseen extensions of the school's facilities and of its classes, introducing the 9 to 12 Montessori stage to the senior class.

In 2002, the school celebrated its fiftieth anniversary, and today the ethos and spirit of the Montessori method, first brought to fruition here by Veronica Ryan, continues to flourish.

Today, the school has around seventy pupils and continues to be a dedicated fulfilment of Veronica Ryan's original vision.

11

SHOPPING

APPLEGREEN

The Applegreen service station on the main road just before the junction with Mount Merrion Avenue, very close to Stillorgan, won the 2013 National Retail Store of the Year Award. It was the first time that a forecourt operator had won the award. The store was described as being first class, exuding innovation and intelligent retail execution, with everything customer-facing and with impeccable service. Keith Ennis, manager of the store, was named manager of the year.

BAUMANNS

Baumanns, on the Old Dublin Road in Stillorgan, just down from the Stillorgan Village Centre, has long been part of Stillorgan's retailing scene. It was founded by Jack and Catherine Baumann in September 1947.

Soon, the shop was successful, selling not just building products and hardware, but toys and garden equipment. The Baumanns also had a newsagent and opened one of the first ice-cream parlours in south Co. Dublin. Jack Baumann became known as the 'king of Stillorgan' and often wore a white blazer and a bow tie, a showman to the last, also noted for running many charitable events.

In 1978, Val Baumann, the Baumanns' son, took over and refocussed the shop on hardware and garden sheds, then expanding into aquatic supplies, fishing supplies and shooting tackle. Over the years, Baumanns became a working place for many local people, some of whom spent their entire working lives at the shop. One particularly dedicated lady was Bess Lambert, who joined Baumanns in 1949, when she was 17. The rest of her working life was spent there and after she retired, she still called in to the shop regularly. She died in 1984.

In the same row of shops as Baumanns, among other occupants, there are an Asian supermarket, a blood donation clinic (close to where the bank used to be) and a firm that specialises in men's grooming products and services.

CATHAL'S COMPUTERS

Cathal Gormley has been running Cathal's Computer Clinic on the Lower Kilmacud Road since 2005 and has built up a very solid reputation for computer repairs, dealing with spyware and malware, networking and data recovery.

C&D SHOES

One of the longest surviving retailers in the Stillorgan Village shopping centre, C&D has been there since the original centre opened in 1966. It has been run since its inception by Trevor Jackman and over the years it has expanded into a wide range of products and services, in addition to its shoe repairs.

DEIRDRE'S VIEWS ON STILLORGAN

Councillor Deirdre Donnelly is a well-known independent councillor on Dún Laoghaire–Rathdown County Council and she has close connections with Stillorgan.

She remembers that the legendary Bewley's firm had a shop in the shopping centre from the 1970s and says she can still smell the fragrance of the Bewley's coffee then. She also says that it was a real treat to go to the Bewley's café on the first floor and enjoy a bird's eye view of all the activity on the ground floor of the shopping centre.

Deirdre remembers that the centre had two excellent record shops; indeed, she had a part-time job in one of them. She recalls how the Stillorgan Plaza was launched in the 1980s, on the opposite side of Lower Kilmacud Road to the shopping centre. The Plaza was hailed as a new shopping experience and one of its shops was a large record store with an incredible collection of music. While the Stillorgan Plaza had promised so much, it never got off the ground. One of the buildings that was developed there, the cinema, now an Odeon, is still there today.

But, Deirdre remarks, some things about Stillorgan remain unchanged. Baumanns has for many years been the place where you could go to for everything from nails for woodwork to a pet snake. 'That shop is still there, as are Fenelon's butchers, Raffertys the pharmacy and C&D Shoes, all in the shopping centre. After all, everyone needs shoes heeled and keys cut at C&D.'

Despite the economic downturn in the 1980s and the property-led crash in 2008, Stillorgan managed to weather the storm, she says. It wasn't long after the most recent crash that the Kilkenny Shop and Donnybrook Fair made brave decisions to set up shop in the shopping centre, by opening outlets that cater for the high end of the market in gift products and food. In both cases, the focus is very much on Irish quality brands.

Another more recent attraction is the regular Wednesday Farmers' Market. Says Deirdre: 'The weekly displays of artisan products and supplies alongside the street food, with Japanese-style stir fries, and Syrian falafels, are certainly a far cry from the Stillorgan of the 1970s'.

DID ELECTRICAL

This well-known chain of electrical goods shops was founded in Dublin in the late 1960s and today one of its largest branches remains its store on the Lower Kilmacud Road in Stillorgan, which opened in 1987.

DONNYBROOK FAIR

This high-quality gourmet-food-store group has its origins in Donnybrook, where its headquarters is still based. In recent years, Donnybrook Fair has expanded considerably in the greater Dublin area, with shops as far away as Malahide and Greystones. In 2011, it arrived in Stillorgan, when it took a big unit on the side of the shopping centre that faces the Lower Kilmacud Road. Before it had opened, Pat Staunton, owner of the Nimble Fingers toy shop opposite the shopping centre, became curious about the man sitting in a car nearby every day of the week. Eventually, Pat went up to him and asked him what he was doing. It was Joe Doyle, the owner of Donnybrook Fair, who was watching the pedestrian traffic flows in and out of the shopping centre, as he was deciding whether or not to go ahead with his planned shop in the centre. In the end, he made a shrewd decision to go ahead. Today, the store remains very busy and popular, selling butchery products, fruit and vegetables, delicatessen items, ready-made meals, grocery and bakery products. It has a wide variety of sections, including an off-licence, a fishmongers, a craft butchers, a charcuterie, a greengrocers, eating-in dishes and desserts, altogether a most appetising selection. Some sources say that the Stillorgan outlet is probably the best performing of all six shops in the Donnybrook Fair group.

DOVE DRY CLEANERS

When Dove Dry Cleaners, well established outside Dublin, opened in the Stillorgan shopping centre in 2012, it was its first store in Dublin. That deal also brought the number of new retailers in the centre over the previous twelve months to twenty-one.

ESMONDE MOTORS

Just at the foot of The Hill in Stillorgan, Esmonde Motors was for a long time an essential part of the motoring scene in Stillorgan, as the OK Garage had been on the site during the 1960s. Esmonde Motors was founded in 1955 and continued trading until 2008, when it closed down. Ever since then, the 0.5ha site has remained derelict. In May 2015, the site, together with an adjoining detached house, was put on the market for over €5 million, but today the site still remains undeveloped.

FENELONS

Fenelons, a local butchers, became the first in the country to open a unit in a shopping centre when the Stillorgan shopping centre opened in 1966. It soon expanded by taking over the next-door fishmongers and began to sell fish and game. In 1996, thirty years after first opening in the shopping centre, Fenelons moved to another, larger location there.

The original shop was started by Larry Fenelon, but when he retired, he sold it to one of his long-time employees, Clif Lenehan (50), who continues to run it with a staff of close on twenty. Some of the customers of the shop have been going there since it opened fifty-one years ago and in 2016, Clif said that his oldest customer was a lady of 105.

The shop has continued to win awards, such as the Bridgestone Best in Ireland, while it keeps up to date by running its own website and Facebook page.

FINDLATER'S

Besides the Monument Creameries shop, Stillorgan once had another of the noted old-time grocery shop chains, Findlater's, but for a much shorter period. Findlater's had a chain of shops across the greater Dublin area and they were noted for the range of their produce and the quality of their service.

When the Stillorgan shopping centre opened in 1966, Findlater's took a shop unit there, but it only lasted until 1968. They had been slow to adapt to the self-service supermarket revolution, and by the time a Findlater's shop opened in Stillorgan, the chain was already in deep trouble. That shop closed in 1968, the year before the last of the shops in the chain closed down.

KILMACUD

Memories of shopping in Kilmacud come from Frank Wallace, who for many years ran a self- service grocery store at Slieve

Rua Drive in Kilmacud. He noted in the *Obelisk* that he had traded for thirty-four happy years in Kilmacud. His own shop was succeeded by the Little Flowers shop until 2015. Frank also recalled seeing a painting done in 1950 of the corner of Slieve Rua Drive and the Lower Kilmacud Road, before any of the shops or O'Dwyer's pub had been built.

Another of the shops mentioned by Frank was the greengrocer's at the corner of Redesdale Road and Lower Kilmacud Road; it was run for many years by Frank Hyland, who died in 1974. Also in the area was a Monument Creameries shop, which had another local connection, since Mrs Ryan, who ran the firm for many years, lived in nearby Burton Hall. After the Monument Creameries closed down in 1966, its Kilmacud shop was sold to a neighbouring shop, the newsagents run by Pat and Nora McKeown. Out on the Lower Kilmacud Road, John and Eileen Conaty had a butcher's shop, renowned for its rashers, roasts and sausages. One of its customers was one of the Overend sisters from Dundrum, who arrived on the dot of 11 a.m. every Saturday morning to buy the weekend roast for herself and her sister.

Among the newer arrivals on the Lower Kilmacud Road in the late 1960s was William O'Dwyer from Co. Tipperary, who bought one of the newly built shop units at No. 118 Lower Kilmacud Road, alongside the chemists and the butcher's, and turned it into O'Dwyer's pub. In those far-off days, men still drank in the bar, while women headed for the lounge.

DOMINIC LEE

Dominic is one of the best-known commercial photographers in south Dublin. He set up Priory Studios, specialising in portrait, wedding and commercial photography, in 1984, and for many years this was a feature on the Old Dublin Road. He was also a founding member of Stillorgan Chamber of Commerce. Dominic retired from the studios in December 2015, but still accepts commissions.

LIDL

Lidl, the German discount grocery retailer, has been one of the larger retailers to open in Stillorgan in recent years outside the shopping centre. It opened in December 2011 on the Lower Kilmacud Road, in what had been a furniture store owned by Durkan New Homes.

LOGUE'S GROCERY SHOP

This shop opened at the end of 1949, run by the Logue family, who had moved to Stillorgan from Northern Ireland. The shop was newly built, part of a row of shops that also included next-door neighbours, the Baumanns, Nolan's pharmacy and a branch of Leverett & Frye, an upmarket grocers and wine merchants.

The Logue family ran their grocery shop in the traditional way, with no refrigeration, which meant that customers had to buy their groceries daily or every other day. In those days, frozen, chilled and convenience foods were unheard of. The line of shops here was known as the 'shopping centre' until the Stillorgan shopping centre was opened nearby in 1966. As for the Logues, they ran their grocery shop until the end of the 1950s, when the old Munster and Leinster Bank, which was later one of the banks that merged to form AIB, bought the premises to open a branch.

PETER MARK HAIRDRESSERS

The Peter Mark chain of hairdressers is another long-established outlet in the Stillorgan Village shopping centre. Peter and Mark Keaveney had started their first shop in Grafton Street, Dublin, in 1961, so their expansion into the Stillorgan centre was a major move on their part. Peter Mark is still going strong in the centre; now, it's by far the largest hairdressing chain in Ireland.

PETER MCCANN

Peter McCann, whose family has important connections with Stillorgan, has two long-established outlets in St Laurence's Park. Stillorgan Cycles is well regarded for the range of bicycles it offers, while Peter McCann Motors, beside it, is an independent car dealers, with a workshop for repairs and service. The motor company also sells a wide range of accessories. Peter's family go back a long way in Stillorgan Village; his grandmother lived for many years in one of Moore's Cottages, demolished to make way for the shopping centre, and Peter's father was born in that cottage in 1917. Peter started his garage business in Stillorgan in 1976 and the bicycle business three years later, in 1979.

MONUMENT CREAMERIES

One of Stillorgan's most upmarket food shops has long gone. The Monument Creameries had been founded in Parnell Street, central Dublin, in 1919, named after the nearby Parnell Monument. One shop became a chain of thirty-three shops, in many parts of Dublin, including one at 25 Lower Kilmacud Road, Stillorgan. The Monument Creameries was noted for its fresh food, including bakery and dairy products, at a time when food shops didn't have any refrigeration or convenience foods. In the Monument Creameries shops, including the one in Stillorgan, one of the familiar shapes was butter being paddled into 1-pound shapes from huge blocks, ready for customers.

The Monument Creameries went into liquidation and closed down in 1966, after the death of Agnes Ryan, who lived at nearby Burton Hall and was the head of the shops for many years following the death of her husband, Séamus, in 1933.

NIMBLE FINGERS

Nimble Fingers, Stillorgan's very own toy shop, has been going strong since 1962, when it was started by Hilda and Robert Tweedy. They had begun by selling wools and crafts, then diversified into educational toys, mostly wooden. The Tweedys kept the shop going despite the opening of the shopping centre across the road, but in time decided to sell out and retire. That was in 1982, and in January 1983, Pat Staunton became the new owner.

He had become involved in third-level educational publishing, initially based in Canada, then in Europe, before moving on to become a publisher's agent. But he had always been interested in toy shops and Nimble Fingers continued to be a popular place for many children and their parents. Pat started importing toys from Germany, which were then a total novelty in Ireland. He kept Nimble Fingers going despite the advent of computer games.

When, in due course, Pat decided to retire, the business was taken over by the two sons of Pat and his wife Jean, Ross and Gareth. To this day, Nimble Fingers is as busy and popular as ever and continues to be run by the Staunton family. It has, as it has always had, a very wide and inventive range of toys, a real Aladdin's Cave for children and their parents from far and wide. One of the new generation of Stauntons, Katherine, is making her mark on the shop.

Next door was highly regarded jeweller's shop, run for many years, until the early 1980s, by German-born Walter Feddern. What was the jewellery shop of old is now Joseph Kramer's hair studio.

POST OFFICE

Stillorgan has had a post office for the past 187 years. The first in the village was located at what is now 12, The Hill. It was run by the Hill family and from them passed to relatives in the Glynn family. Eventually, it passed on again, to the Kelly family. By the early 1960s, the post office was in a grocery shop at the foot of The Hill, close to the then OK Garage. Mrs Kennedy was the last postmistress there and, needless to remark, in this tale of interconnected families, the Kennedys were related to the Kellys. In more recent times, right up to the present day, the post office has been located in the shopping centre.

STILLORGAN SHOPPING CENTRE

Back in 1966, the shopping centre was officially opened by Kathleen, wife of then Taoiseach Sean Lemass, but this seems to have made little impact. The 'unofficial' opening by singer Dickie Rock, in December 1966, has been much better remembered in local folklore.

When the centre happened, it had a total of sixty-three units. Among those were three supermarkets: Liptons, Powers and Quinnsworth. The first two have long since disappeared and Quinnsworth was eventually taken over by Tesco, which today has three units in the centre, one for homeware, one for an off-licence and a third for a supermarket outlet. Tesco is planning to expand its operation in Stillorgan, but declined to comment. Work started on this major extension in March 2017, and is due to be completed before the end of 2017. Dunnes Stores has also had a strong presence in the centre for many years, with outlets for groceries, homeware and fashion.

Other outlets when the centre first opened included Cassidy's fashions, Bolger's, which sold shoes, knitting wool and other items, and the Mary Ann Boutique. The shopping centre also had a branch of the Bank of Ireland, the first non-traditional location in Ireland for a bank branch, as well as the country's first ATM machine, also run by the Bank of Ireland. It even had a pub, The Oyster, owned by Madigans.

Another popular spot in the earlier days of the shopping centre was a delicatessen called À la Française. Iris McGee had married a Frenchman called René Riou and they opened what was to become a very popular deli in the shopping centre. It also had a branch at Killiney and another in Wicklow Street, central Dublin.

Moreover, in the present-day centre there are two bookshops. Book Station sells books, cards and stationery, while Dubray Books, one of Ireland's leading independent bookshop chains, sells books, cards, toys and some stationery items. Dubray Books opened in the shopping centre back in 1997, in what had been The Paperback Centre.

Needless to remark, the present-day shopping centre is strong on fashions for women, with a wide range of international and Irish-owned retailers, varying from Ecco shoes and Carl Scarpa, the Italian design chain, to the Golden Spiderweb, which sells affordable hand knits made by women in Zimbabwe. Ashley Reeves, the Irish- and family-owned retail fashion chain for women, is also there. Men, too, get a look in, with shops such as Best Menswear and Diffney. Beauty and health treatments for women are also prominent and the centre even has its own dentist, not forgetting Specsavers and Brophy Opticians.

The Health Store sells vitamins, herbs and natural cosmetics, as well as health foods. One of the most interesting food outlets is the Natural Bakery, which started in Kilmainham in 2013, tapping into the demand for artisan bakery products. It now has eleven shops, as well as an online store; its outlet in the Stillorgan Village Centre opened in 2014.

Other outlets in the present-day centre include Dealz, where everything is priced at €1.49, the Fujifilm digital imaging service, iFix electronic repairs, The Grafton Barber, and a Vodafone shop. Altogether, the present shopping centre has close to sixty shops. The manager of the centre is Ray Coary. The extensive refurbishment being carried on by its American owners, Kennedy Wilson, is still ongoing at the time of writing, especially on the Tesco side, facing the Lower Kilmacud Road. The centre has 550 free car-parking spaces.

SPORT

GLENALBYN HOUSE

The house here, previously owned by the Wilkinson family, was purchased by the Kilmacud Crokes GAA Club. It was bought in 1965 for just over £30,000 and opened for sporting purposes the following year. In 1996, the house was extended with the construction of a west wing. On the ground floor of this wing are dressing rooms and a gym, while the first-floor bar looks out on the tennis courts. The house is now marketed as Glenalbyn Sports Club and Conference Centre.

While the 5ha of land that belonged to the house are now used by the Kilmacud Crokes GAA Club, other sports clubs are also based here, including the Glenalbyn tennis club and the Glenalbyn snooker club.

GLENALBYN SWIMMING POOL

Much haggling has gone on in recent years over the plans to rebuild the Glenalbyn swimming pool, which was constructed in the 1960s. The pool was closed in 2013 for health and safety reasons; this has meant that the Glenalbyn swimming club, which has sections for adults and children, with about 100 members in all, and the Glenalbyn waterpolo club have had to use alternative pools in the area. However, despite the closure of the Glenalbyn pool and the many delays in replacing it, the

Glenalbyn swimming club has continued to not alone survive, but prosper.

One recent notable member of the swimming club has been Katie Baguley, who in 2015 represented Ireland with distinction in the 1,500m freestyle competition in the European Games in Azerbaijan.

In January 2013, Dún Laoghaire–Rathdown County Council removed the roof of the swimming pool, saying it could become a hazard in high winds. The pool was subsequently filled in. Since then, debate has raged about the rebuilding of it, with two sites in contention. Consultants employed by the county council decided that the least problematic option would be to redevelop the existing pool site at Glenalbyn, but another site has been considered, close to the public library in Stillorgan.

Deputy leader of the Green Party and a TD for Dublin Rathdown Catherine Martin has been very critical of the council. She said in 2016 that the recommendation to refurbish the existing pool is exactly what the local community has been calling for since the Glenalbyn pool was closed down. She said that investigating the use of the alternative site, near the Stillorgan Library, which was never suitable for this type of development, took up valuable council resources which could have been used to fund vital public services.

She also added, 'Given the fact that the council had unanimously agreed the money for refurbishing the Glenalbyn pool more than two years ago, it is incredibly frustrating that the refurbishment didn't begin'.

GLENALBYN TENNIS CLUB

This club, founded in 1965, plays on six new Omni Pro courts, and always welcomes new members. The club is very active and includes ladies and men's spring and autumn doubles, mixed doubles in May and September, captain's day, an Ireland *v.* France match, and club championships. It enters teams in all the Dublin-area tennis leagues, winter, summer, mixed, floodlit and senior. Apart from all the tennis, the club organises a monthly hill walk in the Wicklow Mountains.

The club has a strong membership of around 250 adults and about 160 children.

GROVE GOLF CLUB

Sometimes known as the Stillorgan Park Golf Club, it proved remarkably short-lived, unlike contemporary clubs founded at around the same time.

Stillorgan used to have lots of granite quarry pits; the one at Stillorgan Grove was filled in to form the Grove Golf Club, set up in 1908. It started as a nine-hole course; the back nine holes were added later. The club was advertised as being fifteen minutes from Blackrock railway station.

When it started, the Orr family, who lived at 2, Ulster Terrace, let the new club use their house as the clubhouse for a year. It couldn't have been better situated, as the house was right on the edge of the new course. The Orr family were long noted in Stillorgan for being generous benefactors.

The golf course closed down in 1917. Infighting was said to have been one reason for its demise and trying to run a golf course during the First World War was also too much of a challenge. The Castle, Foxrock and Killiney clubs all started at around the same time and some of the Stillorgan members joined them. Major W.F. Bailey, who had set up the Castle Golf Club, was said to have encouraged some Stillorgan members to join his new venture.

The golf course at Elm Park opened after Louis McMullen bought the Elm Park estate in 1924. Many of the members of this new course had been members of the old club in Stillorgan.

Today, where the old golf course was located in Stillorgan, there's still a small, private pitch-and-putt course, while the ninth hole of the old golf course is still preserved by the St John of God community.

KILMACUD CROKES GAA CLUB

In a relatively short space of time, Kilmacud Crokes GAA club has become one of the leading GAA clubs in the Dublin area. It was formed on 12 March 1959 at a public meeting at St Laurence's Hall, which stood where the Stillorgan Village Centre is now located. The meeting was presided over by local priest Fr Robert Walsh.

A total of sixty people attended that meeting, contributing a shilling each, so that the revenue on that inaugural night was just over £3. Initially, the new club decided to use green-and-white jerseys, but later it was decided to switch to gold and purple, the colours of a local school, Scoil Lorcáin Naofa. Just four years later, in 1963, the club bought a 2.6ha site behind the Ormonde cinema, as a permanent pitch. Within less than a decade of its foundation, the new club had bought Glenalbyn House and its land, and in 1966 Crokes hurling club joined forces with the Kilmacud football club to form the Kilmacud Crokes. The name change was made in 1971. Then the St Benburb's football club from Clonskeagh joined the club.

In 1973, a camogie section was set up at the club, and in 1996 a ladies' Gaelic football section was started. Further developments saw an AstroTurf GAA pitch completed in

2006 and indoor and outdoor hurling walls completed the following year.

Today, the club is run by the executive committee, with separate committees for football, hurling, ladies' football and camogie, as well as the Coiste committee for under-12s. The club has produced at least thirty outstanding players and it has a formidable winning record.

The club has won two All-Ireland senior football championships, in 1995 and 2009. It has also won four Leinster Senior Football Championships, in 1994, 2005, 2008 and 2010, and no less than seven Dublin Senior Football Championships, in 1992, 1994, 1998, 2004, 2005, 2008 and 2010. Furthermore, the club has won six Dublin Senior Hurling Championships, in 1966, 1974, 1976, 1985, 2012 and 2014.

In August 2012, Peter Sobolewski's magnificent book on the history of the club from 1959 until 2009 was launched by noted GAA commentator Micheál Ó Muircheartaigh.

MARJORIE McENTEE

Marjorie, a tall, red-haired bar worker from Stillorgan, captured the sporting headlines in 1985, when she became world bowling champion in Seoul, South Korea. She was described at the time as being the first Irish sports person to become a world champion in any sport. After all the hullabaloo of her win, she disappeared from sight and was rarely heard of again.

OTHER CLUBS

Two very different sports are catered for in Stillorgan. Firstly, there's St Tiernan's Cycling Club, which offers plenty of outings for keen cyclists, then there is Focus Martial Arts Stillorgan. It was started by Daragh Bolton and continued by Stephen White. So far, the club has produced some fifteen black belts, as well as winners of numerous international titles.

SCOUTS

Scouting has been popular in Stillorgan for over a century. The 3rd Dublin (Stillorgan) Scouts were organised in 1911 by J. Arthur H. Water, who lived at Woodview, beside St Brigid's church. This scout troop had got off to a good start, including at least two camps at Powerscourt, near Enniskerry, but the First World War played havoc. By 1917, it was reported that seventeen former scouts from Stillorgan were on war service. By the end of the war, this first scout group in Stillorgan had disbanded.

Another scout troop, which started close to Stillorgan but with links to the village, was set up in 1915 by a man called Roche. He too went on war service and, when he returned home in 1918, his health was so shattered that this scout troop also failed to survive for long.

After the war, Donald Orr, a member of a well-known family in the Stillorgan area, brought all the scout meetings in the area to his parents' house at 2, Ulster Terrace. In December 1923, he started a Rover scout crew in Stillorgan. By 1926, the cubs were going strong in the parochial hall at St Brigid's, but by the end of the 1920s, scouting had all but disappeared from Stillorgan.

There followed a substantial gap of about thirty years in the history of scouting in the area until Gladys Clotworthy of Clonmore Road in Mount Merrion started a wolf cub pack in St Brigid's Parish Hall, Stillorgan, in 1959. By 1969, Roger Beckett was the cub leader, but he died suddenly in 1991. He's remembered by a garden bench in St Brigid's graveyard.

In 1984, after a succession of short-term leaders, Robin McCullagh took over. He had also been active in the foundation of the 3rd Dublin (Stillorgan) venture scout unit in the 1970s. The scouts in Stillorgan have had a turbulent ride through the past 100 years, but the one constant has been St Brigid's. In recent years, appointments have included Karen D' Alton as Beaver leader in 2003 and Colin Roche as scout leader in 2011. Marc Whisker was made cub leader in 1998 and group leader in 2009.

SKILL ZONE

Located on Holly Avenue in the Stillorgan Industrial Park, Skill Zone is a major indoor sports arena, described as the first one of its kind in Ireland.

It caters for ten different sports and facilities and includes a 6m racing wall and battery cages. Sports that can be pursued there include basketball, batting cages, golf chipping, Gaelic games, hang tough, rugby, soccer, target practice and tennis. The vast arena extends to 1,500m² and is even used for hen and stag parties.

STILLORGAN BOWL

Stillorgan Bowl opened in December 1963, on the site of the old Tigh Lorcáin Hall, on the opposite site of the old Dublin Road to the shopping centre, which opened in 1966. It was the first bowling alley in Ireland and introduced the sport of ten-pin bowling; it had twelve lanes.

Among the first to take up the sport were sporting groups from Aer Lingus, who soon started visiting Stillorgan to play the new game. The Aer Lingus Tenpin bowling club was set up the following year, in 1964.

The new bowling alley was so popular that before long, the Stillorgan Winter League was started at the Stillorgan Bowl, which attracted players and would-be players from all over the country. For novices to the sport, instruction was readily available. In many ways, the highlight of the history of the Stillorgan Bowl was the World Bowling Cup, staged at Stillorgan in 1989, when teams from forty-six countries around the world took part, a unique global sporting event that came to the heart of Stillorgan.

In recent years, what had been the bowl has turned into the Leisureplex complex, which continues the bowling tradition, as well as offering other facilities such as Quasar, arcade games and pool and snooker. Leisureplex has also attracted star celebrities, such as Bruce Springsteen. Whenever he is playing Dublin, he usually takes time off to bowl in Stillorgan, which he did in 2012 and again, most recently, in 2016. In 2006, the Leisureplex site was bought by Treasury Holdings, then owners of the Stillorgan shopping centre across the road, for €65 million. The Leisureplex site extends to just under 1ha; nothing came of Treasury Holdings' plans to redevelop the site and it was sold on again, in 2016, to Kennedy Wilson, the US property firm that now also owns the shopping centre. The site had been put on the market in February 2016, on the instructions of joint receivers, for €10 million, but sold for €15 million, a knock-down price considering its earlier valuation. Kennedy Wilson has extensive plans for redeveloping the site and linking it to the shopping centre, and is awaiting planning permission.

STILLORGAN RUGBY FOOTBALL CLUB

This amateur club based in the Stillorgan area has three teams, a 1st XV, a 2nd XV and a 3rd XV, which compete in the Dublin Metropolitan League and cup competitions. In 2013, the club added a minis section, which for the first time facilitated juniors who want to join.

The club plays home matches at the CUS sports grounds in Bird Avenue and has week-night training sessions at St Benildus in Kilmacud.

This club is comparatively young; it dates back to 1973, when a group of former pupils from schools run by the Salesian Brothers set up a new club called Salesian RFC. Most of the founder members came from outside Dublin. Its first pitch was in Maynooth and its first season at J3 level was in 1973/74. By the early 1980s, many of the founding members had retired and the club had to move its home ground to the Royal Hospital in Kilmainham, Dublin. Then, in the 1986/87 season, the club moved grounds again, this time to the CUS sports ground in Bird Avenue.

Before the 1994/95 season started, in order to reflect new local connections, the name of the club was changed to Stillorgan RFC. Soon, it was able to return to fielding two teams.

Although the club is now 44 years old, it is one of the youngest in the Dublin area. During its existence, it has established itself as a worthy competitor in Leinster rugby. From 2005 onwards, the club has experienced the biggest successes in its history and a steady stream of new players have been joining. In 2009, it fielded three teams for the first time.

A steady stream of new players to the club has resulted in stronger squads and more players to cover for injuries and retirements. The teams reached both the J3 and J5 cup finals in 2007, but no silverware followed. However, since then, it has continued to do well, an encouraging result for what is a comparative newcomer to sport in Stillorgan.

13

TRANSPORT

BUS ROUTES

The 46A bus, which is the most frequent bus route through Stillorgan, stopping along the main N11 close to Stillorgan Village, starts at the railway station in Dún Laoghaire and travels to the Phoenix Park. It's complemented by the 145 bus, which starts in Bray and goes as far as Heuston Station in Dublin.

Other bus routes using the N11 close to Stillorgan Village are the 7B, 7D, 46E, 47, 116 and the 118.

Additional Dublin bus routes serving Stillorgan are the 47 from Belarmine Plaza to Pearse Street, the 75 from The Square in Tallaght to Dún Laoghaire and the 84X, which goes between Dublin city centre and Newcastle and Kilcoole, north Co. Wicklow.

In addition to all these Dublin Bus services, the Aircoach service, which started in 1999, serves Stillorgan on a frequent daily basis.

The bus corridor along the N11 close to Stillorgan, and extending from the junction with Mount Merrion Avenue to Loughlinstown roundabout, is the busiest in the country and contributes much to making bus journeys to and from Stillorgan comparatively quick. Bus corridors also extend from Dublin city centre to Mount Merrion Avenue, speeding up passengers' journey time.

Another factor that made a dramatic improvement to bus services was the introduction of real-time passenger information. In the six years between 1997 and 2003, this ensured a dramatic increase in bus passenger numbers of the 46A route, and that increase has been maintained ever since.

N11

The N11 is the only dual carriageway passing through the south-eastern suburbs of Dublin and it's one of the busiest routes in the country.

Originally, the N11 started at the southern end of O'Connell Bridge in Dublin city centre, but these days, the route as far as the junction with Mount Merrion Avenue is the R138. This junction is now the starting point for the N11, which, a short distance later, bypasses the village of Stillorgan and then goes through the townland of Galloping Green.

What is now the N11 was once a single-carriageway road. In 1950, the old Dublin County Council first formulated plans for the upgrade of the road and bought land for a new road to bypass Stillorgan Village. In the 1950s, the first stretch of dual-carriageway road in Ireland was built, between the junction with Newtownpark Avenue and Foxrock Church, but it wasn't until the mid-1970s that the dual carriageway between Newtownpark Avenue and Donnybrook church was constructed.

The present Stillorgan bypass was opened in October 1979, which meant a big improvement in traffic flows along the main road. A plaque on a wall on the other side of the bypass from Byrne's pub at Galloping Green marks the opening of the bypass. This upgrade also meant that the 1950s dual carriageway at Galloping Green was replaced by a more modern dual carriageway.

OLD BUSES

Many people with a keen interest in bus history have observed closely how the bus services through Stillorgan have been developed over the years.

In the 1920s, there was a free-for-all with bus services, with privately owned companies being able to run routes more or less as they wished. The Robin Bus Company ran daily services between Burgh Quay in central Dublin and Foxrock, via Stillorgan. The first bus of the day left Burgh Quay at 8 a.m. and the last at 11.30 p.m. Also in the 1920s, another bus service that went through Stillorgan to Foxrock was run by an entrepreneur called Hoey; he eventually sold his company to the General Omnibus company.

One bus company established in the late 1920s is still running, the St Kevin's bus service, begun by the Roundwood-based Doyle family in 1927 and still owned by them. The service starts in St Stephen's Green in central Dublin and runs as far as Glendalough, passing along the N11 close to Stillorgan Village. But by the mid-1930s, bus services in Dublin city had been so consolidated that the Dublin United Tramway Company (DUTC), which was also responsible for running the city's tram services, had a monopoly on bus services in the city.

Further changes came when CIE was formed in 1945 to include both rail and bus services and, in 1950, it was nationalised. Many developments in bus technology have been seen on the 46A route through Stillorgan. The first seventy-four-seater double-decker bus was the Leyland Titan PD3 bus, which was introduced between 1959 and 1962. The 46A route and twelve other bus routes in Dublin were the first in the Dublin area to get the new buses. In 1961, the old familiar green colour on the buses was replaced by dark blue and cream, but these days the buses are blue and yellow.

After the Leyland Titans came the Leyland Atlanteans, which were in service between 1966 and 1974, although the last one wasn't withdrawn by Dublin Bus until 1996. Then, between 1983 and 2001, Shannon-built Bombardiers were in service. In more recent years, Volvo/Alexandra and Dennis buses have been in service. Present-day buses are far more user-friendly, for wheelchair users as well, while Leap ticketing and onboard wifi are everyday requirements, a far cry indeed from what the old Robin Bus Company provided for its users in Stillorgan back in the 1920s.

RAILWAY

The old Harcourt Street railway line to Bray survived for a century, until the end of 1959, when it closed down. For most of its existence, the line was worked by steam locomotives, but in late 1954 it was converted to diesel. The line was noted for its antique carriages, many of which were up to 60 years old. The switch to diesel wasn't enough to save the line, which in the 1950s faced increased competition from private motorists and from the buses.

In its heyday, the line was also noted for its many excursion trains, not just to the races at Leopardstown, but for the twice-weekly Sea Breezes excursion trains to Wicklow and Arklow, which ran every Wednesday and Saturday. Long before the advent of package holidays by air in the 1960s, for many Dublin families getting away for a short break to Bray, Wicklow or Arklow was the only possibility of a holiday.

The old Harcourt Street line was also noted for its evening express, which left the station at the top of Harcourt Street every weekday at 5 p.m. The first stop was Stillorgan; this meant a journey time of twelve minutes, which has never been bettered. The normal journey time from Harcourt Street to Stillorgan was eighteen minutes.

Another notable feature on the old line was the use of Drumm battery-operated trains, which ran between Dublin and Bray between 1932 and 1949, the precursor of the modern-day Luas trams.

After the Harcourt Street to Bray line was closed on the last day of 1959, work began to dismantle the track and other physical elements of the railway. This job was completed by the end of 1960, but soon, as the southern suburbs began their rapid expansion, it became evident that closing the line with such haste had been a dreadful mistake. It wasn't until 2004 that the Luas Green Line was opened, with a brand-new station for Stillorgan. But the new station, like its predecessor, is well over 1 mile (about 2km) from Stillorgan Village.

14

WORK

DARLEY'S BREWERY

For most of the nineteenth century, Darley's brewery in Stillorgan was the main employer in the area, with up to 300 people working for it. The brewery was beside what was then called the Leper's Stream, now known as the Brewery Stream.

This brewery was extensive and well organised, with a mill, several brew houses, a malt store, malt kiln, a range of stables for its horses, a barn, a beer store, a cooperage for making the barrels for the beer, an office and a millpond. Beside the brewery were two substantial dwelling houses, with yards and gardens.

In 1837, Samuel Lewis, in his topographical directory of Ireland, said that Darley's brewery had been in existence for over eighty years. For over forty of those years, it had been owned by the present proprietors, who also had extensive malting and brewing interests in Bray.

Darley's was located on what is now Brewery Road, where the offices of DCC are based. The brewery produced ale and beer. The Darley family had a connection through marriage with the Guinness family, so for many years the latter took a keen interest in the brewery. The Darley connection lasted until 1853, when two young Catholic entrepreneurs, Andrew and Joseph Carton, took over the brewery. They expanded it and continued to make high-quality ale and beer; their oversight of the brewery was considered at the time to have been very successful, but their tenure only lasted twenty-two years. The brewery closed in 1875 and, after that, few records of it were left.

Few details are left, as well, of the many charitable acts that the Carton brothers carried out for the poor people of Stillorgan.

As for the Darleys, they made so much money from the brewery that they were able to build an enormous house close to where Brewery Road now joins the N11. It was called The Grange and it was demolished around 1960 to provide a site for the headquarters of Esso Ireland. In turn, that building was demolished to make way for the present-day Grange apartments.

DCC IN STILLORGAN

DCC is a remarkable group, founded by Jim Flavin in 1976. Today, it trades in fifteen countries around the world in such sectors as energy and healthcare and has a market capitalisation of around €5.5 billion. When the company was 10 years old, it moved its headquarters to Brewery Road in Stillorgan. It was never that big a building and about fifty people worked there. But it was the headquarters for a group that now employs 11,000 people. In 2014, DCC moved its headquarters to its present location in Leopardstown.

DEIRDRE DONNELLY ON WORK PROSPECTS

Independent councillor Deirdre Donnelly says that employment prospects today in the Stillorgan area are good, with many of those working in Stillorgan, in retailing, hospitality and other sectors, living close by. A number of schools in the area, such as Oatlands primary and college, the Stillorgan VEC, St Laurence's and St Raphaela's, have brought a lot of business to the area over the years and, in turn, the local business community is very supportive of them. She concludes by saying that the geographic location of Stillorgan, in the centre of Dún

Laoghaire-Rathdown County Council, and the proximity of the N11, mean that visitors come to Stillorgan and spend money there, arriving from far and wide.

It's estimated that approximately 8,000 people work in the greater Stillorgan area, which has one of the lowest unemployment rates in the country. Big employers in Stillorgan include St John of God, St Helen's Radisson Blu Hotel and the Talbot Hotel. Many people work in the hospitality and retail sectors. On the fringes of Stillorgan, in Sandyford and Leopardstown (Central Park), many large multinational companies provide much employment, such as Bank of America Merrill Lynch, Microsoft and Vodafone. The Beacon Hospital is a major health-sector employer close to Stillorgan.

DUBLIN COUNTY COUNCIL

The old Dublin County Council, which had responsibility for the Stillorgan area, was replaced in 1994 by three new county councils in the Dublin area, South Dublin, Fingal and Dún Laoghaire–Rathdown. The latter embraces Stillorgan. But in one bizarre decision at the time of the changeover, most of the old Dublin County Council archives relating to Stillorgan were sent to Fingal County Council rather than to Dún Laoghaire–Rathdown County Council.

These days, as part of the Dún Laoghaire-Rathdown County Council, the Stillorgan ward covers a far wider area that that of Stillorgan Village. A total of six councillors represent Stillorgan.

They are Liam Dockery, Fianna Fáil, since 2014; Deirdre Donnelly, independent, since 2014; John Kennedy, Fine Gael, since 2016; Carron McKinney, Labour, since 2015 (she was co-opted to replace Richard Humphrys); Barry Saul, Fine Gael, since 2014 and Dónal Smith, Fianna Fáil, since 2016.

ARTHUR LEE GUINNESS

A grandson of the founder of the Guinness brewery, Arthur Lee Guiness took £12,000 out of the business to buy Stillorgan Park in 1839. He stayed there just over twenty years, leaving it to go and live in Roundwood, Co. Wicklow, in 1860. He died there three years later. But during his time in residence at Stillorgan Park, he did much to help alleviate poverty and unemployment in the area. He employed a considerable number of local people on this estate, probably over 200, while he also gave financial help to many other poor people in the Stillorgan area.

H.R. HOLFELD GROUP

This prominent engineering company has been trading in Stillorgan for many years. The Holfeld family moved to Stillorgan in 1949, then, three years later, in 1952, Hans Holfeld started his business as an import and export trader. In 1955, H.R. Holfeld was established as an engineering business with a speciality in pump sales. The group is based at 2–4 Merville Road in Stillorgan, close to St Brigid's church, and continues to supply a wide variety of engineering solutions.

STILLORGAN INDUSTRIAL PARK

This industrial estate was developed in the mid-1960s. One of the first companies there was Brennan & Company, established in 1966 and still going strong; it supplies instruments for industrial, medical and scientific use.

Other firms on the estate include Aspect Systems, Spruce Avenue (building suppliers); Berendsen, Spruce Avenue (linen hire and work wear); BTW Sandyford Ceramics, Maple Avenue (bathroom tiles and wood floors); Cross Fit Green, Maple Avenue (coaching and personal training); Kenneth Hodgins Interiors, Bird Avenue, (high-quality furniture); Right Price Tiles, Spruce Avenue (tile store); Securall Fastenings,

Rowan Avenue (building materials) and Spirit Ford, Maple Avenue (new and used cars).

In recent years, commercial property experts have noted how the Stillorgan Industrial Park has changed from being largely industrial to having many more stores aimed at consumers. Typical of these are O' Briens, the chain of wine off-licences, and Cellar Master.

O' Brien's began as a grocery store in Bray, Co. Wicklow in 1944 and is now the largest off-licence chain in Ireland, with over thirty stores. Its registered office is at Spruce Avenue on the Stillorgan Industrial Estate.

Cellar Master is of a more recent vintage; it was set up in October 2008 by Alan Crowley, a master of wine who had previously worked for Edward Dillon & Company for fourteen years. His wine warehouse in Stillorgan has a very wide selection of fine wines, and while customers are making their choices, they can sip from a wide range of coffees.

NEW ISLAND BOOKS

This well known book publishing firm has been based in Stillorgan since it was established twenty-five years ago, by Dermot Bolger and Edwin Higel. It is described as Ireland's leading independent publisher of ground-breaking literature from established and emerging writers.

STILLORGAN'S NINETEENTH-CENTURY OCCUPATIONS

In the nineteenth century, a considerable variety of craftsmen and tradesmen, almost entirely male, looked after the needs of the many big mansions in the Stillorgan area. According to Pettigrew & Oulton's Dublin Directory in the early 1840s, Stillorgan had a painter and glazier, a carpenter and a builder, two forges where horses were shod, a baker, a cooper, two dairies, a post office, and a police station.

During the nineteenth century, the Darley family, of local brewing renown, was one of the better-off households in Stillorgan. In May 1835, fourteen men were listed as working on the Darley estate. They worked as gardeners and dung shifters, and had to cut weeds, feed the cattle, mind the lambs and fork straw. They also worked in the kitchens. At the same time, four women were employed to put dung into the turnip drills. Most of the labourers working for the Darleys had to work from Mondays to Saturdays, so that Sundays were their only days of rest. For all their hard, back-breaking work, they were paid 1 shilling a day.

All the other big houses in the Stillorgan area had extensive gardens and, in some cases, estates, so they too provided much labouring work, mostly for local men.

STILLORGAN SHOEMAKING

Stillorgan once had an enviable reputation for handcrafted shoemaking. Shoemaking in the Dublin area has a long history, going back around seven centuries and earlier; shoemakers formed their own guild in Dublin in 1427. During the nineteenth century, they thrived in Stillorgan Village and by 1900 there were still four shoemaker's shops there, each of them making a good living.

In the early twentieth century, a new shop was set up to both make and repair shoes, Licken's, which was begun by Paddy Licken and run by him for many years. Eventually, his son Seán took over, but he found it impossible to compete, closing the doors of the shop for the last time in 1998.

FURTHER READING

F.E. Ball, *A History of County Dublin* (Dublin, 1902)

Bonnie Flanagan, *Stately Homes around Stillorgan* (privately published, 1991)

Bonnie Flanagan, *Stillorgan Again but Different ...* (privately published, 1996)

Maeve Flanagan, *Dev, Lady Chatterley and Me* (Dublin, 1998)

John A. Ingram, *The Cure of Souls: a History of St Brigid's Church, Stillorgan* (privately published, 1997)

Moira Laffan, *St Helen's, an 18th Century Mansion on the Stillorgan Road* (Dublin, 1998)

Samuel Lewis, *A History and Topography of Dublin City and County* (London, 1837)

Canon E.H. Lewis-Crosby, *A Short History of Stillorgan* (Dublin, 1932)

Bryan MacMahon, *Eccentric Archbishop, Richard Whately of Redesdale* (Dublin, 2005)

Ruth McManus, *Crampton Built* (privately published, 2008)

Obelisk annual (Kilmacud and Stillorgan Local History Society, 2006–2017)

Peter Pearson, *Between the Mountains and the Sea* (Dublin, 1998)

Christopher Ryan, paintings by Olivia Hayes, *Dundrum, Stillorgan and Rathfarnham Gateway to the Mountains* (Donaghadee, 2002)

Cornelius F. Smith, *Stillorgan Park Golf Club: a Brief History,* (Dublin, 1908–17)

Peter Sobolewski, *A History of the Kilmacud Crokes* (Dublin, 2012)

THE SHIP OF SULAIMĀN

Persian Heritage Series

THE SHIP OF SULAIMĀN

Other volumes published in the Persian Heritage Series

Persian Heritage Series
No. 11

The Ship of Sulaimān

Translated from the Persian
by
John O'Kane

LONDON
ROUTLEDGE & KEGAN PAUL

*First published 1972
by Routledge & Kegan Paul Ltd
Broadway House, 68–74 Carter Lane
London EC4V 5EL*

*Printed in Great Britain by
William Clowes & Sons Limited
London, Colchester and Beccles*

ISBN 0 7100 7238 4

CONTENTS

ACKNOWLEDGMENTS

I am indeed obliged to Mr Meredith-Owens, Sandy Morton and Simon Digby for their friendly assistance with the Persian text early on and I must extend my particular thanks to Professor Ehsan Yar-Shater for his help and advice during the final stages of translation.

GENERAL EDITOR'S PREFACE

Mr O'Kane's able translation of a difficult text describing a sea voyage to Siam makes available for the first time, through the *Persian Heritage Series*, a work rare in its kind and of considerable interest for the history of Persia and the Far East.[1]

Persian seafaring in the Indian Ocean dates back to the time of Darius the Great (521–485) when as part of his maritime operation Persian fleets, circling the Arabian peninsula, sailed from India to Egypt.

The Sasanids (226–651) expanded Persian nautical activities and established a busy sea trade with China, their vessels often using Ceylon as an *entrepôt*. Setting out from the Chinese ports and crossing the Indian Ocean, the ships of the *Po-sse* (the Persians, according to Chinese sources) sailed to the Persian Gulf, reaching the mouth of the rivers Tigris and Euphrates. Attempts at settling Persian colonies along the route accompanied the commercial activities. Christian Persians sent out missionaries to Ceylon and founded churches in the ports of Male on the Malabar coast and in Calliana near Bombay.

Persian navigation to India and the Far East, together with a flourishing trade with the countries of the region, continued in the Islamic period, well into the sixteenth century. Persian settlements in lands to the east of the Indian subcontinent were established and Persian missionaries, now inspired by the new creed of Islam, went as far as China and Indonesia. 'A very large village of *Po-sse* is found in the Island of Hainan in 748, and in the same year they [the *Po-sse*] are mentioned along with Brahmans and Malayans as owners of vessels on the river at Canton' (G. F. Hourani, *Arab Seafaring*, p. 62).

In the seventeenth century a Persian colony took root in Siam. It became influential in trade and politics and some of its members, by winning the favor of the king, secured the position of chief administrator of the land.

---

[1] It is hoped that Professor Faruqi's edition of the Persian text will soon be published.

The *Ship of Sulaimān*[1] relates the visit of an envoy of Shah Sulaimān the Safavid (1666–94) to Siam and to its Persian community, as a response to a friendly letter by the enlightened Siamese king, Phra Narai, to the Shah. The envoy arrived in Siam at an interesting time when, following the conquests of Albuquerque, the fortunes of the Europeans in the area were on the rise, partly at the expense of the Persian community.

The author, ibn Muḥammad Ibrāhīm, was the secretary of the envoy and with a curiosity born of the novelty of what he saw and a complacency adduced by his religious beliefs and national habits, described the embassy's journey to Siam, which began on 27 June 1685 at Bandar Abbas on the Persian Gulf. The hazards of the sea voyage, the ports along the way, the reception at the Court of Siam, the king and his palace, the Siamese officials, the Siamese food, customs, religion, trade and products, the description of other countries in the Far East, notably China, Japan, the Philippines, some contemporary events in Ceylon and in India, as well as the description of the Iranian community in Siam, their leaders, their background, their influence at the Court and their role in having brought King Phra Narai to the throne, are the chief subjects treated by the author.

Studded with interesting and curious details, the author's seventeenth-century account informs us as much about Siam and the Far East and seafaring in South East Asia, as about the social and religious attitudes and the customs of Safavid Persia.

*   *   *

The *Persian Heritage Series*, which owes its creation to the initiative of H.I.M. The Shahanshah of Iran, is published under the joint auspices of UNESCO and the Pahlavi Foundation's Royal Institute of Translation and Publication. Aiming at making the best of Persian classics available in major Western languages, the translations in the series are intended not only to satisfy the needs of the students of Persian history and cultures, but also to respond to the demands of the intelligent general reader who seeks to broaden his intellectual and artistic horizons through an acquaintance with major world literatures.

---

[1] The title of the Persian manuscript, *Safīna'i sulaimānī*, is an apt one in view of the double meaning of *safīna*, namely 'ship' and 'note book, miscellanea'. Sulaimān is the Safavid king's name, but refers also to the might and wisdom of the Biblical King Solomon, as reflected in Persian legends.

TRANSLATOR'S PREFACE

Iran and Siam

The *Safīna'i Sulaimānī* or *Ship of Sulaimān* is an account of a Persian embassy which went to Siam in the latter part of the seventeenth century. At that time Siam was involved with various foreign powers whose interest varied from purely commercial enterprising to rather unrealistic visions of converting the Siamese king and his people to Islam or Christianity. The atmosphere of the period was generally one of intrigues and conniving. Councilors and court favorites from the several foreign communities in residence all competed with one another to win influence over the king. In the struggle for power, attention and favor from the crown was tantamount to acquiring highly profitable trade concessions and access to the more desirable natural resources.

The present work is a translation of a manuscript which has been sitting in the British Museum for many years now. The style employed by the author is very contrived and would discourage a hasty reading. It is therefore doubtful whether anyone other than Professor Jean Aubin, who will be publishing a résumé of the account's contents in a *receuil collectif* on Siam, has read through the complete manuscript carefully since it was acquired. However, this account put together by a scribe, who accompanied the mission to Siam, has attracted attention from various directions due to the fact that the contents touch on several different fields of scholarship.

As is to be expected from our Persian author, the principal focus is on the community of resident Iranians and the important role which until just before the embassy's arrival those Iranians had been playing in the trade and political affairs of Siam. King Phra Narai seems to have been very progressive by comparison to other rulers in that part of the world and consequently he took great interest in his neighbors and the influential powers of Europe. In the course of his reign he sent out delegations and gifts to rulers in India and other nearby states and eventually succeeded in sending an embassy to the court of Louis XIV. The Persian embassy which our account describes is Shāh Sulaimān's[1] response to the Siamese king's letters of friendship which Ḥājī Salīm delivered to the court agents in Isfahan.

The embassy consists of members of the various divisions of the army and the government administration in the Safavid Empire.

1

Thus the author constantly refers to himself as being employed by 'the honorable Khāṣṣa', the bureaucratic division of the administration which handled the king's immediate property, the royal demesnes. For a few generations the Khāṣṣa had been increasing its own power and encroaching on the Mamālik, or the provincial administration. Certain provinces were governed and taxed by the Khāṣṣa which meant that it was not necessary for the taxes of those provinces to support local governors and elaborate courts but all the money went directly into the king's estates. In his report our scribe also refers quite often to Tufangchīs, Tūpchīs and Qūrchīs who were part of the embassy; these officials were officers from different sections of the army, musketeers, artillerymen and cavalrymen. Other officers are mentioned as well.

Odysseus in Siam

One of the most interesting phases of modern Siamese history is touched upon when the author describes the recent rise to power of an 'evil starred Frank'[2] who was originally only an undistinguished worker on an English ship. The reader is presented with a series of clichés concerning the new minister's character and how he is a pernicious influence on the Siamese king. Such passages hardly manage to arouse any antipathy towards the Frank in view of the fact that, as the author admits on several occasions, the Iranian officials who had previously held the rank of prime minister, with the sole exception of Āqā Muḥammad, were all deficient at their work or blatantly disloyal. This Christian prime minister, who furthered his career by exposing Ḥājī Salīm's embezzlement of government funds and generally showed himself to be at odds with the Iranian community in Siam, is the famous adventurer Constance Phaulkon, and his life story once he became active in the East Indies reads like a seventeenth-century version of Homer's Odyssey.

The strange part of the natural comparison is that Phaulkon was a Greek and happened to be from the island Cephalonia, which is just north of Ithaca. He is reputed to have been shipwrecked several times and lost all his money and goods but one way or another he always managed to repair his situation. His real name was Konstantinos Yerakes which he changed to a French-Greek version by which he is best known. He is given a sizable paragraph in the Eleftheroudakes Modern Greek Encyclopaedia, where his date of birth is recorded as 1647.

At an early age Phaulkon began working on English merchant ships and his name is registered in the log of an English ship in which another celebrated adventurer, George White,[3] sailed to India in 1670. Phaulkon was employed in various capacities by the British East India Co., and although he seems to have made some enemies among the company's staff there are several references in documents of the period to his unusual talent for languages and handling business affairs. Again the comparison to Odysseus is very tempting, for Phaulkon certainly knew the cities and the mind of many peoples and his talent for managing public affairs, in particular his engineering of an alliance between Phra Narai and Louis XIV recalls his Homeric counterpart in the *Iliad*. The French eventually sent troops to Siam and maintained a garrison in Bangkok and Mergui but after a short time they were forced to withdraw in the revolution of 1688.

Due to Phaulkon's wit and unusual ability with language he became very close to the Siamese king Phra Narai. The king spent several hours a day in the minister's company discussing government policy or simply conversing. Phra Narai seems to have been very interested in the European kings and Phaulkon would spend hours narrating battles from history or describing life in the great courts of Europe. Eventually Phaulkon became the most important single influence on the king and acted as a go-between whenever there were to be dealings with foreign powers. In all Phaulkon could not have spent more than eight years in Siam, during which time he rose from the humble office of clerk in the Siamese Treasury to holding a position which is unique in the annals of modern history in the East.

All along his position was precarious and depended on the king's good favor. In 1688 the king fell ill and was confined to the palace. A Siamese faction which was totally against any foreign influence exploited the state's weakness at this moment, and succeeded in launching a *coup* in which Phaulkon was killed.

Concerning Phaulkon's real character, there is much dispute in contemporary documents which reflect his life, mostly due to the rivalry between the French mission in Siam and the Jesuits. Fr. Tachard seems to have been personally very close to Phaulkon and has written an eulogy on him which Fr. d'Orléan's account, *Histoire de M. Constance* (1690), is based on. There are also references to Phaulkon's sexual deviations and it has been implied that his marriage to a Japanese-Portuguese Christian woman was in compliance with the Jesuits' suggestion that he 'settle down'. Phaulkon's conversions from orthodoxy to the Anglican faith and then to Catholicism seem to attest to his adaptability and sense of expediency. English letters have referred to him as a blackguard and French clerics have praised him as a bulwark of Christianity, a stepping stone to the conversion of the Far East. Here we have a Persian account of his activities in Siam, an account which appears to be no less prejudiced than any of the European sources of the same period.

Geography and proper names

A few remarks at this point concerning place names might avoid possible confusion in the text. The author, like many Muslim writers since the earliest days of Islam, is in the habit of referring to both the country and the capital or chief city of the country by one and the same name. Thus Shahr Nāv, which as the author explains means city of the boat and refers to the capital of Siam, is used throughout the account as the name of the whole country. Likewise the author uses the word shahr in the context of China, that is, he writes that he is going to give a description of certain 'cities' which border on Siam but he means 'countries', which is obvious when he mentions how many cities there are all together in Shahr Chīn or the land of China.

When the author says that the delegation is sailing from India to Tenasserim, he means the coastal strip called Tenasserim and that is clear from the fact that the embassy first lands in Mergui, 'the goal of their ship'. Thus they have reached the greater region of Tenasserim but still have to set out from Mergui to the city of Tenasserim. For the purpose of following the present account it is, therefore, very useful to keep in mind that Shahr Nāv means both the country which the author refers to before they arrive in Siamese territory and then the capital which is their destination once they have landed on the western coasts of Siam.

Another name which occurs quite often is the general designation 'Below the Winds'. The term obviously derives from nautical talk and refers to all the countries which one can sail to from Persia and Arabia when the monsoon is blowing east. However, in this terminology India is usually kept apart from the regions of Below the Winds and Hindustan has the special meaning of India north of the Nerbudda River excluding Bihar and Bengal.

There is a curious jumbled passage in which the author, taking into account his own experiences in traveling, tries to make sense out of Muslim geographers that he has read. Chīn and Māchīn are names which derive either from an early confusion over the expression Mahā Chīn, Greater China, i.e. the Empire, or an attempt to distinguish South China as approached from the sea from North China as approached by the land route. Eventually Muslim geographers take these names to mean two different countries. Add to this confusion the name Khiṭā from which we take Cathay and which originally meant North China, being the name of a Turkic or Mongolian people, the Kara Khitai, who had power in parts of the North. The result is the author finds it very difficult to locate where he actually is in the old scheme of things and he struggles to explain the difference between Khiṭā, Māchīn and Siam.

The last point, as far as proper names go, is that in the Persian language there is only one word for Persia and that is Iran. The language, however, is not called Iranian but Fārsī, i.e. Persian, and this second term derives from the fact that in Iran in ancient times several Iranian languages or dialects were spoken. It has remained in the consciousness of the language that what Persians speak and write is the dialect which goes back to the province of Pārs or Fārs. Thus in the English I often refer to the 'Persian' embassy and the 'Iranian' community, freely interchanging these terms for the sake of variety.

In the case of the system of measures used by the author, one is faced with the problem that the value of weights and money is constantly changing and depends on the period being dealt with. I have appended a table of weights and measures at the back which is only valid in a very general way but may offer some help in forming an overall picture of the volume of trade being referred to and the finances involved.

General observations on Muslim literary style

Aside from the specialist who might be interested in gleaning information from this unusual account on Siam, those who are curious about Persian literature or literary forms in general may find the present work worth attention. It should be stated at the outset that what the reader is here faced with is by no means a piece of first rate literature but an ordinary scribe's official report of an embassy. What makes a Persian formal report different from any European counterpart is the author's attempt to combine factual data with a fantastical technique. In this particular case one feels throughout the rambling narrative an odd interplay between the author's concern for the hard kernel of fact which justifies the account's existence and the unflagging attempt to be elegant, clever and entertaining.

For a reader who is impressed with a modern style of narrative like Hemingway's, a terse American telegraphese, it may be very difficult to see any merit in what is often pejoratively referred to as Oriental and dismissed as artificial and turgid. On the other hand one may not be willing to condemn hastily a style which in its day succeeded in influencing the literary taste of the Muslim world from the Bosphorus to the Bay of Bengal.

To approach the author's style realistically it is necessary to appreciate certain general characteristics of Islamic letters and then to locate his position in relation to the whole. It is perhaps worth giving a brief description of some of Muslim literature's basic features which are too easily misunderstood by the Western reader. What would otherwise appear to be rather arbitrary novelties or, worse still, pompous, self-indulgent rhetoric on the part of the author, may be more readily acceptable when viewed as clearly defined variables of an age old tradition.

First of all the scribe's introduction may seem tedious and drawn out. We are confronted with very contrived passages praising God, then the Prophet, then 'Alī, the personage most revered by the Shī'ite sect which was then predominant in Iran and finally, a long section which praises the Shāh and accords him all the Muslim ruler's stock epithets in a rather mechanical manner.

This kind of opening is extremely familiar to the Muslim reader and what appears contrived to us is cliché or cliché with a twist for anyone used to such required literary formalities. I have made an effort to put the author's introduction into as readable English as possible and still retain the details of each image. What is lost to the reader who is unaware of basic Muslim attitudes is the conceptual aspect of a great number of the images, concepts relating to Islam's view of the Prophet, revelation, the importance of God's oneness, king-ship's relation to God and the world order, etc.

Our scribe is a small man in a big bureaucracy and he has been schooled, if not inspired, by a set of very restricted conventions. It is, however, worth noting that the prevalence of clichés and thematic passages is not so much due to lack of industry and imagination as to a strong belief in the superiority of a particular sensibility which the tradition cultivated. Then again the style we are dealing with here is at the end of the tradition and what makes it even harder to define and evaluate is that this late style has the added dimension of trying to go one step further, of developing within the conventions.

The Muslim attitude towards imagination

Islam begins with the Arabs and the Arabs bring their language and its orally preserved creations with them wherever they go. If we read an early Arab literary critic today, we feel a certain lack of aesthetic directive in his criticism. He will use phrases like bayān, balāgha and faṣāḥa—clarity, aptness and elegance—but these terms do not really help us as outsiders to enter into the peculiar qualities which, we sense, distinguish Arabic poetry. There is the problem of invention and the place accorded to imagination in a good poet's work. The stronger tendency from earliest times on was to play down the poet's personality, the poet's subjective imagination *vis-à-vis* the traditional mode of expression. At least this is what we are led to believe by Arab and Western critics alike.

It is claimed that invention borders on fashioning idols and infringes on the oneness of God, on God's prerogative as the Creator. Therefore, the good poet is the schooled poet. He focuses on acquiring the right vocabulary words for a stock scene. He perfects the accepted form and puts emphasis on displaying the extent of his learning and the facility of his craft. And when it comes to learning, knowledge is looked at as a stable, fixed corpus of facts which can be embraced as a concrete entity. One form which this attitude manifests itself in is the view that the Quran is stylistically perfect, in fact a miracle, displaying every virtue style is capable of.

As such the Quran becomes the Arabic literary absolute, equivalent to what Plato would call the *eidos* or the form for a perfect book. But thanks to revelation the Semite sees the form materialized where the Greek is left to speculation. In more modern terms one thinks of 'the book' which Mallarmé envisaged, the *Grand Oeuvre* which would end the evolution of writing and stand as the final statement, the ultimate work which all his other poetry was only leading up to.

In view of these attitudes, the creative struggle for the good poet consists of fitting the fixed ideas, the maʿānī, to the precise, correct words, the alfāẓ. If the poetry which is produced in that manner requires an elaborate commentary to be understood that is all the more proof of its poetic validity and excellence. The emphasis is by no means focused on psychological expression, for this would appear almost sordid. Just as Aristotle assigned a relatively low value to imagination in his system of psychology, ranking this faculty of man with the animal functions, so Muslim theology fostered the same view by confirming man's weakness and mistrusting natural genius. Only in the case of the Muslim mystics was there a possibility of articulating a position which put trust in man's poetic creativity. Poetry could provide symbols and images which would facilitate man's transcendence over nature and reason.

Poetry may be the archives of the community, then it may instruct; finally it is allowed to delight, and indeed the Arabs as well as the Persians are typically pictured as taking incredible delight in the sound of verse. Beauty, however, if one is forced to externalize the concept, is not so much the creation of fine ideas in apt language but a decorative gown draped over the well-known themes. Thus, Western critics are often to be heard condemning what they believe to be a fundamental flaw in most Arabic verse, namely that it is uninspired and shallow, mere outer decoration. A Muslim critic like al-Qazwīnī would seem to justify the Western attitude when he defines the 'ilmu'l-balāgha, or the science of elegance, as the science of the various methods of representing themes.

Conventional themes and metaphor

To give an example of how tradition prevails over Muslim literature it is worth mentioning a well-known work which was meant to aid poets or students of poetry to grasp the accepted conventions used in describing a beautiful woman. It is also important to keep in mind the fact that very much of Persian as well as Arabic poetry plays with the possible ambiguities which arose out of praising God or longing in an elegiac tone after God's presence. Thus, every detail of the beloved's appearance can be enjoyed sensually or deeply interpreted and yet the device is often purely literary, that is, it is not meant to document or explore mystic experience but functions as an additional dimension in view of the reader's consciousness of basic mystic attitudes.

The literary textbook I have in mind is Sharafu'd-Dīn Rāmī's *Anisu'l-'Ushshāq* or the *Lover's Companion*. The author flourished in the latter part of the fourteenth century and his manual was translated into French by Clement Huart in 1885. The purpose of the book is to list and explain all the similes and features of the beloved which may be legitimately employed by the poet.

The example drawn from this work is directly pertinent in the case of our scribe, who employs images which a reader unfamiliar with the technique finds hard to understand. When the embassy is entertained by the English in India and the author becomes elated with the presence of unveiled English women, he immediately describes their beauty in terms of the conventions which will be referred to below. The same passage is a clear example of how a non-mystic author will play with the ambiguity that exists between the sensual and the transcendent. The women are depicted as flirting with the delegates and calling them to enter into the Garden of Paradise.

Sharafu'd-Dīn's book contains nineteen chapters treating respectively of the hair, the forehead, the eyebrows, the eyes, the eyelashes, the face, the down on the lips and cheeks (the beloved can be a boy), the mole or beauty spot, the lips, the teeth, the mouth, the chin, the neck, the bosom, the arm, the fingers, the figure, the waist and the legs. Each chapter catalogues the terms which Persian and Arabic authors commonly applied to these features, as well as their corresponding epithets and metaphors. To take one example in particular, the eyebrows may be either joined together above the nose (muttaṣil), which is esteemed a mark of great beauty, or separated (munfaṣil), and the schooled Persian poet has at his command thirteen metaphors or metaphorical adjectives to describe this one facial trait.

Thus the eyebrows may be compared to crescent moons, bows, rainbows, arches, the prayer niche in the mosque, the shape of various letters of the Arabic alphabet (Mīm, Qāf), the curved head of a polo stick, the curved mark branded on horses or the royal seal as if imprinted on patent letters of beauty. In the case of the beloved's hair the number of metaphors and metaphorical adjectives is much greater. Sharafu'd-Dīn cites sixty as used in Persian but the hair is generally known as the feature of one hundred attributes. A copious list is appended.

Rhymed prose

Quoting from the above-mentioned manual is merely meant to give a partial idea of the elaborate conventions which rule over the realm of Muslim poetry. To the convention of imagery or themes we may add conventions of form. For the purpose of this introduction it is not necessary to go into all the different forms of poetry and literary prose. It will suffice to explain that much of our scribe's account is written in rhymed and rhythmic prose. That is, in distinction to verse where there is a regular foot which occurs throughout a whole stanza or a whole poem and where rhyme may occur according to various patterns, in saj' or elegant prose there is not a metrical foot but simply a rhyme. There are three kinds of saj'.

Mutawāzī is when the two clauses that bear rhyming words also bear a similar pattern of consonants. That is to say the two clauses agree in measure and number of letters. An example from E. G. Browne's *History of Persian Literature* is 'Give the spender health and the lender wealth.' Even more interesting for the novel effects it can produce is the muṭṭaraf or 'lop-sided' prose. Two or more clauses differ in measure and the number of letters but the rhyme still occurs. Again an example from Browne, 'He awakes to reprieve us from the aches which grieve us.' The third form of elegant prose is the mutawāzin or symmetrical. Here the words in two or more successive clauses correspond in measure but may not rhyme exactly. 'He came uplifted with joy, he went dejected with woe.'

The more exacting reader may reply that this is nothing new, this is no 'mode of perception'. We have our own examples of this

artificial, clumsy style in English. The difference is that in Arabic and
Persian the syllable patterns of words and the grammatical morph-
ology make saj' a natural style for an author to employ. The fact
that certain kinds of consonant clusters occur in Anglo-Saxon words
surely encouraged the use and development of alliteration. Whereas
in English we can only manage to produce a limerick effect or become
euphuistic, the Quran and many other great prose works produced
by Islamic culture have been able to communicate seriously and
poetically through this device. The refinement which they attained in
that direction has no counterpart in Western literature. An informed
critic who persists in maintaining that this rhetorical device took
root in Islamic literature only because of the Quran's religious prestige
and that because Islam was inflexible it had to be content with what it
inherited, runs the risk of being accused of literary provincialism.

Persian metaphor as mystic transformation

The writer in Islamic letters is confronted with clearly defined conventions both of form and content and the Westerner will feel an
unfamiliarity with that tradition from the start, but there is another
problem perhaps even more difficult for someone who is approaching
a Muslim author through translation. Given that the reader is
prepared to accept as conventional what may at first seem to be a
bright, far-fetched image, the reader is still at odds to follow the kind
of transformation which often takes place through the conventional
metaphor. Here we may point out that one of the big differences
between Arabic poetry and Persian poetry is that Persian most often
uses pure metaphor in place of similes. Arabic poetry is more often
concerned with recording precise detail or building a clearly divisible
image based on two distinct parts. Thus in Arabic poetry the phrase
'as if' occurs very frequently. Persian poetry, however, tends to be
concerned with a transforming vision in which the two parts are
pictured as relating to each other in a vital or mythic way.

The result for Persian poetry is that, in the case of depicting nature,
flowers, trees, animals and astrological bodies react and behave like
people, or some distinguishing quality of an object in nature is
explained or related to a corresponding aspect of human life and
experience. This transformation seems to preserve in a highly refined
form a basic yearning in man to be one with nature or the outside
world. It is very much a subjective or poetic view of the universe
although it is built up through convention and not reforged personally
by every new poet. This view of nature, however, is very distinct
from a European romantic view, where nature may be depicted in a

hazy, frightening manner which is meant to suggest some greater dynamic workings perceived through the mists.

In Persian poetry nature metaphor will always be optically clear and bright, much the same as the handling of landscape or portraiture in Persian miniatures, which contrasts sharply with the use of tone and shadow in Rembrandt. Thus the outer forms in nature are the basis for animation. The poet's eye is insatiable and drinks in details which are then transformed to intensify the visual perception. Here art accredits the fixed arbitrary characteristics of nature in all its fulness with a deeper *raison d'être* and the new relationship between natural phenomena, the appearance of objects, is based on an implied necessity.

Metaphor of this kind can be of two different types. In a garden scene the eye is led from object to object, flower to flower, setting up pairs of relationships. Or the eye may fall upon something which monopolizes its attention. A description of glowing coals in a brazier may hypnotize the eye, hold it in a trance of perception and evoke a series of discrete images as if the eye could not satisfy itself and pass on. There are many examples of this technique in our author such as his description of storms at the beginning of the embassy's journey or his list of images of the drought in China towards the end of the account.

Another point which may be irksome to the Western reader, especially in the case of a work which purports to be narrative, is the apparent lack of unity or organic development in the whole. Our author, as a typical Muslim writer, jumps from episode to episode, from one strange event to another. In some passages he merely piles up sundry bits of information or observations of novel foods and customs. There is a total lack of internal structure or symmetry such as one finds in Homer's *Odyssey*, where the hero arrives home in Book XIII, the center and pivot of the epic. Neither does the Muslim author feel that his medium offers a challenging stone-like resistance, such as Ezra Pound speaks of in 'Rock Drill' where the poet is pictured as a sculptor. Instead the Muslim is concerned with piercing pearls and proceeds to string distinct, colored jewels, novel remarks and strange events, on to one glittering necklace.

The ubiquitous presence of religion throughout the author's account may seem strange to modern readers but it would not be difficult to find a parallel for this trait in European writers of the seventeenth century. Thus our author is always quoting from the Quran or the canonized traditions of the Prophet's life or simply interpolating his own remarks about the squalor and depravity of the Siamese infidels.

2

The scribe courtier

Finally, it is worth pointing out a certain tendency on our author's part to display an almost chivalrous image of himself. His style attempts to convey the image of the scribe as a man of letters, endowed with balanced views on everyday morality and generosity. Even an occasional whiff of literary piety may emerge. He will avoid using the direct pronoun 'I' or 'we' and generally writes in the impersonal third person or speaks of himself as 'the slave', 'the least', 'the most humble'. This form of writing, however, is not intended to give a picture of the author as groveling and all self-effacing. The audience familiar with those details of style is able 'to read between the lines' and tell when the scribe is being clever by pointing something out which is to his credit or meant as a sly observation.

As an indication of his courtly learning the author's metaphors derive from many different fields of Muslim letters and science such as medicine, theology and alchemy but he will never delve too deeply into any one of these studies for fear of being burdensome or unintelligible. The overall effect which is aimed at is to appear elegant, clever and somewhat learned and above all, worldly. Yet, the author's way of displaying such qualities can more often than not appear quite humorous today, when many of his criticisms and reactions in face of a foreign environment seem rather provincial and inexperienced.

Peculiarities of the late style

What remains to be said in the case of our author is that his style is very much influenced by what was popular in the new poetry of his period, the Sabk-i-Hindī or the Indian style. The emergence of this late, florid style can be traced back to authors of the thirteenth century but it does not really appear in its fully mature form until the sixteenth century when it begins to dominate the poetry of the Turkish and Persian courts from Anatolia to India. Since the Safavid regime was always more involved with patronizing religious writing, many poets from Iran found it more to their advantage to move to India and write for Mughal benefactors. Thus the famous poets who used this style often lived and wrote in India and the style became known as Hindī. However, the Indian style as applied to Persian poetry was never a phenomenon limited to India and the name should not be mistaken for a regional designation. This style grew up and developed within the matrix of Persian literature wherever it was being written and appreciated and the fashion for florid phraseology, learned puns and far-fetched images became the accepted norm throughout the Ottoman, Safavid and Mughal empires.

There is hardly any critical analysis to which the modern student can turn to acquire some definition of what makes the Indian style of writing distinct. Most descriptions of that poetry are based on the degree to which it diverges from accepted usage in earlier Persian styles, that is, it is called overly ornate, researched and too clever. To anyone even vaguely familiar with this style, however, it is clear that something new has become the focus of the author's attention, something essentially different from mere excess and exaggeration.

Recalling the role that tradition and convention play in Islamic literature at large, one could rightly raise the question as to what indeed would happen if a Muslim author did try to break away from the basic rules of his profession. In the *Cantos* of Ezra Pound or the *Ulysses* of James Joyce the West has examples of a phenomenon which never occurred in Islamic literature. A modern Western reader has come to accept a situation in writing where he is utterly incapable of understanding a contemporary author. Much *avant garde* writing in the West has become obscure and the audience requires a commentary, just as in the case with Arabic poetry, only in the West the situation is a result of the opposite circumstances. On the one hand the Muslim is faced with a fixed tradition, the intricacies of which are not familiar to him through his everyday experience or a normal degree of education. On the other hand the modern Western reader, by tolerating subjectivity and psychological introspection in his literature, is faced with a maze of unmarked paths which he will only be able to maneuver through with 'A Guide to James Joyce' etc.

The Indian style added a new dimension to previous styles employed by Muslim writers. It attempted to develop itself in terms of an inwardly directed spiral based on the familiar conventional images of poetry. Thus the new poet might take a pair of images, each composed of two elements, collapse them into one line and present the result with a new twist. He might take what were elements of earlier metaphor, decompose them and rearrange the parts into a totally new, striking image. It would never occur to a Muslim poet to do away with the ma'ānī and the alfāẓ, the concepts and vocabulary but he did feel it would be a sign of his intelligence and quite acceptable if he juggled the glittering pieces of the old mosaic. The traditional word pictures are made the components of a new word game. Adaptions, extensions and unexpected twists occur, all of which can become florid or appear sheer exaggeration.

The reader will undoubtedly consider many of these passages which our scribe uses very contrived but find such passages startling and sensual, characteristics not normally preserved when an author values cleverness over directness. The storm scenes, the English party in India, the tiger hunt and the long anecdote about the revolution in China, all bear signs of the Indian style's influence on our author and stand as specimens of a kind of writing which is very foreign to the average non-Muslim reader.

Throughout this translation I have especially given attention to any passage which I felt has pretensions to being literary and in such cases I have tried to keep as much of the original wording and feel as English will allow. For, although we are by no means here dealing with a great work of literature, this account does partake of many of the unusual characteristics of the Persian classics. If this sample of style from an ordinary scribe appears curious and sympathetic in part, it could hopefully arouse a wider interest in the modern reader for the great works of Persian literature and help create a demand for more new translations from Persian poetry.

J. O'KANE

INTRODUCTION

Doxology to the one God who is endowed with many attributes

Ship of Sulaimān, adept at bearing travelers on the sea of true religion, over ranks of swelling waves, through limits of confusion, till they reach the shores of their salvation, you are the pride, the glory, the pious acknowledgment of the one great King, our eternal Lord.

From unfathomed seas beyond existence the ship of His omnipotence brought forth creation's present forms. So efficient is His overflowing bounty, behold, two essence-producing drops from His cloud of generosity have been the source, the moisture of all these seas of varied being.

And merciful. When He saw their hearts disturbed, their well-being floundering on the seas of probability, straightway were these travelers granted consolation with 'See the ship sails on through stormy seas blessed with the grace of God.'[1]

And He is mighty to have launched the tongue's trim sailing ship upon the rising ocean of the word. And He said, 'In the name of Allah be her sailing and her mooring.'

He is the guide who rescues aimless wanderers lost in waves of illusion, for He has declared, 'Fear God and He will steer your course to safety.'

Is He not ingenious? With esoteric wisdom He exclaimed, 'In it I have breathed my very essence', and thereupon exhaled a soul-bestowing fragrance into this rosebud of creation.

As Regulator He bears order into nature's varied elements that fight like spiteful children in their cradle. His compassion is the conciliating nurse whose breasts give forth the milk of peace.

And He fosters the weak and humble. When the dark moon had polished her face praying at the threshold of His illuminating grace, He raised her from the pallor of obscurity and made her illustrious in the heavens of creation.

And He is king of kings. For, in the field of possibility He has raised monarchy's banners to the zenith of command with the empowering statement, 'The sultan is the shadow of the Lord.'

He is above all earthly sovereigns. The splendour of mortal kings is small part of the courtly pomp and state of His divinity.

He is the source which generates all light. World-conquering sultans radiate a brightness from their countenance. This light is but the dust they gather with prostrations to His throne.

His force invests the kings with kingship. All rulers of title, bearers of a regal crown, submit their wills, entrust their souls, to the gracious yoke of His bounty.

He is the one true inventor. This realm of sky and earth, which dazzles us with strange events and wonders, is an unimportant corner of His limitless creation. To manifest the hidden mysteries, bring forth spheres devoid of time and place, this is but one facet of His full invention, The nadir of His greatness is the zenith in this world's sky, the two worlds but two waves in the sea of His magnificence.

And He is all-wise. With sympathy and balance He can harmonize the needs of Adam's offspring and the force of nature, all inside a single household.

He is the great composer who has ordered that the collected hearts of world-ruling kings be bound and prefaced with the Prophet.

The Builder, who has laid the foundations of love's flourishing paradise, here in the realm of existence. The Artist who has painted the portrait of disaffection with the color and complexion of pure union.

With all her streams of gratitude the Ocean still falls short of doing justice to the Lord's two drops of grace. And so her shores retain their dust for penance. The rain storm's liquid wealth is spent. She has showered all her pearls of praise. Her lips are dry. Her heart is thundering.

Indeed, the book of Your praise is large. The thumb would drain the ocean dry to count through all the contents. Then how may we come through successfully, sailing with this raft of pages over seas of His unbounded praise; how surmount our limitations to achieve the scope which equals His full glory?

In praise of Muḥammad, the Prophet of God

There can be no hope unless we call to mind, 'Let the sea turn into ink and write the Lord's due praise', and with apologies humbly made, take our refuge at the Prophet's foot. For, he is the pilot of mariners lost at sea. He is the guide of beginning and end. His value is beyond a reckoning.

They say the sea shell of this temporary world would shatter like a fragile bubble bursting in the surf of non-existence, if he were not the pearl within its center, the jewel of all creation.

His dignity rises far above all mankind. Had Noah's ark not borne the seed of his future coming, no anchor had secured us Mount Ararat's deliverence.

He is the captain of this world's ship, steering the course of sight and knowledge, He bears the noble title from the Lord, 'I have sent you as a comfort for both worlds.'

Men past and present find in him their elemental cause. He raised the inscribed banner, 'Adam, you were only dust and water but I was the prophet even then.'

Holder of the unique honor from our Lord, 'Oh Muḥammad, if not for you . . . !' Adorned with the unique epithet, 'Mankind never realized the full extent of your greatness.' Aḥmad is king,[2] mounted on the throne entitled, 'Oh Muḥammad, if not for you, I had not raised up the heavens and created earth.' Allah's grace and peace be on him always and on his family and his faithful followers.

In honor of ʿAlī, the fourth of the orthodox caliphs

And peace be on our Prophet's twin, the Prophet's most intimate companion, second visionary of inspiration, conquering Lion of the Lord, manifestation of wonders and of mystery, subduer of infidels, captain of the ship of worldly chance and fortune, ʿAlī ibn Abī Ṭālib,[3] prince of true believers, yes, peace on him and all his family and companions.

In accord with held tradition he has rightly said, 'The elect house of my people is like the mighty ark of Noah. Those that ride therein are saved. Those left behind will drown and perish.' All who take refuge in the salutary ark of love will flee God's wrath, that fatal floundering, but those who disobey are even now hastening to the depths of black perdition. The path is cleared of obstacles.

Author's name followed by eulogy of the present king, Shāh Sulaimān the Safavid

At this point may the humble author, ibn Muḥammad Ibrāhīm Muḥammad Rabīʿ, scribe to the contingent of royal musketeers, take the opportunity to praise his mighty king, for the present sultanate, this twin of justice, springs from a king whose fate is written boldly in the stars.

He spreads before mankind the carpet of fulfillment and security. He is Chosroes[4] conquering this world and not unlike a second Alexander. Founder of the solid structure of a world dominion. Preserver of the kingdom and the faith. Bezel in the ring of equity.

He annihilates the elements of sin and heresy throughout the world. Architect of eternal rule. He is like the magic signet ring of Solomon,[5] his honored name-sake.

Noble rulers everywhere take our king as the model for behavior. He distributes for the Lord the bounties of this world. The divine King's court maintains him as the earthly representative.

He is the living surety for covenants on which hinge the desires and hopes of all mankind. Unrivalled sovereign of the sphere of creation. Highest, most awesome of all Khāqāns.

He is the sky's bright sun risen to the zenith. We may rightly say of our king what God said to the Prophet, 'We have raised him to a noble post indeed.'

He is the full moon resplendent in the zodiac. 'Above all others we have chosen you.' Other kings rule through his endowment. He assigns all crowns which wield authority and might.

In the arts of war he ranks highest of all horsemen here on earth and with purified spirit he rides through the heavens on his fire steed.[6]

The Khāns[7] of far-off China bow; they kiss the earth to do him praise. His very presence is sublime.

He is the dignitary of the age, the source of every ruler's power, the Lord's shadow here on earth. Sultan,[8] son of sultans. Khān, sprung from a line of Khāns. God is his strength.

Abū'l-Muẓaffar, Abū'l-Manṣūr, Shāh Sulaimān, the Safavid, descendent of the Imām Mūsā[9] and the martyr Ḥusain,[10] valiant and heroic—God perpetuate the shade of his mercy, the comfort of his generosity, up to the very day of judgment.

Our king holds the noble banner, 'We have established you firmly upon the face of the earth, throughout the seven climes, across its length and breadth.'

This king of kings shades all classes of men with justice and compassion. Destiny has sounded the drum of his prosperity from the peak of heaven's dome. His justice flows forth with the force of spring, causes Iran's broad lands to mirror Paradise to come.

But it is God who gave mankind kingship, God, the eternal King, who ordered that the firman[11] of this everlasting dominion of Iran be adorned with our king's august name followed by the inscription, 'Give Me the kingdom and seek none in My stead.'

For from God's being is composed the substance of the world. And as the shadow closely hugs the body, so the world is bound to God. To insure stability He fashioned kingship and caused all beings from the fabled fish[12] that props up the earth to the moon that glides through the Heavens, to render kings their due obedience.

God, whose fame has reached the young and old, whose rule is known to big and small through all six corners of the earth. The tasty honey of His justice delights the palate of man's soul.

The goal of every enlightened ruler

And so it is that every ruling chief in the civilized world who assumes office with the shining crown of understanding, who keeps his sight sharp with the collyrium of humility, who polishes the inner mirror of self-knowledge with the saying, 'The man who knows his own soul . . .' to catch the beloved's cheek reflected in his heart, 'that man knew his Lord', who has not clouded up the mind's window with the smoke of boastful conceits but has raised intimacy's divine-most banner in the field of God's love and come to sit on the high throne of self-contemplation, who has clasped the belt of wisdom round the waist of his soul and has cultivated the fruit-bearing tree of communion in the Prophet's garden and with the nourishing texts of truth revealed has caused the tree to yield a sacred closeness to the Lord, all such rulers recognize this one great truth that the ultimate purpose, creation's final goal, is none other than conciliation, attainment of harmony in the relations between all elements of society, especially the relations between the world-ruling sultans and the potent Khāqāns;[13] for, they are honored with life's most noble places at the banquet of superior station. They are the chosen few whose lucky star has presently risen.

For this conspicuous reason the prosperity of wordly sultans is attentively recorded in Time's register of months and years and there can be no doubt that the ruler's prosperity is the cause of the land's flourishing and the population's repose.

The Siamese king

Good rulers, therefore, take a further step on the path toward world harmony. With ambassadors and delegations as their key they unlock the doors of world-wide friendship. Such was the intent of the Siamese king, possessor of the white elephant and the throne of solid gold. For he loves all Muslims and was overawed seeing that our king, the brilliant luminary of world rule had risen into the Heavens of eternal sovereignty, our king who is the noble planet of good fortune, adornment of the throne of omnipotence and bearer of Chosroes' crown and the cap of Kayān.[14] Thereupon the Siamese monarch hastened to open the accounts of friendship and affection. 'May Allah bless him and guide him into the fold of Islam.'

Ḥājī Salīm, the Siamese king's envoy to Iran

It is sufficient in his praise that he has placed his forehead on the threshold of Chosroes, orderer of the world. Indeed, he set his needy foot into the arena of petition and snatched away the palm of striving from all contenders. Making purity of heart his introduction to our king, again and again he sent out his courtiers entrusting them with marvelous gifts and letters of affection. Alas, some drowned in nameless seas and left no sign behind, others caught by pirates on the main failed to reach their destination. But in ītyīl 1093,[15] Ḥājī Salīm Māzandarānī was delegated to attempt the great voyage and present to our king a letter of friendship which professed all forms of good will and sincerity and was accompanied by the finest gifts the Siamese king could procure. The letter prayed that the limitless sea of true affection be stirred up with happy waves as delegates and embassies passed between the monarchs, that love and lasting attachment rejoice in the freshening breezes thus created.

Shāh Sulaimān responds to the Siamese embassy and Ḥusain Beg is chosen as the Iranian ambassador

Our king has a character of special generosity and general compassion. The world stands dazzled before his practised virtues. His bounty exceeds all proportions of description. His compassion is like the compassion which brought back sight to Jacob, the old man of Canaan.[16] His indulgence is as renowned as the indulgence which Joseph of Egypt practised in this world. And though our king, a constellation in the firmament of power, would be seen to deal with merchandise of lesser stuff, he resolved to condescend; remembering the pious words, 'For if they salute you, salute them back the best of salutations', he saw fit to grace the Siamese king with the glances of his bounty and thereby raise that king above his peers. Therefore Muḥammad Ḥusain Beg, officer of the honorable Khāṣṣa, was appointed the head of a delegation made up of Qūrchīs, Ghulāms, Tūpchīs and Tufanchīs, all of whom were to travel to Siam.

The author expresses his joy at being chosen the embassy's official scribe

As for my humble self, ever since the day that Destiny played clerk and entered my name in the register of existence along with the rest of mankind, I have cherished a single unrelenting passion to pierce the jewel of virgin service, to undertake a duty as yet unrealized among my peers and thereby gain my king's special affections. Bearing in mind that one must never hope for what one seeks with insincerity, for therein lies the cause for much remorse, my heart was honestly overcome with joy when I attained at last my life's desire and was appointed to the special task of composing this journey's official report.

> In my heart I felt elated.
> My soul is coin to scatter at the king's fair feet.
> What breath of life this soul contains
> We spend in serving thee.
> My head is bobbing like a bubble tossed on the sea.
> Now is the time to plunge amid the swirling waves,
> Either sink and drown or bear back news to thee.

We have tried our best. With hope, sincerity and devotion in our heart we undertook this difficult task. Our pen, the twin of clarity, has rendered explicitly all that happened on this journey. If there be some elegance herein, praise be unto God. For our part, as was our king's command, we have aimed at brevity, retaining relevant detail as one finds in the famous tale of the Locust and the Ant or the Bedouin and the Brackish Water.[17] We are full of hope that this priceless jewel, the outcome of our king's inspiring command, the pearl of our unworthy efforts, will find before his sun-like gaze that complete approval which we seek.

> You are Sulaimān, lord of the age.
> I am as a wretched ant.
> Do not reject this humble gift
> Which I bear home from a distant unknown land.

The account has been named after Shāh Sulaimān and divided into separate gems

We cherish the hope that this jewel may be acceptable to our king when weighed in the balance of his judgment. When he has journeyed through the sea of our narration, sailing with God's grace, may it please him to remember that his name is proudly entered in the title of our work. As for the cargo, God has given this captain of Sulaimān's ship such little merchanise of natural genius and yet no captain sets sail for his destination without some goods of value. So I have loaded the ship of my account with all kinds of priceless wares, tales which sparkle like bright gems and thus we call each anecdote which comes before the elixir of our king's gaze, a threaded jewel.

The Ship of Sulaimān

Hear how the swift sailing ship of the mighty king Sulaimān bore us across the open sea and we were led to a strange and distant land. Such a journey is a fabulous rose that blossoms before the traveler's charmed sight. Day by day we breathed in a scented bouquet of marvels and adventure, all of which is herein contained. We also bore our share of hardship and were forced to gaze upon the face of Death but thanks to our humble vessel and the prevailing gale of God's almighty grace, we have returned to present our incredible tale. Praise be to God, the ever present pilot, whose hand and breath guide every purified soul along its course through life.

PART I FIRST JEWEL

The embassy sets out from Bandar ʿAbbās[1]

Here our pen begins the task, composing on a sheet of clarity, and the story sets out upon its course like a ship that plies the sea. After six months of various delays in Bandar ʿAbbās we set sail on the 25th of Rajab 1096,[2] entrusting our souls to the limitless sea. It was just evening twilight. The Sun like a distant ship cast anchor in the waters of the West and thereupon the wind of our desire rose. The captain and the officers passed on orders to the members of the crew and roused them to their stations. When the sky's great Captain had made fast the shining chain of night to moor the drifting heavens, we cast off and were heading towards our destination.

The ship sails into a storm

For several days we were in sight of the shore with its mountains but suddenly a rough wind bore down on us. The passengers became alarmed and began to moan with low voices. Their hearts were, 'Like a sailor in a ship and his ship is floundering at sea'. The buffeting increased. Waves began crashing all around us. The heart was choked in Despair's tight claw. The clear face of Endurance was swallowed in the sea's gulf.

Every man aboard drenched his shirt with weeping. Like a sailor who gives up the sinking ship, the vital spirit perched on the heart's edge. The immortal soul was ready to desert the body like a captain when the ship is lost.

To look at the passengers you would think they were a crowd of dizzy drunkards, their hands clasping their heads. Their eyes were tomes wide opened where the frightened pupil reads the Quran's fatal warning,[3] 'Black perdition, darkness piled on darkness through descending levels of the underworld.'

In the end that night of discomfort passed and the all-commanding Sun brought his head up from the sky's hold, leading back light to the upper world. The Officer of the Heavens hung the sun's lantern over the celestial maindeck and the road ahead was bright. Night, the Helmsman of the stars, exchanged his watch with breaking Dawn.

25

A reef at sea

But at that first light a clamor of grief arose from the fore of the ship. The crewmen wailed and shouted, hurriedly unfurling the sails and maneuvering the rigging. When we asked what had happened we were informed that the night watch had carelessly fallen asleep and forgotten his duty and all through the night the ship had been drifting. In this part of the ocean there is a certain reef which is barely covered with water at high tide or during storms.

With the aid of God, later on we shall give a detailed description of such aspects of navigation in these waters. As usual there was not nearly enough water for the ship to pass over. Had we drifted just a bit further we would have struck rock and split asunder. Our poor ship would have broken into pieces the way sheets of paper fly apart when a book's binding breaks. All these passengers on the sea of life would have perished there and then as in the saying 'All things return to their constituent elements.'

The ship is hauled to safety

With that for the journey's beginning everyone aboard broke out in tears and washed their hands of life in the sea which held them prisoners. The eyes were drowned in the midst of streaming tears and everyone sat waiting the fated moment when he would meet with death at sea. Then in accord with 'Pray unto Me and I shall answer you', we were sent comfort and security. Our piercing cries, our lamentation so full of misery brought the Lord's sea of compassion to a boil. Divine kindness was our Khiẓr,[4] who guides all mariners through dangerous waters.

The crew managed to launch dinghies and attach our ship to these smaller boats by a series of anchor chains. They rowed and hauled us the length of two maidāns[5] and finally put us back on course. We only escaped from that reef of destruction due to the never failing luck which accompanied us throughout the whole voyage.

The winds die down

Now the sun like a tired deck hand went down into the hold of the West. But the Wind, who was competing with the musical spheres of Venus,[6] suddenly changed the direction of his melody. For two full days and nights he blew against us and then he stopped and held back his voice completely. He would not perform for anyone but wrapped himself in the cloak of silence. Thus he caused further suffering for these travelers caught in the sea of confusion.

We were caught in unbearable heat

This unhappy event took place when the Dog Star had climbed to his fullest ascent. It was the hottest part of the year. The winds ceased rushing to and fro. Even the morning breeze, fair Zephyr, drew round itself the skirt of stillness.

The heat which followed was so great, ocean's realm of water became a mountain of blazing magnesium. The Dog Star itself caught flame, turned into a roasted kebab. The sea burned like a blacksmith's furnace. The region of water changed into the flaming sphere of ether. It was so hot you would think destiny had brought forth a second Hell.

Such fire is beyond my humble capacities of description. Yet, if in the furnace of my imagination I could raise one spark of that weather's blaze, my account would burst into flame and brand you with meaning. When the poet's mind seeks to pluck a rose of metaphor in a garden of such fiery visions, like a lit branding iron the flower falls from the gardener's smarting hand. Praise be to God for that ocean's mighty heat! For as I struggle to depict this scene I feel the tongue's candle catch fire in the lantern of my mouth. And that is a God sent marvel!

This heart could rightly shed a stream of tears simply recalling the plight of those days. The ruthless heat turned the whole realm of water into a Sahara of shifting sands. The waves arched their backs and threw up heat like glowing coals. Our ship in the sea of 'Ummān[7] was crisp kindling tossed on a fire. The poor souls aboard were bereft of all sense and life, mere corpses at large in a floating coffin. This was no ship but a sailing Hell; one huge coffin with a thousand dead.

All along the powerful sun caused springs of sweat to gush from the base of each and every hair. Each hair was a distinct wick aflame with the touch of air. Had storm clouds let fall a mighty shower, such heat would turn each drop into a separate, brilliant spark. At last the Sun himself went reeling in that heat and such a sight scorched Ocean's heart with pity.

The water aboard runs low

With this went a companion calamity. Suddenly the water bearer of our English ship, who as a Christian rides the ass along with Jesus, dripped sweat from his pale face unto the ground of impatience and desperately ruffling his hair like a grief stricken mourner, announced that this was the end of the monsoon, the wind was finished.

3

There is no means of allaying the present heat other than with scorching sea water which is a cure worse than the ailment. From now on you shall each be given one drop of drinking water a day to keep the body's river flowing with life and the soul's cup full of spirit. Half of that drop is for the heart's kettle of emotion and the other half is for the body's kitchen.

Concerning the need for water, there is a view held by atomist doctors and even the opponents of atomism, that if the thirsty do not first drink the vital drop of water, their bodies will not assimilate particles of nourishment.

Oh Lord, keep us from that other water, the brackish water of the sea, for it distils pain and grief into the weak and thirsty who drink it. They imbibe a single drop and hear the doleful murmur of their heart, 'this is molten lead that boils straight through the stomach.' The lips that touch the edge of such a bitter cup are blistered, 'now in poisons, now in scalding water'.

Each drop contains a hundred maggots busy at their swirling dance. This water's chemistry is concocted from some heavy essence out of rock or soil. Its clotted multitude of snake-like worms dams up the body's stream of life. The tormented sufferers feel their insides burning and cry forth, 'My liver roasts in liquid fire.' Their tears flow forth abundantly and finally quell the flame of speech.

It is no consolation that this water boasts of equal footing with the force of fire. Still tears pour forth from the sufferer's storm dark eyes like rain dropping to soothe a season's heat. And yet the burning plaintiff cries, 'How can my broiling heart take comfort from these salty tears. Thirst's very flame grows brighter with the salty water of the sea.'

But we saw clearly why the wise saying, 'All living things are sprung from water' is current among the flourishing peoples of the earth and that wasting good water is to risk the very substance of life and is against God's explicit command. Hence we fortified our wills with keen determination and made do with the few drops of water then available.

I do not pretend that we suffered during this dry spell nearly as much as the thirsty of Karbalā[8] but in our biting the ruby lip of endurance we earned admittance to that company of martyrs and became their drinking companions at the Euphrates of patience. In accord with 'Those whose way of life resembles a certain people are accounted of that people', our hearts entertain a hope in the bounteous waters of Kauthar to come.[9] One particular thought from the Quran's great spring contents the palate of our souls, 'Have patience and endure for God esteems the patient.'

'Praise be to God for all events', but may my pen be shattered and
my page be blackened over if the purpose of my narration seems
to be complaint. I have mentioned this incident only for the sake of
recording the facts. Now let the nightingale of my tongue sing the
following praise in return for our king, the merciful Khān's attentions
and be hopeful of attaining to the shade of his affection:

What sorrow can we know
From the sun of hot events.
For our shade we have the refuge
Of your all consoling grace.

The ship arrives at the port of Muscat

Fourteen days after setting out we arrived at the port of Muscat.
And this is a port controlled by the Nāsib Arabs and Khārijites.[10]
Formerly it was held by the Portuguese Franks but a few years ago
these Khārijites took to their slyness and caught the cursed Franks
off guard. It was during one of the church services when the Franks
had no weapons on hand. In accord with 'We have sent devils against
the infidel to strike him with devastation', the Arabs came down
upon them like the final judgment. Large numbers of Franks were
killed or taken prisoner and their fortifications as well as the port
were seized.[11] And so this port has remained in the possession of the
Khārijites from that time up until now.

The case of these contemptible Khārijites is as the scholars have
recorded in their various histories. When 'Alī prince of true believers
sought to purify the flower-bed of religion and had cleared the soil
of the thorns and brambles of the Khārijites at Nahravān,[12] there
were nine of the multitude who eluded his sword. From this number
the Arzāqites,[13] followers of Nāfi' ibnu'l-Arzāq, fled and settled
around Ahvāz and Fārs and two other survivors made their way to
'Ummān.

By today the Khārijites have managed to repair their broken
lineage and these lost travelers in the desert of religious error claim
to represent Islam. In accord with 'We have sent false Imāms among
you who call you into the flames', they continue in their ignorance
and hold their own chief to be the true Imām. He lives in seclusion
but has appointed delegates to guard over and maintain the harbor
lest the Franks come back.

The harbor is strongly fortified indeed with mountains to all sides
and the local ships are well outfitted. It is worth noting that one may
find the same fruits here in the market as in India. Despite their
debased character these Khārijites do not inflict the wickedness of

their religious beliefs on the merchants and travelers who happen into the port but they do exact a 3 per cent tax from everyone including Muslims.

Indeed their hatred towards the people of the faith's great leader, king of men, 'Alī, may God, the one gracious King, give him peace and their hatred towards 'Uthmān ibn 'Affān and Mu'āwiya ibn Abī Ṣufiān,[14] those thorns and brambles of the desert of insolence and rebellion, upon them both be God's curse and Hell fires, is so great that they go to the following lengths.

Whenever a child from this improper line of Khārijites reaches an impressionable age the parents give him three different kinds of animals as pets. But after two or three years when the child has become quite attached to them, they steal the animals and kill them. When the child finds out what has happened they explain that one animal was carried off by 'Alī and the other two were taken by those wolves 'Uthmān and Mu'āwiya, all because these three men have a special hatred for you. In that manner from childhood on they cultivate this carefully planted tree of enmity and thus it will continue until it is plucked up by the roots along with each individual Khārijite.

It may also be mentioned that their religion forbids tobacco and anyone who is caught smoking in public is punished with a whipping. The water pipe of his body exhales the smoke of anguish.

The embassy sets out from Muscat to India

When we dropped anchor in that port the Franks of our ship had row boats sent ashore to fetch fresh water and a little later we took on the necessary provisions. We remained in Muscat for three days and at dawn on the fourth day when the sun's ship broke into the sky's Indian ocean we cast off and headed out to sea.

The ship is a young bride and the winds are musicians

The ship was a newly wed just come out from behind her veil. As her fair form came gliding through the sea the waves rose up to splash her with their happy rhythms. The waves brought forth their bubbling heads to scatter as gifts before the bride's swift feet. And so for twenty days the ship proceeded smoothly beneath the winds of our desire. But alas, this breeze gave out before we reached the shore of our destination.

The Loosener of the winds, who had been entertaining his assembled guests with the dulcimer of indulgence, gave new orders to his servants that they play in a different key, contrary to their earlier performance. It was of no account that this change brought grief to the heart of harassed travelers on the sea of light and heavy rhythms. The servants were quick to obey his commands. They came forth from every far flung corner of nature nor did they dally along the way. The sea's proud wave was the groom who sang and struck his drum to set the bride, our ship, into a swirling dance. He even leapt to strike the rigging's harp strings with his flashing plectrum.

A black night fell portending a storm

Meanwhile the strongest night fell about us, more black than a black day of ill luck and darker than inside an evil man's heart. The black iris reads the white of the eye like a page from the Tafsīr,[15] 'Like the black depths of the fathomless sea, a sea where wave mounts over wave and mist clouds over all. Darkness heaped on darkness.' The illuminator, Destiny, had painted the night's page with the black pen of his decrees. The scribe of Being recorded this translation with annihilation's ink and the pen of non-existence.

For all the night's obscurity the iris could not distinguish its own black from the eye's white. Tears, the children of the eye, ran down the face, seeing what black humor resided in the iris' heart. Night's darkness traveled forth from the shadows of the West and settled over all the world. At the sight of such unaccustomed blackness even the eye of the inkstand brought forth tears of fear.

Mother Time blackened her breasts with pitch to wean this babe, the child of darkness. The night bore raven black hair that rivalled the dark down of waxing young men. Beholding such pure black, the locks of the spoiled beloved curled upon themselves with jealousy.

What apt metaphor can the merchant of imagination bring before the bazaar of elegance and not come home with a face turned black in shame. And the gardener of words, what pepper seed of speech can he plant in the course of this account that will not cause the page's face to blacken over.

The storm hits at dawn

When the fierce wolf, black Night, had bedded down in ambush of the pale ewe of Dawn, a forceful wind blew up, indeed a gale which would rival the famous blast which layed low the ancient 'Ādites.[16] This wind was so powerful that by comparison any typhoon would be a transparent illusion, a mirage seen at sea.

The ship was tossed to the zenith of heaven, borne up by ranks of climbing waves. The next minute the ship fell, dropping to the innermost center of the earth's pit. God's hand alone was responsible for our deliverance. The typhoon reached such a pitch of rage the author's imagination must take refuge in the saying, 'Any amount of words is only a drop in the full flood of that calamity.'

The waves rose and fell in blind succession, disappeared into the crazed force of the sea. If Noah had ever seen such a storm, he would not have placed his hopes in a ship. If Noah had entered the vessel knowing her to be his sure salvation, once aboard he would have lost all courage and drowned in waves of limitless fear. Even if Noah calmed himself with the foreknowledge of God's intentions, where would he find the patience of a Jacob[17] to abide through that disheartening sea of grief.

One passenger is drowned

It happened that a certain man who traced his family line back to Māzandarān[18] had come aboard in Muscat. He was returning to India after visiting Mecca. That night of the storm he fell into a sleep of neglect and with all the sea and wind, the ship of his being plunged into the waves like a bubble and the fox of his life swam off into the dim waters of non-existence. The wave of doom clasped onto his skirts and he, poor man, went under in the tight embrace of death.

Everyone aboard weeps and prays for deliverance

Whirlpools opened all across the face of Ocean like so many watery eyes of mourning and every traveler on the stream of suffering wept for those gone down to the depths and wept as well for himself calling to mind, 'When the wave like an impenetrable shadow has covered them over, pray to God and make manifest the sincerity of your faith.'

And so they raised a great wailing and besought the ears of the Heavenly Council on high.[19] Their abundant tears formed a great sea. The eye's iris drowned in the water of dismay. 'Such is the flood of my tears that had one drop escaped from their train and rolled down to the sea, the wide sea herself would be engulfed, lost in the greater liquid volume.'

Thus they wept until the Gospel-like message, 'We delivered him from dire sadness', reached the soul's inner ear. These were the all-powerful words of God, whose voice inspires every penitent sinner but whose form remains upon the waters.

However, our crossing over that sea of divers afflictions is tedious to recount. Let it be sufficient if my pen writes out this final phrase:

'I was sore afflicted, struck with every kind of misery, misery enough to turn bright light of day into the darkest of nights'. And so we close our account of that painful stage of the journey.

The embassy arrives at Chinapatan in India

Now our story goes forward and like a ship as swift as wind steers a course through new waters towards her destination. After forty-seven days at sea we arrived at our next stop, the port Chinapatan. This is one of the ports of the territory of Carnatik in the vicinity of Ḥaidarābād. The English have rented it for twelve thousand hūns and have built themselves a fort there and established a city.

As soon as we dropped anchor we announced our arrival by firing a thunder-voiced cannon and the tarakī came out to the ship. Tarakī is the Indian term for a kind of special courier. He came out to meet us in a thin canoe and was wearing a hat made of woven reeds. He shot across the water faster than the waves. He was all efficiency and speed. When he confirmed the fact of our arrival and learned our port of embarkation, he hurried back to the governor whom they call the gundar.

He presented the governor with a detailed report inscribed on a good sized leaf. This is the custom in most of the states of India as well as in the countries of Below the Winds. The habit of copying all letters, documents and government reports on the face of leaves has become the accepted practice because the officials are so often coming and going on the water. Another factor which makes this system necessary is that the rainy season in India is very long and there is an unusual dampness in the air. Under these circumstances leaves are by far the best writing material since they offer the greatest security for correspondence and keeping records. Once the governor had the report of the tarakī, our ship's captain was escorted ashore.

The embassy comes ashore

Early the next morning several dinghies brought out various fowl, meats, local fruits, pan and betel nut. And the day after, when the Sun brought forth his head from the castle of Heaven, the governor of the city sent his deputy with a group of the captain's close associates to escort our embassy ashore. We took our seats in small boats which were specially provided for us and then set out towards the land.

We were still two maidāns from the shore when about fifty different rowers appeared in their own boats to accompany us the rest of the way. In certain places the waves were breaking with such violence some rowers were tossed into the water. You would think they were drowned but they always managed to swim to their boats and climb back in. It was explained to us that because the waves were so rough, dashing upon the shore one after another, it was best to have many extra boats on hand to insure a safe landing. If one boat was over-turned there was no danger of the passengers drowning. The other boats all around would quickly collect the people.

A procession from the shore to the fortress

When we landed the gundar came down from his fort on foot and met us at the shore. There we were provided with traveling litters made of ebony, a separate litter for each of us. Once inside our litters we formed a procession and at the head singers, tumblers and musicians were busy playing and dancing. It may be noted that throughout all these ceremonies we were accorded the greatest care and esteem. At both sides of our litters were servants who despite the heat kept us cool with enormous fans. As we moved along the road other servants with fine white cloths skillfully dusted all our clothing. Artillery men and musketeers were stationed in the towers of the fort and all the cannons were loaded and ready.

A tour of the fortress

As we entered the fort the soldiers fired a resounding salute. Straight-way we were taken on a sightseeing tour along the walks of the fort and we were allowed to visit and inspect the various apartments. Finally they took us to the royal lodgings where the gundar lives. These rooms are kept in perfect order and were particularly beautiful and from this height the whole fort and the surrounding city were visible. When our tour was finished we approached a large tent-like pavillion with several doors on both sides.

Our first formal reception

Chairs of ebony were placed before us. In fact it is the custom of Franks and most other infidels that when they come indoors they sit on chairs and not on carpets. As soon as we arrived large amounts of wine and *hors-d'oeuvres* were brought out. At this point the gundar and the other Franks felt the time was right to stand up and toast God, the qibla[20] of all mortals. The gundar made a special sign and all at once the cannons of the fort fired a salute.

Inside this large room they had set up a table which was seven cubits long and resembled a golden throne. It was covered over with a white cloth and was set with plates of silver, silver spoons, knives and napkins. Next they brought out various kinds of preserves and sweets as well as almonds, pistachios, hazel nuts and raisins.

It is one of their customs that when they wish to honor someone they select his food and serve it to him personally. And so the gundar, their governor, took up the knife in his own hand and neatly cut us separate portions which he placed over a specially prepared rice dish.

But before they extended their hands to partake of the outspread food, they stood up once more, removed their hats and gave thanks to God in their own language. Only when the prayer was over did they begin to eat. They consider this practice of removing one's hat to be the highest form of showing respect.

Visit to a garden on the way to our lodgings

Later we were informed that a house had been prepared for us outside the fort. When the meal was over we stood up along with the other guests and everyone took his leave of the gundar. Then we returned to our litters along with the men who were to escort us to our lodgings, but first we were carried to a beautiful garden in the middle of which there was a large building.

On one side of this building was a park and on the other was an orchard and on the top of the building's walls were colored statues, creatures so skillfully wrought you would think they were real birds roosting there. After our guides had given us a tour around their own wonderful house, they brought us to the accommodations which had been prepared for us. Then they left and returned home by themselves.

We were sent quantities of food, fruits and various other commodities and a group of their servants was assigned to look after any of our needs. They were there to guard us and generally maintain our apartments. The gundar and his associates visited us from day to day and indeed they offered us hospitality in every possible way.

Description of the port

Chinapatan is blessed with an abundance of vegetation and extreme fertility. The town is divided by avenues of houses and gardens and stretches for about a quarter of a league. The port's inhabitants are of various racial backgrounds but most of them are Telegu Hindus. There is also a group of Portuguese Franks residing there.

Not long ago these Franks had possession of a nearby port, Mailāpūr, but because of some unseemly act which they brought to public view, the Wālī[21] of Ḥaidarābād sent an army and destroyed their fort. The survivors came to Chinapatan to take refuge and re-established themselves.

The English governor had made no attempt to confiscate their goods or extort money from them. In general he has treated them well, being very satisfied with the port's prosperity. Day by day these Franks arrive from outlying districts, taking note of this governor's leniency, and they are able to settle in quite easily.

It is the king of England, however, who holds authority over the buying and selling of the port's inhabitants and he has arranged that every year several ships with money and various goods come to the port to trade and accumulate merchandise.

It may be noted that the Franks maintain a high standard of discipline and are very cautious when it comes to manning their forts and protecting their cities. Night and day the artillerymen and the musketeers are at their stations on the towers. The wicks are lit and the cannons are loaded and ready to fire. They do not neglect their watch or other duties for a single moment.

News arrives that the king of England is dead[22]

A few days after our delegation arrived, a ship came from England, which is the home domain of their king. The ship brought a letter announcing that the king's soul had removed its seat of repose from the undistinguished throne of the body and turned the face of its attentions to conquering the realm of eternity and such is the goal of all heroes of noble spirit. The king's soul threw the body's transitory cloak to the ground. On the chessboard of time his soul was check-mated by the raging elephant of death.

The new king wrote: 'The puppeteer, Fortune, has smiled his bounty on me from behind the double colored veil of the chess game, and the backgammon player, Chance, has shaken the dice of hope and thrown the number of my wish. So I am king. Be happy and rejoice and continue to fulfill your accustomed duties. May any requests or complaints be presented before my sight that they receive the honor of my attention and indulgence.'

When the news was made known to the gundar and the other government officials, that whole day they wore black to display the sadness in their hearts, but the day the new king came to sit upon the throne everyone strove to wear his finest clothes.

On the coronation day messengers were sent from the gundar. He requested that the delegates of our embassy fix a convenient time to come to a party in the garden which we had visited previously. The messengers explained that it was indeed a day of joyful celebration for the English. They also requested that we send our cooks to prepare the meal that evening. None of their caterers had a knowledge of the food and dishes which would please us and they were interested to try our kind of food. Since it was the blessed month of Ramaẓān,[23] the 22nd in fact, we arrived towards evening.

The Franks' feast and a description of their manners and behavior

May this account not be kept secret from all those who are wont to sit at the banquet board of grace and joy and pluck the rose of festivity in gatherings of good cheer. To begin with the twelve delegates were installed in their litters and brought to the home of their generous host. On the porch of that building rugs were arranged in profusion and chairs rather than cushions provided. The party was to take place under a large tent which was attached to the porch.

As we were about to enter the porch and expected to take off our shoes, we observed that everyone there was walking about on the rugs wearing his shoes. They even had their dogs along with them. So in accord with their custom we kept our shoes on and walked straight into the tent area where we were offered chairs.

When the guests had assembled, the musicians who were stationed behind a wall and could not be seen, began playing their instruments and then the wine was brought out. First the English toasted the Iranian king, who is the almighty omniscient King's shadow on earth, and that was a soul intoxicating toast. Next with shrewd maneuver they balanced the score by toasting their own king and finally after toasting the king of Siam, the cannons fired a salute.

Description of the Frank women[24]

With a show of humility the host proceeded to explain: 'Although it is a Muslin practice to keep women from associating with men outside their kin, we feel that to keep the dazzling Frank women, whose faces beam like the sun and are round like the moon, hidden with veils of modesty would be the height of blasphemy and exceed the bounds of all propriety. Such a sin would be inexcusable, pure abomination.'

And they were right. If Fakhr Rāzī,[25] the theologian, beheld these pages, whose surface is made of rosy cheeks, his guiding finger of orthodoxy would raise the modest veil from codified indulgences and grant these brilliant faces admittance to our sight. With zeal he would waive accepted regulations and, retreating from the field of modesty, unfurl the banner of decreed indulgence.

He would surely grant these beauties free entrance to our gathering and would not fear the consequent disturbance which arises in our hearts. Then if he were wise he would abolish the illusory difference between various religions and preach with the radiant beauty of these moon-like faces. He would defend his new theological position with the texts of these gleaming eyes, the scriptures of flowing hair and the sayings of their colored lips.

And if the high flying hawk of Imām Ghazālī's noble thought caught sight of these lion breaking gazelles, the swift dog of infatuation would loose its neck from the leash of orthodoxy to pursue this wild game with reckless abandon. If he saw that the Muslim ascetic, who is vigilant through all the night had finally come to converse with the true-born Hindu, who wears the Brahmanic thread, and these two religious sages were become sincere companions like two nuts in a single shell, he would look upon their conciliation with indulgence and approve their apparent heresy. He would not be at a loss to dress their unusual behavior in the clothes of propriety, calling forth certain forms of proof, citing precedents and pointing out analogies with the scriptures.

Indeed if Ghazālī was faced with such beauty, he would renounce his position as Imām, join obediently with those heathens and follow their form of worship. He would bewail the wasted piety of his former days, scratch his face and pull out his hair in a rage. Yes, he would reproach himself the rest of his life and shed salty tears of regret from his visionary eyes.

Surely such women must be encouraged. Their beautiful straight backs sway like cypress trees and bring a rush of sap into the dry garden of these old lover's hearts. The rose-red glimmer of their cheeks, cheeks like those of heaven's Houris,[26] sparked new life in the breasts of the company of friends. Thus the light of their beauty was admitted and they participated in the festivities despite the fact that they were women.

Suddenly these moon-faced idols entered and an indescribable charm was radiated throughout the room. They were all joy from head to toe. The magic of their eyes bewitched our sight and this gathering became the very envy of eternal paradise. Their flashing appearance was the key which opened up the doors of paradise. The garden of joy and spiritual union stood before us. We beholders with our dearth of wealth, our paltry means, stood at the threshold and gazed within.

They set the clear-throated nightingale of flirtation singing and he called to us from the tree of intoxication, 'Enter with faith and peace.' The bird chanted promises, 'If ye repent, enter this garden for all eternity.' There is no doubt but that party was the rival of the garden of Paradise thanks to the presence of those Houri-like creatures.

As is their custom the men salute the women first. The men stand up from their places and lift their hats and at the same time pronounce courteous greetings. The women have their own way of returning the gesture by bending down a bit and making a slight movement of the foot.

The party continues with dancing and professional entertainers

After these formalities the mart of hugs and kisses began to warm up. Everywhere slim-waisted women were being embraced while faces grew red with the rose-colored wine. The festivity reached such an intensity the veils of modest restraint were on the verge of bursting into flame and burning away. It is another of their fixed rules that the degree of friendship one has for a person is expressed by the amount of affection one shows that person's wife.

Now the guests filled up a large beaker of wine and came before the gundar to offer him a toast. He took off his hat and drank from the cup and then the beaker was passed among the guests. The men and women joined hands and did a dance after their own fashion and instead of happy exclamations when a turn was well done they plucked throat-burning kisses from one another's honeyed lips.

After the party had advanced and even the late guests had arrived, expert performers entered and did various dances. They juggled fire and sang with drums. Their melodies thrilled the bird of the soul and made it take flight. Finally the fuel in the hearts of the lovers was kindled and burst into flame.

> Come forth and caress these curly locks.
> Here are the flashing eyes that soothe the lover,
> Here are the flirting glances,
> The graceful form and gracious manner.

Next came the entertainers and each one had a special act.

One unusual entertainer was a woman who was a tight-rope walker. She performed various feats of skill on top of a high building. There was a fine rope attached to the roof of that building and joined to a pole in the ground. The woman went out on the rope and stood on her head without using her hands for support. Then she did a summersault and repeated the same trick on her stomach and her side. Another performer tied a wooden pole three cubits long behind his neck and did a summersault. He dived from the rope and landed safely on the ground. Another carried a donkey on his back all the way up the rope and down again.

The food and how the Franks eat

At sunset the food was brought out and as is their custom it was placed on a wooden table with wine and *hors d'oeuvres*. So we broke our fast with these dishes. Indeed it was a splendid night whose only equivalent would be 'the Night of the Decree'.[27] Each exciting minute was 'better than a thousand months'.

One of their customs is to maintain a full table constantly. During the course of the party they serve themselves several times. They take a small portion each time and return to their conversation. After the main course they brought out sweets and preserves along with betel nut, milk and large pitchers of a drink they call gul bakh,[28] which consists of lemon juice, liquor and nutmeg mixed with an equal amount of clear water. They drink this special drink to cool the heat of their liquor. Then they start in to eat.

One of their outstanding delicacies, which I might pause to serve up on the plate of my narrative like a sugar plum among the dainty anecdotes, was a white rooster, a skillfully executed masterpiece of sugar confection. Every single feather was in place. When it was brought out before us we were obliged to examine it twice to be sure that it was in fact made of candy. That day and night they must have fired the cannons a thousand times. They have no greater pleasure when dining in society than to fire off salutes, which is also their way of displaying the highest respect.

Description of the religion of the Franks

As is recorded in the works of the scholars there are seventy-two Christian sects in all and they have three basic points of difference. Some Christians claim that Jesus is the son of God, some say he is God himself and still others believe that he consists of three separate persons whose aspects are substance, knowledge and life. The latter group considers Jesus to be the very essence of creation and not merely one of creation's attributes. They maintain that the person which is knowledge entered into the material body of Jesus.

Others hold that the Messiah has a double nature, part divine and part human. They believe that in Jesus the divine became manifest in human form and that both aspects, divine and human, suffered death and crucifixion. However, there is also a group which believes that the death and crucifixion only happened to the human aspect of Jesus and not to the divine, since divinity cannot suffer pain.

Although these sects adhere to the same Gospel, they do not follow the same principles and interpretations and are only loosely affiliated. On enquiring into the matter further it was made clear that today most sects and particularly the ordinary people firmly believe that Jesus is the son of God.

Those Christians who hold that Jesus is divine also maintain that in rank and position women are higher than men in the eyes of Heaven. That this is the case is clear from the fact that a woman was the immediate cause of Jesus's existence, for it was a woman who bore him into the world. It follows then that Christian men have a duty to respect women above themselves.

Indeed the Christians have very trusting natures and in most cases they view their brethren's actions in a wholly favorable light and they never suspect one another of treachery. Even if they catch one of their friends in the same nightshirt with their wife they interpret such behavior as an indication of the respect and affection which their friend has towards them. But if this friend abuses their hospitality and they catch him in the very act they are still obliged to provide two eye witnesses whose testimony must concur and only then do they have a legal case. In such circumstances the priests condemn the wife and the other man to death.

However, only some sects observe this procedure. It is the custom of the Portuguese for instance that every week, month and year the men and women go before a priest in private and confess all their sins. The priest tells them to repent and metes out to each one of them whatever punishment he feels is appropriate. 'God protect me from the evil of their wicked thoughts and deeds.'

Mention of such iniquities has no place in this narrative but I have been bold to include these details in order to encourage the faithful to be all the more diligent in rendering God thanks for the benefits which they enjoy.

Unusual events

Two of the dancers who were more good looking than their companions had decided earlier in life to renounce this world and dedicate themselves to the idols. Now they would not accept payment but having set out on the path of charity performed with the sole intention of pleasing the idols and amusing the idolaters.

Another strange incident which occurred involved a Brahman who claimed to be a fortune teller. To amuse themselves the delegates called him over and had him read their fortunes. The fortune teller held out a bunch of leaves with small signs written on them and when you chose a particular leaf he would read it and tell your future.

When he came around to my humble self, he explained in a whisper that he had been afraid to divulge everything he saw when he read the fortune of the other delegates. He predicted that the ambassador would die shortly after we reached a certain place that would have water and vegetation on all four sides. He also predicted that the Siamese king would become angry and put one of his envoys under arrest.

He went on to tell of various events which actually did take place when we arrived at Shahr Nāv. How he was able to predict our future with such accuracy, I am at a loss to explain. 'Only God knows, for God's wisdom is infinite and all-inclusive.'

PART II SECOND JEWEL

The journey from India to the coast of Tanāsurī[1]

The course of our narrative has now reached its next stage. On the 17th of Shawwāl 1096,[2] after we had taken on supplies, our ship set out for Tanāsurī, which is one of the regions of Sharh Nāv. It would be too tedious to describe all the details of our ensuing troubles, especially as you have read about our previous suffering at sea and so I hold back my double-tongued pen from giving the full account and I am recording only that fraction of our experience which I feel is indispensable.

The ship runs out of provisions

As our port of destination was not very far off the captain did not think it necessary to take on large amounts of food but as it happened the wind died down, the food became scarce and all aboard were reduced to the most dire circumstances. During those days a useless piece of bread six months old, all sour and full of worms and ants would be eaten without the least hesitation. That old crust seemed to be the finest honey.

We were almost shipwrecked on the coast of Paigū[3]

At the same time we came near an island called Andaman and the wind and water, as is the nature of the warring elements, rose up against our earthly bodies. The flames of fear were kindled in our souls while the currents drew us towards Paigū. Paigū is a country situated in the land of Khiṭā[4] but has a separate king. We barely escaped being dashed to bits on a rocky island. God willing, this same pen will present a detailed account of all these places when we compose our bright pages on foreign countries and the islands.

The ship arrives at the port of Mergui[5]

The crew was all in an uproar. They placed the anchor in a dinghy and everyday thereafter hauled the ship like a stubborn she camel. Finally we were clear of that dangerous spot and thanks to our never fading luck we came in sight of the port of our desire, Mergui. 'Praise be to God for his mighty decrees.'

Only local sailors are able to pass safely through the hidden rocks and reefs of this harbor, so when we were still a few farsakhs out at sea, we sent ahead to announce our arrival the cannon's voice, our fiery, wind-swift messenger. As soon as our loud message was received, natives came out to meet us and guided the ship into the port.

The way the natives show their respect to royal documents

At this point Ḥājī Salīm explained to Muḥammad Ḥusain Beg that in this country the natives honor any object connected with a foreign king in the same manner that they do homage to the person of their own king. This was certainly the case with the most lofty letter of favor from our own king, that majestic gift which, 'indeed is from the mighty hand of Sulaimān and comes in the name of God, the merciful, the compassionate.' It is a bright token of kindness, the most eloquent of confirmations like the glorious, merciful Quran itself.

The natives place such priceless jewels in a special receptacle, the pāīdān, and the pāīdān is seated on a throne which they bring on board the visiting ship. There the document sits, shaded with gold brocade. In this position it receives the various forms of respect from all who come aboard. The visitors from ashore prostrate themselves before such awe inspiring monuments. Indeed that high station suited our letter's dignity and just as Ḥājī Salīm predicted, our inspired tablet, 'like a message sent from heaven' was given its worthy position on the foredeck.

The local officials come aboard to pay their respects

Shortly after our arrival the rajah, their governor, with the commander of the port and other Siamese officials, came out to the ship. On their first visit to our official document they fell down on the deck as if they were offering worship to God. They raised their hands and joined both palms with their fingers carefully spread apart. First they touch the ground with the tips of their two little fingers and raise them up again. Then they touch the tips of their two thumbs to their head and prostrate themselves once more. They repeat the whole procedure three times in exactly the same way. In fact this is the very manner in which they worship before their idols as well as how they honor their king. They call this affected manner of showing respect uluk in their own language.

Now these infidels were genuinely happy at heart for at last they were worshipping before the true word and not before their vain idols. They busied themselves polishing the mirror of self-awareness with the unique document of truth and made sparkle with jewelled adornment the saying, 'Metaphor is the bridge to reality.' Upon completing these introductory ceremonies they made haste to be of service to our ambassador and quickly had small boats brought for us.

The embassy is escorted ashore with festive music

In this strange land there is a musical instrument which always appears at parties as a welcomed guest. It is actually shaped like a pot but it is made from iron and glass and the natives play upon it with a heavy metal rod which looks like a pestle. Unfortunately this instrument is capable of producing such a strident noise, a man of sensitivity would be driven to insanity. The only escape is death. The melodies which emerge from the throat of this instrument are so far out of tune that the instrument is known as the 'squawking partridge'.

Another of the slender favorites present at the local festivities is the flute. Alas, it is sad that round holes have been drilled into the poor flute's heart but this is clearly a punishment for the evil company which she keeps with shrill, deafening notes. And the irksome drums? They beat the war drums so madly you can scarcely refrain from attacking, attacking the musicians. We would have liked to flay the drummers and stretch their skins.

The care and respect accorded our noble document

When all these instruments of gaiety were assembled, the escorts installed our noble document in a very shapely and distinguished boat which was beautifully decorated with red shīla cloth. The delegates were seated in the other boats which were provided and we all went ashore together. At the beach there was a large ornate structure waiting for us. It was shaped like a boat but it had an impressive throne built in the middle. The throne resembled the chair of a pulpit. The Siamese call this litter-like conveyance a kanam and it is only used by the king and other important dignitaries.

This noble throne was especially provided for our royal letter and required four men to lift it off the ground. In accord with their rank, the Siamese officials were stationed on all four sides of the dazzling throne. They lifted up the kanam and carried it along while the delegates followed from behind on horseback.

Accommodations for the delegates and the royal document

On top of a hill in the vicinity of a temple the natives have constructed a bridal chamber for their chief idol. The splendid interior of this house is decorated with fine gold brocade from China. Here our document was domiciled as if a young maiden awaiting her marriage day and in accord with the local custom a group of guards watched over the spot and all through the night fires were kept going.

There is another building named Dhu'l-Fiqār[6] built by an Iranian who had little good fortune while in Iran. But he came to Siam and was made governor and chief over this whole forest region. This building, as well as a bath, was such as had never before existed in the domain of the infidels. The great architect, Imagination, had never conceived such a blueprint in the edifice of the heart, and scheming Thought had never ventured forth from the mind's treasury to dip its foot in the pool of such a bath. It was the very pinnacle of beauty and ceremony and was furnished with choice rugs and cushions for the delegates.

Muḥammad Ṣādiq was our host in Mergui

Since there is no native in those parts who has a proper understanding of foods, Muḥammad Ṣādiq, the son of the above-mentioned Iranian, was assigned to entertain us as his guests. Indeed he discharged himself of this duty with the greatest propriety in every detail. Through all that morning and evening we were feasted and accorded the utmost consideration.

Ḥājī Salīm arranges our food

The next morning Ḥājī Salīm visited our ambassador and informed him that in this country there were no markets or shops for buying and selling. He insisted that we allow him to procure our basic provisions and whatever else was possible to find. It may be mentioned that nothing grows in Siam besides rice, and rice is what most people live on exclusively. Since the natives avoid wheat like poison, it is extremely rare to find even a single grain.

Ḥājī Salīm took it upon himself to see that a sum total of fifty meals a day was put at the disposal of our entourage and he looked after our other needs as well. We were assigned about fifty Siamese servants to wait on us and feed and water our horses. Although we had so far escaped the dangers of the sea, suddenly we were drowned in an ocean of legally unclean filth.[7] 'God, the Pure and the Manifest, remains our final judge.'

The embassy departs for Tanāsurī by boat

After spending a few days in Mergui we set out for the town of Tanāsurī. Since most roads in that country traverse great rivers and fearsome jungles and the surface of the terrain is not smooth, it is impossible to travel overland by horse or on foot. If the Siamese wanted to construct one straight road it would cost more than all the present state revenues and they would have to clear a path through the den of wild elephants, leopards and wolves and still there would never be any comfort in traveling that way. Thus the standard form of transport in that country is boat and indeed this means of travel is very comfortable and inexpensive.

Two men paddling a small boat can easily carry one hundred mans of merchandise and cover a distance of ten farsakhs a day. And so boats are the mainstay of the populace, the very pivot of these people's lives. Their boats are their houses as well as their markets. They ride their boats wherever they wish, tie them up alongside one another and do all their buying and selling without going ashore.

So a number of boats were procured for us and loaded up with our luggage and horses. When we were all aboard, our boats set out for the port of Tanāsurī traveling on a river which flows down from Khiṭā. From Mergui all the way to Shahr Nāv there were no settlements, villages or buildings to speak of, but the authorities arranged that some houses of wood and cane be built along the riverside every few farsakhs. Inside these modest huts the ceiling and the supporting poles were covered with cloth to appear more neat and clean. We only made one stop before we reached our destination.

Description of Tanāsurī

Tanāsurī is a town of lush greenness and has a population of about five or six thousand householders. The inhabitants are made up of Siamese, Indian Muslims of the Shāfi'ī[8] and Ḥanafī[9] schools and Hindus and Franks. Since the town is situated between mountains, the mist and the frequent rains create a climate which resembles a dewy morning but the haze persists throughout the whole day. The aforementioned Muḥammad Ṣādiq accompanied us to Tanāsurī and as before he assumed the task of entertaining us.

The Ambassador Ḥusain Beg is seriously ill

When we were held up in the blessed port of Bandar 'Abbās, we were all subject to a climate which is wholly different from that of Iṣfahān, the glorious House of World Rule. Every one of us succumbed to sickness but the case of the ambassador, Ḥusain Beg, was especially grave. His illness during our stay in Bandar ʿAbbās had reached an extreme intensity and the effects remained with him when we went to sea. He also suffered very badly in that first storm during our crossing to Muscat and now his aggravated condition was growing worse day by day.

The ambassador dies in Tanāsurī

In Chinapatan Ḥusain Beg was afflicted with dropsy and by the time we reached Tanāsurī his condition was more serious than ever. Upon our arrival the noble king of Siam received word of the ambassador's illness and with the utmost haste sent two doctors to cure him. One was Siamese and the other was Chinese. There was no use in doctors. 'When their time is come, they shall not be slow nor dally for a single hour.' The ambassador's soul heard the fatal voice of the Collector of souls, 'Return unto your Lord!' and he was forced to swallow that bitter prescription, 'Every soul must taste of death.'

   Other members of our delegation had already passed away, some in Bandar ʿAbbās and some out at sea. Still others died at a later date during our sojourn in Siam. On the 12th of Muḥarramu'l-Ḥaram 1097[10] the ambassador set out for the regions of the Ruler of all men. May it be recorded that those who died on this voyage, died as a sacrifice for our blessed, most noble king.

The surviving delegates

Those who were still bound to life were two Qūrchīs, two Ghulāms, one Tufangchī and one Tūpchī, not to mention my humble self, who was only spared by the heat of these hardships in order to render this account to our awesome king. A few days after the death of Ḥusain Beg a group of trusted Siamese attendants arrived from the king. They made all the necessary provisions for the next stage of the journey and sent us off to Shahr Nāv in a boat.

The devious journey to Shahr Nāv

The different countries of Below the Winds do not possess great length and breadth and from ancient times every forest has been held and inhabited by a separate landholder, nor has the present king of Siam deviated from the accustomed paths of his forebears in this respect. In order to be shown the extent of the kingdom, how the land

and merchants flourish and especially the defenses which would foil any attack or cause the enemy to lose his way in the wilderness, we were conducted to the capital by a very roundabout route. The voyage, which took us a month and a half, normally takes the merchants twenty-five or twenty-six days and messengers can cover the ground in ten or twelve days.

The elephant that went berserk and ran to Tanāsurī in one night

We were informed by a reliable group that a while back, during the reign of the present king, a brutish elephant was accidentaly struck a nasty blow with the prodding hook. The elephant went mad and reared its head from the collar of obedience. It withdrew the foot of submission from the path of tame behavior and raced forth from Shahr Nāv, breaking its own straight road. The elephant cleaved through the great jungle fastness that separates the capital from the sea and carried his keeper to the port of Tanāsurī in a single night.

When the king received news of this event his cheeks flamed with anger. The king moved the queen of his intellect out of the square of clemency. He sent his pawns with all haste to the harbor. They goaded the rider's poor elephant-like soul until it rushed forth from the city walls of life and surrounding the rough elephant they checkmated its rebellious, rider-like existence. The king's pawns were swift to fly across the chessboard of Siam and fulfill the royal commands.

Jalang, the first village along our way to Shahr Nāv

But let the story-teller continue the tale. For our part we set out from Tanāsurī and spent about twenty days floating on a great river which was hemmed in on both sides with forest and hills. Every day we spent the whole morning traveling with our boat. At noon we would alight at the stations constructed along the shore. At nights, for fear of the wolves, leopards and wild elephants, a group of the men stayed up and tended the fire until the first light.

From Jalang to Paj Purī by elephants

We came to a village named Jalang where female elephants, which the king had sent ahead, were waiting for us. They were swift and smooth-paced and they bore painted, throne-like seats made of wood. Our royal letter was placed on top of the best-looking elephant. Then we all mounted our own elephants and trod along the road for the next fifteen days. At every station which we came to, we were provided with delicious local fruits and so we proceeded in comfort until we reached a village named Paj Purī. Here we were received by Sayyid Māzandarānī, who was the local governor and holder of royal favor in that area. He hastened to fulfill his official duty and served us graciously.

Sūhān, a flourishing town along the river to Shahr Nāv

Again we boarded boats and in one more day we came to the town of Sūhān. This community is attached to Shahr Nāv and is extremely fertile and beautiful. A wondrous river of fresh water flows through the town and continues down to the sea. On both sides of the river for several farsakhs are orchards which are not partitioned by walls or fences. There grows every sort of fruit tree, lemon, orange, coconut and mango, as well as the betel tree, which for beauty and grace rivals the free, swaying cypress. In fact, every fruit native to Siam was available in that village.

All around us were trees that never feel the withering touch of autumn, trees as flourishing as the youthful hopes which old men nourish in their hearts. Most countries of Below the Winds evade the grip of autumn. The meadows and the trees keep their skirts free from the chill touch of winter. But this garden spot is surely the most blessed of all these regions.

Throughout the whole year the countryside stays fresh, the meadows are full of roses and the heavy trees bend with fruit. The leafy branches swayed and whispered all around us holding their outspread arms one above the other. Juicy fruits shake and glisten in every gentle breeze.

Here were trees more pleasing than the Ṭubā tree of Paradise, foliage speaking in the winds more sweetly than the orators of honey tongue. Indeed there is no spot in all Shahr Nāv which thrives like this village or displays such plentiful riches and bounty. The climate is pleasing and uplifting to the heart. Here is a resting place for a traveler's weary soul, a place of good fortune for those who have left their home.

The embassy is received by the rajah, Chelebī, and presented with finer boats

When we arrived at the outskirts of the town we were met by a man called Chelebī. He was from among the people of Rūm,[11] had settled in this country and enjoyed the honor of lately converting to Shī'ism. Chelebī was presently the rajah of that region. He came out to meet us in a long boat which the natives call a kamūcha. This kind of boat is a conveyance of honor for ministers and officials in Siam.

After bowing down before the seal of Sulaimān's signet ring, Chelebī ordered forth a gold-painted ship of great length. It was made from one huge piece of wood and contained a high throne in the middle. Fifty sailors rowed this boat with gilded oars. We were informed that this special boat was the king's 'parade horse' and that it was only fit and proper that Sulaimān's firman honor her humble throne.

Attendants also brought before us seven other boats, each of which had two house-like constructions built in the middle for seating. Ten people could easily sit in each house. The interior of the cabins was furnished with rugs and cushions and the doors were decorated with curtains of landra material. The officials cordially announced, 'Each of you is to be allotted a separate boat. Indeed, we appreciate that your journey has been full of hardship but that is all over now. Board these boats with peace in your hearts and enjoy the king of Siam's kind indulgence.' After boarding the boats the curtains were drawn open for the view and we proceeded up the river past the gardens and the orchards.

Some Iranians meet the embassy outside Sūhān

When we had traveled a certain distance several of the members of the Iranian community in Siam came out to meet us. One of the party was a Yūz Bāshī[12] of the right wing and another was an official scribe who is regularly employed by the Iranians. They came out to receive us with their own group and escorted us into the town. Lodgings had been prepared for us in the fort and our rooms were newly furnished with rugs and cushions. The Siamese displayed the utmost respect and deference in accord with their own protocol.

When we reached the fort a cannon salute was fired in our honor and we were received with hospitality and all possible friendly concern. The officials announced that the king sent us his welcome and expressed his deepest sympathy for the hardships we had suffered on our journey. The king also made it a point to offer his condolences for the death of Muḥammad Ḥusain Beg.

In response we forwarded our greeting to the king, 'Peace be upon you, who are the goal of our long pilgrimage. We see no other purpose to our existence but to scatter the coin of our lives before our Iranian benefactor's feet. Long live our worthy king and may he cherish his friends and loyal servants.'

The Siamese concern for reporting details

One of the customs in Siam is that a special body of Siamese interpreters and scribes at the court prepares reports on everything anyone says or does, no matter how insignificant. The reports are then presented to the king. The Siamese seem very eager over details and there is nothing which they consider to be more low and mean than telling a lie. They are so concerned with the exact truth that if a person changes the slightest detail when giving an account of an event, he is considered an out and out liar. This preoccupation with being precise even leads them to condemn exaggeration in literature and poetry.

An Iranian poet who came to Siam

Once there was a great poet whose empty stomach brought him to Siam to sell his talent. He decided to dive into the sea of fantasy and bring up a splendid pearl from the jewel box of his mind. He hoped to string his priceless wares on the cord of verse and stir the king's wealth as one stirs a maiden's beauty with a sparkling gem. Thus the inspired poet carefully opened the lid of his thought's treasure casket and by way of displaying the precious gems of his verse, recited a fine qasīda.[13] He recited this half line in commemoration of the King's favorite elephant, whose name was Full Moon.

> Oh king, the Full Moon is your splendid elephant,
> The crescent moon your driving hook.

When he brought the qasīda with its clear and adept metaphor before the king and it was translated into the language of Siam, instead of receiving an award, he was given the title 'sap lap', which means liar. They punished him with this name which is one of their worst terms of abuse.

The delegates are advised to choose a replacement for the late Ḥusain Beg

After we had been shown to our lodgings and the formal reception was over, the Iranians informed us in private that the king thought it best that we appoint one of our number as our official leader now that Muḥammad Ḥusain Beg had passed away. Someone must formally present our dignified letter at court to fulfill the mission. But the late Muḥammad Ḥusain Beg had been careless and assumed his office without foresight, for he had never enquired from the authorities in Iran what should be done in such circumstances as these.

When Ḥusain Beg died we were all eager to be of service but each of us felt he lacked the ability and the qualifications to dare assume the leadership. Therefore, when this matter was brought to our attention it seemed fit that this most humble servant write a letter to the king explaining our position.

The author's letter to the king of Siam

'May it be known to the elevated corps of the king's attendants that ever since your honorable administration first conceived the pure sentiment of opening the doors of friendship before our king who is guarded by the angels, whose chosen family is like into 'Alī's and whose threshold is as the Heavens, your kingdom has remained a fixed object beneath our ruler's sun-like gaze. Indeed he is the very qibla of the world, the Ka'ba[14] of mankind.

Thus when Ḥājī Salīm was sent to the threshold of our holy country, as surety of our king's friendship, he was received with limitless affection and honored with our highest forms of respect and generosity. In compliance with Ḥājī Salīm's petition, the late Muḥammad Ḥusain Beg and his group of servants from the honorable Khāṣṣa administration were appointed to undertake this journey.

The delegates have made a great sacrifice in leaving Iran

It will not escape the attention of the noble king of Siam that these deft horsemen of the field of achievement, these charioteers in the arena of power and success, have up until now lived their lives in the indescribable paradise of Iran where the fields are broad and ample and the climate is delightful. There the foods are tasty and the fruits delicious and the flowing waters cool.

When the soul becomes accustomed to that kind of luxury, if it once drops the reins of control over the mare of happy leisure, it is lost in dark suffering. Such a wretch is like a bird trapped in the narrow confines of a cage. There is no remedy but to drown in the sea of death, for giving up an ingrained habit only brings on misery.

Yet fortunate are those who reach the appointed goal and taste the sweet elixir of self-sacrifice on behalf of their noble benefactor. And so others of our group have died along the way, serving their worthy king in the same manner as our ambassador. Of all those who began the voyage, seven individuals have arrived.

Now that this thriving state has opened the gates of friendship before us, your noble authorities have requested that we choose one of our number as head of the mission. However, we feel that this matter is the concern of your own high authorities and that they should make the final choice. Your king knows best and whomever he elects will surely be most suited to undertake the incumbent task.'

The embassy departs from Sūhān and heads upstream to the capital,
Shahr Nāv

This letter was forwarded to the king and the next morning we were installed in our new boats and departed from Sūhān. When we reached a point along the river which was only one stage from Shahr Nāv, most all of the native officials and ministers of the city came out to meet us.

From here on the rest houses along the shore instead of being made of simple cane and reeds, as I described earlier, were of a much finer construction. They were plastered over with red clay and for neatness the inside walls and posts were covered with various kinds of cloth, such as chīt or red shīla. Another improvement was the fact that they were all furnished with rugs and cushions and contained such refined conveniences as incense braziers and silver perfume sprinklers.

That evening our party was provided with silver candle sticks that held one or two candles each. Since it is not their custom to use regular torches, they had installed brass lamps throughout the rooms for lighting and each lamp had several spouts. That same evening we were also provided with a fresh quantity of basic supplies.

The Siamese king is not in Shahr Nāv but has gone to Lubū

The next morning we were informed that the king was not in Shahr Nāv but Lubū, a city which is a number of farsakhs away from the capital. Lubū is a spacious city with a pleasant climate and in former times had been the capital and prospered greatly. The city itself is surrounded by seven fortification walls, one within the other. A diagonal through the city's center would measure about a farsakh. To one side of the town flows a huge river.

As time passed, however, the city's ramparts fell into ruin. Recently the present king rebuilt the city, being very pleased with its climate, and now he resides in this comfortable spot and has made it the base of his power. He regularly spends nine months of the year in Lubū. It was then the king's wish that we come to present ourselves before him at Lubū. Thus according to orders we by-passed Shahr Nāv and headed towards our new destination.

Ḥasan ʿAlī comes out to meet the embassy on its way to Lubū

At this stage of our journey Khwāja Ḥasan ʿAlī came out to meet us. He is originally from Khurāsān and claims kinship with Khwāja ʿAbduʾl-Laṭīf, the former vezier of Khurāsān. Khwāja Ḥasan ʿAlī presently holds the ministerial post which Āqā Muḥammad held and as such is the head of the Iranian community in Siam. He had our royal document transferred to a golden throne which he brought especially for that purpose.

Then we all set out from that station and headed up the river together. When we came to the settlements which lie just outside Lubū, a large number of Siamese came out in their boats to receive us and they brought with them the king's boats of state which are built in a special distinctive style. At different points along our route the royal letter was transferred from boat to boat each more magnificent than the other.

The embassy arrives in Lubū and is escorted to the palace

When we arrived in Lubū, there was a gold-painted kanam ready and waiting on the shore. The Siamese officials raised our all-commanding royal document on a gold throne and moved it from the boat to the kanam. Meanwhile, other Siamese attendants transported the trunks of royal gifts to a kanam and the trunks were carried on ahead. We mounted our horses and followed the officials and by now all the Iranians and the local dignitaries had come out to welcome us.

We proceeded in this manner until we reached the first city wall. At this point a throne was brought out more splendid than the first. This kanam was normally used to convey their vain idol when they think he wishes to go to a different temple to visit his fellow idols. The king himself does not have the right to ride in this revered seat. Our letter, more miraculous than all their idols, was promptly installed and the attendants carried it along until we reached a spot two maidāns from the king's residence.

The king of Siam's processional throne

Then the king's own touring throne was brought forth. This magnificent kanam is known as the royal parade horse. It is built of wood and plated with gold and has curtains of gold brocade on all four sides. It is mounted over a good-sized cart but the cart itself is covered with drapes in such a way that the horses and driver are hidden from view. When the vehicle is actually rolling along, the source of its movement cannot be perceived. The Siamese king's throne enjoyed the honor of submitting to the foot of our excellent letter and the letter and the throne were carried to the king's palace. Along the route of our procession there were many decorated elephants standing at attention.

The Siamese do not wear any clothes

Except for the king himself all the natives of Siam of whatever station in life, men or women, consider their bare flesh to be sufficient clothing and they expose their bodies without concern. The sole blessing of clothing they avail themselves of is the lungī, a small cloth which veils their private parts. Their apparel is the same through spring and autumn and, despite the fact that they stumble through the rocky wadi of idolatry, they wear no shoes on their unsure feet.

Their attitude towards dressing their hair is much the same as the case of the hudhud[15] and his crest. Having no hair at all is a sign of poverty and lack of connection with the royal exchequer, whereas the élite make it a point to keep their hair well groomed and consider elaborate hair styles to be a sign of good fortune and wealth. Such was the strange appearance of the populace that had gathered to welcome us. Both men and women wore no clothes or veils.

The silly appearance of the Siamese soldiers

There was also a large group of soldiers present who were standing at attention on both sides of our path. They had on hats made of wood and reeds and wore a kind of one-piece robe which they wrap around themselves. This robe is made of red muslin and resembles a short tunic, but it looks so strange that you would think it was something Iblīs found in the ancient days of Idrīs.[16] It would seem that up until today Iblīs has kept this primitive robe as if it were an article of great value and on such occasions as these, he uses it to dress up the king's bodyguard. The troops feel proud to wear this simple uniform and think it rivals the chain mail of David.[17]

Some of the troops who were stationed about were armed with guns for the sake of maintaining security. However, the king's army is in fact nothing more than the peasantry which is assembled at special times. Thus the foot-soldiers wear no uniform except their nakedness and have no horse to ride beside their bare feet.

Our official letter is brought into the palace estates

Next we came to the king's palace. The great outer gate is made of stalks of cane joined together as if forming a huge reed mat and the surface is plastered over with red mud. As is the custom of all the kings in the countries of Below the Winds the gate is always kept closed.

Just when we arrived it was announced that the king considered our noble document as his beloved guest and wished that the letter honor his household by residing within the royal estates with the other gifts. Another kanam was brought, which was of a most exquisite construction, and our noble letter was placed upon that high seat. Then the great gate slowly opened and the attendants bore the kanam inside the palace estates.

A special pavilion was erected to house our official document

The royal estates contain a large garden and a charming pavilion which one of the Iranians built on the grounds when news of our arrival reached the king. The Iranian architect considered his work to be a marvel equal to the dome of Kasrā[18] and the fabled palace of Khavarnaq.[19] With this and other such works he sought to place the Siamese king on a well built pedestal and raise him above the other kings of those regions. Thus the Iranian worked to engineer a widespread respect for the great king's wisdom.

Our worthy document and the official gifts were brought into this newly built pavilion. The honorable letter was raised up to a high position in the inner part of the building and the trunks with the gifts were safely stored away. The pavilion was well furnished with rugs and cushions. In the middle stood colorful Chinese screens and the interior of the walls and the arch were decorated with gold brocade from China.

The lodgings and entertainment for the delegates

We left the pavilion and the Yūz Bāshīs and the king's ministers escorted us to a pair of houses near by. These two buildings which had been especially constructed for us in the Iranian manner contained several rooms and had a hammām[20] off to one side. Each room was well furnished with rugs, cushions, velvet drapes and embroidered coverings from China and Gujerat.

That evening the Yūz Bāshīs came and on behalf of the king they announced, 'You are cordially invited to be entertained at the house of my minister. Your presence will give my minister much pleasure.' Thus we spent that night at the Iranian minister's house, which was located near our own lodgings.

The minister himself and two of the Yūz Bāshīs as well as other Iranian servants were appointed to look after our needs. Every day they were diligently occupied to see that we were happy and comfortable. Two days after we settled into our new home they brought us the following message from the king.

The king wants the delegates to appoint an ambassador

'Your petition has reached me and it has been explained in Siamese. The contents are understood and the sincerity of your friendship is clear, but it is not customary or befitting that I choose one of your number to undertake the official presentation. You yourselves must make the choice as you know which of you is competent to handle this matter. My part as king is to accept or reject. Whatever you feel on this subject, put in writing and have delivered to me immediately.'

The author's disappointment—Ibrāhīm Beg is chosen as the new ambassador

Though at first I thought, with the help of God, the gracious King and merciful Benefactor of mankind, I myself would be best suited to perform the presentation, I came to see how it was expedient that Ibrāhīm Beg be chosen. Ibrāhīm Beg was a Ghulām of the worthy Khāṣṣa, the official guardian of the royal gifts and had been honored with an appointment to the office of 'crown and accounts'. His desire to render service was already aroused in these other capacities and so he was eager for further duties. As he was bold to express his desire to undertake the task of the official presentation, I wrote to the Siamese king and told him of our decision.

Concerning the Iranian's recent loss of power

As I will describe in its proper place, from the beginning of this king's reign up until just recently, all important business and matters of state were in the hands of the Iranians. They were the very source of the king's power. But since the death of Āqā Muḥammad Astarābādī,[21] who was the king's minister and councilor, a great disorder has crept into the country's administration and the channels of procedure have shifted their course. This change of power is due to errors committed by the Iranians, their hypocrisy and their total lack of agreement among themselves.

The rise of the sly, ill-begotten Frank minister

There is one other cause of this deplorable situation. To begin with the Siamese themselves are much like the fabled Nasnās,[22] devoid of intelligence and any practical abilities. Since they can scarcely undertake the simplest task with a hope of success, the king is cautious and never confides to any great extent in the natives. When Āqā Muḥammad passed away, the king was in need of foreign support. Taking advantage of the situation, an ill-begotten Christian rose to power and filled the empty position. Formerly this Frank had been employed as a humble worker on ships. Thus he illustrated the true saying, 'Once the lion leaves the jungle the jackals venture forth.'

The Frank's talents and evil influence

In a very short time this Christian learned the language, customs and laws of Siam and day by day, in the eyes of the king, he cultivated a reputation for managing affairs. The Siamese king has made this man his chief minister and confidant, without bothering to test the coin of his character or establish to what degree his opinions or abilities are an advantage to the state. In accord with the firm rule that the low and base resent the good fortune of others, the Frank has endeavored to weaken the king's character and encourage the royal fickleness. He causes the king's sight to stray from the straight path of practising justice.

The bad behavior of Āqā Muḥammad's sons and the king's suspicion of the Iranians

The sons of Āqā Muḥammad gave clear proof of their ignorance, incompetence and reckless nature by becoming involved with the following foolish scheme. When their father died, they became intoxicated with the wine of their own pride and they soon swerved from the path of diplomacy. They stumbled onto the crooked ways of conniving and spite. In secret they met with the king's brother and gave him tokens of their friendship. This kind of behavior on their part naturally gave the king cause to suspect that they were plotting to push him out of power and bring his brother to the throne.

It could appear that the arrival of an embassy from Iran was also part of such a plan, that our visit was aimed at strengthening the position of the king's enemies. It might seem suspicious that an Iranian community has been residing in Siam for such a long time

5

and certainly the whole world knows of Iran's military exploits, and has good cause to fear the glorious Qizilbāsh[23] who are so fierce in battle.

For these several reasons the king revoked the high rank of the late Āqā Muḥammad's sons. Indeed the king was finally so angered by their behavior, he had them arrested and sent off to an island. At the time of our arrival it was not known whether these young men were dead or alive. 'God alone is all knowing.'

The king would not meet the Iranian embassy en route to Lubū

Thus the king is mistrusting and he is especially cautious with people he has not met before. Even so, at first he agreed to come out and meet our official document despite the wish of his unscrupulous minister. But that ill-begotten Christian convinced the king to change his mind. He planted a fear in the king, warning him that something might go wrong during the reception. Thus, having caused the king to be overly cautious, he deprived him of an elevating and auspicious encounter.

The Siamese king does not want the delegates to present their document to him by hand

When two or three days passed and we had not received any specific instructions, the Christian minister sent a group of officials to our lodgings at night to speak to us on the king's behalf. We were asked what day we would care to present our document to the king and we answered that we were waiting on the king's convenience. Then they asked us in what manner we wished to make the presentation. We replied that we thought the letter should be presented in the ancient way, that the king take the letter from Ibrāhīm Beg's hand, fulfill the requirements of goodwill and sincerity and perform the ceremonies of respect. Our reply seemed to confirm the Frank's warnings and the king's suspicion increased.

The king goes off hunting and the Frank minister summons the author

The king postponed granting us an audience and at dawn he rode off to go hunting for several days. In the meantime orders were issued that no one from the Iranian community was to come to visit us in our lodgings. Twenty days later a messenger came and announced that the king wished my most humble self to go to the house of the Frank prime minister.

When I went to the Frank minister's house he acted out the usual formalities and made conversation with me but eventually he asked me what the purpose of our visit to Siam really was. I answered: 'Our king, the benefactor of mankind, has sent us to this country for the purpose of increasing goodwill and strengthening the foundations of accord and love and there are absolutely no other motives attached to our mission.'

The Frank replied: 'If what you say is true you should put aside the idea of Ibrāhīm Beg handing your document directly to the king and, as is the practice in Iran, you should stand at a respectful distance from the king and let the honorable chief minister make the actual presentation.' I returned to our lodging and reported to Ibrāhīm Beg exactly what the Frank had said.

The Iranians agree to the Siamese king's wishes

In the midst of these difficulties of language and our lack of information concerning local protocol, Ibrāhīm Beg agreed to present the document in the manner that the Siamese king wished. Our ambassador adapted to the situation in accord with the saying, 'If you make friends with elephant drivers build your house big enough to admit the elephants.'

The formal ceremonies begin

Ibrāhīm Beg informed the Siamese that we were ready to comply to their form of presentation and thus the official ceremonies began. All of us including our servants were provided with fine looking horses, each horse outfitted with the best possible gear and trappings, and we set out for the king's palace.

Once again, all along the path our procession took, there were colorful elephants stationed at attention. When we arrived before the palace estates, the barred gate was opened and we saw that a large number of the king's soldiers were present on duty. They were dressed as we described previously.

The Siamese king's palace guard

Each soldier was drowned in the chainmail of his nakedness, such that his whole body was visible. The only cuirass they bore across their front was the chest's four humours. The invisible helmet which protected their head was a headstrong temperament and for boots they made do with their wretched bare feet. They were content with a scanty loincloth, just large enough to cover up their private parts, and a few of them were wearing a kind of hat made of woven reeds and wood. This is the kind of hat Franks wear also. Their spears were merely pieces of cane and their sword and shield consisted in their uninviting poverty. For firearms they had the thunder and sparks of pure imagination. In place of the sash of Hātim[24] they wore belts of woven reed around their waists.

Our official letter is carried to the throne room

Such were the soldiers standing at attention before the king's residence when we passed by. We went straight to the pavilion which had been housing our royal document, that scripture of inspiration. When we came before the letter again it was with the respect of pilgrims who have arrived at their goal.

Ibrāhīm Beg transferred the document to a special container made of gold. This vessel is especially fashioned to bear rare contents which are studded with pearls of precious wisdom and like an elegant oyster shell it closes tightly over the written word. As soon as Ibrāhīm Beg had possession of our rare document, he set out for the king's throne room and we servants of the honorable Khāṣṣa followed behind him.

The Siamese prostrate themselves before the entrance to the throne room

The Siamese consider the king's throne room the most sacred edifice there is and on religious days they all gather at this spot to perform their idle ceremonies. When we arrived the Siamese officials and translators who were accompanying us all prostrated themselves, as if they were worshipping God, the one true King. We were still a good distance from the door but they had already caught a glimpse of the throne so they fell to the ground.

The authorities were considerate enough to excuse us from this form of homage and we paid our respects in the normal manner. But our Siamese escort were all engaged in performing the uluk and they proceeded the rest of the way on their knees and elbows although the building was still sixty paces off.

The first half of the distance was covered with the kind of woven mats that are commonly produced in Siam, while the half closest to the building was covered with rugs. It is obligatory to observe the uluk and no native is allowed to stand up or walk about in the king's presence. Even the servants are obliged to remain on their hands and knees while they hurry about attending to their duties.

This huge mass of people, face down on the mats and rugs, looked like a large congregation of Muslims saying their prayers. They were arranged row after row like a collection of dead bodies and not a single person made a move or showed the least sign of life.

The Siamese wash their feet before entering

When we came closer to the threshold, we noticed a vessel for water and a piece of stone. On entering we were told that the king is very particular about maintaining cleanliness and order. Since all the men of state as well as the servants go barefoot and arrive with dirty feet, they are obliged to wash before they are admitted to the royal presence. Their good sense has let the following saying fall from its grip and now they tread with heavy feet upon its meaning, 'Water poured on top of filth will only spread the filth out further.'

A description of the throne hall and the king's elaborate throne

At the very entrance of the throne hall there are several steps which rise about three cubits from the ground. The building itself consists of one long room covered by a gabled roof. The hall is about ten cubits long and six wide. The floor of the throne room is built of wood and the ceiling and the inside of the walls are painted rose and vermilion. Six mirrors are fastened to the walls as well and the bright glass shines like gold leaf. The innermost part of the hall is plated with sheets of tin and is ornamented with gilded tiles. The king's throne house is eactly like a large pulpit with the usual pulpit steps removed. It is made of wood and decorated with pictures of devils. The whole of the outer surface is plated with sheets of gold. To the left and right are stairs which the king uses to climb up into the portico. The portico is richly furnished with hangings of gold brocade and contains the actual throne. There is one other door at the very back of the whole building and there are two gilded doors which lead to the throne house. The king had already seated himself on his throne and was awaiting our arrival.

The Iranian delegates enter the throne room

When we entered we saw that the gifts were all spread out across the length of the room in rows and the ministers and officials were lying prostrate, arranged according to their rank and dignity. However, a sofa was provided for us, which the attendants placed directly in front of the throne. When we reached the sofa, we were told to do obeisance and pay homage to the king after our own fashion. At that moment there was not a single native left standing. We faced the throne and lowered our heads. Then two attendants got up from their knees and took our document from Ibrāhīm Beg. Another attendant brought a jewel-studded pāīdān with a long, gold handle which was able to reach up to the window of the throne. The pāīdān is the special vessel which they make use of to present the king whatever he requests.

The official letter is passed to the king

The officials indicated to Ibrāhīm Beg that it was time to transfer our document from the litter it arrived in to a second pāīdān. He did as they bid him and the attendants took the empty litter into their charge. This first litter was a pāīdān more delicate than a rose petal and the attendants took it back to the treasury. Then the document was raised to the throne in its new glittering pāīdān. At the right moment the king brought forth his head from the throne and received the document with his two hands. He kissed it and raised it to his crown, then pressed it to his eyes and breast and gave it a place to rest on the throne.

The Siamese and the Iranian way of addressing the king

The Siamese rajah, Pi Ta, and the translator announced that the king wished the delegates to be seated. The king spoke to the rajah, which is their term for commander, and the rajah performing the customary uluk, recited the following prayer: 'Pūrbudī chau kāsīka lāsīka mūm kūrāb kān'. These words are the very essence of religious error. 'Divine protector of Heaven and earth, your command hangs over my head. Be merciful to me.' It is their practice to say this phrase of adoration before every question and answer which they pose to the king. The Iranians, however, employ the saying, 'Oh my lord and my refuge, your indulgence is the essence, the very height of mercy.'

The king converses with the delegates

In this way questions were put to Ibrāhīm Beg and the Kalungs who accompanied him. Kalungs are the servants who have the right to come into the king's presence. We were asked whether our lord the king was in good health and happy when we last saw him in Khurāsān. It appears that the Siamese imagine that Iran is limited to the region of Khurāsān.

In reply Ibrāhīm Beg explained: 'At the time we were excluded from the threshold of the paradise of Iran, our king of noble descent, whose armies rival Alexander, whose power equals that of Jamshīd,[25] bezel in the signet ring of Sulaimān, in brightness like the very sun, conqueror of distant lands, was making the capital of Iṣfahān the seat of his world-governing power and the house of the Caliphate.

"Praise be to God the source of all bounty." Iṣfahān is the mighty pivot on which hinge the doors of prosperity and abundance and the doors of the blessed capital open wide before all the governors of the eternal kingdom of Iran. There the wine of fulfilled hopes and desires flows as at the banquets of Paradise.'

Next we were asked whether our king, the lord of mankind, was presently engaged in war with anyone. Ibrāhīm Beg replied: 'Even though a fool of the lowest nature would shrink before our potentate's scorching anger, lest the mighty king wrench up the mean brambles of such a man's existence by the roots and reduce the harvest of his life to a heap of ashes—for indeed all the enemies of our blessed state perish in the desert of their error—at this moment the king's supreme commander has marched into the region of Āzarbāījān with an immense army and is installed there waiting for further orders from the throne. It is still not known what the commander's exact task will be.'

The king indicated that he was aware that the proper season for our return voyage was still a long way off and he entreated us to consider ourselves his personal guests while we remained in Siam. Any needs which we might have should be related to his minister, who would diligently look after our well being.

Then the king closed the door of his throne and the audience was over. We returned to our lodgings and two days later translators came with the Yūz Bāshīs and announced that the king had invited us to come on an elephant hunt. We were to set out that evening.

The ceremonies of the outing and the elephant hunt itself

We mounted our horses and departed from the city. On the road we came to a pavilion with a porch built at the front and rugs layed out under the porch. Our escort explained that during these outings the king is not waited on in the usual elaborate way. This pavilion was constructed especially for the Iranians and here they awaited the arrival of the king. The Iranians were to pay homage to the king at this spot before the expedition actually started and then they would follow from behind on horseback. After the hunt as well, they were to return to this same spot ahead of the king and repeat the same formalities as he passed by. This was the only form of attendance required of the Iranians during the whole hunt. We were informed: 'This pavilion has been furnished in your honor. When you receive the king, you have the choice of standing or remaining seated.' Thus we waited where we were until the king's banners came within sight.

The king's procession

A group of Siamese foot soldiers preceded the king's elephant and another group marched in the rear. They were barefoot, without hats, and carried spears, firearms and unsheathed swords. Another group marched along beating various kinds of drums which they carried slung over their shoulders. Others were busy playing pots and pans, flutes and a kind of curved trumpet, similar to the trumpets played by the kings of the clime of absolute poverty.[26] There were also two other kinds of trumpets present which were like the ones the Franks use.

The king's elephant was preceded and followed by several other elephants with decorated faces and elaborate trappings. All these elephants bore thrones and were guided along by their keepers. The king himself sat on a throne of splendid construction which was mounted on his elephant. When he came near our pavilion, we stood up and bowed our heads before him as a sign of respect.

The hunting site

As soon as the king passed by we mounted our horses and rode on to an open plain which was prepared for catching the wild elephants. In the midst of this open space the workmen had built an enclosure of firmly implanted posts. In the middle of the enclosure were four tall, thick columns which supported a roof of wood and reeds. The roof and posts were covered with cloth. The king remained seated on his elephant and installed himself under this large pavilion. We sat outside the enclosure under a similar construction, which they had built especially for our delegation. The Siamese princes all knew their proper positions around the hunting ground. But in the beginning everyone present was lying face down in his assigned place. My most humble self remained standing and I saw that the people to every side of me, whether they were on elephants or had come on foot, were all prostrating themselves.

The king sends messages to the delegates

The Frank minister was lying at the foot of the king's elephant and the king was speaking with him. Then the minister talked to the translator in a whisper and sent him to Ibrāhīm Beg to announce the king's message. The king said that he felt it was a great shame that Muḥammad Ḥusain Beg had passed away. He had hoped to go hunting with him but that was no longer possible. Ibrāhīm Beg replied that he had wished to give his own life in service, but such had not been God's will. He would seek to sacrifice himself in the future.

The king enquired which of the royal gifts had pleased our illustrious king most when Ḥājī Salīm arrived at the Persian court, that refuge of all the world. The reply was made: 'In the sight of the sunlike gaze, which is the light of mankind's eyes, what found favor above all other gifts was that bouquet from the gardens of love and friendship, the gift of first fruits from the orchard of blissful accord, the very letter you sent in sincerity and entitled with true affection. When our noble king inhaled the fragrance of such pure intentions, he was charmed with thoughts of friendship and his mind was perfumed with the amber of union and accord.' Then the king gave the order for the hunters to go after the elephants.

How the Siamese catch wild elephants

There are certain elephant trainers who keep herds of female elephants. They take a few of the females which have just given birth, tame them along with their children and train them for hunting. To capture more elephants, these keepers go out into the jungle with their own herd and spend several days wandering about in the thick of the forest until they catch sight of a wild elephant, male or female.

The tame hunting elephants are herded together in one place and attract the wild elephant to join them. All this time the keeper stays more or less concealed, lying flat on his own elephant off to the side. If the encountered elephant is a male, he is immediately attracted towards the group of females. Once his animal lust is aroused, in accord with his nature, he sets off boldly to follow their tracks.

The females run away and head in the direction of the hunting grounds. Just like rose-cheeked women that stir up men, these female elephants fix the firm lasso of their attractions about the male's neck but off they run.

The male is charmed and follows after them in accord with the saying, 'Even an old camel once it starts flirting, will prance about like a fool.' The male elephant charges after them and though he is blindfolded by the bands of attachment he is sure-footed in his passion.

The female elephants lead him by the hand to the 'peh niat', which is what the Siamese call the open arena where they capture the wild elephants. When the females bring him to this spot and have bound the foot of his will in the chains of their affection, if it so happens that he is large and fierce, the keepers drive him and the females into an enclosure of flattened ground. Then the attendants lead out the females through a different door and leave the male alone in the middle. Keepers enter the enclosure and tie down the wild elephant's hands and feet with lassoes.

If the male captive is not too fierce, men mounted on elephants approach him while he is still outside the enclosure on the plain and catch his hands and feet in leather lassoes and tie him between fixed posts. Then the keepers ride up and close in around him from all four sides with their own elephants. This way they force him to remain still and they fix a sturdy lasso around his neck. The lasso is tied to the necks of two other elephants placed alongside him and a third elephant with tusks pushes him along from behind. In such a position he can only move forward and has no choice but to insert the neck of his will into the chains of obedience.

Thus he is taken off to the stable in the company of the trained elephants. After being tied up this way and struggling against his companions for a few days the wild elephant becomes more tame. At this point the attendants untie his neck and free him from the other elephants but they still keep him tied to sturdy columns.

Twice a day they tie his neck between two tame elephants and he is escorted to a pool to drink water. With this method it does not take very long before the Siamese tame the elephant completely.

While we humble servants were present, an elephant that was not very fierce was attracted to the hunting ground. He was bound and held fast outside the enclosure. We sat checkmated with amazement as the king gave orders, the ministers supervised and the foot soldiers, like pawns on a chessboard, achieved their tasks with skill and speed. After we returned to the city and several days went by, the king invited us to a party.

A party given in our honor by the king

The food of the Siamese, which I shall describe in its proper place, in no way resembles normal, proper foods and the natives are not familiar with intelligent methods of preparing meals. In fact no one in Siam really knows how to cook and eat or even how to sit correctly at table. The Siamese have only recently arrived 'from the world of bestiality to the realm of humanity.'

The king, having had much contact with the Iranians when he was growing up, has acquired a permanent taste for our food and every so often, according to his mood, he will make an exception and incline to eat in our style. For this reason he has had a cook brought over from India, whose sole occupation is to prepare real food for him when it is required. But since the king is not practised in our table manners and the proper forms of society, he closed the doors of banqueting upon himself and did not make an appearance during the party. That day the banquet ceremonies were delegated to the Iranian attendants.

When we entered the palace there were all sorts of large and small cushions arranged in the customary manner on the floor. We sat down and a water pipe with gold accoutrements was brought from the king's stores for Ibrāhīm Beg. It was set on a gold tray and came with its own spitoon, a special cover and a pair of tongs. The rest of us were brought the same sort of water pipe made of silver. In the center of the gathering there was a brazier for aloes wood, a perfume sprinkler and a hashish pouch as well as several bottles of rose water. After we had drunk coffee and tea, the attendants set out the food.

The food

There were several large, deep plates which bore smaller, silver cups full of jam, sweets, pickled preserves, pickled ginger, firnī,[27] warm milk, oranges, sugar cane and fālūda[28] and instead of being served with one of these dishes of dainties at a time, two or three such plates were placed before each of us. That was only the first course. Next followed a course of fifty more trays.

The food was served in china dishes which were set on saucers and covered with tiny silver lids. Because of the constant heat in those parts it is the local custom to keep the bulk of the hot food at a distance and serve each portion individually, and so we were served. When we finished eating and the food was cleared away, the Iranian scribe gave praise to God, the one true Benefactor and Source of all grace, and then pronounced a prayer for the Siamese king.

The only members of the king's official staff who were present were the minister Ḥājī Ḥasan 'Alī, two Yūz Bāshīs, a physician, a scribe and a secretary. There were also some Siamese in the group but the servants who waited on us were Iranians. When the gathering was over we were escorted to our lodgings by some of the officials who had dined with us.

The next hunting expedition

It was not long after the formal dinner that the king ordered the minister, Ḥasan 'Alī, to take us all hunting. The king's administration made all the necessary arrangements. We were taken two farsakhs from the city to a certain spot near the hunting site. Here a tent had been set up alongside a river. It was a tent with a pointed top and flaps which fold back at the entrance. Inside were assembled all the prerequisites of a fine entertainment. About 1,000 Siamese along with all the Iranian attendants accompanied us on this expedition. Some were on foot and others were mounted.

In the rainy season, which they call mahiyā or the herbage rains, which we will describe later on, all the land is transformed by the great downpour of water. When the rains are over, vast tracts of grass grow up and the elephants are put out to pasture, but the tramping about of these heavy beasts causes the land to become very uneven and with so much grass growing over everything the broken surface is not clearly visible.

There are various kinds of game available at that season such as mountain cows, mountain goats and another animal similar to a stag which they call 'little short-foot'. But, contrary to the stag, this animal is a very poor runner. He is found in large numbers in the plains and can be caught easily if you chase after him on foot.

When we arrived at the great plain we saw that a net had been set up at one end and from the other direction riders and men on foot were closing in, while they shouted and made as much noise as possible. In the short time between dawn and noon we caught about thirty head of these different animals.

At noon we retired to our comfortable tent and dined and drank coffee and tea. After we had rested a bit and performed our prayers, we returned to our lodgings in the city.

A man was killed during the hunt

There was a young man of the Iranian community, a Georgian in fact, who was a member of the king's corps of attendants and he was endowed with no small skill and daring in the arts of horsemanship and hunting. While racing after game in the field, his horse fell and the lance which he was carrying stuck fast in the ground and caught him in the chest. He was thrown from the horse of life, which is a steed as swift as the wind and the quick paced charger of death carried him out of the field of existence. A few more days went by and we were invited to go hunting again. That hunt passed in the same manner as I have described.

How the Siamese capture tigers

When the Siamese desire to hunt the tiger they send out two or three thousand men on foot to the part of the jungle where the animal has been seen or they believe he is hiding. All day the natives shout and yell and fire off guns. At night they keep large fires going. As in other hunts where beaters encircle the game, all paths out of the middle are blocked and the beast is driven towards a pre-arranged arena. At a certain clearing workmen have constructed high, firm enclosures of wood and cane which are about one maidān long. This construction is arranged so that there are three circular enclosures, one inside the other, each one joined to the other by a narrow passage way. The innermost enclosure contains a strong wooden cage. The door of the cage is left wide open and faces the entrance to the enclosure in such a way that when the tiger enters he is forced to take refuge in the cage.

When everything is properly prepared, the beaters drive the frantic tiger towards the enclosures. In the meantime dogs have been placed inside the enclosure walls and when the tiger hears them barking, he rushes in to catch them. Once the tiger is well inside, attendants sneak up and close the door behind him.

The wall of this enclosure is about four cubits high and the workmen have strengthened it by draping a net over it. The tiger is kept inside the stockade for a few days and nights and is allowed to glut the hound of his greed by devouring all the dogs. But when the Siamese desire the hunt to begin, attendants gather outside the enclosure and the elephant keepers mount their elephants.

For this kind of sport the elephants have their head and trunk covered with leather padding. Then the elephant keepers drive their elephants into the enclosure, surround the tiger and the fight begins.

The elephants are specially trained to use their tusks with skill and whenever they can, they catch the tiger, lift him up on their tusks and toss him through the air. In this way from all four sides they checkmate the tiger with their bold maneuvers. But the tiger is not afraid and does not shrink from direct encounter with their tusks. He advances roaring and hissing and in his heart he says:

> Why should I fear the elephants' raised trunk
> It is only a wretched sleeve with no arm inside.

And so the fierce tiger attacks, striking the elephants stinging blows with his claws and the slow elephants endure much suffering and grief. There are times when despite the elephant's protective padding the tiger grips the trunk so fiercely and clings so stubbornly with his claws that the elephant falls to its knees in pain. On other occasions the tiger will succeed in snatching the rider from the elephant's back and it is a sad sight to see the beast going about his work. In such cases the elephant rider is forbidden to protect himself with any weapons. He can only save himself by fleeing as best as he is able. If he is not quick enough to escape, he speeds to the lowest depths of Hell.

When the elephants have tired out the tiger with the thrusts of their tusks, he is forced to take refuge in the second enclosure, which is joined to the first by a narrow passage. Thus the tiger flees before the elephants from enclosure to enclosure and the elephants follow after him. Finally he is forced to enter the cage. Once the tiger is inside the narrow prison, attendants on foot come out from hiding and lock the cage door. Then the captured tiger is carried off, kept in the cage for a while and eventually all his teeth are pulled out. When this beast is no longer very dangerous, the attendants put him in a special enclosure which is not far from the king's residence and every day they use him to train the new elephants.

A tiger hunt which we witnessed

When we arrived at the enclosure, everything was ready and we went straight in, mounted on our elephants. The tiger was napping in the midst of some trees. He perceived our crowd with all its tumult and the elephants coming towards him, but did not immediately advance for the fight. He gazed about him in all directions, calmly taking account of the situation. Indeed he was a great tiger! The heavenly sign Leo would fear to set foot in the sky's broad meadow at the sight of such a ferocious beast. Taurus would not dare draw a single breath for fear of this tiger's claws.

Then suddenly the tiger decided the time was right for an encounter and he leapt forth and began roaring like thunder.

Struck with terror Heaven itself was transformed into a mad elephant and took to flight. None the less hunting elephants closed in and the tiger was quickly surrounded.

The splendid elephants towered over the tiger. Their limbs rose up like Mount Alvand.[29] Just as the brave on day of battle roll up their sleeves and wave their angry arms, the elephants raised their trunks and dodged the claws of this lion-hearted beast. They tossed the tiger back and forth through the air, using their tusks like weapons. The tiger raged like a mad crocodile and gave full account of his bravery and noble spirit. He joined battle with the elephants and continued fighting until he was driven into a feverish frenzy by the sun and the excessive activity. By now the temperature had risen and for fear that the tiger would die of exhaustion, the sport was postponed until late afternoon.

We departed from the hunting site and were escorted to a pleasant spot near by which had been furnished with cushions and arranged for a social gathering. Here were assembled all the requisites for a banquet. Everything on hand was provided from the king's own stores. We enjoyed ourselves, indulging in the various foods, and had a comfortable rest. Then towards evening, the worthy minister and his attendants mounted up and we all returned to the hunting site.

The fight is resumed but the tiger will not surrender

The elephant keepers mounted up and the elephants were driven into the enclosure once again. However, as much as the hunters endeavored to weaken the tiger and drive him to flight, the noble beast refused to shame himself. Relying on the strength and endurance of his lion-hearted nature, he persisted in the battle and would not retreat. Great suffering arose from the claws of this tiger. He sprang into the arena of battle like a raging lion and the dazed elephants let go the grip on their souls. In the end one of the elephants who was renowned for his daring and unusual strength, firmly planted his foot in the arena of manliness and managed to wound the tiger.

In accord with the proverb, 'If enough mosquitoes join together they will even attack an elephant', the elephants overcame the noble tiger. The elephants were many and the tiger was all alone. Thus the leopard of his Soul was driven out of the body's enclosure by the mighty elephant of Death. The tiger refused to go into the cage and fought so fiercely that his soul finally left the cage of his body.

That evening we returned to the same spot where we had rested during the afternoon and we were accorded all the formalities of hospitality and a fine banquet. The following morning we returned to our lodgings in the city.

Birds used for hunting in Siam

Siam has many birds of prey besides the falcon, the royal falcon and the hawk. Consequently, the king ordered his hunters to deliver several pairs of baḥrī, royal white falcon, sparrow hawk and pīgū to the Iranian attendants, for he knew that the Iranians are always interested in hunting and wished that they train these birds and return them to the court.

The king also gave orders to Ḥasan 'Alī that he was to continue to look after our needs and see that we were taken out hunting again. And so we went riding and hunting with the Iranian minister several times. In Siam the region around the city and even the very edges of the city itself provide much game, especially blue and white haqārs.[30]

A second elephant hunt and an interview with the king

It was not long before the king invited us to come elephant hunting again. The procedure was the same as I described previously. On this occasion, however, favor was granted to my unworthy self above the others present, for the king invited me into the enclosure to sit near him.[31] Through the minister and the translator the king asked: 'Why are you always preoccupied at home? You should come hunting and riding more often.' He added: 'My orders to Ḥasan 'Alī are that you are never to be left alone and unhappy but every day you should be amused with hunting. Today I myself have invited you to the hunt.'

I answered: 'The king's generosity is great indeed and we are continually happy due to his kindness. Today we are even more happy because it is our good fortune to be invited to the hunt by the king himself and we are honored to serve at his stirrup.'

That day one wild elephant was captured right where we were sitting. Another more fierce one was captured after being driven to the spot which I described before, where they tie up the strong difficult elephants. After the hunt we returned home in the company of the king.

Besides amusing us with hunting expeditions the minister, Ḥasan 'Alī, on several occasions arranged to take us on a tour of the temples which are situated in pleasant open areas alongside pools. We were shown all the sights, honored with many banquets and were always looked after with the utmost consideration.

The king moves to Shahr Nāv and the embassy follows him

As soon as the monsoon started, the king left Lubū to take up residence in Shahr Nāv and a few days later he called us as well to the capital. In the city of Shahr Nāv there are several houses of exquisite beauty, comfort and spaciousness which are better than any others in the whole country. Each of them is well furnished with cushions and sofas and contains a recently built hammām. These houses were allotted to us along with a large number of Siamese and Iranian attendants.

Preparations for the return voyage to Iran

A few days after we had arrived, Ḥājī Ḥasan 'Alī visited us and announced that the monsoon season had begun and that the choice was ours whether we wished to remain or depart. Our reply was

> My heart swirls in ecstasy and so it should,
> For this good news brings new life to an old spent soul.

While life remains within me, what greater happiness is there than to set my tired sight upon the heavenly threshold of Iran? Perhaps these eyes will take on their former brightness before the healing virtues of that threshold of Paradise. Ḥājī Ḥasan 'Alī asked which route we would prefer, whether we wished to go overland again to Tanāsurī or to depart by ship from the capital.

The sea route from Sharh Nāv

We were afraid we would waste too much time traveling overland and then waste more time in Tanāsurī trying to outfit a ship, so rather than risk losing the monsoon, we chose the pain and misery of the sea route. We replied that it would be best if we could board a ship where we were. Ḥasan 'Alī went to the king and informed him of our decision. Although the officials originally indicated that a ship from the worthy king's administration was at our disposal to take us to Tanāsurī, now they began negotiating to hire a different ship from a merchant and outfit it for the journey.

Report of the king's munificence

A few days later the members of our mission were given gifts of money and cloth in the presence of the aforementioned minister and a group of Siamese officials. The gifts were brought before us in separate lots. One lot was brought in on three silver trays, another on two trays and the last lot on a single tray which was very highly decorated. Ḥasan 'Alī, the Yūz Bāshīs and a group of Siamese carried the trays.

Ibrāhīm Beg, the treasurer and guardian of the royal gifts, received a sum of twelve kātīs in cash and twenty-nine rolls of Indian cloth valued at five kātīs. The two Qūrchīs received fourteen kātīs cash and six kātīs worth of cloth. The Ghulām was given nine kātīs in money and cloth. The Jazāyerī and the Tūpchī received seven kātīs of money and four kātīs worth of cloth. My most humble self received ten kātīs in money and twenty-eight rolls of cloth worth four kātīs. The Siamese officials who presented this splendid gift were paid four tūmāns worth of money and goods.

Boating at Sūhān

A few days later the king boarded one of his boats and went to Sūhān for his amusement. He took us along with him to show us how the boats are run and what kind of maneuvers they are able to

6

perform. We were installed in a large pavilion which was built by the waterside and well furnished with cushions. The king boarded his boat with the customary pomp and passed along the surface of the water in splendor, like the reflection of flying sunbeams.

A parenthetic remark about money

May the following information not remain hidden from the experts of accounting nor veiled from the studies of those who pursue secret knowledge. The great scholar and author of 'Rauẓatu 'ṣ-Ṣafā'[32] has drunk deeply from Jamshīd's[33] world illuminating wine, has plucked facts like thornless blossoms of seventh heaven from works as wondrous as the picture book of Mānī.[34] He is a learned sage intoxicated with choice aromas of historical bouquets. He trims the pithy contents of the world-adorning chroniclers, extracts and preserves their purest cream. The studious seekers of the Mecca of style and veracity flock about this master, for he is the guide who conducts the pilgrim through the rites of study to the Ka'ab of recorded knowledge.

That author's marvel-depicting pen has left us with a description of the embassy which the late and pious Shāhrukh,[35] royal-born appointee to the Sultanate and the Caliphate, sent to Khiṭā. In the account it is mentioned how Mīrzā Bāysunghur[36] made the arrangements and chose a group of men to go on the mission. Khwāja Ghīyāthu'd-Dīn was the scribe who accompanied the mission and he mentioned, in his account, that when the delegates had accomplished their task and were taking leave of the king, they were honored with a gift of so many measures of silver and goods.

The amount of that sum was recorded in terms of a foreign system of reckoning and the scribe did not bother to explain the accounts in a way which modern men would understand. Instead he placed the sum in the drawn purse of silence. When I originally read the particular passage, as hard as I tried, I could not lift the latch from the author's purse of money. As much as I assayed that coin in the crucible of my imagination, I did not succeed in establishing its true value. In the end I was not able to judge the extent of the honor which the gift was meant to bestow.

The Siamese king's gift was not very generous

Now the decrees of heavenly fate have made me familiar with that system of reckoning values and I am in the position to see that the honorable king of Siam, in view of what would suit his high station, comes out at a loss when placed in the scales with other generous patrons. In my humble position, however, I felt that it would be out of place to bring this to the king's attention and I have sealed my observation in the purse of silence.

In fact this incident was not the fault of the king nor did he once commit the slightest indiscretion in any of his formal dealings with us. The responsibility in this case goes back to that illegitimate-born Christian and the deep-rooted personal and religious enmity which he bears towards all Iranians. Our lack of familiarity with the Siamese protocol and the fact that we were not led by a clever ambassador or counselled by an intelligent guide who knew the Siamese language made our situation all the more difficult. Otherwise this innocent king is known to be unique among his peers in generosity and freedom with his purse.

Invitation to a special elephant hunt

To return to our account, a few days after the king had cheered his Hātim-like[37] soul with that display of generosity, news arrived from the outlying countryside that the beaters were all ready and had drawn tight their circle about the wild elephants.

This was a special hunt which occurred once a year and beaters were employed to drive the elephants out of their den in the jungle. The king immediately returned to Lubū and despite the fact that we did not have much time left to catch the monsoon winds, we were called to Lubū to witness the hunt. The king himself went on into the jungle to encourage the hunters.

The Iranian community puts on its mystery play

The present king of Siam actually came to the imperial throne through the help of resident Iranians who at the time of the change in power were performing the ta'ziyat[38] in honor of Abū 'Abdu 'llahu'l-Ḥussain. I will describe the details of that whole situation later in my account. In gratitude for their past service the king has accorded these Mughals the right to perform their religious rites of mourning once a year. The king even demolished a pagan temple in the vicinity of the royal residence and had a mosque with an adjoining upper court built here in honor of the late Āqā Muḥammad.

It was also agreed that every year the king's administration would provide the Iranians with whatever they needed for these ceremonies in the way of furnishings, provisions, drinks, candles, oil lamps and a certain sum of money. This year, as well, the king ordered that these arrangements be carried out, and the Iranians went ahead with their celebration.

We were all invited to attend the Iranian performances and were escorted to the mosque every day. The preacher mounted the pulpit and in a loud voice cursed and mocked the infidels and idolaters. In previous years the preacher would stand on an elephant and ride about all night long delivering sermons.

Following the ancient rule and the established custom, at the beginning and the end of the mosque service these Muslims would pronounce a prayer to God, the true Benefactor and Guide of the world and religion. They also prayed that God send down destruction on the enemies of the Prophet's house and that their preacher be blessed with Divine support. On the very day of Ḥusain's death the king summoned us to the hunt which was to take place two farsakhs from Lubū.

Hunting elephants with beaters

This particular form of hunting elephants is carried out in an unusual way. When the 'herbage rains', which will be described in detail later, have subsided, vast quantities of grass spring up throughout the fields and plains. At that time the wild elephants come out of the jungle and the hills and go down into the fresh, grassy plains. Then the king sends out about two or three thousand auxiliaries to penetrate the hills and valleys where the elephants are known to wander.

The natives cut off all the paths which the elephants could possibly use for retreat. Night and day the beaters carry on shouting, making noise and firing off rifles and cannons. When the elephants perceive that their path is blocked from behind, they set off in the direction of the city and the cultivated fields. At nights the beaters light great fires to drive them on and the elephants continue their flight towards the city.

At a certain point the elephant keepers mount up and begin to surround the wild elephants. They force the confused elephants towards the open field with the wooden enclosure which I described earlier. There a group of elephant riders with lassoes are ready to capture them and they are able to rope several wild elephants in a very short time.

When we arrived near the field where the hunting site is, in accord with the king's orders, we changed our horses of choleric nature for female elephants which are smooth-paced and cheerful. Our elephants bore seats and trappings that were gilded with pure gold. The king had not yet arrived and we waited along the roadside for his honor-bestowing presence. During that time we remained mounted on our elephants. The minister and other Iranian attendants dismounted and prostrated themselves on carpets which were spread before the feet of their elephants.

In that manner they waited, like humble pawns, until the king made a move from his chess square. Finally the king came forth in the company of his queen and presented himself in the square where he formally receives attention and service. He was riding a female elephant which bore a gold throne and when he reached the spot where we were waiting, the ceremonies of greetings and polite exchange were performed.

Then the king called the minister, who promptly went before him, prostrated himself and recited the usual praise and benediction. The king ordered the minister to take us on to the hunt. The minister returned and seated himself on the neck of an elephant which had no seat or trappings and he led us into the hunting enclosure.

The king was sitting on his elephant in a special part of the hunting enclosure and we sat stationed on our own elephants off at the side, a certain distance from him. The Frank prime minister was also present. He was mounted on an elephant which bore no seat and was positioned right by the king.

Another interview with the king

When the king caught sight of us, he called the minister over and said a few words to him. The minister returned and announced that the king had summoned Ibrāhīm Beg and my humble self before the royal presence. The minister escorted us to where the king was stationed and despite our deference and hesitation the king persisted in his generosity and ordered us to approach him more closely. For this purpose our elephants were stationed very near his.

Then the king made display of further beneficence and summoned Mūsā Beg Pīrzāda, the Qūrchī, who is indeed a man of wide experience and the most refined manners. The king had already heard of the extent of his noble character.

Next the king gave the order for the hunt to begin. The dexterous elephant keepers mounted their elephants and carrying firm lassoes in their hands, they came up behind the wild elephants from left and right.

Once the wild elephants are stirred up and on the move, the keepers form their lassoes into nooses and fling the nooses around the elephant's limbs. Then they tie each beast's legs together with sturdy ropes.

When the lassoes have been made secure, the elephant keepers bring two other trained elephants, which they join to the wild elephant's neck from both sides, and in this way they lead the captive out of the enclosure. An elephant with tusks frightens the captive from behind and pushes him along towards the stable.

The Siamese king asks the delegates about hunting in Iran

While the sport was underway the king stated through the minister and a translator: 'This is the way we hunt in Siam when we use the beaters. How is this kind of hunt carried on in Iran?' We gave an explanation of the Iranian method.

Then the king asked us how we captured wild horses in the jungle. We answered: 'Only beasts and wild animals live or take their refuge in the jungle. The horse, which is close to man in times of hardship or times of ease and after man himself, is the most noble of animals and the best of almighty God's creatures, is found in large numbers in the kingdom of Iran, for Iran is the best part of the inhabited world. Horses are especially numerous in the herds of the king's honorable estate. They are beyond count or reckoning.

Description of the Iranian king's horses

Each herd has its own master, overseers and herdsmen who take care of the horses and when the herd's colts become old enough for riding the overseer notifies the Bāshīs and the Bāshīs have all the young horses brought to the capital. If the heart of the blessed king is inclined towards the sport of hunting, he orders that the state horse be outfitted with the richly decorated saddle cloth and saddle and such trappings would indeed rival a Chinese picture house. In this fashion the hunting site is honored with the presence of the royal steed and the very Heavens on high have cause to be jealous. If the king is not disposed towards this sport he appoints one of the close attendants of his heavenly court to take care of the matter.

The herders drive all the horses into a wide field. There the lasso throwers pursue these wind-swift creatures without attempting to drive them into an enclosure. The horses race about in a whirlwind of fire and dignity.

> To what shall I compare these fine bred beasts.
> Behold the eagle turning in the air,
> The gazelle that jumps across the plains.
> Now they are the savage shark at sea,

Now they are the sleek mountain-lion,
Ranging through the mountain heights.
The unseen wind can scarcely gallop faster.
The rain drop can not fly with such speed.
They are solid and sturdy when they stand
But light as air when they make haste.

These Lailī-like[39] beauties are so wild, the mere thought of their neck in an imaginary noose stirs them to a frantic gallop and they race out of the arena of conceivable speed. But the rope-twirling horsemen are busy plying their curved lassoes with the utmost skill, the way sweet maidens use the ringlets of their hair, and soon the horses find themselves bound like lovers in the beloved's snares.

The lasso is so efficient at its work you would think the brocade-weaver, Fate, had woven it from the threads of his decrees. Soon each roper has caught himself several deer-like creatures in the lasso's noose.

Those horses which appear worthy of the king's honorable estates are selected and taken to the stables. There the horse breakers and grooms tame the beasts and train them for riding. If a horse is lucky enough to heed the reins of good fortune, it comes to enjoy the honor of bearing the king's noble saddle. Of the remaining horses, some are given as gifts of charity to the princes and the rest, in accord with the accepted practice, are divided among the king's armies which are renowned for their world-wide victories.'

The Siamese king's wish to be remembered to the king of Iran

When we had finished our description of hunting in Iran, the Siamese king charged us to communicate his sincerity and good intentions to our sovereign when we arrived home. The Siamese ruler ordered us to see that our king, the beneficent lord of mankind, increase his affection and kindness towards Siam.

Our reply to the king's request was: 'My most humble self and the others of this group are not so much in the king's close favor that we are able to promote these matters personally. I am only one of the many insignificant servants of the court. However, if good fortune is our guide along the way and, God willing, we manage to reach the glorious court, we will present your wishes to the high ranking agents of the prime minister. He is the support of the bright Sultanate and the lofty Khāqānid state of 'Alī and in accord with his better judgment he will forward your petition to the king when the time is right.'

Then the Siamese king said: 'Whoever brings about the friendship of kings is like a person who builds a mosque or a temple. He will

82   THE SHIP OF SULAIMĀN

be illustrious in both worlds.' We replied: 'Our religion views the engineering of charitable works in just such a way. He who strives in the path of conciliation will receive his reward in the end.'

The king of Siam asks which of his gifts was most pleasing

The king added: 'Before I sent the disloyal Ḥājī to the Iranian court he was not sure what would make an appropriate gift and what he brought with him was only a sample. I ordered Ḥājī Salīm to make note of which gifts were most suitable and to inform me on this subject. But Ḥājī Salīm was occupied with his own interests while he was in Iran and neglected our important command. Despite my enquiries on this point, you have not given me a satisfactory answer.

It is clear that this world and all its trivial affects are of no import in your blessed king's sight and that as much as I contrive to impress him I will not find anything which is not already included in his vast wealth. Still I am greatly concerned over this matter and wish through some novel gift to succeed in making myself remembered to his Majesty.'

I replied: 'This humble servant lacks proper information on the subject but I do know that what you sent reached the king's blessed sight and your gift was accepted. I should add that when our king's agents sent out the late Muḥammad Ḥusain Beg they did not possess much knowledge of Siam or your customs. However, rest assured that the king's ambassador was sent in a spirit of complete generosity for the sole purpose of facilitating the speedy construction of an edifice of friendship and affection.

What gifts our king sent along with his embassy are only meant to be a selection to find out what pleases you most and what you might accept in the future. Once our king is better informed he will send a gift worthy of your rank and dignity, for our lord and sovereign is eager to give clear proof of his generosity and kindness.'

The Siamese king answered: 'The Iranian king's intentions are known to me through the contents of his honorable letter and I am very happy to receive your great king's consideration.'

Elephants for Iran

The king asked us what the elephant was used for in Iran. We replied: 'Our king's possessions and property are not simply intended for practical uses but it is a requisite of his power of state and world rule that one of every kind of God's creatures be contained within the royal estates.'

The king declared that he wished to send a few young elephants to the Iranian court and that he had transported them to the outlying regions to be shipped but during this season he could not arrange the passage. He told us that he would send them on later. He added: 'I have been the first to start this friendship and I intend to carry on in the same way. I will consign a few of the elephants we have caught today to my attendants and they will see that these elephants are sent along with you.' We replied: 'Whatever the king sees fit to undertake is the very essence of propriety.'

Every day before our departure the Siamese were making arrangements to transport these elephants but when we boarded our ship and were about to depart they said they would have to postpone the shipment and it was never made clear exactly why.

A gift for the author

By the time our interview at the hunting site ended, several large and small elephants had been caught and the king, by means of his translator, granted me the privilege of choosing an unweaned baby elephant to keep for myself. But it is impossible to take care of such a beast and the transportation would be very difficult, therefore I made my apologies and declined the generous offer.

Then the king set out for his royal residence and was followed by the minister and the infantry. The Iranian minister announced that we were to be the king's guests and consequently we proceeded to the king's palace, which was not very far from the jungle and the hunting site.

Entertainment at the king's palace

The royal residence was situated in a beautiful meadow by a lake of fresh water. The lake water was like the invigorating fountain of youth or Salsabīl,[40] the sweet spring of Paradise. The setting all about us was the essence of grace and beauty.

A silver fish glides through the dark pond.
The new moon passes silently through the dim heavens.

The king had chosen this exquisite spot to build a temple and a residence for himself. Just recently he had had a chamber constructed near his house for our entertainment. All the refinements for a party were assembled there and the necessary arrangements for a banquet and entertaining guests had been made. We were informed that all the utensils and foods which were provided came from the king's own stores and this was a special sign of his favor.

That afternoon the king boarded a boat and rode across the lake to the hunting site. Boats were provided for us as well and we followed after the king. When we arrived at the edge of the jungle, we mounted elephants and spent the day watching the hunt. In the evening we all returned to the royal residence and there a lavish party was given with a notable display of generosity.

When morning came we mounted up again and went back to the elephant hunt in the company of the king. That was the last day of the hunt. We returned and dined once more in the royal palace and that night we took our leave of the king.

Honorary clothes given to the delegates as gifts

One afternoon at the end of Muḥarramu 'l-Ḥarām[41] gifts of clothing were sent to us. Each of us received one robe, a turban cloth, a sash and a cloak. These were meant to be items of honorary dress in accord with the Iranian practice and indeed they were fine gifts, worthy of the king. At the time we were also informed that the king wished us to appear before him the following morning.

The final audience with the king

When we were given an audience, the king was seated on his throne in the manner I have described previously. He asked us, 'Have you accomplished the business of your visit?' We answered, 'We have no other concern here in Siam but to be of service to your Majesty.' The king asked if we intended to leave now and we replied that we would depart if he gave his approval.

A letter from the Siamese king

Suddenly the king said something in Siamese and two attendants, who had been lying prostrate, rose to their feet and approached the throne. They extended the jewel-studded pāīdān to the king in the manner described earlier and when the king placed his letter inside, they carried it off. The letter was transferred to another pāīdān made of gold and thus the royal document was passed into Ibrāhīm Beg's hands.

Then the king declared: 'May God look over your lord's life and increase his prosperity. May he live a thousand years, for that would give me the greatest joy. Make every effort to communicate my good-will and sincerity and convey my wish that, God willing, his friends may prosper and his enemies be destroyed. May the king of Iran not

forget us in time to come.' Then the king closed the portals of speech
and closed the door of his throne.

The ministers and the Siamese escorted us out and led us to the
building where our letter was originally installed and there they
took the Siamese king's letter from Ibrāhīm Beg and placed it in an
elevated position. They had us sit down inside this building and
a formal banquet was given in our honor. Then we retired to our
lodgings.

The delegates sell their horses at a loss

The late Muḥammad Ḥusain Beg, as well as the other servants of the
honorable Khāṣṣa, had each brought several horses with them to
Shahr Nāv and it would have been very burdensome to transport
them back to Iran. Of necessity these horses became gifts to the
Siamese king's estates. Each of us had lost a few horses on our way
and spent about twenty tūmāns on them in addition to their initial
price. The Siamese, however, have no interest in good Arabian-
and Indian-bred horses. They knew the market value and what we
had paid for these fairy-like beauties but they pretended to be ignorant
and only gave us ten to twelve tūmāns in money or goods for each
horse.

The way the Siamese train their horses

Although the Siamese, contrary to proper usage, do not groom their
own hair and tails, they cut the manes and tails of their horses.
They consider the mane and tail to be bad luck for the horse as well
as for the rider. Even more strange, a horse is expected to keep his
head lowered and tucked between his two front legs. That is considered
a sign of respect for the rider. The horse is never allowed to raise his
head.

To encourage the horse to acquire this posture the natives first
tie the horse's head to his front legs with a short piece of rope. The
horse remains tied up in this manner until he is accustomed to holding
his head down and eventually he learns to walk about like an old
draft horse. It is not the custom in Siam to train horses to run at
different paces or to perform any of the maneuvers of finer horsemanship.

The embassy takes the Siamese king's letter and departs

A few days after we had sold our horses we were all ready to depart
from Siam. First we were taken to the house where the king's letter

had been lodging. The letter was transferred by means of a pāīdān into a strong box and the officials ordered that Ibrāhīm Beg and my humble self put a seal on the box. We applied the seal and with little further ado they lifted up the document, placed it upon a litter and escorted it to our boat. The ministers and the court attendants themselves carried the litter to the boat. Finally when all the officials returned ashore, we raised anchor and set out for our destination. That was the 22nd of Ṣafar 1098.[42]

PART III THIRD JEWEL

Now that our pen has sailed through the straits of a condensed report and the official events of our embassy have been described, it is permissible if we turn our attentions to recording some facts about the local conditions. To begin with let us explain where Siam is located in the scheme of world geography and what different names the country is known by.

Chīn and Māchīn

May it not be hidden from those that travel the great road of research that the regions of Siam are what voyagers have called Māchīn. At least this would seem to be the case but the humble author must admit that as much as he has made enquiries it was never perfectly clear whether that region is or is not the real Māchīn. Some learned writers have stated in their various works on travel and geography that Chīn ibn Nūḥ[1] had a son of good fortune whom he named Māchīn. But by the time Māchīn grew up his brothers and other relatives had become so numerous that the young man decided to take leave of his father and eventually built a great city adjacent to China. As was natural the natives named that city Māchīn in honor of his memory.

The geographers all concur in describing Māchīn as an extensive country that borders on China. The author of Nafā'isu'l-Funūn[2] writes that Māchīn is located 'beyond the island Lāhūrī in Bandbanās (Nabdnabās), which is one of the provincial districts of Havāmaka (Javāmaka), and very fine aloes wood comes from there.' In Siam there is a jungle and a mountain known by the name Banā which might be related to Bandbanās.[3] It is therefore possible that Shahr Nāv is actually the port of Māchīn. The same author has written that Khiṭā is a walled city with a diameter of ten farsakhs. A small stream flows through the middle of that city and later on the same river passes within six farsakhs of Māchīn.

Ḥamdu'llah Mustawfī in his work Nuzhatu'l-Qulūb[4] has undertaken a description of the inhabited portion of the world and, following the calculations of Abū Raiḥān,[5] he states that part of Māchīn is in the first clime[6] and part is in the second. According to that system of reckoning China is placed in the third clime and Khiṭā in the fifth. Thus Māchīn lies beyond Khiṭā and China and is described as a very large and prosperous land. The present author feels that the rumor that Shahr Nāv is the same as Māchīn simply derives from the Iranian travelers. They realize that Siam is near China and therefore they assume it must be Māchīn.

The name Shahr Nāv

The mainstay of travel and transportation in that whole region is the boat. In fact the name of the country and the capital means city of the boat. However, the local inhabitants call the city Ajaudīā, which in their language means big city. Finally, the Franks and men of learning who have gone more deeply into this subject refer to the city in their books as Siam.

If some effort is made at conciliating these various views, we may arrive at the conclusion that Shahr Nāv is one of the cities of the greater district of Māchīn and that the whole district is sometimes referred to as Māchīn because it is near China. Actually Siam is adjacent to the land of Paigū, which is ruled over by a separate king, and Paigū borders directly on China. 'God alone knows the real truth in these matters.'

However the case may be:

>Indeed there is no matching
>The fair maidens of Māchīn
>But this unlucky traveler never won a kiss
>Or made a happy match.
>I did not pluck love's flower
>In the meadows of Māchīn.
>And yet that lusty sounding name
>Is taken from the ancient hero Chīn.
>When the great flood receded,
>The flames of his passion
>Repopulated the damp and empty world.

Description of the inhabitants of Siam

The Iranians and the Franks call the natives of Shahr Nāv, Siamese, but the natives themselves trace their stock back to Tai, whom they hold to be one of their devils and genii. They tell many fables and foolish tales concerning their lineage and in the end none of it connects or makes any sense. Although the natives do not trace their line back to Adam, it is quite possible that in accord with the view of the local Iranians, the lost people of Siam go back to Sān ibn Yāfuth ibn Nūḥ.[7] The Siamese language is very imprecise and most words are not pronounced clearly anyway. Every sound is confused with another sound especially the 'm' and the 'n'. Thus it is very possible that Siam is a mispronunciation of Sān.

There is also another opinion held by several historians that Sīāmak, the son of Kayumarth,[8] sired children and that the Siamese can be traced back to this progenitor. Supposedly, as time passed by his name was shortened to Siam. In the end there is no guiding pilot through this sea of fantasy. 'Only God knows the full history of His creatures.'

The war between Siam and Paigū[9]

The present king considers himself to be Siamese and of the same stock as his people. However, the rule of his ancestors does not go back more than two-hundred years and the city walls and the fortress were constructed about that time as well. There are some temples and other buildings which the natives reckon to be more than a thousand years old but these constructions were the work of another age.

Before this king's family came to power the city was under the control of the king of Paigū and Paigū was alternately under China and Khiṭā or occasionally had a separate king of its own. One of the present king's ancestors was the chief of an important local tribe and thus the king of Paigū found it convenient to make him the governor of Siam and in fact the king entrusted the whole country to that man's care. As time went on the family managed to retain this high position, at least up until one of them met with the following troubles.

It happened that the son of the Siamese governor was at the royal court employed in waiting upon the king but unfortunately the young man's honest character and the large amount of favor that the king accorded him only served to arouse the jealousy of the king's son, for such was the faulty nature of the crown prince. It was not long before the relationship between these two young men took a turn for the worse.

Goaded on by jealousy, the prince was constantly on the lookout for means to inflict some harm on the honest, young man. When the governor's son took leave of the court to visit his father and relatives, the prince, quick to exploit the opportunity, formed a plot with a certain group of statesmen and devised a plan to eliminate the other young man for good.

The prince went before the king and boldly declared, 'Someone who enjoys your generous patronage and highest favors has suddenly

become your enemy. Even now he has thrown off the yoke of obedience, returned to his own kingdom and is busy hatching several
schemes against you.' A group of the king's councilors was on
hand and they were eager to confirm the prince's accusations.

Without taking the pains to look further into the matter, the king
ordered that the governor and his son present themselves at the foot
of the royal throne but before this order reached the accused father
and son, the nobles who were plotting with the prince sent ahead a
tricky letter of their own. The letter stated: 'The king intends to arrest
you immediately and has decided to take away your kingdom and
give it to his son. For this reason the king is about to call you to the
court. You have been warned. Act as you think best.'

Shortly thereafter the governor received the king's summons but
fearing for his life and the life of his son, he answered with excuses
and begged to postpone coming to the court. The sly prince had
thrown the dice of deception and his lucky number had appeared.

When the governor's excuses reached the court, the king was
furious and promptly declared war. Orders were issued that the
renegade governor and his son be captured at once. As it was the
prince who had instigated the whole affair, it was natural for him to
be appointed leader of the army and so with high hopes and numerous
troops he set out to wage war in the territory of Siam.

When the prince reached the borders of that country the compliant
governor came out to receive him. The governor professed his
loyalty and obedience and performing all the ceremonies of duty
and respect, approached the prince through the portals of humility
and petition. The governor exclaimed: 'Perhaps we have committed
some error unknowingly. If so, I am hopeful that you will be indulgent
and overlook our shortcomings, that you will even become our
intercessor before the king, for as you see there is no question of our
rebelling or being disloyal.'

But as much as the governor endeavored to pursue a course of
conciliation, there was no advantage to be had. In the end all he
received in answer to his polite entreaty was reproach and harsh
abuse. Thus the governor and his son were caught in a tight net of
circumstances and found themselves forced to conclude on war,
which was just what the prince wished.

It should be mentioned that in all the countries of Below the Winds
the peasantry and the army are one and the same and if the army
suffers the country itself falls into ruin. Consequently, when the
natives of this region wage war, they are extremely careful and the
struggle is wholly confined to trickery and deception. They have no
intention of killing one another or inflicting any great slaughter

because if a general gained a victory with a real conquest, he would be shedding his own blood, so to speak.

The fixed custom is that when two factions have lined up before one another, a group from each side comes forward, beating kettle drums and playing flutes and the infantry and the horsemen on both sides begin dancing and shouting and raising all the noise they can. Every so often one army advances and the other retreats and in that way the one that has some luck manages to catch the other off guard. They rush up and surround their rivals and when the victorious group like a pair of compasses draws a line around the other army, the vanquished, being the dot in the center, admit defeat and place their will in the circle of obedience.

This being the usual style of waging war, it was only natural for the governor's son to take refuge in trickery. He wrote to the prince declaring: 'Since you have clearly decided on war and refuse to quench your anger with the waters of clemency, know that a state of war now exists between us. But my army is made up of your peasantry and they are in no way at fault in this matter and if they suffer losses, it is a loss for you as well. If you are sure of your cause and have any pretentions to manliness, let us face each other alone in the field of battle tomorrow morning and we will see what hidden things the Creator of this world will make manifest. If you are victorious over me, this whole territory is yours. If I triumph, I will deal with you as I see fit.'

Since the prince was bold and a man of great physical strength, he was very satisfied with this arrangement and consented to the wish of the governor's son. They say that the prince was so strong, the elephant goad he used weighed thirty kātīs, that is six mans according to the king of Iran's weights and measures. It may be added that the famous goad of the prince has remained in the Siamese king's treasury up to this day.

However the case may be, when the Sun, who is prince of the realm of being and possessor of all the earth, mounted the white horse of morning to destroy darkness with a crack of his glittering whip of light and the battle ranks of day were drawn up in full order, the prince of our tale mounted his horse and rode into the field. There was no hesitation in his mind, no sense of caution in his thoughts.

> First youth is fair and strong,
> Set high upon a thundering elephant.
> Now here, now there, he rushes through the field of battle,
> As fierce as a raging lion.
> Behold the bright faced hero riding on a mighty elephant!
> Behold the radiant sun rising above the tall black mountains!

He drives forward the heavy beast,
Striking with his crescent shaped goad.
Does he not appear the shining half-moon,
Perched on the dark blue Nile?

The ministers and men of state beseeched the prince on their knees but he would not turn back from battle. His mind was set and his purpose was firm. Eventually the governor's son came forth and positioned himself opposite the prince. He sent the prince a messenger declaring, 'Your army is great beyond a reckoning but if you intend to be fair and set aside deceits, return now to your camp and swear before the idols that with or without you, this army will not move against me, that they will observe the agreement we have made.'

The prince was compliant and did as the young man requested. When the armies were facing each other once again, the governor's son came forth and proclaimed, 'What really is the purpose of our fighting? If you want this domain, have it and if you wish to arrest me, I will submit and go along with you to the king. Let the king do as he sees fit.' But the prince was afraid his whole plot would be exposed and he answered the young man with harshness and abuse.

At last when the governor's son could tolerate the situation no longer, he was aroused with anger and violence in accord with the saying,[10] 'In time of mortal danger when no hope remains, a man will pit his hand against a sword, insensible to pain.' All along he realized the extent of his adversary's strength and had no hope of overcoming him in an even match. But as a bent wheel cannot roll along a straight path and only makes its way with crooked maneuvers, the governor's son decided to attach a firearm beneath his elephant prod.

When the two combatants were close to one another and the eagle-like prince swooped down to snatch his victim from off the elephant, the governor's son took aim with his goad and before the prince knew what had happened, he fell from the happy elephant of life on to the earth of humiliation and was dead. In accord with, 'The evil doer is snared in his own deceits' the prince caught his foot and was held fast in the net of his own schemes.

When the prince's generals and ministers learned what had happened and thought over the situation they were in, they realized that they were not free to wage war and they did not feel they could return home and face the king. In this predicament they decided to join forces with the governor's son. Thus they promptly pledged him their allegiance and settled down in Siam. This turn of events greatly increased the young man's power and brought prosperity to his country.

The next stage of Siam's conflict with Paigū

When a certain amount of time had elapsed, the king decided to take revenge for the loss of his son and sent a general and another huge army to Siam. The general arrived at the Siamese frontier and sent a messenger to the governor's son declaring: 'My army is immense and beyond reckoning. In accord with "Do not be the cause of your own destruction", refrain from any forms of resistance and put your neck under the yoke of obedience.

If my superiority is not clearly manifest and you wish to learn the extent of my power, let us both submit to the following test. I will command my troops to build a temple within a certain period of time in this field, a temple of stone which will be of such and such dimensions. Undertake to build a similar temple yourself, as this is your own domain.

If I complete the task before you, it will be clear proof that the gods are on my side. You would have no other choice but to render me obedience. If I can not build this temple faster than you, however, you will have the upper hand and the victory will be yours.'

After exchanging messengers both sides accepted this test of strength. And so, relying on their great numbers, the troops of the general's awesome army began to build the edifice as agreed. But the governor's son knew that no amount of effort on his part would enable him to compete with such an army. There was no other remedy but to draft the blueprints of deception with the aid of that master builder, Imagination. Since it was impossible to construct the building in so short a time and still keep to the agreed specifications, he decided to build a simple construction of cane and wood. A certain amount of work was done each night and before daylight the workers would cover over the wooden dummy with white plaster to conceal the trick.

On the morning designated for the unveiling of their work, even before the master craftsman, Destiny, had streaked the arch of heaven with the whitewash of dawn's light, the Siamese completed their temple and stood ready for inspection. The general's foolish troops laboured in all fairness and were almost finished with their sturdy construction, an edifice which the wrecker, Time, has still not breached with the pickaxe of his decrees.

But when the invaders beheld the finished monument of their rivals, they were stung with grief and they did not take the pains to examine it very closely. The local inhabitants of that part of Siam had already made their plans to give up the struggle and flee but now the enemy soldiers were thoroughly tricked. The invading army felt that their superiority of number was of no avail if the natives were capable of finishing such an edifice so quickly. 'The idols are surely on their side. There is nothing to be gained by waging war. We must abandon this campaign if we expect to return home in safety.'

Thus they set out for the districts of ignorance and returned to their king. The general explained to the king what had really taken place and as the general was the key to figuring out the deceit of the Siamese, so his cleverness became the key which opened the king's heart. The general presented his explanation like a pretty bride before the king's sight and the king decorated the beauty of his wit with an ornament of generosity. Thus the general even managed to receive an award.

Shortly after these events the king died and since the kingdom of Siam was of no immediate value to the court, the war was forgotten. Day by day the local governor of Siam grew more firm in his independence and his domain began to prosper. It was not very long ago that the ancestors of the present king strengthened the walls of the city.

Iranians in Siam before the present king's reign

Since Siam is close to the ports of India and is situated on the sea route to China and Japan, merchants have always been attracted to settle there. It is also possible to make great profits buying and selling elephants. From the time merchants first arrived until just before the present king came to power, about thirty Iranians had settled in Siam due to the great profits to be made in trade. Each of these Iranians was honored with the utmost respect, presented with a house and given a specific position in the Siamese king's administration.

How the present king came to power

When the present king was still a boy, he used to visit the Iranians regularly and he took great pleasure in their social manners and their foods and drink. In that way he became quite familiar with the Iranian style of life. When the father died, the oldest son was seated on the throne in accord with the father's will but the present king was jealous and plotted to overthrow him. He adopted the following plan.

He went to his uncle and addressed him with guile. 'How is it that my brother sits on the throne while you are still alive? Are you expected to prostrate yourself before him? Do not accept and obey such an outrageous convention and do not be afraid. I will give you all the support you need.' Thus he won over his uncle. Early the next morning, without any warning, the ambitious prince went to his brother's private residence and killed him with his own hand. Then he put his uncle on the throne. By that time the Iranian community had grown to about one hundred individuals.

Shortly thereafter the present king began to deal with the affairs of state without consulting his uncle. He did whatever he pleased and paid no attention to the fact that his uncle was the king. This state of confusion continued until one day he even killed a minister in front of his uncle for no apparent reason. Then the prince left the palace, went home and refused to attend the court any longer.

When the king felt he could no longer tolerate the situation, he called together a group of supporters and made plans to eliminate his nephew. But he did not pay heed to the saying, 'The wise man does not draw his sword until he is ready to draw blood.' And it so happened that one of the servants present had grown up with the prince as a child.

This servant warned the present king of his uncle's intentions declaring, 'Take care not to go before the king or if you do, be on your guard lest he kill you.' Thus informed, the present king decided the time was right to rid himself of his uncle and he drew the Franks and the Iranians into his plot.

The Iranians perform the taʿziyat and help the present king come to the throne

As it was then the month of Muḥarram and the Iranians were about to perform their mystery play in honor of Ḥusain, the following scheme was devised. The present king told the Iranians, 'The day your performers go before the king, I will follow after you with my own men and we will see what can be accomplished with you at work within and my men and myself pressing from the outside.' The Mughals went to the king and announced that for them it was a day of sorrow and mourning. 'We must perform our religious ceremonies and we wish to come before you to offer up prayers in our own language.' In this way they explained their request for an audience.

The palace guards

As I mentioned before, the king of Siam does not have a standing army like other kings but the peasantry act as his soldiers. In times of need he orders the peasants to assemble and gives them his particular commands. Among the Siamese, however, there is a group well known for its loyalty and courage. The members of this corps of élite stand out above all the rest of the king's troops and their daring and fierceness is famous. They are even reckoned among the close confidants and councilors of the king.

These guards have requested to be allowed some sign of distinction to vouch for their superior rank, a sign which would not be subject to the inroads of time. Since they do not wear clothes or armor, they have taken to tattooing themselves with certain words of their own script, much the same as the Turks and the bedouin Arabs who decorate themselves with dots and lines. Of the officers who have the highest rank and are in charge of making arrests, executions and torturing, there are some who wear their sign on the right arm and others who wear it on the left. Those in the courier service and the office of roads have their own particular insignia. All these posts are passed on from father to son.

As a measure of safety these select guards who are similar to the Ājarlū,[11] have their residential quarter near the king's lodgings. The shrewd prince, as part of his conspiracy, arranged that his men set fire to the houses of the élite corps and a fire is indeed a serious danger, as all the dwellings in Siam are made of cane and wood.

Once the flames of the prince's conspiracy were well ablaze and the smoke of confusion was rising from the household of the guards' heart, the élite corps would certainly desert their posts in the palace and rush off to save their homes. That would be the moment of opportunity when the prince and his supporters could gain the upper hand. And so the conspirators went to work.

Once their houses caught fire, the guards and courtiers were filled with fear and busied themselves trying to put out the flames. The prince was quick to exploit the situation. He mounted up with his group of followers and set off for the palace. When news of the fire reached the king, he was greatly alarmed and despatched his closest guards thinking they might offer assistance. But the king only sent his guards a few at a time to fight the fire.

It is the belief of the Siamese that their princes and kings are divine and no native would ever think of fighting with them or killing one of them. Thus it was easy for the prince to placate each of the guards that came forth from the palace. In this manner he avoided a real struggle and convinced the guards to join him. Little by little he approached the throne.

Meanwhile the Iranians took advantage of the situation and, using their religious rites as a pretext, they entered the palace with complete freedom. Then from within they launched their attack and the king's palace fell under the siege of their guns and cannons.[12] When the prince made his way to the interior and joined the Iranians, he encouraged them by raising a loud cry shouting, 'Oh 'Alī', and thus they all pressed on to the king's apartments. There was absolutely nothing the king could do to offer resistance. Fearing the flames of rebellion, he jumped into the river and took flight. The prince ascended the throne and after a short time he captured his uncle and relieved him of the burdens of his life. The prince rose to the imperial throne on the 8th of Muḥarramu 'l-Ḥarām 1068.[13]

Description of the present king's rule

As soon as the king of Siam assumed the power of state he appointed 'Abdu'r-Razzāq, whose family is from Gīlān,[14] to the post of prime minister. 'Abdu'r-Razzāq became the king's councilor and a holder of favor at the court. But this Iranian proved to be devoid of character, low-bred and vile. Abusing the privilege of rank, he spent all his time furthering wickedness, immorality and oppression of the weak. After several years of heavy drinking he had distorted his mind and was crazed for the purple wine of innocent blood. He always carried a gun and whoever had the misfortune of greeting him at the wrong time, he pushed aside and answered with his deadly aim.

The rank of Fū

It is the custom in Siam that if the king raises someone to the rank of Fū, which means being near the throne, and recognizes that person as a close councilor and a favorite, no criticism of that individual is tolerated. No matter how unjust he is or how oppressively he behaves, the king does not allow anyone to speak against him. Once the king awards such a high position, all accusations, true or false, are disregarded. The king thinks that when royal favor is accorded to someone, other people are jealous and strive to ruin that person's reputation with their insinuations. These detractors simply wish to employ trickery and seduce the king from the path of nobility. Thus certain factions aim at creating a bad reputation for the king and would like to point to his infidelity and disloyalty towards his friends. They attempt to make the king weaken the pillars of state.

These being the royal suspicions, no one dares inform the king of such a favored person's blameworthy behavior, at least not until the king's attitude begins to change towards that person. For these reasons despite 'Abu'r-Razzāq's tyranny, dishonesty and harmfulness to the state, no one spoke up against him in front of the king. To deliver such information a courtier would have to feel very trusted by the king and imagine that the evil deeds in question were already notorious. The only hope is if the king is awakened from his sleep of negligence by the cries of the populace.

In fact matters did reach that point eventually and the king forbade the Iranian minister to continue his vile behavior. The royal warnings produced no change and in the end the king was greatly angered. Finally the minister was imprisoned and a little later the captive's soul escaped its confinement and left the prison of the body.

The rise of Āqā Muḥammad

After that Āqā Muḥammad, whom I mentioned earlier, came into office. It is more than evident from his works and deeds that he was a man of noble character. He possessed the laudable manners and fine integrity of a truly well-bred man. He is originally from Astarābād, the abode of the faithful. Wise and loyal, and a man of practical skill, trained in the school of experience, he originally settled in Siam to carry on trade. After learning the language and customs of that domain he rose to a position of authority and became a minister and favored councilor of the king.

Indeed he was a sensible man with much talent and quite learned in history and letters. He worked for the prosperity and good order of the affairs of state to the utmost of his ability and this was clear to everyone around him. He had much knowledge of the real workings of politics and governing and was well-versed in matters pertaining to kingly magnificence and the regulations of food and drink in formal gatherings.

The Siamese king receives instruction from Āqā Muḥammad

Making use of his store of wisdom he endeavored in every possible way to familiarize the king with all the foreign men of importance in the world and he instructed him concerning refinement of character, management of the household and governing cities.

The king was diligent in his studies and neglected no points of education however subtle. He particularly applied himself to the lessons concerning moral aberration, injustice and tyranny, which in the end only lead rulers into misery. He delved into the precepts on the natural disposition and lusts of man but when it came to beholding the beauty of the true Beloved and mastering the Perfect Subject, which consists in knowing the one God, his inner eye of understanding remained limited to the bare exterior of this world. Despite the breadth of his studies, the king held firmly to the path of ingratitude before his Maker and to this day he continues on the road of ignorance. However, a certain degree of change did take place. Contrary to the fixed attitude which his father displayed, the present king has made certain concessions and the most basic beliefs he held, have been shaken to their foundation. His pagan faith is no longer so firm and the hatred which usually exists between the non-believers and the faithful, has disappeared.

The king's character

Contrary to all the other kings and overlords of Below the Winds, the king of Siam sincerely was interested in raising himself, of acquiring distinction and improving his way of living, his household and his possessions. He was eager to learn about the other kings of the inhabited world, their behavior, customs and principles. He made a great effort to enlighten himself and sent everywhere for pictures depicting the mode of living and the courts of foreign kings.

When the Siamese king finally came to gaze at the illustrations on the page, which the artist Destiny painted with the pen of Fate's decrees, and there beheld the heavenly court of the Khāqān, the ruler with a lucky star and that court was depicted in accord with, 'Indeed He painted your face and great was the beauty of your portrait' and he heard of the noble life and refined manners in Iran, guided by right reason, which faculty distinguishes man from beast, the king grasped the clear fact that perfect kingship, glory and higher forms of government are the exclusive privilege of Iran.

Thus dressing himself with sincerity, he has abandoned his former style of clothing and he has started to wear Iranian clothes, our kind of long embroidered tunic, trousers, shirts and shoes and socks. When his servants ask what kind of weapon he wishes to wear, he replies, 'What one wears must conform to one's rank and I find the Iranian style dagger alone worthy of my waist.' But he has turned his head aside from wearing the turban because of its weight. He declares, 'My head has no desire for the elaborate crown of Jamshīd. This simple cap of felt is proper to my station.'[15]

Since the king first broadened his horizons with education up until this present day, he has been secretly devoted to Iran and has cherished hopes of effecting friendly contacts with our royal court. Now these hopes have been fulfilled. According to the king's own statement, he has often sent gifts to the governor of Ḥaidarābād and different rulers of India, as well as to kings of various other regions. He has been especially practicing this sort of diplomacy since his present prime minister has facilitated contacts for him with the Christian kings.

Iranian guards brought over to Siam from India

As I mentioned briefly at the beginning of this account, the kings of Siam are devoid of power in the absolute sense and they do not maintain a corps of real attendants and a professional army. Since the present king came on to the chessboard of government neither mounted on the elephant of absolute power nor riding the steed of effective rule, the queen of Āqā Muḥammad's mind sent to India and recruited 200 Iranians, mostly men originally from Astarābād and Māzandarān. They had migrated from their homeland with high hopes but lacking the integrity necessary to succeed, they were checkmated in the tricky land of India by the elephant of unfavorable chance.

Āqā Muḥammad consoled them in their state of despair and engaged them to attend at the king's stirrup. He hired each of them for a sum of not more than twenty and not less than twelve tūmāns. The king's administration allocated each one of these Iranian attendants a separate house, two peasants and a horse with a saddle, the proper accoutrements and fodder. Once every year they receive good sets of clothing and other basic items.

Due to their lack of integrity, which is a commodity always wanting in the low-bred, they were quick to stumble into the meshes of mischief and sedition. They became embroiled in mutual hatred, malice, jealousies and all manner of perverseness. Despite the king's manifest affection, they opened the register and accounts of treachery.

They repeatedly complained to the king declaring: 'In India we are all called by one name, Mughal, and originally we all came from the same country. We all hold the same rank and, finally, we are all Iranians. No one of us holds a higher distinction than the other. But Āqā Muḥammad persists in showing favor to those of our group who are related to him and he sees that they are paid more money. All along he has been merely wasting your finances. In India we were satisfied with half our present salary.'

The king punishes Āqā Muḥammad

Since the king had never had this kind of expense in his administration before, the soldiers were easily able to make him feel dissatisfied.

Their bickering encouragad the king to foolishness. His Majesty became angry with Āqā Muḥammad and accused him of not telling the truth. 'You told me the Iranians' present salary is very little but they have revealed to me that it is much too much.' The king ordered attendants to sew Āqā Muḥammad's two lips together with strips of cane and they kept the wretched minister in that painful condition for a whole day. Then the king made everybody's salary the same, reducing it to twelve tūmāns a year.

Two members of the group who were Yūz Bāshīs, one of the right flank and the other of the left, were allotted thirty tūmāns. They consider the left flank a higher rank because the heart, which is the sultan of the body's city, is located on the left side. However, at that time it so happened that the Yūz Bāshī of the right flank had gained a higher rank due to his personal qualifications.

The only duty which this Iranian group had was to accompany the king when he went riding and every year they were paid their full salary in cash. But they have put aside their pride and made display of such improper behavior that any esteem and rank which they might have gained has since been forfeited.

Āqā Muḥammad's two sons

The poor Āqā Muḥammad has been dead for a while now and thus he has escaped from the low company of the Iranian Guard. He left behind two sons who were still under age at the time of his death. They have both turned out to be very foolish and immature, being intoxicated with the wine of recklessness. The king himself undertook to raise these boys and consequently acquired a warm affection and real kindness for them. He kept them continually by his side and named one of them Chū Chī, which means 'apple of my eye' and the other he called Chū Kīā, which means 'the heart'. When their father died, the king passed on the old man's office to the two sons. As head of the Iranian community and a minister their father had been in charge of all business transactions. The sons were now assigned that job.

However, the other Iranians were jealous and hostile and they encouraged the young men's debauchery and caused them to be unsuccessful in their work. The king became aware of the situation but as much as he forbade them to continue in that fashion, his warnings did not effect a noticeable change. The young men even undertook contact with the king's brother and appeared to be his good friends by spending all their time with him. Such a state of affairs caused the king to fear that in the same way as the Iranians had originally aided him to the throne, they might now support his brother. The late Āqā Muḥammad's sons were all the more suspect since they were at liberty to come and go in the palace and no one had the authority to question them. Such a privilege would be of great use to an enemy.

The courtiers who were pursuing their own advancement all along played upon the king's suspicions and thus managed to decrease the young men's rank. It was not long before the king became very angry with the two boys and had them tortured and abused. Then the king presented an account of their behavior to the Iranians and his messenger announced, 'Look at the comportment of these young men and bear witness to how they have returned my good favors.'

The lack of unity in the Iranian community

Certain of the Iranians, who were trying to further their own interests and had spread calumny against the boys, were quick to take advantage of this opportunity. The most jealous of their number put their heads together and actually wrote out an order for the boys' execution, declaring, 'According to our religion any one who behaves in such a manner and is disloyal to his lord, must be put to death.'

Others of the Iranians, who had a small amount of religious faith left and still held on to a shred of the divine law, disagreed with the first faction and although they knew they would incur the king's anger, they wrote a decree stating, 'The accusations which have been recently formulated against Āqā Muḥammad's sons do not hold credence with us. There is no sin upon these boys according to our religion and we think it would be much better if the king chose to be kind and passed over their faults.'

The king acted nobly in this matter and through his messenger he announced, 'I have raised these boys myself. I will neither kill them as some of you suggest nor will I pardon them. I have decided to send them into exile in a certain part of my kingdom which is in the jungle far from the path of all travelers.' While we were in Siam it was not possible to ascertain whether these boys were still alive or had already died.

The Iranian successors to Āqā Muḥammad

After these sad events the king entrusted the premiership to a man who was originally from Shūshtar. He was distinguished among the Iranians for the background of his family as well as for his own personal ability and manliness. His family traced its lineage back to the Mullā Ḥasan 'Alī of Shūshtar and indeed this man proved to be very clever and endowed with much practical ability. He possessed an excellent understanding of the language and protocol of Siam. Unfortunately, shortly after he was appointed as minister, a perverse man from Khurāsān assassinated him in broad daylight, raving on about, 'It was you who deprived me of my rank and position. You did not care that you were the cause of my ruin nor would you offer me the least help.'

The lack of a qualified Iranian leader

The group of Iranians which was left was neither worthy nor capable of assuming higher rank and thus they were kept in a position of ill-fortune. Two or three persons who were actually offered responsible positions by the king would not accept, fearing the jealousy of their Iranian peers. Meanwhile the affairs of state were beginning to slow down.

Everyone whom the king entrusted with tasks and sent abroad fell into debauchery and never came back to Siam. Soon the situation reached a point of urgency. For the above-mentioned reasons the king was not able to find an Iranian to act as prime minister and since the Siamese are not capable of handling the affairs of state, the king never used them in the past and was not prepared to use them now. The only candidate who remained was that one Frank who had originally worked as a sailor.

The rise of the Frank minister

While Āqā Muḥammad was in office, the Frank was first hired to work in the king's administration. At that time the man's job was to procure ships. Since he is in fact an extremely clever man and full of shrewd tricks, from the beginning he took great pains to acquire the appearance of a good character, at least what is taken for a good character in Siam. The important factor in that country is to know the language well and to be versed in their protocol.

Thus the Frank applied himself to learn the local speech, the laws and customs of the land and he had the luck to be in a position where there were no capable rivals to oppose him. Day by day he impressed the king with a show of practical abilities and a counterfeit integrity. After a short time he rose to the post of prime minister and he has held that office for three or four years now.

The Frank minister has succeeded in penetrating into the king's affections to such an extent, by means of shrewd trickery, that there is never a moment in public or in private when he is not at the king's side. To the world at large this Christian minister displays a record of service, integrity, thrift and sincerity and makes every effort to increase the state revenues and cut down expenses.

However, it is a fact that every year he sends huge sums of money from the king's treasury abroad to the Frank kingdoms, supposedly for business purposes. Up until now there have been absolutely no visible returns from that money.

In accord with the spirit of hatred which exists between Islam and the infidels, the Christian minister is ever competing with Muslims for the upper hand and in accord with, 'If you give help to a wicked person, God soon arouses that man against you', the Frank has tried to drive the Iranians out. By way of harming their reputation he is always on the lookout to expose their improper deeds and find some sign of their disloyalty to the king.

Ḥājī Salīm exposed by the Frank minister

Only recently that illegitimate-born Christian succeeded in gaining the upper hand over the envoy Ḥājī Salīm, exploiting the latter's short-sightedness and neglect. When Ḥājī Salīm returned from Iran the Christian stirred up the king's displeasure by criticizing the envoy's behavior in the following manner. 'Ḥājī Salīm, whom your Majesty sent on a mission to Iran, spent about five thousand tūmāns and yet he did not manage to effect his business in the manner that you ordered. In addition to his lack of efficiency as an envoy, he has tucked away in his own home certain of your Majesty's provisions and materials which were supposed to be used on the mission.

Now he has returned naked and cannot offer a satisfactory explanation for himself. He was given bills of credit to borrow what he needed from the Dutch and English and indeed he borrowed one thousand tūmāns. It is a known fact that he also received huge sums of money and various presents from the Iranian king's honorable administration. But despite such gifts and despite the great expenses which he incurred, he has returned with no clothes or apparel to his name.'

The scribes who had been sent along with Ḥājī Salīm agreed with most of what the Christian minister said. They were dissatisfied with the envoy's behavior, especially the fact that he had not allowed them to attend to their own duties. Thus the scribes presented a full report of Ḥājī Salīm's breach of good manners, his confiscation of official goods, all his irregular expenditures and, finally, how he had transported his own freight back to Siam on the embassy's ship. With such reports it was easy for the minister to fan the flames of the king's anger.

The king declared: 'I would not care if my envoy spent many times this money, if he increased my name at the Iranian court. Indeed, I would be grateful. But when he returned with the ambassador of Iran, he had no proper accounts to present. I put my trust in him and he has acted ignobly. Now I am very angry with him.'

A few days after we arrived in Siam the king arrested Ḥājī Salīm and when we were about to depart the king sent him to us in the company of the Iranian minister, a group of Siamese courtiers and Iranian attendants. They had the following message to deliver.

'From the beginning of my rule to the present day I have entrusted my affairs to the Iranians and relied upon them for support but each one has turned out treacherous and disloyal and eventually has stolen from my treasury. Ḥājī Salīm, who escorted you to Siam, has given me a bad name. He has returned in disgrace after squandering large sums of my money.

Since my sincerity and good will have been made manifest to the agents of the Iranian court, I wish you would please check his accounts. Whatever you reckon were his legitimate expenses, write out in the form which I have explained to him. I will accept your statements in this matter.'

Ḥājī Salīm did in fact spend large sums of money living in a style higher than his station but he claimed: 'When I was sent to the world-consoling court of Iran, the Siamese agreed, through the Iranian minister who has since passed away, that whatever I thought fit, I should do and in that respect I only did what I thought was proper.'

But since the minister was no longer present the king was not satisfied with this explanation. After much ado, even though the king gave him the benefit of the doubt in certain matters, Ḥājī Salīm still came out owing two thousand tūmāns in face of his claimed expenses nor did he have a document from the Iranian agents to account for this sum.

The vilest sort of men have been going to Siam and they have borne themselves without the least sense of modesty and propriety. Thus they have made the Siamese suspicious and it is common for any foreigner to fall from esteem suddenly and encounter the retribution of God. Poor Ḥājī Salīm suffered from the bad reputation which such scoundrels have left behind. Yet it is not so much that the various foreigners are to blame. The situation in Siam is like the proverb, 'Bad waters flow forth from a polluted spring' and 'An old fish goes rotten in the head not in the tail.'

This is certainly a true description of conditions in Siam, for why does the king continue to entrust the reins of power to the hands of such deficient men? Why does he not investigate them more closely and test their qualifications? After a short time he only comes to regret his choice and lament his circumstances.

All rulers need the advice of capable ministers

To those acquainted with the secrets of true wisdom and the teachings of political science it is perfectly clear that if it were possible for rulers by dint of sheer effort and endeavor to manage the affairs of this world and the world to come, if it were not necessary that they prune error from the annals of government with the keen blade of learned men and councilors, then the kings and sultans of ancient times, whom God supported with His grace and a fair share of the divine bounty, would not have felt themselves insufficient in face of the tasks of state and they would not have been obliged to rely so heavily on sharp-sighted scholars and men of learning, on their councilors and the princes of insight and sound judgment.

Sultans who are graced with good character and the attributes of virtue make every effort to maintain, within the confines of the royal domain, a group of princes and ministers who will apply themselves to their work with the utmost diligence and who are endowed with the capacity to render wise counsel and appropriate service before the foot of the heavenly throne.

A good ruler must maintain a large army and be endowed with a courageous spirit. He must possess the virtues of generosity and mercy, wield his power with diplomacy and endeavor to cultivate a subtle judgment, which will enable him to estimate the worth and rank of his attendants. It is also important to know what degree of importance to accord to each of the arts.

How a ruler acquires talented ministers

The coinage of every servant's character must be checked with tests and observation and the currency of his sincerity and goodwill should be clearly established. If the king has reason to believe that someone is capable of providing the state sound assistance against the ravages of Fate and is ornamented with perfection of intellect and chastity of spirit, endowed with upright character and the qualities of goodwill and sincerity, he should hasten to entrust that man with the office of minister and make him one of his close councilors.

It is not proper that a base, characterless, low-bred person be admitted to the king's intimacy or granted a position of closeness at the court. Such a careless policy only invites loss and disaster. It is indeed a great danger to encourage men of little or no personal resources. Only the divine grace of God can transform a man of no natural talent.

> If God pours down His grace,
> Upon the man devoid of talent,
> Behold, water in a pimple,
> Becomes a pearl within the oyster shell.

Reference to events in India, discussed at the end of the account

In this manner only recently, due to a lack of trustworthy diplomats, certain powerful sultans have lost control over their dominions. In its proper place at the end of this account I will explain just what happened.

How to choose an ambassador

A sultan must also be familiar with the abilities of his servants in the realm of public speaking and practical management and be fully informed concerning their background from earliest education onwards. Such information is especially necessary in estimating the talents of someone who will be sent abroad as an ambassador. The sultan's ambassador must be a man of perfect intelligence, a clear-sighted councilor who knows his job thoroughly and has spent much time in the past acquiring experience. He must be a man who has already proved his worth, who is quick to appraise a new situation, is true to his word and has an honest reputation. Only a man who has been tested with previous tasks and proved himself a sure support for the king can be considered for such a responsible post.

The importance of having a qualified ambassador

Wise scholars and men of learning have pointed out that the ambassador is the king's own tongue. Whoever wishes to judge the intentions of a foreign king reads an ambassador as if he were the title page of the king's heart and tongue. Rulers all judge one another in accord with the saying of 'Alī, the prince of the faithful and testator of the

8

Prophet, and 'Alī has declared, 'The envoy is the king's interpreter, the representative of the king's most secret thoughts.'

Indeed, there is no other way to assess a distant ruler but through the discrimination and skill which he has displayed in choosing his envoy. If the envoy is eloquent and succeeds in impressing his host with praiseworthy behavior, that is a sure sign that the king has ability in evaluating men's character. Illustrating this important point is the story which occurs in various histories, how Alexander, possessor of the two horns,[16] desiring to send an envoy somewhere, changed his regal clothes to disguise himself and went on the mission himself in disguise.

Every wise councilor declares that the ambassador must be brave, clever in his speech and generally forceful. He must be able to answer with grace and expediency whatever questions may be put to him. He must speak out directly and speak well in whatever manner the occasion requires.

> One word destroyed a flourishing people,
> Behold, a whole world came to its end!
> Another word cleared the field of battle,
> Two sworn enemies became the best of friends.

Diplomacy among the Christians

Upon investigation it was revealed that among heathen rulers none are so industrious in observing caution in diplomatic affairs as the Christian kings. When they decide to entrust someone with a particular office, they first assign him simple tasks to accomplish and then observe his capabilities closely. If he performs his duties well, every two or three years they raise his position a little, advancing him one step at a time.

Another of the Christian practices is that from an early age princes are put to studying history and biographies and are often appointed to difficult posts in order to acquire practical experience. Sometimes they are sent out along with veteran generals, governors, ministers and envoys in order to gain a working knowledge of diplomacy abroad. Thus the Franks cultivate specific talents in their young men so that when the need arises they have several men of experience and are not forced to depend on deficient employees as the king of Siam must do.

It must be added that when the Christian kings do send one of their trained diplomats abroad serious attention is given to the circumstances of his mission. Before they send him on his way, they are careful to explain all the particulars of his task and exactly how he is to carry it out. They inform him of the customs and the manners of the country he will be visiting and they also explain what he should do in case of an accident. If anything serious happens to the ambassador it is already understood who will take his place and how the other diplomats are to behave. Even if the second ambassador dies, another man is ready to assume the empty position. In general the Christian diplomats have been instructed as to what to do and where to seek help, no matter what difficulties arise.

The effect of employing characterless officials

If the above-mentioned formalities are omitted and characterless men who lack the talent to serve sultans are appointed to high positions, men whose family background is connected with the lowly pursuits of farming and business, they will forgo conducting a thorough inspection of prospective diplomats and for the sake of their own immediate gain they will engage poorly qualified men in the affairs of government. What follows is inevitable. The deficient ambassador is first scorched by the holocaust of riot and sedition and then bursts into flame and burns like stacked hay, consuming a crowd of others along with himself. The stubble of his barren existence is burned to the ground, for his mind is dried out and dead. He perishes through carelessness, like the man who digs a well and then falls into it. The Sultan who relies on such types will gain no profit from their services. By associating with these men he is only weakening the power of his state.

The evil influence of the Frank minister

There are times when such unfit men of state deceive their lord and seduce him from the path of virtue and thus the king acquires a reputation for breaking his agreements and for being untrustworthy. Despite the fact that the Iranians have long taken the trouble to help the king of Siam and have displayed their generosity and fairness by instructing him about the outside world, that illegitimate-born Frank, that Christian, whom I have mentioned before, has caused the king to alter his attitudes and now the king's inner thoughts wander on the path of error. Outwardly as well the king appears beguiled.

The Frank minister exercises a great influence on state policy and is continually provoking the king to injustice by saying, 'How long will you continue to squander your benevolence on merchants and travelers who appear from every land and especially from Ḥaidarābād and the states of India. People imagine your kindness is due to your weakness and lack of power. If you were wise you would hire a group of Franks, build several ships and proceed to capture the merchants and travelers of these parts no matter what their business is or where they are going. Confiscate all their cargo and supplies. That will give the foreign kings cause to take note of your rank and position. Once you make a display of your power, wherever your attendants go, they will be treated with respect and civility.'

The king uses certain Franks as pirates

This kind of remedy is a rare medical prescription which consists of an emulsion of rubies mixed with the elixir of gold coins and the king was quick to appreciate its economic value. Thus the king outfitted several ships and had them manned by Franks. These Franks have since captured many merchant vessels, put large numbers of people to death and in the process have amassed a great quantity of goods which have still not been turned over to the king. The Frank pirates are smart enough to deliver a small amount of the booty to the king's administration but the greater part remains in their own hands.

Rubies from Paigū

It was heard that among all the ships which have been captured there was one that belonged to an Armenian who resided in Ḥaidarābād. The Franks caught him and his ship as he was returning from Paigū where he had bought a good quantity of rubies. As usual the Franks presented the king's administration with a mere sample of the spoils and kept the greater part for themselves. Worse yet, when it came to dividing up the valuable rubies, the Franks gave the king some glass beads for his share.

The Frank minister is executing Siamese officials

Besides this kind of dishonest practice, everyday the Christian prime minister has several Siamese officials and councilors killed, giving various false reasons for their execution. He has introduced all sorts of new practices into that kingdom and has succeeded in greatly limiting everyone else's business. As I explained earlier no one dares speak to the king about what a prime minister is really doing. Thus the Christian minister has become all important and manages to keep the reins of state power in his own hands. He wields a greater influence over the king than anyone else and consequently has freedom to do absolutely anything he wishes.

War with England

The result of this calamity is that lately fewer and fewer travelers and merchants have been coming to Siam. The prime minister's misbehavior has even caused the English king to open the doors of war and it is a standing order amongst the English to capture Siamese ships wherever they appear. The English king also gave the order that no Englishman was to remain in Siam. If this Christian stays in favor and continues along the same path, the Siamese king's power and kingdom will soon go into serious decline.

A description of the religion of Siam

At this stage of the narrative's journey the author feels it is appropriate to point out that, as is recorded in published texts, the general mass of mankind agrees that this world must have a Creator but concerning the details and the attributes of our Creator and the nature of His agents, men differ. In this matter all mankind can be divided into two groups.

If people adhere to a distinct religious body and a particular form of God's law, they are known as people of faith and religion. If such is not the case, they are rightly referred to as people of lust and contempt. There can be no doubt that the Siamese belong to the second group, being most blind and hopelessly gone astray, for it is clear that they do not adhere to any form of divine law or specified practice.

Idolatry and transmigration

During our stay in Siam it was ascertained through conversation with their learned men, who actually make direct use of the devil in teaching falsehoods, that the local practice is idolatry plain and simple, as well as belief in transmigration.

Transmigration is when a soul goes from one body into another. The various people holding this belief are divided into several sects. Some of them believe that the soul can only pass between human bodies. Some say the soul is capable of descending into the body of other animals. Still others claim that the soul can become attached to plants and finally there are those who believe that the soul can even inhabit minerals. Those believing that the soul only inhabits human bodies, are called, Naskh, those accepting animal bodies, Maskh, those who accept plants, Faskh and those who include minerals, Raskh.

Certain sages and authoritative philosophers who are unusually clever, discriminating, learned and clear-sighted such as Anaxagoras,

Democritus, Socrates and Plato[17] are known to have professed the doctrine of the temporal progress of the soul, based on transmigration. These thinkers have said quite a bit in the way of demonstrations and proofs and they were able to exhibit much ingenuity. None the less, those philosophers still fall short of the absolute truth. This is not the proper place to undertake a full account of the demonstrations and arguments which they have expressed in their deep works, but a brief summary is as follows.

Some of the philosophers have claimed the soul pursues perfection and is ever in a state of developing. Every soul which finds itself embodied in a material form necessarily strives to perfect its own nature and to become free from the body. When the soul quits the body at death, if a human character and human nature is uppermost in that soul, it will again attach itself to another human body and resume its pursuit of self-perfection. Whatever qualities it had not yet perfected in its previous form, it continues to strive after in the new body until it passes through various stages and reaches the form of an angel.

However, if the animal nature is predominant at the time of death, the soul becomes clothed in the form of that animal which it most resembled in its former life and thus it will remain until it reaches perfection appropriate to that station.

There are those who believe that the form you return in after death, depends on your works and deeds in this life. Thus, if during the days which the soul spends in the material form of some particular species, the days when the soul is sultan ruling in the palace of the body's four elements, there is but one object which it longs after and that, the acquisition of knowledge of the higher world, and it is fully pre-occupied with praiseworthy pursuits in accord with virtue, envisaging nothing of lower status in its inner eye, sketching no other portrait than the good in the private chambers of its heart, then shall the soul return with a splendid countenance and in its next life be embodied in some higher form.

Another of the wretched beliefs of the Siamese is that whatever a person owns and has striven to acquire should be buried under the idols' feet and when that person returns in the next life, it will still be there ready for him to reclaim.

Refutation of the doctrine of transmigration

Indeed the people of the true religion and the fixed divine law have in no way ever given credence to the doctrine of transmigration. The refutation which the true believers hold forth is this. It is clear that the soul is contingent and its contingency is dependent on the contingency of a body which has the capacity of receiving it. Therefore, whenever a contingent body attains perfection, a soul flows into it from God, the all abounding source, and this process is due to the universality of the creative bounty and its primary prerequisite, contingent body. Thus it follows that if transmigration could take place, a second soul could attach itself to a body and there might be two souls inhabiting and regulating one body. Such a situation is obviously ridiculous. Any sensible person knows that there is not more than one manager of his body.

If transmigration did regularly take place, why does the soul not remember the particulars of what happened in its earlier body? Again, according to the doctrine of transmigration the number of destroyed bodies must always be equal to the number of existing bodies. This simply is not so, for it is evident that there is not now a number of living equal to all those who have died for different reasons in previous ages nor will there be a number born in the coming centuries which will equal them.

Each of the great sages, by way of affirming his own claims and refuting contrary positions, has brought forth in his books convincing arguments and cutting proofs which are not at the disposal of this humble, deficient author. For fear of being prolix I have pulled in the reins of speech and held back my ink-tipped pen from entering into a detailed discourse on the subject but in accord with the saying, 'What is not understood completely is not to be omitted completely', I have given account of their positions and hope this to be all for the best.

While I was face to face with the learned men of Siam I had no need of proofs and arguments. They are so backward and clumsy in their thought that they offer no better argument for their particular way of seeking God than, 'We found our fathers this way in religion and we shall follow them.' When it came to discussing these matters with the Siamese there was no other final remedy but to avoid the whole subject. The Siamese, who are only one of the many peoples who adhere to the foolish doctrines I have described, see themselves as truly religious and despite the clear deficiency of their own beliefs they regard everyone else as infidels. Indeed they expound much confused nonsense concerning all such matters.

The Hindus

Perhaps the best of these peoples is a group of Hindus who make it a point to refrain from all forms of violence and oppression. They are very careful to avoid causing even the slightest disturbance. They refuse to kill any form of life and abstain from eating meat and in order to repress their lusts they practice asceticism continually. But the Siamese themselves are the worst of these peoples and more vain in their meaningless practices than all the rest. In fact they do not adhere to any fixed doctrine but will admit into their creed whatever is convenient. Hence you never see a Siamese follow an honest straight course, no matter what the circumstances may be. He does exactly what he wishes and omits whatever he finds personally unpleasant.

Idolatry and superstition

The Siamese persevere in worshipping idols, burning the dead, eating animals of land and sea, carcass or freshly killed, drink to their fill and debauch themselves in every wicked manner. They are not even like the other idolators who worship one special idol which has a determined shape and form. In Siam anyone who pleases makes an image out of plaster, wood or mud, sets it up in a particular spot and worships it. Nor are they content with idolatry alone but they take every kind of wicked falsity to be their truth. Neglecting the almighty Creator, the Siamese worship everything else in creation: the sun, water, fire, everything from the fabled fish that props up the world to the moon that glides through the heavens. They also believe that certain land and sea animals are gods.

The scholars of Siam exclaim, 'Since we cannot experience direct contact with God in all His glory and perfection, we are obliged to seek Him through substitutes, which we can behold with our own eyes. Therefore we make the idols our masters and gods.' Thus these idolaters argue in favor of their evil practices and just as the divine scriptures have described them, they declare, 'The idols are our intercessors before God and our means of approaching the Lord of lords.'

Some Siamese also maintain that the sun and moon and the stars have a soul and a reasoning mind. There is a small number of true sages who claim a particular kind of soul is to be assigned to the stars and undertake a learned explanation of the subject. However 'Human speculation cannot penetrate to the essence of such matters.'

Divine incarnations

Some Siamese maintain that God manifests Himself in the form of various persons. In fact if one examines this question with the eye of truth it is possible to complete their deficient doctrine with the

THIRD JEWEL 115

fuller statement, 'Though God's full beauty is hidden from our sight, it is partly visible in everything we behold. Praise be to God for the noble and the lofty truths which men have uttered.'

The king himself is considered to be a benevolent god who has entered mortal flesh and since the fiery sun is also held to be a god, the natives have brightened the king's heart by conferring on him the title, 'Brother of the Sun'.

The truth is that none of these peoples believes in the everlasting Lord, the all-powerful, all-seeing Creator but they are devoted to the general process of fate and time. They proclaim: 'Mortals are like the herbs and plants. Man springs up suddenly but just as suddenly he passes out of sight. After a few thousand years two human beings come back into the world, one male and one female and then the whole cycle starts again.'

The Siamese say nothing concerning the final day of judgment or the resurrection. In fact they are all worshippers of the devil. When someone dies, they make a likeness of him and set it up before the other idols and they proceed to worship him along with all the others.

The monks in Siam

In their own language the Siamese call their religious wise men rūlīs, that is, servants of God. These holy men inhabit the temple and pay no attention to the considerations of this world. They have dedicated themselves exclusively to the works and rites of idolatry. They give up the common necessities of life and retain no personal possessions, not even food or clothing. Thus they proceed along the path of vanity with determined steps.

All members of this community renounce marriage and if one of their number is caught neglecting this restriction, they drive his soul forth from the body and hurry it on its way to Hell, just as one drives a false god out of a holy temple. One of the requirements of their religion is that all young men, whether of high or low birth, even the sons of princes, must spend time in the temples attending on the rūlīs, cleaning-up and taking care of the idols.

How a man becomes a monk

During this stage of their general education they are expected to discipline their corporal lusts and acquire the training and better manners which their faith purports to teach. When they have spent the required amount of time striving to attain piety and their own idea of the good, which is sheer nonsense and a waste of valuable time, having reached their highest level of religious development, if animal lusts prove to be dominant in their character, they return to their parents and relatives and attend to their household, farming and arranging a marriage. If such is not the case and the devil finds that some of them have a use for his purposes, he makes them his assistants and helpers. Indeed if the devil discovers the tell-tale signs of devilry in their character, he seduces them with beguiling suggestions and helps them become religious guides and leaders of that nation.

Having brought these men to set up their camp in the desert of moral error, the devil then excludes them from enjoying wordly pursuits and they are forced to renounce all the simple pleasures, as I have mentioned. Day and night they are kept busy within the temple performing prayers, giving sermons and studying the rules of piety.

In brief what they preach is that the wise man should renounce this world with all its false pleasures, indulge in as little sleep as possible, be moderate in his eating habits, never neglect worshipping the idols, never covet other men's wealth and finally, strive in building and maintaining the sacred temples.

Despite the fact that Siam is only a small kingdom it contains more than five thousand temples and as if this was not enough the monks encourage the natives to build new ones. In this manner the monks encourage the people to bury their possessions under the idols' feet, offering what is clearly faulty evidence that such pious acts lead to a great advantage.

The good man who died and returned to life

One of the stories the monks tell is about a man who died and in accord with transmigration returned to life. This man was asked how it was that he had managed to return to the world in such fine circumstances. He answered: 'One day during my previous life I saw some mud which had been thrown on an idol. I washed off the mud and cleaned-up the whole temple, leaving it in good repair. Thanks to that one pious act I have returned to this world in a satisfactory human form.'

On the other hand this same man testified: 'The fellow who was disrespectful and threw the mud on the sacred idol returned to life in the shape of a dog. Indeed such an animal body suited his sinful nature.'

Furthermore, the man who returned as a dog was confronted and asked what had been the cause of his unhappy situation. He was explicit, stating that his present misfortune was a punishment for the contemptible way he had behaved in his previous life. These are the kind of simple tales that currently circulate in Siam.

How the Rūlīs gain their livelihood

The rūlīs do not engage in acquiring the necessities of life such as food and drink but they are given whatever they need by the people. Each day at the break of dawn all the temples ring their wooden gongs and this is the signal for the natives of Siam to rise from sleep and begin preparing their food. Later on I will come back to their food and their manner of eating and present an account of this subject on the plate of my narrative.

Upon waking, the natives set aside a certain amount of their provisions in a special vessel. When dawn has given way to the fulness of day, the servants of the idols come forth from the temple one behind the other, much the same way a string of beasts is led about in a single file. 'Indeed the extent of a people's ignorance is clear from their customs.'

Each rūlī carries several bowls of wood, brass and copper which he holds under his arm. He wears two separate pieces of muslin. One piece is wrapped about his loins and the other is thrown over his back like a cloak. With the end of this same cloak he covers up his various food bowls.

All the monks carry a kind of fan made of woven reeds. This fan has a special shape and is one of the distinctive signs of their vocation. Some of them shade their naked head with a rather modest, simple parasol. They do not wear shoes or a hat and their bodies are clothed in the most meagre way. In contrast to the other Siamese, they shave their head, eyebrows, eyelashes and their somewhat skimpy beard. Dressed in this manner and using their fan to hide their face, which is never to be looked on, they enter into the streets, squares and markets.

Without uttering a word they display their needs to the populace who respond with politeness and respect, placing small amounts of food in the monks' open bowls. Since their religious men have renounced the world and all its finer pleasures whatever foods they have thus acquired, no matter how incompatible, they mix together into one lump before they sit down to eat.

During the space of one day and night they are content to consume a single meal and otherwise they observe complete abstinence. They are capable of reaching the point where they eat very small amounts of food over a period of several days. Thus by diminishing their food and sleep they subject their bodies to ascetic discipline.

The natives of Siam believe that these holy men are guides on the difficult road of error and salvation. It is claimed that without these devoted men all the daily pursuits of the ordinary people would go wrong and end in failure. For this reason the monks deserve a share of everyone's wealth and it is strictly forbidden to borrow or consume anything which has been allotted to this religious group.

The Siamese day of worship

Just as we have Friday for our holy day, the Siamese have a particular day and night of the week which is their day of worship and this day is called Vām Prā. However, their special day does not recur regularly but is the first, seventh, fifteenth and twenty-seventh of their month, a month which is calculated by the ancient system. When the time comes they sit on the floor in the temples and face the idols. In the company of their teachers and religious leaders they recite and worship from evening through to the next day. During this time no one engages in work or pays the least attention to business.

The form of worship in Siam

That evening the king himself goes to his temple and place of worship and he gathers the indigent monks before him. The monk who is deemed the most learned is given a place on the royal throne and in the same way that the people prostrate themselves before the king, the king prostrates himself before this fool of a wise man. The king accords him every form of respect and politeness and whatever the wise man orders, the king accepts and has carried out.

The other monks, who are still engaged in pursuing the absolute of ignorance in their studies and have not yet perfected their perfidious knowledge by the Siamese faith, are not granted admittance to the king's presence but are arranged in rows and seated in their own part of the royal temple.

Throughout that whole day and night the king regales the monks with feasting and bestows gifts upon them in accord with the occasion and his sense of generosity. In no circumstances will the Siamese suspend or postpone the ceremonies of that holy day. They consider this observance to be one of the most important ordinances of their religion. That same day other groups as well carry on the ceremonies in various temples throughout the land.

There are also special occasions when the idols are mounted on traveling palanquins and brought in from the outlying temples to the city temples where the king and monks worship. In such a case the Siamese say that one idol has come to visit another or a certain impoverished monk is visiting one of his religious colleagues. Then the city population gathers together and they play drums and flutes. The devout bring flowers and leaves from the trees and fasten them on to the temple walls to make festoons. They also fashion artificial flowers from paper, which their poor taste considers a splendid decoration.

After the monks are all assembled inside the temple, the natives arrive accompanied by the din of flutes and drums and carrying bowls made of reed or wood. Each person brings as much rice, fruit and yellow muslin as he can afford and bestows these commodities on the monks. The yellow muslin is destined to be made into the monk's clothing. When the people have all arrived, they sit down on the floor in the middle of the temple, men and women together and the women wear neither a veil nor any real clothing.

At this point one of the monks who has just reached the stage of admittance and learned their ceremonial nonsense in the prescribed manner, climbs up into the throne, which is like the throne of a king, and he begins reciting all sorts of ridiculous vanities into the face of the idols. Everyone sits facing this novice. They join their palms together, keeping the fingers spread apart, and in that manner they hold their hands and finger tips poised beneath their forehead. In this pose they follow the sermon of the monks and whenever the name of one of their devils is mentioned they raise their poised hands to their forehead as a sign of respect.

After the preacher has kept his congregation busy for a while, like a group of waiters serving up the nourishment of recitation, though he is by no means sated or finished with the fare, he pauses a moment to catch his breath. In the meantime he gives a sign for his audience to begin eating betel nut and for the entertainment to start.

A group of musicians specially brought together in the temple for the benefit of the worshippers begins to play on the lyre of Cathay. They are not paid with money but perform for the sake of higher rewards. Unfortunately, their instruments are most inharmonious and their melodies range about somewhere outside the realm of recognized scales.

When this discordant nonsense is over, they busy themselves tuning the mouth harp of gibberish, load it full of air and resume their preaching. This goes on until nightfall and even during the night the lanterns blaze brightly as they mumble on. The rūlīs all sit to one side in the temple. When they have heard the preacher's stupidities to the end, they allot him a special name, title and rank.

The poor preacher is fully engrossed in these silly ceremonies all that day and night.

Restrictions on becoming a monk

Since the kingdom of Siam is not of great extent and whoever becomes a monk deserts the peasantry and enters the temple there are not many people who actually work. Therefore, the king has ordained that whoever resides in the temple and wishes to be excused from the responsibilities of everyday life must do several years of study. If the candidate really applies himself to his studies, fine and good, but if this is not the case, if his only purpose is tranquil seclusion and a life of ease, he is not left to such dreaming but is forced back into the ranks of the peasantry. Once his name is inscribed in their registry, the revenue agents exact the taxes from him as from anyone else.

This demanding practice has acted as tax collector in its own right and exacts a high standard of effort and application from the religious students who strive to extremes in their vain pursuits. We entertain the hope that in view of the way the devil aids these heathens to endeavor and persevere, the one, true God will display His pride and by means of His grace support the faithful and pious who are following the pure Imāms and practising virtuous and charitable acts.

The king's personal faith and creed

As for the faith of the Siamese king the situation is not very clear. Outwardly it would appear that he is also cursed with a weakness for idolatry. But every so often he shows interest in the faith of his particular prime minister. This is especially true at the present moment and due to the Christian prime minister many Franks of different nations have come to Siam and they have brought their priests with them.

It is a fact that the Siamese are not at all firm in their own religion but in accord with, 'the people follow the religion of their overlords' Siamese men and women will join whatever religion their employers adhere to. Thus the Iranians who have settled in Siam and begun to raise a family, brought all their household into the fold of Islam. In the same way the Christian community has managed to convert about five to six thousand natives to its faith.

When this fact is brought to the king's attention, he says that he has no interest in the matter and that the people may adhere to whatever religion they wish as long as they remain part of his peasantry. Thus every nation which comes to Siam converts some of the natives to its own religion. What faith the king really holds in his heart, 'God knows best the secrets of His servants.'

Description of the legal system in Siam

Although the Siamese do not really possess an amount of property, money, wealth or power sufficient to warrant the existence of a real legal tribunal or proper law suits, it is their custom to carry out investigations and prosecutions in their law courts but to apply legal terms to that procedure is as meaningless as to call the Siamese generally civilized human beings.

When someone wishes to make a legal complaint he goes before the officials of the secular and religious law. These officials make up a body called the Kurūm Kān, which means those who ascertain the truth. The plaintiff either writes a petition or presents his case verbally. The officials sit before the plaintiff and write out his statements or receive his petition. Then they proceed to question the plaintiff and they write down in his own words everything he has to say. The plaintiff's statements are recorded in a black surfaced notebook with a pen made of chalk. Next the officials summon the defendant and in the same manner they register his responses to the charges.

The following morning the two parties are summoned separately before the court and once again questions and answers are recorded. If the parties involved are wealthy and influential and their case is considered a legal controversy, the court will continue its proceedings in this manner indefinitely. The natives call this process Kawām.

All along the court exacts its fees for the investigation and these costs are levied each day before the formal questioning begins. Thus the whole procedure continues until one of the parties satisfies the officials with his testimony or is incapable of meeting the expenses.

When the formal interrogation ends the register of statements is brought forth and the officials compare the testimony given by the two sides since the first day of the case. If the investigators come upon a place in the records where one of the parties has said something inconsistent, has mixed up the sums of money in question or the dates of certain events, they conclude that he has been lying all along. The court declares, 'You are lying and your claims have no substance to them. This is clear from the conflicting evidence in your statements. Your testimony, as we have recorded it, shows disagreement.'

If the two parties involved have great power, then the controversy is handled in the following manner. All during the lifetime of the two rivals the interrogation continues and the legal dispute is never actually resolved. The recorded testimony of the two sides is never brought forth for a final examination and after a while the court sessions are only held on certain days when no one is busy. All that time the court goes on exacting its legal fees and eventually the parties of the dispute have nothing left but the empty words of their argument.

The Siamese look upon defeat in a legal suit as a serious stain on their character and the source of great shame. Both sides hold out as long as possible and being very stubborn in their anger, they refuse to stop and compare their testimony. They put off the final reckoning of the evidence and are incredibly slow at furnishing the details of the case.

The result is that a law suit becomes interminable and the truth and deceit of the case is never quickly brought to light. They will even go to the point of selling or pawning themselves, their wife and their children, if they have no other way of maintaining the costs of their court case. Indeed this practice is a regular occurrence in Siam and the other countries of Below the Winds.

The public hearings are run in accord with the same principles. When the king's natural disposition is stirred up in anger against one of the ministers or high officials, an order is given for the court to start interrogating that unlucky individual. The poor soul might just as well wash his hands of all he owns, including his life. The moment he is arraigned he is finished.

Once the king's favor has deserted a man and that man is called to give an account of his behavior and his property, the court does not seek to establish the validity of a specific plaintiff's claims. Anyone in Siam, whether a truthful claimant or an out and out back-biter, may charge the defendant and expect the case to be formally received. Everyone in the country, the good along with the bad, appears in court and opens the register of testimony. The Kurūm Kān record the statements and collect fees from both sides.

Normally the pitiful defendant is kept bound in chains unless he can afford to pay a bribe. But if the plaintiff puts up a bribe the guards will tighten the chains about the victim until he is forced to yield and breaks down crying, 'Yes, what the plaintiff says is true; I have been lying all the time.'

Even then the case is not finished and the defendant's only hope is to regain the favor of the king. There are several lawsuits which have been going on since the time of the present king's grandparents and still no settlement has been reached. Every few years or so the proceedings are renewed and further testimony is recorded in the court register.

The case of an Iranian merchant

One of the several lawsuits which arose before the wicked tribunal of Siam while we humble servants were present is as follows. It is mentioned as a strange case, not totally devoid of interest. There was a man from Iran, who could not succeed at home and to make up for his past bad luck had come to India to seek his fortune. He was also in the habit of visiting Siam and not long ago he was residing in that country, carrying on his business and trade.

The merchant falls asleep[18]

One night the thief, Sleep, with the help of a twisting lasso of mist, climbed into the hanging balcony of the palace of the good man's mind. The invisible intruder slipped down an inner passageway, eluding the guardian outer senses and crept into the innermost chamber where the heart takes its repose, the very center of the body's basic humors. With the art of a practiced pickpocket he eased open the purse of the gentleman's conscious wit and lightly plucked forth the coins of wakefulness.

A servant enters and steals the merchant's life savings

Just then the gentleman's servant came home and found his master fast asleep, propped up in the throne of careless neglect. Trusting to a slave's black luck and giving into the lusts of the moment, the servant as bold as the hour of death snatched the purse of the poor man's life savings. One by one he extracted the tawdry coins which the merchant had received for the priceless goods of his daily existence.

The merchant wakes up

But when the night watch of the intelligence had finished its tour through the market place of the body, the merchant, Thought, opened up the shop of the wakeful state. The good man rose to find his purse like the soul of the pure at heart, bare and empty of the evil influence of money.

9

The grief-struck merchant suspects his servant

Never before had his business schemes with the merchants of chance ended in such a complete and sudden failure. He was on the verge of closing up the shop of his life and emptying out the merchandise of his very soul. He wandered about in a daze, turning now one way, now another, until the inspector, Imagination, together with the officers of his reason, picked up the tracks of the disloyal servant.

The gentleman's threats

The master summoned the slave before him. He maimed him with threats of punishment. He tortured him with the violence of recalling their former friendship. Finally, after the master's prolonged fits of hot and cold abuse, the servant found himself on the rack, pinned fast with the four spikes of the investigation.

The gentleman's friendly appeal

In excitement the gentleman swore oaths, citing all the instances of his past generosity, the pinch of salt for the servant's broth, the sliver of old cheese that accompanied his bread and thus the servant was gradually drawn into the chains of a confession. All along the slave sensed that behind the blazing furnace of his master's anger there was a glimmer of indulgence. The iron heart of the stone-natured slave began to melt and he confessed to having stolen the missing cash.

The innocent blacksmith

But his story was that he had handed over the money to a certain blacksmith. Now the Iranian merchant did not have the power to deal with the smith directly and so he presented his case to the Kurūm Kān of the port. These Siamese authorities summoned both parties before their tribunal.

The authorities torture the blacksmith

The slave repeated his confession in public but the poor blacksmith naturally denied having anything to do with the matter and, as is the custom, they took to torturing the blacksmith. Although this lost soul could not understand a scrap of what was happening, confused and frightened, he was quick to confess to all the charges.

Only when the judges saw that he could not lead them to the money, did they realize that he was not the actual thief.

They torture the servant

At this point they released the blacksmith and turned to torturing the slave. After the slave had experienced a sample of their torture, he abandoned his lies and adopted a policy of honest truth. He admitted that the blacksmith was not to blame, that the blacksmith had been falsely accused. In the end this snake-like slave uncoiled his secrets and informed them of a ruin where he had hidden the stolen money.

The money is recovered

The whole assembly proceeded to the spot indicated and sure enough they recovered the money, which was a sum totalling thirty-two tūmāns. However, when the attendants brought forth all this money, it seemed to glitter with an irresistible sheen in the eyes of the officials. They had recourse to the practice of their religion, a practice which they call tan mīm.

The merchant pays a fine

A religious decree was issued, stating that since the slave had given false testimony against a native and the merchant had consented to having the slave tortured, whatever the court extracted from the slave would revert to the estates of the king, who is related to the idols. But in this case, since the slave owned nothing himself, the master was obliged to pay a fine, which it just so happened amounted to the recovered sum of money.

The merchant pays the court fees and loses his slave

In addition to that the court claimed three tūmāns, 2,400 dinars for the general costs, taxes, rights of the tribunal and fees of the officials and attendants. This is the way the Siamese uphold the law and after going through much trouble the merchant was forced to pay every bit of the above-mentioned sum and his slave was confiscated for the king's estates.

The law has become corrupt

This event took place during the office of the Frank minister, whereas previously such corrupt proceedings were unheard of. Legal matters

which concerned the foreigners living in Shahr Nāv were well looked
after by Āqā Muḥammad. Each foreign group was under the jurisdic-
tion of its own religious and secular judges and that way everyone
felt he was treated in accord with his own customs and beliefs It
is true that the very same law still stands but unfortunately it is no
longer put into practice.

The trial by fire

When the Siamese are unable to establish the facts of a lawsuit
through the usual procedure of interrogation, they have recourse
to their own strange form of swearing oaths. There are two different
oaths which they can administer, one involves fire and the other,
water. If the two contending parties are at a loss to produce conclusive
evidence by any other means, they agree to test the honesty of their
former statements by placing their foot on the path of the first kind
of oath.

The officials mark off an area of specified dimensions in front of
one of the temples and there they pile up a good amount of wood and
start a fire. Each of the parties takes an oath swearing that his own
story is the truth and then they put their sincerity to the test. But
first the authorities examine the foundation of the whole case and
take a close look at the feet which bore evidence in the courtroom.

When it is clearly established that these feet are clean and pure and
have not been tainted in any way, the rivals are ordered to walk
barefoot through the burning coals. Whichever one of the contestants
has been sure-footed all along and spoken the truth in the court,
passes over the fire like a light, morning breeze and thus the burning
flames verify his testimony by the weakness of their tongue.

But the party who has greased his feet with the fat of lies and
hypocrisy suffers in the fire and his feet are caught in the lasso of the
flames. He is unable to pass through the fire and as his feet burn
and recoil in pain the lawsuit drops from his hands. He has lost the
case.

The king's justification of the trial by fire

The king of Siam, contrary to the other rulers of Below the Winds,
has made a great effort to find out about the history and culture of
previous ages. He has ordered that the jewelers of the bazaar of
imagination and the bankers of the market of artful speech string the
gems of world literature on the necklace of the language of Siam.
However, since the Siamese men of letters compose with clumsy
verse and prose and are never able to produce works worthy of the

king's praise, Sayyid Dardmandī, who is from Khurāsān and not wholly lacking in perfection of style, was commissioned to present a written summary of the Shāhnāma.[19] It goes without saying that this masterpiece, which is more pleasing to the society of perfected hearts[20] than a hundred clear-sounding lyres, was well suited to the nature of the noble king and more than worthy to be published before the natives of that distant corner.

Thus the above-mentioned writer undertook the great task of translation and in the course of his recital they reached the spot where the hero, Sīāvakhsh,[21] is falsely accused and to prove his innocence has recourse to the test by fire. Sīāvakhsh is pure of heart and shoots through the burning fire like a bolt of lightning and comes forth unscathed.

Here the king of Siam remarked, 'This is indeed a book of great repute among you and the passage which we have just heard proves the validity of the trial by fire. Why have you declared that such practices are improper?'

But the Sayyid who was present produced examples and proofs more dazzling than the sun and swifter to the mark than the fire's jumping flames. I am humbly omitting a full account of his obvious replies for fear of being tedious.

The trial by water

When the two parties of a lawsuit cannot settle their case one way or the other and the particular lawsuit is not considered very serious, they have recourse to the oath of water. They carry out this test in the big river which flows through Siam, at a spot where the water is only a few hand spans deep. Both the plaintiff and the defendant are required to dunk their heads under the water at the same time and hold their breath as long as possible.

The man who has been truthful in his testimony is calm and remains under water as long as he can but the liar immediately becomes upset and cannot control the head of his lawsuit. The falsehood of his testimony rises up through the water like a hollow bubble and bursts. His case is lost.

This test is really more effective than it sounds because the Siamese claim that whenever they put their heads under water they see all sorts of frightening things. Since there are no hammāms in Siam, the common practice is for the men as well as the women to wash themselves in the river every day, but it may be observed that during their whole lifetime they will never once put their head under the water. They consider such an act to be a grave sin.

A Siamese wake

Now that the author has given an account of the Siamese legal system it is fit and proper if he moves on to a description of their wakes and cheerful holidays. In Siam song and music go with mourning and mournful wailing pervades the festive occasions. Therefore, following their practice of reversal, I will present first what is best put off till the end.

When someone dies the corpse is kept in the house as long as possible and set upright, as if sitting on its toes. The palms of the deceased are bound together and tied to his forehead with a rope. Then the corpse is seated on a large metal tray, a tray made of gold if the deceased was a prince or a rich man, or one made of silver or lesser metals, depending on the importance of his family. So he sits and is looked after in the middle of the household and every day friends and relatives gather there.

The rūlīs come from the temples and install themselves in the sad house where they recite their assorted bits of sermons and aphorisms. When the rūlīs are finished reciting, the relatives award them assortments of rice and fruit and quantities of yellow muslin and then send them off. But during all these proceedings there is absolutely no loud wailing or shedding of tears. No one seems the least disturbed. In fact everyone is having the finest time, making his heart merry. Musical instruments are brought in and the musicians play away all day long. Members of the family carry on in this manner as long as the wake lasts and give out charitable gifts in accord with their status and the extent of their wealth. There is certainly no haste to pack up the dead body and get on with the funeral. In fact if these ceremonies are not sufficiently drawn out, it is considered an insult to the deceased and a cause of reproach for the family. A short wake is taken to mean that the relatives lack wealth and substance and are not able to afford elaborate entertainment. Some families maintain these celebrations for a whole year, others six months, some one month, others only ten or five days.

The cremation

Next, all the paraphernalia for the cremation is assembled in front of the family's own temple. Friends and relatives provide caskets, artfully carved wood, paper flowers and gold-plated thrones. In the middle of the temple square they set up a pavilion, magnificent in its dignity. It is covered with wood and reeds and all the supporting poles are decorated with colored paper. When all these arrangements

have been made and the materials necessary for a bonfire and fireworks have been provided, the corpse, still sitting on its tray which I
have described, is removed from the house on to a traveling litter,
where it is tied firmly to its seat.

The children of the deceased mount horses, the boys as well as the
girls, and the girls do not wear veils or conceal themselves with proper
modesty. The chain of the procession is clasped about the children's
neck and they lead the way to the temple. The relatives follow from
behind, each linked to the procession in accord with his status in the
family, for such is the practice in this transient world. The rūlīs
followed next, some in litters and some on foot. They open their holy
books and recite as they march along.

To show that this day is no ordinary day the relatives shave their
heads and if this were a funeral of one of their kings the whole nation
would observe this practice. When they arrive at the appointed spot
before the temple, they set up a throne and place the corpse on this
seat of honor. For several days and nights they remain there, lighting
small fires and setting off fireworks. Meanwhile music is played
and the immediate relatives indulge their generosity by giving gifts
to the rūlīs.

It is the customary practice that the different relatives, close
or removed, lend assistance to the immediate family which is conducting the ceremonies. Every day all the relatives send whatever
they can afford as contributions. After spending a few days like
this in the temple, on the appointed date they set fire to the sumptuous
pavilion. The litter, the caskets and flowers are all burned up, along
with the corpse which is still sitting on its precious tray.

When the bonfire is lit the rūlīs and all the relatives of the deceased
sit before the flames, reciting from their holy books. The smoking
stench perfumes their filth-exhaling lungs. When the cremation is
over, the children of the dead man go before the rūlīs who bless them
with the saying, 'Carry on your father's memory, as you now carry
about his smell.'

After the cremation they throw the man's ashes to the wind, water
and air and fashion a statue from the funerary tray. This likeness of
the deceased is placed inside the temple where it receives the family's
veneration.

The false justification of cremation

The Siamese justify practising cremation by pointing out that man is
composed of the four basic elements and once he dies the components
of his body should return to their source in nature. This final debt

is an obligation to be filled by the dead man's friends. Since fire only burns that part of the body which is its due inheritance and fire is not greedy in this matter, they have honored fire above the other elements and give its claims precedence.

The scholars of history have recorded in their works that when one of the children of Khazar ibn Yāfuth ibn Nūḥ[22] passed away, Khazar did not know what to do with the body. Since his own father had been drowned at sea, along with other relatives, Khazar decided to vent his anger on the element of water and ordered all his people to assemble around a great fire. Lutes and other musical instruments were playing away wildly and as Khazar sang out with a booming voice, he consigned his son's body to the flames. And this reproachful practice is still carried on by certain backward peoples.

Even more strange than cremation is the Siamese custom of fashioning a likeness of the dead man and placing it among the idols. Once the new statue is admitted to the temple the natives prostrate themselves and worship it in the same way as they worship their other idols.

Sorrow always follows after good cheer

Thus we have visited their cheerful funeral but there is an old custom that whoever attends a party goes on as well to a sorrowful wake. Hence if I present an account of their festive celebrations, which are meant to be light and gay but are sheer mourning and lamentation, I will have honored a traditional practice.

Siamese festivities, marriage

The celebrations of the Siamese have no fixed form or protocol. For example, they have no clear idea of a marriage contract, wedding ceremonies, or what is sanctioned and what is forbidden by the universal laws of religion.

One of the ways the despicable people of Siam differ from the Hindus in these matters is that a Hindu will not court a girl or even think of marrying her unless she is at least seven degrees removed in kinship. The Siamese, however, regularly arrange marriages with their closest blood relations. A father will marry his daughter, his sister or his niece and indeed no one indulges in these incestuous practices more than the kings.

The royal family feels that its most important duty is to maintain the purity of its blood and therefore avoids contracting a marriage with anyone outside its own caste. The present king, who is the most sly of all these people, has a daughter by his sister and he is now offering her in marriage to his brother.

The way the Siamese generally arrange a marriage is through their parents. The parents sit down and have a friendly discussion but do not go into the expenses of the wedding clothes and the entertainment or ask whether the girl has a house, furnishings, money, chattel and jewelry. On the contrary it is all very simple. Once the mother and father say they are satisfied with the bridegroom the marriage takes place and from then on the couple live together.

The way a young couple may elope

However, if the parents do not consent to the marriage but the man and woman are agreed among themselves, the young couple adopt the following plan. The girl arranges a certain day or night when the lover is supposed to come to the house armed. He breaks in and carries off the girl in the direction of his own house. The girl shouts and screams for help to give the appearance of propriety but off she goes quickly enough.

The mother and father and all the other relatives of the girl are obliged to follow after the young pair and, if they are able to arrive soon enough, they begin fighting to recover their daughter. But if the rescue party is late, the bolt of war will have been spent. What has been entered has been entered already and for their part the parents give up beseiging the young man's house.

The young women of Siam have no other dowry than their own nakedness. The trousseau they bring to their new husband is their total lack of means. Moreover, the men are content with a pretty face and do not search to find a deeper spirit underneath the skin. No one thinks to himself that marriage is a question of family honor and so they take their women from any nation or religion and show no qualms.

The practice of pawning human beings

Here it may be mentioned that pawning men or women is one of the most common practices in Siam. For a certain sum the Siamese will pawn themselves or their sons and daughters. An attractive girl will go for ten to fifteen thousand dinars. Whoever is doing the pawning keeps the money as long as he wants, one day or ten years, and when he has attained his end with that capital and regained his dignity, he pays back the loan in full. No interest has been subtracted in advance. Thus he frees the pawnbroker from the binding agreement and recovers the person who was the pledge.

It is a lamentable fact that Siamese parents are like wild animals and feel no close ties with their children. Even if they have several sons, which makes their life easier, they show no signs of humanity and do not raise their children with affection.

It is also common for men to pawn themselves and while they cannot pay back the loan, they work for the pawnee as if they were his slave. Only when they have paid back the borrowed money in full are they free from their servitude. Otherwise they may remain in their master's chains until the true Proprietor, God, claims the cash of their existence and forecloses on the loan of their life.

Even after such a bankruptcy the wretched obligation still stands and the deceased's children are obliged to work for their father's creditor if they cannot pay off the debt immediately. This is the way the Siamese accumulate capital to enter business and carry on trade. Their commerce is based on the unfair advantages that this system accords certain individuals.

The purpose of giving an account of these practices is to show how the people of error are caught prisoner in the nets of their own ignorance. This world with all its far-flung, inhabited regions is full to the brim with men who violate the laws of God. They will be excluded from the joys of the after life just as they suffer and choke in the squalor of the transient world. The possessors of the true religion and the lords of wealth and security, who sit upon the couch of leisure and amass the riches of this world along with the promises of the resurrection, when confronted with the facts of the affairs of the heathen nations, will be quick to strive with a more profound sense of thanksgiving for all the mercy and wondrous bounties which our almighty Creator has bestowed upon them.

The scapegoat

One of the more curious Siamese festivities takes place on a day which the wisemen and scholars designate as a day of special astrological significance. The astrologers claim that when the stars and planets move into certain positions, the horoscope of the king and the other inhabitants of Siam indicates the advent of grim events. Before any calamity actually befalls the land it is necessary to take the proper precautions.

Therefore, they elect a person who is like our Mīr-i-Nau Rūz[23] and he is made king for the day. They sit him on the baseless throne of his momentary sultanate and accord their verbal obedience to the power of his command. The real king does not come outdoors but folds up his foot under his skirts and sits all day in seclusion.

The whole population of the city gathers about the temporary king and pledges him loyalty and obedience. Then certain traditional festivities and celebrations follow during which everyone gives himself over to banqueting with the utmost spirit. Towards afternoon the king-for-a-day is escorted out of the city with great pomp. All of the city's populace follows, some accompanying the king in litters, some riding on elephants, and others in boats.

When the procession arrives at a certain spot, they dismount and proceed on foot to a specially prepared temple. There they fall to their knees and worship before the idols, beseeching the lifeless statues to make that day's ceremonies a success. After the prayers they gather together in an assembly and set up a mock court where their king metes out meaningless punishments and rewards. Towards the end of these proceedings the order is given to pillage and destroy certain rice paddies which are near the temple.

Finally, when they have engaged in various other antics, the king-for-a-day heads back to the city along with his crowd of followers. However, just outside the city the multitude is met by a large force of the real king's troops. The two factions face each other and begin to shout and hurl their loud threats back and forth. Now evening is approaching and the sun begins to sink from the zenith of its glory and in a like manner the fortunes of the make-believe king begin to sink. His lucky star crosses the path of the planet of failure and obscurity and suddenly his prospering name is eclipsed. Perceiving his situation he takes to flight and the victory of the day rests with the real king.

The small amount of expenses and damages which occur that day are met by the generous bounty of the king, who orders his administration to pay out compensations. These costs are considered slight in face of preserving the prosperity of the kingdom. The Siamese call the temporary king, Rīdnūk, which means king of the forest. As incredible as it may seem, these are the senseless rites which certain lost heathens perform. 'Woe unto him whom the infamous idolator, Nimrud,[24] would call an infidel.'

Spring, the boating festival

Another one of their festivities comes after the rainy season. When the sign of Leo first rises to prominence heavy rains begin to fall in Siam. Several great rivers which flow from Khiṭā pass through

Shahr Nāv to join up with the sea but, due to the high tides during that season, the sea flows inland and blocks the river's course. All the excess water is forced back into the region of the city.

The continuous rains only add to the growing flood. Because the atmosphere is humid and the rainfall excessive, mountain streams are created which rush down into the valleys and the open fields. But the land of that region is already saturated with water and cannot absorb any more. The result is that everything becomes completely inundated and large boats ply up and down the city streets and squares. Even large seagoing vessels are able to enter the city. Just to visit a neighbor you must book passage on a great ship.

The situation remains like that until the beginning of Sagittarius. Then strong cold winds blow down from the direction of China, which is north of Siam, and the tides begin to diminish. In a short time all the waters are flowing towards the sea. The land is slowly drained off and rich juicy plants spring up everywhere.

When the season of floods drowns and is washed away by the ebbing tides, it is the custom that all inhabitants high or low born, men and women, the latter without their veils or any modesty, board boats and go for pleasure cruises on the river. They also take strolls through the fields and gardens for amusement and all along the way gather up fruit from the beautiful orange and lemon trees which grow in Siam. Carrying the fruit with them they board their well-made boats and race each other as if riding on fine-stepping, wind-swift horses and during the races they fling oranges at one another.

At that time as well the king and his ministers and close attendants board their boats of state and cruise about taking in the sights. The king rides in a well-outfitted boat, which is gold-plated and of the finest construction imaginable. His boat is preceded and followed by other fine boats which are his reserve parade horses.

On this occasion the ministers and councilors also race each other in their boats and two referees are especially chosen from among the king's servants and are stationed in boats at both ends of the racing course. They record whichever boats win and present the king with an account of the crews and the owners. The king is the starting point and the goal and in the end he decides who is given preferment and who will win prizes.

All in all the king has about a hundred boats of his own. Crews of fifty, sixty or seventy men drive a boat along by means of oars. Indeed this holiday was a magnificent sight but due to the base character of the Iranians and the low manner of conduct which they displayed to the women who were present the order was given for the delightful celebrations to stop.

Devil worshippers

There is another rather strange festivity which is indulged in by certain of the inhabitants of Siam, who are indeed notorious for their debauchery. With the help of God the following description of their scandalous practices will be ample proof of how this particular sect worships the devil and they make no effort to conceal this fact.

At certain times of the year the devotees assemble in a temple and slaughter a pig in a way which accords with their foolish rituals. Then they bring forth a woman who claims she contains the devil inside her stomach. She rises before the gathering and begins to dance and spin about. Eventually she passes into a trance and if anyone questions her she will make predictions about the future.

On rare occasions she declares that the devil wants to leave her and now desires to enter a certain other young girl. They summon the new girl to their assembly and both the woman and the girl get up and dance about. Soon both of them enter into a trance. After an hour or so the woman who was the devil's mistress changes and is no longer able to utter a single word. Now the young girl assumes the woman's former qualities and is able to give prophecies in the same manner.

This is the extent to which the devil and the pagan co-operate. However, the truth of these events and what really does take place was not made clear to this humble author. 'Knowledge of such matters rests with God, who sees all and knows all.'

The dance of the Macassars

Another festivity which is worth mentioning is the dancing of the men of Java and Macassar. The Macassars are from a separate country which lies near Siam and has its own king and they are all Shāfiʿī Muslims. Despite the fact that they live in Siam they still preserve their own way of life and in general this is the case with all the foreign nations that have settled in Siam. These Macassars had their own neighborhood in Shahr Nāv and there they lived and followed the creed of their own religion.

For instance, it is their custom that both the men and women always carry weapons with them. They walk about with daggers fixed to their lungī, which is a tunic they wear to cover their private parts and they do not even put aside their weapons when they go to bed at night. When they have a party, male or female musicians play wild music and arouse the men who take up sharp daggers in their hand. The Macassars call their dagger a krīs and it has an excellently wrought serpentine blade. In the manufacture of such daggers they are great craftsmen and they are known to temper the blade by dipping it in poison.

In general the science of mantras, spells and incantations is practised to a great extent in Siam but no one surpasses these Macassars who have put a special spell on their daggers. If someone tries to stab a man with the man's own dagger, the blade has no force. Another effect of their spells is that while the dagger is in the possession of the owner, no thief or enemy is able to overcome him and if a stranger steals the dagger he only brings harm to himself.

The Macassars employ these same daggers in their dances and when they swirl about in ecstasy they stab at each other and make such vigorous thrusts that anyone witnessing this performance for the first time would believe that they are really wounding each other. In the realm of entertainments there is absolutely nothing which can compare to these dances for intensity and fierceness.

The Macassar revolt

It so happened that while we humble servants were present in Siam certain brave exploits were perpetrated by these Macassars. Having beheld these events with our own eyes we feel justified in presenting the following brief description in our narrative.

A while back one of the Macassar princes who had trouble in his own kingdom, decided to come to Siam with a group of his men. They settled down in Shahr Nāv and the Siamese king accorded them the various courtesies customary in that country. However, when for some reason or other the king left the city the Macassar prince, finding the arena empty, came to entertain the idea of capturing the city for himself.

He called his men together to inform them of his intentions and indeed, with the king away, the city was without sufficient protection. His plan was to set fire to the houses of the natives and while they were busy trying to save their property, he and his men would proceed to the king's residence and take possession of the throne.

The attitude in Siam is that even though the king himself may still be free and have his army intact, if his house and throne are captured, the buttress and mainstay of his power is considered destroyed.

When the prince and his men had agreed to this undertaking among themselves, they sent a letter to other Macassars who were living near by and solicited their support but it so happened that three of those people were dissatisfied with the whole affair and they took the letter before the Siamese king. Thus the plot in all its details was exposed. However, the king reflected on the situation and felt that there was still some doubt. It was always possible that the evidence was not genuine but forged. He decided to postpone condemning the accused rebels until he could investigate the whole affair more thoroughly. The king had a letter sent to the Macassar prince ordering him to come before the royal presence at once to explain this matter and answer to the alleged charges. The prince realized the difficulty of his position. He was stuck in Shahr Nāv with no chance of retreating, had no army to speak of, a mere three or four hundred men and did not even have a definite plan of action and the king was only five or six farsakhs away. Despite these unfavorable circumstances he showed no signs of fear but was bold enough to send back the following answer.

'With respect to appearing before you I must state that I have no trust in your Majesty, for at the present moment the prime minister is a Frank and a state of mutual hatred based on religious differences exists between him and me. I have no knowledge of any conspiracy but if you suspect me of such intentions, it is clear that your treacherous minister has planted the idea in your head. I know that he bears a grudge against me and that you hold him in great esteem. If I present myself before your court, he will denounce me with false accusations and you will accept whatever he says. So far you have made no errors meting out punishments and bestowing pardons. Do not begin practising tyranny now.

However, being convinced that you intend to kill me and calling to mind the saying, "In time of mortal danger when no hope remains, a man will pit his hand against a sword, insensible to pain," I am prepared to fight to the end nor will I surrender like a fool and give myself and my men over to death until I have shed some blood in compensation.'

This bold reply was sent to the king and the vile Christian minister had no difficulty fanning the flames of the king's anger. The Siamese troops were assembled and in all about three or four thousand men were sent against the rebels. The Macassars understood their plight. They proceeded to burn all their possessions and even kill some of their women and children. Then they sat down with determination and waited for the hour of their death.

However, despite the fact that the Macassars were few in number and cut off from any allies, the Siamese lacked the daring to attack. They were afraid and rendered helpless by the cowardly suggestions of their imagination. Thus for several days they remained in confusion as to what course they should pursue. They simply sat where they were surrounding the small group of Macassars.

This state of affairs continued until the king arrived with the Frank minister. Then a hugh mass of Siamese along with many Franks boarded boats which carried several cannons on the deck. They easily managed to sail round to a point opposite the Macassar's homes and blew the houses to pieces with heavy cannon fire. Thinking that the rebels had all been killed, the Siamese were content and felt the danger was over.

However, earlier on the Macassars had evacuated their quarter of the city and moved into an open stretch of farm land where they dug graves and hid themselves. There in the graves they led the life of ghosts. After the useless bombardment the king's troops landed and approached the ruined houses but just then the Macassars fearlessly rushed upon them with daggers in hand and managed to kill large numbers of Franks and Siamese.

The rebels aimed their attack in the direction of the Frank minister and came close to ridding the Siamese of his evil influence but fate did not lend them assistance. The incompetent minister, born under a star of evil, was quick to flee. Just before the Macassars could reach him, he jumped into the water and escaped the flames of destruction. Thus, although the Macassars were only a small group, it seemed impossible for the Siamese to overcome the heat of such fierce resistance.

In the end, however, the Macassars fell into despondency. Since their prince, who had stayed behind in his house during the bombardment, was dead and their food supply was cut off, the remaining men realized that it was futile to continue. They threw down their daggers and tied up their hands, calling the Siamese to come and finish them off. And, indeed, when the Siamese arrived they slaughtered every last one of these brave Macassars.

One of the rebels, who was shot and had a broken leg, hid among the dead bodies. When an important Frank attendant took a stroll to see the remains of the massacre and happened to walk near him, the wounded man suddenly rolled over and stabbed the Frank. I have been bold to include a description of this uprising in order to illustrate the lack of internal organization and the extent of weakness which pervades the government of Siam.

The life and daily routine of the king

As was mentioned earlier, the rulers and governors of Below the Winds have no real majesty and power and they do not maintain a grand entourage or a professional army. What they call an army is really only a mob of peasants assembled in times of danger. The population at large is divided into small groups which are represented by a minister and each minister has his own corps of officers. The ordinary people are forced to work like slaves for the king's administration and they receive no pay for their time and labor nor are they able to raise the least complaint or refuse to serve. Only when the administration has no need of them are the natives free to pursue their livelihood, but the population is small and there is so much work to be done that the Siamese men would never be able to do everything just by themselves.

For that reason it is common for women to engage in buying and selling in the markets and even to undertake physical labor, and they do not wear veils or cover themselves with modesty. Thus you can see the women paddling to the surrounding villages where they successfully earn their daily bread with no assistance from the men.

In the past there were absolutely no craftsmen in Siam but recently a few people from outlying regions have come and established themselves in the city and they now produce some of the basic commodities. But there is a dearth of skilled workmen and for this reason it is not common to come across many fine buildings or other elaborate constructions. In fact all the houses in Siam are simple and are made of reeds and wood. Only the king's estates have been planned with any degree of care and skill.

The king's estates include temples built of wood and brick as well as private houses which were actually constructed by the Iranians. The latter buildings are not lacking in taste and beauty but the Siamese go so far as to think these works rival the palace of Khavarnaq or the achievements of Chosroes.[25] The interior of the king's apartments are painted with vermilion and red clay and the roof, which is made of wood, has been plated with sheets of tin and gold. These buildings are the king's actual living quarters.

The king's daily routine

Considering himself an upstanding idolator and a god in his own right, the king lives a life of the strictest devotion. His nights and days are divided into fixed parts and he never deviates from his schedule. He sleeps no more than five hours, but contrary to good sense he takes his sleep at precisely the wrong time of night, from before dawn until two hours after sunrise.

As soon as the king wakes up, he washes and changes his clothes. Then he goes to the temple and prostrates himself before the idols

10

and the carved images of his relatives, living and dead. After morning prayers the king leaves the temple and proceeds to a special room where he receives several learned doctors.

The doctors are from many different lands, men of China, Siam, India and one is even from Gīlān. Each doctor sees the king separately. First the doctor presents himself and pays his respects before the throne, praising the king and uttering a series of benedictions. Then the doctor conducts a routine examination after which he administers whatever medicines or special nourishments the king might need.

When these consultations are over the king proceeds to yet another private chamber where he receives the palace superintendent, the chief scribe and two or three of the higher ministers. During this interview the king asks whether these officials have any matters of importance to bring to his attention and likewise, if the king requires any of their immediate services, he issues them orders and sends them about their business.

Next the king goes to the main throne room and there he opens a general session in his court. Members of every important group or faction of the state who hold the rank of fū, that is, who have access to the king's person, now enter the hall of the royal court. The interviews which take place, follow in order of the ranks of the participating officials.

Each dignitary prostrates himself at the foot of the throne and there on the ground he spends an hour or so groveling before the king. These pretentious court ceremonies merely consist in the king bestowing his affection on the loyal functionaries and there is no clearer indication of the royal affection than when the king calls out the name of each member of the court, employing the specially awarded titles which go with the various offices. The following is a list of the more important titles which are current at the Siamese court.

A list of the Siamese ranks and titles

The lowest rank in any office is akūn and then in ascending order come the titles umunk, ulunk, ūprā, then ūyā and chawpīā but the highest of all is the title chakrī. These titles correspond to prime minister, general, khān, minister, sultān, mīn bāshī,[26] yūz bāshī and dah bāshī.

If a man rises to be prime minister he may hold any one of several titles such as ūprā, chawpīā, barkalān, ūyā or chakrī. These titles do not indicate a particular office. Any office which requires the official to come into the king's presence will bear one of those titles. Thus the title of a minister and that of a bodyguard are both ūprā. Even the king's elephant keeper holds the rank of ūprā. The head steward of the palace and members of the police corps as well as the mayor of the city all hold the rank of ūyāvang. Then there is the harbor master and he bears the title ūprātan tabūrī saimhā ṣabūt which means 'highest khān on the great sea of God'.

However, the various posts of the king's administration do not carry with them very much prestige, income or power. The revenues which come into the prime minister's coffers each year do not exceed two or three hundred tūmāns and this is due to the fact that the king simply does not have much property or money.

The wretched Siamese nobles have been forced to roll up their sleeves in poverty and reveal their nakedness. They are not even accorded the honor of a decent pair of shoes, much less the kind of income which normally accompanies good breeding. They have learned to be content with the revenues of poverty and do not complain about their state of destitution. There is really only one sign of magnificence which the Siamese hold to be of supreme importance.

When a man or woman goes for a stroll, if the person's rank is high, a retinue of one or two hundred attendants drawn from the peasantry will follow along. The attendants are generally people who have pawned themselves or whose parents sold them when they were young. It is also possible that they were originally part of the king's peasantry and that the king bestowed them upon a particular noble. These humble servants without hat or shoes follow after their master like a train of obedient camels. The number of a man's attendants is his surest guarantee of distinction.

When the Siamese king heard that in India the Iranians received certain titles along with their posts, he though he would be generous and he added a handful of Indian titles to the ones he had already bestowed upon his Iranian attendants. But there are really no posts in Siam which deserve any esteem or distinction and all such titles are empty and meaningless.

The case of an Iranian who was awarded a Siamese title

Of all the Iranians who have been accorded posts and titles at the Siamese court, it is perhaps worth mentioning the case of a poor soul from Shīrāz who previously had been a traveling business man.

After many years of buying and selling he was dissatisfied with his lot and decided he would try to double his fortune over night.

The merchant gathered all the material wealth which he had earned by bartering and exchanging the years of his youth in the market place of life and he risked the whole amount in one big transaction with the agents of Chance and Fortune. He set his cash down on the world's board of events and day and night he threw the dice of conniving and deceit but the sly old competitor, Destiny, matched every move.

The wretched Iranian was stunned and confused by the unscheduled arrival of Calamity, the express messenger who rides the interchangeable ponies, Care and Affliction, and it was not long before the queen of the poor man's mind, sound Reason herself, was boxed in and could not make a single move. There on the chessboard of time and events he beheld himself checkmated by the knights of Trickery and Deception.

The invincible backgammon player, Fate, forced him into exile, blocking all six squares of the inhabited world.[27] Now he learned to drink deeply from the cup of bitter days which the wine-pourer, Time, served him from the vats of failure. His hopeful palate was stung by the poisons of sharp disappointment.

Desperately seeking relief and consolation, the merchant clung to opium, the short-termed medicine extracted from the poppy. He craved after opium as if it were the body's vital fluid, the very sustenance of life. In the end this passion emptied out the purse of his health and squandered all his coins of mental fitness.

Reduced to such a helpless state, he was forced to remain in Siam and the Siamese king, who is like a king without a kingdom, made this Iranian one of his princes and entered him in the nobility of the land. But instead of being allotted a prosperous fief and rent free lands or a fixed income along with a rich post, the poor merchant was merely honored with the lofty title 'most worthy Khān ūprā.'

Thus he remained trapped in Siam and addicted to his dreams. The heart within his breast was spotted like the petals of a poppy. He branded the red flesh of his heart with a hundred black wounds. Each burning mark was a separate token for the mistress opium.[28] He was oppressed with grief and sorrow. His breast was like a poppy which the druggist has drained, slit in a hundred places and bleeding to death.[29]

The wretched fellow sank so low he found himself begging for a simple pair of shoes but once reinstated by modest allowances of charity his feet chose to wander down the blistering path of apostasy. All along his one valuable pledge was that rare heirloom which so few recognize as the only legal tender, his high priced, God-fearing faith.

Out of sheer stupidity he threw these bank notes before the wind for the sake of his bare necessities. To climb into favor at the Siamese court he sold himself to the Devil and betrayed his foremost duty which is towards God.

There was another Iranian whom the king specially honored. This man was awarded the high-sounding title 'support of the Khānship ūprā'. And indeed the fellow was greatly pleased with himself and his new position. He beat the huge drum of his incompetence and played the trumpet of his naked poverty until the din could be heard echoing through the upper Heavens and the Sphere of Crystal.[30]

This Iranian bore forth the yak tail insignia from the camp of his morals and character and there upon the fluttering banner were inscribed the words, dearth and deficiency. As he marched through Siam with this display of pride and inability, he drew into his ranks the militant hosts of beggars and traitors. Instead of assuming office with authority and strength he let impotence become the real ruler of his province. Even within his own family he chose dallying and neglect as his household superintendent.

Throughout his career he held aloft the banner of his close ties with the Siamese king and thus he seemed to be prospering in the public arena where men fear punishments and reprimands. But due to the man's jackass-like lack of intelligence he was most careless with the affairs of his private life. He propped up the fat backside of his lusts with a fluffy pillow of thin air and it was not long before the winds of destruction blew away all the supports of his independence.

Debt collectors descended on him from left and right demanding that he pay them with desirable posts in the left and right flanks of the imperial guard. Thus the Iranian was drawn further and further into Siamese intrigue and in the end was obliged to lay aside his former religious duties. Every day he would attend the humiliating ceremonies at the king's court and by dint of sheer flattery he acquired a certain degree of success and in the end rose to the rank of fū. But such a post is nothing more than proof of a man's degradation and a sure sign that he has abandoned the one true faith.

The king rewards such men with words. The whole meaningless kingdom is based on words and nothing more. The king's kindness and generosity are like a poorly constructed sentence which begins with a splendid dependent clause but never finds a main verb to complete the sense.

The court ceremonies

When the court favorites come into the royal presence and perform their prostrations, the king deigns to call out their name, ūprā so and so, or ūyā so and so. They in turn respond with certain customary greetings of respect and proceed to recite phrases in honor of his greatness and glory.

Since some of these ministers do not know the Siamese language, they are allowed to recite in their own tongue: 'My master and my refuge, may God increase your prestige and power and may He always guide you in this life.' By now the king has had much contact with foreigners and understands some foreign expressions but if a case arises where there are grounds for misunderstanding, translators are on hand who can solve any difficulties of communication.

When the king has heard the courtiers deliver their proper greetings, he smiles and returns the honor by pronouncing out loud the names of everyone who is present during the audience. Indeed this would seem to be the only purpose of all these formal proceedings.

The king meets with the Iranian minister

When the court ceremonies are over, everyone is dismissed and the king receives the incompetent Iranian minister who is out of favor at the moment. Instead of using this opportunity to give the king any sound advice, the minister simply passes the time narrating anecdotes and light stories like the tales of the hero Ḥamza.[31] And although the Iranian minister is supposed to restrict his discourses to the subject of politics and the system of world rule in India and Iran, he is not capable of bringing the matter to a head and will not give the king practical advice. He simply goes on and on in the most vague manner praising the virtues of nobility, justice, bravery and generosity.

Every morning and evening for twenty years the Iranian minister has been narrating the details of history but the conclusion is always the same, that kingship is indeed the mainstay of nobility and justice in this world. If not for kings every two inconspicuous villages would be up in arms and pitched against each other with a drum and flag. And so the interview goes and when an hour has passed by and the Siamese king has been exposed to these wise sayings long enough the Iranian minister is dismissed.

The Frank minister's audience with the king

Then the king's vicegerent, that Christian of illegitimate birth, the minister of evil star, comes before the king for a private audience. The Frank minister's full title is ūprā rīd kima hin bakdī sīn surī sīnā which means 'the king's khān of full favor, general, first companion of the king, intelligent and competent devotee to the crown.' This despicable minister is busy handling matters of state in a way which will soon destroy the finances of the realm and greatly humiliate the king.

The Frank merely has to declare, 'In such a case a Christian king would never act that way but would adhere to the following plan' and the king is immediately persuaded to alter the accepted procedure. The ignorant, inexperienced king does not pay proper attention to the affairs of state and is not in the habit of examining an issue deeply. Without exercising any discrimination or seeking any better advice he gives his approval to whatever the minister proposes and is ever bent on imitating the Christians.

Every day this Frank of debased origin heaps slander on the Siamese who are in the higher circle of the royal court. By concocting a series of false accusations and exerting personal influence with the king, the Christian minister is able to eliminate anyone who opposes him. Since he has become a minister he has ruined and murdered about two to three hundred of the top men of Siam for no other reason than to increase his own power.

By noon the king finishes his audience with the Frank minister and retires to take a meal which is regularly prepared for him at this time. Seated in the dining room is a young man, a minister's son, whom the king has raised from childhood. He is called the pālank and as a protective measure he tastes whatever food or drink is brought before the king. Only when the pālank has thoroughly examined the food does the king indulge.

When the king finishes his meal, he stays on in the dining room and rests until the afternoon. Then he rises again and calls either the Iranian minister or the Frank minister and spends the rest of the evening in conversation. At the ninth hour he has something light to eat. By then the king feels he has fulfilled his duties and he brings his day to a close.

Modes of punishment in Siam

Since the methods of punishment practised in Siam are a bit unusual and not without novelty, the author sees fit to include their mention at this point in the account. When it is clear that a man is lying, they sew the guilty man's lips together with thread-like reeds and he is kept that way for a number of hours depending on the king's orders. An instance of this practice is as follows. At the beginning of the present king's reign several Siamese went on a visit to Ḥaidarābād and when they returned, the king questioned them about their trip. He specifically asked them how many cavalrymen the king of that country had. The poor souls replied that the Indian king presently had about twenty thousand horsemen ready to go into the field.

The inexperienced king of Siam was greatly surprised and due to the limited scope of his imagination, the arena of his thought would not admit an army of such great size. The storehouse of his mind did not have room to contain the truth of such a statement. He accused his envoys of lying and ordered that their lips be sewn together.

There is another punishment they call 'clearing-up the matter'. When someone commits a crime and is caught the authorities proceed to clear-up his head. First they shave bare the criminal's head. Then they raise a bare sword a certain height in accord with the king's orders and let it drop on the man's exposed scalp. The height the sword drops may be a hand's span, four fingers, two fingers, or more or less depending on the weight of the crime.

If the crime is very slight, it suffices to conduct the offender to the spot where this form of punishment is usually meted out. Having heaped shame upon his head in this manner, they are content and spare his scalp.

Another form of punishment is called ṣūlī ṣūlī and consists of piercing holes in the nape of the criminal's neck and passing through separate slivers of cane.

Another punishment is the hafta kām which consists of tying the victim's limbs together with chains as if he were being wrapped in a cummerbund. The chains are placed around the arms, legs, waist and neck of the prisoner but instead of being put in a pillory, he is hung on a tall structure which is made of cane. They call this kind of cane bam bū. No matter what way the suffering man turns or moves it is impossible for him to find any relief.

The Siamese also practise throwing people to the elephants. The criminal's hands and feet are bound together and specially trained tusk-bearing elephants are brought out into an arena. The elephants lift up the criminal on their white tusks and throw him through the air as far as his crime deserves, one cubit, two cubits or more or less. If the particular crime is great, the elephants will eventually destroy the man but if the crime is slight, they roll him about on the ground rather slowly so that he is not badly hurt.

In the case that an elephant administers punishment which was more or less than what was called for, the keeper himself is thrown beneath the elephants. The beasts trample him, break his bones and crush his limbs into a pulp. This harsh treatment is meant to set an example and put fear into the other elephant drivers.

If the crime in question is so slight that the Siamese only wish to frighten the offender, the elephants shove their victim about on the ground nudging him with their tusks, the way you would push someone when you are in a hurry.

A criminal never cries for mercy

There is an inflexible rule in Siam that when a man is condemned before the king or is actually suffering punishment and torture, he will never let out a scream or make the least sound. Even if a prisoner is naked and defenseless and is struck a thousand blows with a wooden club, he never draws a single breath of complaint. If someone screams it is taken to be a sign that the punishment is unjust and this increases the ruler's wrath.

The Siamese take their king to be perfectly just and claim whatever punishment he chooses to mete out is most certainly what is deserved. Therefore, crying forth in pain will gain no advantage but runs the risk of provoking further torture.

Another of their practices and the worst of them all is the public execution. When someone is condemned to death, the important men of the country are called to witness the execution. Everyone sits down right where the criminal is beheaded and the following announcement is made: 'May all present take heed and have fear lest one of you meets with this same end.' There are times when the head of the executed man is hung about the neck of another criminal and the criminal is kept that way for several days and nights.

The chain gang

If someone who is from the peasantry or generally of humble origin commits a crime, no fuss is made but he is immediately condemned to life imprisonment. Whether it is a man or a woman the prisoner is bound in chains and a heavy yoke is placed about his neck. All these wretches are tied together and form a long, human chain like a group of slaves whose ankles are chained together and who are offered up for sale in the market place.

For the rest of their life they are forced to work as laborers and there is absolutely no escape possible. They are divided up and chained together in separate groups, 'In accord with their rank and category of their sins.'³² A special guard is set over them to see that they do their work, which mostly consists of farming, digging clay and collecting fodder. The people of the market place supply these convicts with food and basic necessities but only enough to keep them barely alive. Once at dawn and once again in the evening the prisoners are brought to the bazaar. They clank along in their chains from one shop to another and whomever they meet gives them a small bit of food.

The convicts accept these terrible conditions because they know there is no possible escape. To both sides of Siam there is only the sea and the interior of the country is all jungle. A man cannot take to the sea without arranging a ship and provisions and without first having the king's permission. If a prisoner ran away and took refuge in the jungle, sooner or later his path of escape would lead into the jaws of wild animals.

Therefore, they have no choice but to go on living in their wretched condition and submit to the yoke of forced labor. 'Indeed, the infidel's soul is cheap merchandise, destined for great suffering.'

Official procedure when the king issues an order

When the king decides to give an order, it does not matter whom he is directing his order to or whether the order pertains to state affairs or private affairs, the king addresses himself to the jāvank, who is the equivalent of our state master of ceremonies. The jāvank communicates the order to the mahālak, who is the personal attendant to the king, and he passes it on to the mahtābī. Each of these officers writes out the order and forwards it by hand.

When each of them has recorded the letter in several places, it is delivered to the mahtābī, who is like a gate-keeper or a doorman. He brings the letter to the ṣalah lakūn, their name for the guardhouse, and hands the letter over to the scribes who copy it in the register.

Even if the order concerns the simplest of matters this elaborate procedure is always observed. Only then is action taken and the order is passed to the executive branch concerned.

The court scribes

Another Siamese practice pertaining to the king is that day or night several scribes are on hand to record every detail of the king's conversations, whom he addresses and exactly what is said in reply. It does not matter how trivial the talk may be, it is meticulously recorded.

The scribes also keep record of whatever service a person renders to the king. Even if it is only a question of the king drinking water, they record who brought him his drink.

Appeal to higher authority

Concerning complaints and petitions of redress, a person is not able to approach the king directly but every department of affairs has its own minister or superintendent who must be consulted first. If the official in charge does not forward the complaint or take action himself or if the petition is stopped for no good reason, the claimant can draw up a more serious petition and send it to the higher authorities. In the same department where he has been applying he accumulates a group of discontented colleagues and they appoint a deputy who has the right to present their complaint to the king.

When the case is examined, if the claimant has good grounds for seeking a redress and the law court had dismissed his case unfairly, the authorities proceed to punish the judge. If on the other hand it turns out that the claimant has been wasting everyone's time with unwarranted demands, he is reprimanded and subjected to a harsh punishment. However, since the Frank minister has taken power upholding justice in this manner is no longer practiced and no one is bold enough to raise a complaint before the king.

Description of the Siamese king's income

Since it is the custom for accountants, once they give a general explanation of a business, to add a detailed list of what money comes in and goes out, it will be true to form if this humble author now presents a summary of the Siamese ruler's revenues and expenses. Here is the inventory sheet of the king's gains and losses which we have computed and published along with certain side remarks and marginal notes.

To proceed with the account let it be noted that in Siam there is neither a landed gentry which maintains large estates nor is there the usual practice of collecting revenue from the land and conscripting a quota of farmers for the army. All the land is made up of wide plains and there is absolutely no need to irrigate the soil by drawing off water from the rivers. It is true that the rivers are continually draining water from the higher terrain but the yearly rainfall is so plentiful that the land remains moist and fertile.

Every piece of land in Siam is considered the property of the government and if anyone wishes to undertake farming, he is obliged to pay one-third to two-thirds of the produce to the king. Despite this oppressive situation the present prime minister has gone even further and imposed new restrictions on the natives. As we have often mentioned the natives of Siam are very dependent on canoes and boats. All the Siamese have their own boats, even the women, and every day they shoot along paddling through the water. Thus they delight their souls and manage to get around to the various rivers. But now the Frank minister has appointed road officials who exact sums of money from every little boat that goes by.

There is hardly anything grown in Siam except rice and rice is the staple food of most of the natives. Aside from the rice crop and the small amount of produce from gardens and vineyards, no other food is collected for the royal estates. The bulk of the king's revenues comes from the various other sources which we will now describe.

Trade in elephants

One of the important sources of income is elephants and there are indeed many elephants in the jungles of Siam. For a long time now the Siamese have been exporting elephants to the Dekkan and Bengal since these countries are not very far away. The heart of all Hindustan has been captured by the idea of leading about elephants in chains. But the cost of the elephant is so burdensome and heavy that the Indians have fallen ill. Their limbs suffer with elephantiasis and they are obliged to ride an elephant if they expect to move about.

Every year merchants have been coming to Siam bringing commodities which the Siamese desire and in exchange the foreign merchants take away elephants. The king's administration itself makes money exporting elephants to India. Every year the king catches about three or four hundred elephants in the jungle and has his men tame them. Once the elephants are tame and can be ridden, they are sold.

A while back almost all the elephants sold in India were from Siam and the Siamese were prospering with the trade and maintained large numbers of elephants for themselves. In the last few years, however, there have been disputes and uprisings in Siam and the Indians have been buying elephants from other countries. Therefore, of late there has not been so much revenue from this source and elephants are selling at a very low price.

A large sized elephant, five cubits high, will bring thirty tūmāns if the animal survives being shipped by sea to a foreign buyer but the merchants are doing well if they sell one in Siam for seven or eight tūmāns. There is also the tusk-bearing elephant and the peasants form into large groups to hunt this beast. In accord with the famous saying, 'A fool kills his cows for the sake of the pasture lands', the natives slaughter this valuable wild elephant for the sake of his tusks. The tusks are sold at the rate of one thousand royal dinars for one man.

Aloes wood and how it is collected

Another item of their economy is aloes wood and very good aloes wood comes from Siam. It may be noted that aloes wood is not produced by a special, distinct tree but is found in the jungle inside the hollow stump of rotting trees. Since it is difficult to enter the jungle in Siam because of the insects and snakes and poisonous mosquitoes, once a year at a fixed date two or three thousand men assemble to penetrate into the jungle together.

The men cut down trees which the saw of their mind reckons will contain aloes wood and if they choose correctly they are able to extract what they are seeking. If the wood of the trees which they have felled is not dry enough but it is evident that aloes wood is forming inside, the wood is buried under the ground until it reaches maturity. Otherwise they separate the aloes wood from the rest of the tree right away.

The aloes wood of Siam is of three kinds. The substance which is contained inside the branches of the tree they call the head and this is heavy, distilled and mature. Another variety comes from the trunk and is called the waist and the third kind is from the root and is called the foot. There is a great difference in the price depending on which of these three kinds of aloes wood you buy.

At first the Siamese did not appreciate the true value and price of such a commodity. The fragrance of this aromatic had not reached the merchant of their sense of smell and the foreign merchants were making great profits. Āqā Muḥammad rented the area where the aloes wood forms and consigned it to his own administration but after his death the aroma of its worth and price reached the nostrils of the natives.

As attendants install braziers throughout a banquet hall, the Siamese cleared a space in their hearts for their new love of this incense and were quick to take over the source of the aloes wood. Now they export it to all the countries of the world. They sell one man of the highest quality for three royal tūmāns. During a good year they probably collect about four to five hundred mans of varying degrees of quality.

Sapanwood

Another commodity is sapanwood and this wood can be found in great quantities in the jungles of Siam and is not highly valued by the natives. It is so inexpensive no one undertakes to sell it. At most it costs five dinars for one man.

The exportation of jarang

Another item is jarang which is the sap of a certain local tree. The tree is very common in the jungles of Siam and the other countries of Below the Winds. Jarang is exported to Japan and China where it is used by the natives in a peculiar way which no one else understands. Every year the Siamese make a certain sum of money selling this commodity to merchants.

In fact jarang is used to protect wooden furnishings. When applied in its liquid form it will preserve wood for very long periods of time. Lāk is another commodity and is similar to jarang, being a juice extracted from another kind of tree.

Iron and animal skins

Iron exists in Siam and recently the Siamese have begun to market a small quantity each year. There are many wild animals in Siam which have valuable skins such as deer, bison and mountain goats. A special group of natives is continually engaged in hunting to acquire these skins. The Siamese collect the skins and sell them to the Franks and the Dutch who transport this kind of merchandise to such places as Japan where they are able to make good profits.

Camphor and how it forms

Another commodity is camphor, which is generally found around the regions of Japan and Siam. However it was explained that contrary to the common belief camphor is not a fruit that grows on a camphor tree. In fact there is a tree which the Siamese call the mūz and it has large, thick, green leaves. Some days the leaves are all rolled up like an accountant's scroll and other days the leaves are spread out flat like the pages of a manuscript. Each leaf is about one and a half cubits long and three-quarters of a cubit wide. When the spring rains come, whatever raindrops penetrate into the hollows of the folded leaves, eventually crystallize and turn into camphor.

This process only takes place in the lands of the Macassars and the land of Java which are separate countries where other kings rule. The kind of camphor described above is known as jaudāna or camphor of eternity and is extremely white and of fine quality. This is the best camphor to be had in Siam. It is very concentrated and expensive so that one man is never sold for less than sixteen royal tūmāns.

The kind of camphor which most people use is not really camphor at all but a substance concocted from several cheap ingredients. This camphor of lesser quality comes from China and Japan and is not very high-priced.

What we have just stated concerning the origin of camphor is not consistent with what scholars have written in their learned works; none the less, in the annals of absolute truth our account must stand and we have recorded the real facts. Other authors have written that camphor grows on a real camphor tree which is of great size and wondrous proportions, so large that a hundred noblemen could lounge beneath its shade or a thousand servants crowd in underneath its spreading boughs.

Admittedly, there is a tree in India called the kīla which also has good large leaves and yet when the spring rains fall on this tree it does not produce crystals of camphor. But this is not proof that camphor is not produced by rain in the lands of the Macassars. Rains fall in many places in the world and have a different effect in each clime. For instance, the rain which falls in the oceans is believed by some to turn into pearls. It is very possible, therefore, that in the country of the Macassars the weather conditions are unique and rain will crystallize on certain kinds of leaves, 'God alone understands all the secrets of nature.'

Since the Macassars do not live far from Siam, they regularly transport camphor to Shahr Nāv and sell most of it ot the administration of the all-powerful Frank minister.

How the Siamese grow rice

As we have mentioned above, Siam also yields a rice crop and this is the way they grow the rice. When the time is right for planting, they plough the land in a very careless manner and scatter seed all over the surface of the soil. Then they depart and wait for nature to provide them with results.

The monsoon arrives just after their ploughing and the fields become saturated with water. Every day the water mounts up until it finally covers all the land. Under water the seeds turn into green plants and raise their heads up through the earth. They actually spring to the height of five or six cubits. When the plants reach maturity, the farmers return in their boats and gather the harvest.

Betel nut

Another item of the land is betel nut which is also consumed in huge quantities by the natives of India, Japan and China, since they eat it along with their pān. In fact during one day the Siamese eat about a quarter of a man of pān, betel nut and lime.

Porcelain

Porcelain, carved woodwork and other such items are brought to Siam from Japan and China but this kind of merchandise is all bought up by the lofty king's administration. The administration buys it in one big purchase and eventually sells it somewhere else at a great profit.

Pepper

Another commodity is pepper. In general there are two kinds of pepper, ordinary pepper and Dār pepper which the Indians eat as their main food. Both these kinds of pepper are sold in Siam. The tree which produces ordinary pepper belongs to the family of bindweed ('ashiqa) while the Dār pepper comes from the family of myrtle (mūrd). They have so much pepper in Siam that they are able to export a certain amount and make a reasonable profit.

Ambergris and its mysterious origin

Every now and then ambergris is found in the ocean around Siam. Some of it is good but some of it is the bad kind which has no aroma. By now the Siamese business sense has caught whiff of the profits to be made selling such a luxury product. This humble author has heard and read many conflicting reports about the origin of ambergris but has not come across an account which makes clear sense. As a result the author remains perplexed on this subject. But a certain man from China, a country which we will describe later on in its proper place, explained the matter in the following manner.

In the ocean around China there is a particular kind of ambergris which a huge serpent-like fish swallows and when the monstrous fish dies and is washed ashore, the natives extract this substance from his mouth. It is extremely white, has a strong, fragrant odor and is of great value and price. This ambergris also has a most strange and striking quality.

When any other ambergris, incense or aromatics are burned at social gatherings, the smoke which rises from the several braziers is overcome and attracted toward the brazier where this rare kind of ambergris is burning. Large quantities of this expensive ambergris are said to be kept in the treasure chambers of the king of China. Further knowledge of this matter rests with God.

Mining tin

Another item found in Siam is tin. The truth about the metal tin is that it is always found in moist places such as an ant colony where the ants lay their eggs in the ground. Tin looks like a black seed and lies hidden beneath the moist earth. When the natives of Siam succeed in tracking down this substance, they lay siege to its stronghold, extract it by force and batter it into shape. Once they dig it up and melt it they can make use of it directly. This whole process is carried out on one specially appointed day.

The king's total income

All the commodities which have been mentioned above, are reserved for the king's administration. In this manner the income of the administration during a good year, counting the profits made from trade, will come to a total of about 7000 kātīs.

A description of the Siamese king's expenses

If, having composed a list of the king's profits and revenues, the author proceeds to write a bill of the king's expenses, the balance sheet of this account will be completed in full. It so happens that none of the kings of Below the Winds have extensive expenses which can be compared to the money spent by real kings. Those counterfeit rulers do not incur the usual financial burdens of royalty such as endowments, salaries, fiefs, pensions, grants, charities and alms nor do they lay out great sums for fine clothes, elaborate foods or maintenance of grand palaces. Praise be to God that they have no share in these matters.

Once the kings of those regions enact the requirements of official politeness, they make simplicity and poverty the mainstay of their life and thoughts. However, the king of Siam has had much contact with the Iranians and by comparison with his peers throughout

11

the rest of Below the Winds, he has broken with tradition and adopted what he imagines are proper manners, fine food and drink and clothing worthy of a mighty ruler.

He has endeavored to acquire fine furnishings and has learned to make use of proper utensils when dining and thus, in general, he is striving to raise his name before the world and establish contact with powerful, world-ruling sultans. As was mentioned earlier, the king of Siam has repeatedly sent envoys to the threshold of Iran, the noble threshold which angels guard day and night. He has also sent delegates to the potentates of India as well as to the rulers of many other lands and seeks to understand Siam's position in the world.

The king's Frank employees

Recently the king of Siam brought two hundred more Franks to the country and having made them his attendants, pays them a regular salary. All in all he spends about three thousand tūmāns a year, exporting government merchandise and importing his personal necessities, maintaining the temples, consecrating new idols and providing for the rūlīs.

Thus the king's yearly expenses amount to seven or eight thousand tūmāns. What is left of his income after these expenses are subtracted is kept in the royal treasury.

The life of the Siamese

In Siam the natives themselves have no wealth or power to speak of. Their way of life is not at all affluent nor have they any luxuries or leisure. They are all naked and penniless without estates or large homes. Abject poverty is the mainstay of their daily life nor do they indulge in elevated ceremonies, cultivate refined manners or entertain themselves with sumptuous banquets.

It is a curious fact but all throughout their lives the Siamese will not allow the taste of oil to reach their palate and though there are many cows and buffalo in Siam the natives will not milk them and extract butter. Because of their religion they consider these foods sinful. Consequently the Siamese have no idea of what tree or animal produces oil.

The small amount of oil which is required in Siam for the Iranians, is brought from India. Recently when it came to arranging for the provisions of our humble embassy, the king was at a loss. The amount of oil which he promised us was not available and he began to think how he might procure more.

The king ordered his peasantry to milk the cows and buffalo and extract butter and oil from the milk. The peasants were aghast. They screamed and ranted, 'Never in all the history of the kings of Siam has such tyranny and oppression occurred. You would even confiscate the food of young calves.'

The food in Siam

The Siamese normally restrict their diet to plain rice. They add no salt or meat or spices but they eat their rice with a little boiled water and a cooked fish head. People of all classes, high and low, make this food their mainstay. If by chance they come across the body of a dead animal no matter of what species, even an old dead crow, they will eat it without hesitation but they would never kill an animal for food themselves. That is considered a grave sin.

Once an animal has died of its own accord, it is religiously pure and may be consumed. If they intend to entertain important guests, they grip the neck of a bird with their hands and hold on until the bird of his soul flies out of the feathery cage of his body and he dies. Then they boil the bird without adding rice, seasonings or oil and in that plain way they swallow it down.

Local delicacies

Every now and then the natives are inclined to roast lizards and snakes and this is quite a common practice in Siam. In all the market places you see these repulsive animals on sale instead of partridge and lamb. Another dish is the tortoise and in general they do not abstain from eating sea food or for that matter any land creature either. One tribe of these people eats the meat of elephants and wolves.

There is another group known as the Lāvand who have a separate ruler and kingdom. It is said that their king is so wealthy and has so many hunting falcons that it takes two whole buffaloes to feed his birds each day. Although the men and women of Siam and the countries adjoining China do not have hair, the people of this tribe are the most handsome of them all and amongst their young girls you will find beauties such as in Cathay.

A curse upon the barbarous infidels

It was heard that this people which has come and settled in Shahr Nāv condescends to eat the meat of dogs and thus they disregard the old injunction, 'Would you dare eat your dead brother's flesh?' Praise be to God that the greater number of non-believers lives in such foul conditions. In the same way they are denied a part in the joys of the afterlife, they have no share in the clean and holy practices of this life. 'Oh God, make them firm in their error. Make short their lives. May their necks be twisted and their death be brought on in haste. Give them pains in their bowels and punish them with ruthless, awesome punishments.'

PART IV FOURTH JEWEL

It is not hidden or veiled from the vestibule of the hearts of scholars and men of wisdom that the seas of this world embrace a multitude of islands and flow around coasts both flourishing and desolate. Each of these separate realms is ruled by its own king and maintains its independence. In this manner God, praise be to His mighty name, saw fit to create and divide the terrestrial globe.

The various kinds of islands in the world

God has chosen to abandon some islands to harmful weeds and brambles so that the clutching roots and sharp thorns might extract their own profits and gains. Other islands, which God recognized as more valuable, He bestowed upon the race of man, while still others are the abode of tribes of genii. There are islands inhabited by savage beasts and other islands where wild birds make their headquarters. Last, there are the deserted islands which contain rare minerals and treasure, gold and silver and other valuables which are hidden there for safe-keeping.

Scholars of learning and insight have often given their attention to geography and their books provide detailed accounts of the islands of the world. Concerning their opinions let us recall the old saying, 'How is the man who only hears about a marvel like unto the beholder?' Thus this humble author makes bold to undertake a description of the islands and the coasts and the wonders and the miraculous sights which were encountered during our voyage.

The author will also include observations on the areas near Siam and information which he was able to acquire from reliable travelers who have visited the countries adjacent to Shahr Nāv. With the aid of a wonder-depicting pen the author writes upon the sheets of clarity and presents the facts of his account as follows.

The sea between Iran and Siam

We mentioned earlier that our ship set out from the sea of Fārs and 'Ummān and the terminus of our long journey was the sea of China but there is not really a clear separation between the seas we crossed. An ordinary traveler would not be able to perceive where one sea ended and the next began. As for the various great gulfs, although they are usually designated by separate names, they are really all joined together. They flow down from the same direction and merge in the Great Ocean.

The scholars of travel and geography, confronted with many different place names, some near to each other and some separated by great distances, have wandered into the discords of choppy seas, doldrums and foul winds and they divide the great expanse of waters which lies along this path into seven distinct parts. They insist that each tract be defined as separate and distinct and have decided to ascribe a different name to every section.

The distance from Bandar ʿAbbās to Siam

However the case may be, the full distance from the blessed port of Bandar ʿAbbās across all seven seas to Shahr Nāv amounts to 1,320 leagues and each league, as they call it, is equivalent to about one farsakh. But this reckoning is only true when there is clear weather and the proper wind is blowing. If the winds are contrary the ship is forced to maneuver to the left and right of its desired route. The ship may have to spend much time sailing in the wrong direction before it can come back on course again. If the wind is not compliant, the distance of a voyage can be doubled or trebled.

On the way to Siam we humble servants managed to traverse the great road of water in three months and a few days but the return voyage took five and a half months. We learned the deeper meaning of the holy saying so full of guidance, 'When God blew winds upon their ship, on they sailed with His command.' All travel rests in the hands of the Almighty, the one majestic Lord, the lofty Protector of mankind.

If God wishes, in one day and night a ship can sail one hundred farsakhs but if the wind of His holy indulgence does not caress the ship's sails, the voyagers on the waves of resignation will not come one step closer to their goal even after a whole year at sea.

Storms and rough seas, as well as the ebb and flow of the tides, also play an important part in the ship's progress. Even when there is no wind, if the tide or a strong current pulls in the direction of the ship's destination, good speed will be made. If conditions are just the opposite, no matter how much wind the ship has, it will not make headway.

One of the great miracles of God which this author has seen with his own eyes was an incident which involved two ships sailing in opposite directions, A strong wind was blowing and should have hindered one of the ships and advanced the other. But both of them passed each other, one sailing out of the west and the other coming from the east.

Description of the tides and currents

This author acknowledges the fact that scholars of geography and history have all made mention of the Great Ocean and other seas and they have undertaken to explain the ebb and flow of the tides but their explanations are contradictory and incomplete. Here is a summary of what they have said and this explanation certainly comes closest to the truth.

The Great Ocean surrounds the globe of earth and seven distinct gulfs branch off from it, each one of them being known by a separate name. The Great Ocean even bites the coasts and penetrates into the continents of land. Each of the gulfs, as well as the Great Ocean itself, changes in accord with its own particular tide. That is why the seas are always in the process of rising or falling.

The influence of the sun

As for the ebb and flow of the tide of the Great Ocean, during the course of a year that huge mass of water will gradually rise and fall once. What causes the high tide is the fact that the sun is busy climbing in its circuit and transports itself into the furthest constellations of the north. The water begins to rise once the sun rolls round into a position opposite the ocean's surface.

The sea rises at this time because the sun's hot rays heat up the stones and massive rocks which are at the bottom of the ocean's bed. This growing heat creates pockets of air underwater and stirs up waves which flow towards the shores and thus greater amounts of water build up and are drawn towards the east.

An ebbing tide simply consists of the sea's mass of water shifting towards the west. This process is caused by the sun's sinking and returning to the furthest mansions of the south which eliminates the conditions described above.

The moon's influence on the tides

Celestial movements are also the cause of tides in the smaller gulfs. The tides in the seven principal gulfs are caused by the rising and setting of the moon and by the moon's climbing and sinking through its heavenly circuit. When the moon goes through her phases and varies the amount of her light or when the moon crosses the path of bright comets, the behavior of the gulf tides is greatly influenced.

When the moon rises and inclines towards the highest point of its yearly circuit, the gulf waters are set in motion and the tide begins to rise. As the moon goes higher and higher the sea swells and the tide rises until both moon and tide reach their maximum height.

When the moon goes into its decline and heads towards the west, the ebb tide begins and by the time the moon reaches the western horizon the tide is at its lowest. The process continues in the same way even while the moon is passing under the earth. When the moon reaches the midway mark and is directly under foot, the high tide is at its peak. When the moon begins to surface at the eastern horizon, the tide is at its weakest.

The relationship between the sea and the heavenly bodies

Scholars have postulated that this peculiar relationship exists between the sea, the sun and the moon because their separate essences partake of the same purity. Thus the sea is attached to these heavenly bodies and when they rise and fall, the sea's waters follow them. Therefore, all in all the ebb and flow of the tides depends on the increase and decrease of the moon's light, the moon's drawing near or crossing, the path of comets and the stormy force of winds, especially winds that rise from the south.

Heat is created in the sea

There are also those who point out that the seas contain many rocks and that the wide surface of the water reflects the stars when they turn round in their courses. Both these characteristics are said to cause the water to heat up. The sea is also stirred up by the fact that the moon's rays meet on the surface of the water.

When this new heat is generated, motion is created and the sea desires a wider field to range about in. The sea's waves beat the surface of the water and roll towards the coasts until the moon reaches the middle of the sky. But once the moon begins to decline, the sea's boiling subsides and the constituents of the water return to their former state of balance and calm.

Then the sea rests until the moon arrives at the western horizon and the high tides begin again, this time drawing towards the eastern coast. Thus the whole process repeats itself and high tides abide until the moon rounds the great peg of the earth's axis.

A traditional explanation of the tides

There is a tradition which quotes the noble Prophet as saying, 'The seas are watched over by a giant angel. He dips his foot into the waters and thus creates the high tide. Then he extracts his foot and the tides recede.' It is possible that this angel is a symbol for the moon and the angel's foot represents the influences of the presence or absence of the moon's rays. 'Only God understands all the mysteries of life.'

Reefs

As we mentioned earlier, during the return voyage our ship sailed into a region of the sea where there were many reefs and yet there were no coasts or shores visible in any direction. The ship had just enough water to pass through the rocks and had the captain been the least bit careless, the ship and all the passengers aboard would have perished without leaving a single trace behind. We were only in that dangerous spot for a short time and once we were clear and back in a proper depth of water, we sailed on unimpeded.

The great expanse of water

It is not possible to measure the full extent of that sea except with the eye of fantasy. No one will ever delve to the bottom of that sea except by plunging into the waves of his wildest dreams. We were surrounded by a limitless desert of water. The days were white and the nights were black. You could not spy a single speck afloat on those fields of water, only the dark blue of the heavens reflected on the blue back of the sea.

In the midst of the ocean we encountered several uninhabited islands and large masses of projecting rocks. Most of those islands were green and flourishing and covered with thick clumps of trees. On some islands there were sweet-flowing, fresh springs and we were able to stop and replenish our stores of drinking water.

Forms of life out at sea

Way out at sea, a month's distance from any land, we would come across birds and other forms of wildlife. We beheld many fish of the most unusual shapes and sizes. Some fish even had legs like land creatures. There was one kind of fish that was shaped like a pig and an elephant and another fish whose body was so perfectly curved, he resembled a large, round dish. This particular fish had its eyes located in the center of its body. In fact this whole fish looks like a big eye swimming in the water and there is no difference between its back and stomach. Then there was another fish that was about forty cubits long and five or six cubits wide.

The flying fish and the Āmbūs

We also saw a fish that can fly and it had wings like those of a bat. These flying fish are regularly hunted by a particular fish which is called the āmbūs. The āmbūs is beautifully colored and has a very delicate and fine shape. Its body is covered with bright stripes and dots. The one food which this fish lives on is the flying fish. When the āmbūs catches sight of the flying fish, it sets out in pursuit and tries to swallow it. To escape, the flying fish swims to the surface of the water and jumps into the air, flying for a distance of as much as two maidāns. Thus it thinks it has eluded the whirlpool of destruction, being negligent of the adage,' The spider never goes very long without a fly. The bounty of our provident Lord is endowed with wings.'

Despite the fact that the āmbūs is about one whole cubit long and devoid of wings, this fish possesses the power of all-conquering, divine wisdom. The āmbūs is so quick that when the flying fish takes to the air, the hunter keeps sight of it from under water and follows wherever it flies. The flying fish finally lands but, like the confused hen sparrow of the jungles, in the end it flies back into the captor's hands. Thus the winged fish drops into the net of the larger fish's mouth.

Over and over again we watched the swift āmbūs pursuing his game, which flies through the air in flocks like pigeons. The sailors take the āmbūs as a sign of good fortune and proof that their ship will arrive home safely. When the āmbūs comes up alongside the ship the crew fishes it out of the water and offers the catch to the passengers. Those who accept the fish pay the sailor in accord with how much the frying pan of their generosity heats up. We also caught sight of a sea tortoise which was about twenty cubits long.

The makramaj or crocodile

Another fish is the makramaj, which men generally call the crocodile, and this creature is extremely large, very violent and full of strength. However, we never sighted one which was actually big enough to overturn a ship. These fish usually inhabit the fresh water of rivers in Below the Winds and India.

When we were leaving Shahr Nāv and sailing through fresh water on our way to the sea, we encountered a heavy makramaj. We hit it and caused it to roll over suddenly and in the commotion one of the crew members fell out of the dinghy. The huge crocodile carried him off into the canal of disaster and swallowed him down.

Capturing crocodiles by magic

In India and Below the Winds the science of incantations, spells and mantras is very widely practised. These forms of magic are also very popular amongst the Siamese and they employ their spells to hunt elephants and trap wild beasts of the jungle. They especially hunt the crocodile in this manner. When they wish to catch a crocodile, they get in their boats and recite a special spell or mantra over the petals of a flower. They tear up the flower and throw the pieces into the water and follow after the scattered petals wherever they float. Thus the hunters are led to the spot where the crocodile is hiding.

When this huge beast sees the floating petals it surfaces and swims around the flower and the boat in a charmed, senseless state. The men have no cause for fright. They wrap their ropes around the dazed crocodile and take it prisoner and without any trouble they bind its snout and hands and tie it to the back of their boat. In the end they lift it right out of the water. Some Siamese actually eat the meat of this fish, despite the fact that it is putrid and extremely tough. We may add that it was heard that the oil extracted from this fish is a wondrous cure for colic.

Casting spells on elephants

Some people are so clever at practicing the art of spells that they are able to bewitch a fierce elephant which would otherwise take two or three years to tame. By simply casting their powerful eye upon the elephant when the beast is still at large in the jungle they apply such a strong spell that it becomes more tame than the fully trained elephants. Then these sly magicians take their catch to the merchants and make huge profits. But after a few days the spell wears off and the elephant returns to its former state of madness. It must be captured all over again and handled like any other wild elephant.

The worm tree

We saw a tree in Shahr Nāv which had very unusual properties. When they pluck a leaf from its branches, the leaf, on being separated from the tree, turns into a worm which has the same shape as the leaf. The worm has hands and feet and once its insect soul enters its body, the little creature begins to move. But not just any leaf of the tree has the ability to turn itself into a worm. Only some leaves behave this way and then only on the days from the first of Sagittarius to the appearance of Aries. Why this happens or how this happens 'Only God the all-wise Creator understands'.

The worm that looks like a rooster

We saw another kind of worm but this one was white and extremely small. It was shaped like a tiny white rooster and its whole body, including its two arms, was covered with feathers. Like a rooster it bore a cock's comb on its head, had plumes and a tail and it walked about on its hind legs.

The flying cat

Another strange animal is the flying cat which we only heard about. It is like a bat and is covered with feathers from its feet to its ears. It is found in all the countries of Below the Winds, including Siam, and always remains in the jungles where it flies from tree to tree. They are generally so wild it is impossible to capture one alive. We heard from the group of trusted Iranians that they had seen many of them but because these creatures fly so quickly, much more quickly than any known bird, it is not possible to capture them.

The cat with the evil eye

We heard that there is another kind of cat which lives on one of the islands of China. It is extremely valuable and its peculiar quality is that whatever other animal it fixes its glance on falls under the affliction of the evil eye and is incapable of moving or flying. Many men have actually seen this creature at its work.

The Nasnās

There is also the Nasnās who has been observed in the jungles and mountains of those regions. In every aspect of his outward appearance he is like an ape but in distinction from other animals he walks erect on his two feet like a human being and he shrieks and screams with a shrill voice like a woman.

Other oddities

Another strange sight we came across was a piece of wood which was half wood but half turned into stone. There were many pieces of such wood lying about. We also saw small fish which were brought from China. Some were bright yellow and others were white and they appeared as if they were plated with gold and silver.

An anecdote we were told

The following story was told by a Dutch captain who was in Shahr Nāv for a while. 'Once on our way to China we dropped anchor in the bay of an island to avoid a heavy storm. There was a strange collection of people inhabiting the island who only barely resembled human beings. Their feet were three cubits long and just as wide and they were completely nude and had very long hair. At night they all climbed to the top of their own trees in the jungle, even the women who bore their children with them under their arms. Once up in the tree they would tie their hair to a branch and hang there all night resting. This is the way they slept until dawn when they climbed back down to the ground. We went before these people with a display of strength and force. They were very frightened by us nor would anyone dare do us harm.' It is possible that this island is the very same island the author of 'Ajā'ibu'l-Makhlūqāt[1] describes and refers to as Ar-Rāmī.

Another anecdote

The same Dutchman recounted another tale from his voyages as follows. 'We came to an island inhabited by a tribe of wild men who had very large feet and went about totally naked. It was their practice that the more important a man was in the tribe, the more gashes he inflicted on his limbs. They even cut their noses in such a way that the inner cavities were visible. Then they would pierce the neighboring bones and insert a ring.'

Description of the islands

The authors of 'Ajā'ibu'l-Makhlūqāt, Ṣuwar-i-Aqālīm, Tuḥfatu 'l-Gharā'ib, Nuzhatu'l-Qulūb,[2] as well as other writers on geography, have been keen in describing the various islands. Since this humble author of lesser merchandise wishes to be reckoned as a member of that learned group, in accord with the saying, 'One who acts like a particular people is considered of their number', he will make suffice what has so far been reported of the actual mission and turn his attentions to facts concerning the islands in these waters.

Ceylon

The first island which we encountered on our voyage was Ceylon, which is located near the mountain Sarandīb. This mountain is known to the scholars of history as Mount Ad-Dahūn and it is often mentioned in their learned books. As long as sailors are not in the vicinity of this mountain and can not actually see it, they are unsure of their way and it is not possible for them to orient their course.

Fertility and valuable mines

The island contains broad fields, plantations, mountains and jungles and is extremely green. There are also several rivers and fresh water springs in the interior. The very tree of Paradise is only one of the many off-shoots from this island's well-watered stem. The garden of Paradise draws its fair breeze from the meadows of Ceylon. Rubies of every shade are found in the mines as well as saylonīs, sapphires, crystal and diamonds. Add to those resources the mines of precious metals such as gold, lead and iron.

Elephants

In the jungles of the island there are elephants but the Ceylonese elephants are not very large. Standard-sized elephants in India and other countries of Below the Winds are about three and a half cubits tall. The best of them, and they are rare, are never taller than five cubits. Only in Abyssinia do they grow much bigger. In Ceylon the elephants are never more than two and a half cubits high but it may be added that they are very fine-looking, pleasant animals. This author has also read that the fabulous bird, the Rukh, has been seen in Ceylon.

Pearls

On the coast of the island as well as in Tūt Karī, which is a separate port near by on the mainland of India, the natives do a large trade in pearls. Unfortunately all other pearls when confronted with the pearl of Bahrain[3] lose their bright countenance out of shame and grief. The jeweler of Time and Chance has relegated these Indian jewels of lesser lustre to a low shelf in the bazaar of happiness.

Here live the sly money changers of the world market of Fate but how will they convince the pearl merchant of Baḥrain that for purity and value the Ceylonese pearls can be ranked as equal with his wares?

The quality of any other jewel when weighed in the mind's balance by a merchant of insight and experience is proved lacking in gravity and comes out with a pale face and a light reputation.

Men of learning who have strung the cord of their mind with the gems of the science of jewelry, recognize the worth and price of the pearl of Baḥrain and they will not string this orphan gem on the same thread with any other foreign pearl.

The king of Ceylon

The king of Ceylon lives in the midst of more splendor and wealth than the kings of Below the Winds but still his army, servants and court attendants are drawn from the peasantry. Even though Ceylon is an island and it should be easy to control, we heard that a certain faction would not keep its neck in the yoke of obedience and rose in rebellion. It would seem that the king does not have sufficient power to root them out and destroy them.

The Dutch took control from the Portuguese

For a long time the Portuguese Franks held Ceylon and up until a few years ago they had been extracting great profits from the island. They built themselves a fort and constructed a beautiful town which they kept well defended. It is a well-known fact how the Dutch Franks recently defeated the Portuguese and took possession of the port themselves. The Dutch have seized all the important ports in the kingdoms of that region and they always employ the same method. First they win over the local king and make sure he will support them and then they bombard the harbor and the fort with their cannons. At present they appropriate all the profits which result from trade and commerce on the island and they insist that this is their exclusive right.

Cinnamon

Cinnamon of the finest quality comes from Ceylon but only the Dutch administration is allowed to buy or sell it and they have fixed the market price. The new law states exactly how much it is to cost in each place it is sold. If one year no one buys cinnamon in a particular market, they burn it all rather than let the price go down. They have only allowed a fixed number of cinnamon trees to remain on the whole island, just enough to meet the demands of a good market. The rest have been burned so that cinnamon might not become too abundant. They apply the same controls in the case of nutmeg, cloves and several other products.

Adam's fall

As has been recorded in written texts the fall of Adam, peace be on him, took place on the famous mountain of Ceylon and the imposing peak can be seen from the sea for several days before landfall. The noble sire of man has left his footprint on the summit and we were informed that once every day this footprint is cleansed with drops of rain. God, the undoubted Lord of mercy, sees fit to send the nursing clouds with the rain of His compassion.

The beliefs of the Nahādān sect

Jewels are found in the vicinity of that holy spot and Hindus and yogis of the Nahādān sect reside there. These people are described in various books. The author of Nafā'is in his chapter on religious groups and false sects has given a brief account of them which is worthy of attention.

The members of this sect believe that there once was a great angel, Nahādān, who became visible in human form, but he had two brothers and they eventually killed him. After his death they fashioned the sky and earth from his skin. From his bones they made the mountains and from his blood the seas.

A religious leader is born[4]

Another of their tales is that in India in the city of Gīlūs once lived a king by the name of Shadhūdan and his name means the man of pure heart. He had a wife called Māhā, that is, big or great, but little else is known about her besides her name. Māhā had a dream one night and in her dream the king devoured the sun and the moon. With one draught he drank up the sea and he took the lofty mountain Qāf for his throne. When she woke up she told her dream to Shadhūdan and he sought an interpretation from his councilors. The dream was interpreted as meaning that the king would have a son who would rule over the whole world and all forms of creation would worship him as a god.

Not long after she had that strange dream Māhā happened to be in a garden passing the time of day. To amuse herself she reached up and hung on to the branch of a tree. While she was swinging herself back and forth, she suddenly gave birth and brought forth a child into the world. Then and there before her eyes the babe stood up and took seven sure steps. Each step produced a flowerbed of blooming roses and uncovered a separate sum of treasure.

The child spoke out declaring: 'I have been born 8000 times before in different forms and shapes but this is my final birth. Now I am clean and purified and I have reached the highest spiritual stage.' Four angels appeared and washed the child with clear rainwater and carried him to the temple. There all the idols fell down before him and worshipped him.

When he grew up and reached manhood he had no interest in the world and kept to himself inside the castle. Eventually angels came down from Mount Qāf and led him forth from his home. But for six months he only sat meditating on top of a tall rock. He fasted and was able to sustain himself on one grain of lentil a day. An angel named Indar, who has a thousand eyes, came down from heaven, stood before the young man and declared, 'Go and preach to all mankind.' The young man rose and until the day of his death he continued preaching to the world.

The adherents of the local sect believe that the footprints and the tomb which are on Mount Sarandīb are from this holy personage.

Though the natives consider themselves to be human beings and part of the human race, they will not admit being descendants of Adam, the first man.[5] There is a famous tooth which the Hindus call Shārmal and this sect insists on attributing the relic to their saviour. The king of Ceylon and all the Indians living on the island believe in this nonsense and are fervently engaged in idolatry.

Purpose of describing the idolators

It is perhaps not altogether appropriate for the author to include such sordid details in his account but mention of how these heathens are lost in the error of their ways should encourage the faithful to strive in rendering God thanks for the gift of true religion. It is hoped that this brief excursion into the folly of pagan beliefs will fire the passion of the true believers for pursuing the Almighty's manifest guidance. Thus the present narration, dressed and adorned like a pretty bridesmaid, is offered up as a prayer in praise of God's numerous names and attributes.

12

An anecdote on the Indian pilgrims

The following account was heard from a group of Indians in Ceylon
and there are indeed many Indians living on the island. Years ago it
used to be that if the grace of God happened to favor an Indian with
the means to visit this holy island, he would perform the pilgrimage
with thanks and devotion. Thus many visitors from India came to
Ceylon whenever their position and wealth would allow them to
make the journey. A person who completed the ceremonies of the
pilgrimage and had the honor of beholding the sacred footprint
would have a strange experience.

Jewels uncovered in a dream

At night a message from the realm of dreams would be delivered to
the pious man while he was sleeping. 'Rise and go to the spot which
you now behold in the eye of your imagination. There you will find
something valuable. Take a just portion of that treasure for yourself.
Such is the reward which is to be bestowed upon you.' And this
happened to all the pilgrims in the same manner until one of them
who was a fool abused the divine bounty.

The soul is a jeweler

A certain pilgrim who came to Ceylon and performed the ceremonies of the pilgrimage, received the usual message in his dreams.
When his immortal soul, like a prospecting jeweler, finished delving
in the rich mines of the world of dreams and returned to the market
place of the body, the pilgrim opened the shop-door of wakefulness
and rose to hunt for the sumptuous gift he had been promised in
his sleep.[6]

The thief, Greed, waylays the modest soul

Greed and Desire who are always on the look out to waylay the
traveler, Equity, fell in with the pilgrim's soul and, prodded by
their covetousness, he opened the purse of excess and stretched
forth his hand from the sleeve of propriety. Thus the pilgrim stole
a large quantity of jewels over and above what had been bestowed
upon him as a gift. Then he set out for home.

The king sees the dagger of greed in his dreams

However, just as the pilgrim received a message from the world of dreams, the king while sleeping was informed of what had happened. 'A certain man was granted a generous gift but he has overstepped the bounds of modesty. With a display of vulgarity he has ornamented the dagger of greed with an excess of jewels and has plunged the blade into the sheath of his heart.'

The thief is caught and the jewels are recovered

The king summoned the thief before the throne. The thief realized that the king knew everything and, bowing his head in shame, handed over the jewels. The king's attendants took the jewels to the shore of a river and threw them into the flowing treasury of the almighty Creator and from that time up until now the pilgrims have not received messages of this kind from the world of dreams.

The king's omniscience

It is also related that the natives occasionally come upon a pile of jewels when they are farming or out in the countryside. But if they try to sell them or take them out of Ceylon the king immediately perceives what they are up to. No one actually tells the king about the jewels neither does he see them with his own eyes; none the less, he knows every move the thief makes and every detail of his schemes. The thief is ordered to come before the throne and whatever he has taken is recovered and put back in its proper place. No one knows how the king acquires this knowledge but nothing ever escapes his scrutiny. Even stranger than this is the fact that the king does not collect any of the precious jewels which are to be found in the local mines.

Foreigners in Ceylon

Now the Franks dominate trade in Ceylon and aside from a few merchants and councilors from India it is unusual for other foreigners to settle on the island. Two or three Iranians have gone there representing the business interests of Indian princes and the local king has been generous to them. They have been provided with houses and fine furnishings and are generally well looked after but they are not allowed out of their lodgings. Further than this there is not much to relate concerning Ceylon. Let us close this description with the wise words, 'God knows best the truth of all matters.'

Āchī[7]

Another of the flourishing islands which we passed on our way to Siam was the island of Āchī. From Ceylon to the port of Āchī takes five or six days if the winds are favorable and this island is considered part of Below the Winds. As is well known Saifu 'l-Mulūk and Badī'u 'l-Jamāl[8] lived here and their palace and throne can still be seen. The island is located on the equator and thus it is constantly spring. All year the trees bear fruit. On some of the branches the hanging fruit is already ripe and on others it is still maturing and some trees are just beginning to bloom.

Most of Below the Winds enjoys a continual spring season but Āchī has a climate which is even more unusual for its balance and beauty. There are many fountains and rivers whose sweet water is a delight to the palate. The plantations as well as the uncultivated fields are continually in full bloom and the hills and plains are always green and flourishing. The whole island is like the dazzling garden of Iram[9] and the beauty of such a climate can only be described by the verses of the poet Ẓuhūrī.[10]

> Evening is never sultry, noon is never hot
> And trees sway gently in cool breezes.
> The happy grove smiles to see new spring
> And raises a canopy of dew-fresh branches.
> Everywhere the trees are heavy, laden with bright fruits.
> Their heads bow to the ground to thank God for His bounty.

Āchī is indeed a very prosperous and splendid island. At one time it was the abode of genii but now every corner shelters a separate king or governor and all the local rulers maintain themselves independently and do not pay tribute to any higher authority.

The ruling dynasty of Āchī

Earlier there was an Arab king on the island. He went to Āchī, succeeded in establishing himself and even after his death several members of his family held the throne. This state of affairs continued up until the crown passed to one of that Arab's descendants who was an insufferable tyrant with a passion for bloodshed. His rule was distinguished by the number of murders he perpetrated. After his death the ministers and councilors were desperate to preserve the peace and prosperity of the island and they decided to place the late king's daughter on the throne. It also happened that the surviving son was too young to rule.

Unmanly deceit

Thus the councilors kept the reins of power in their own hands and governed the island without any problems. Their hypocrisy did not balk at this unmanly solution. They simply hid their heads under a female kerchief of shamelessness and disloyalty. These woman-hearted men of state seated the maiden of their virgin thought on the throne of deception and from that time on this kingdom, which is the twin of Paradise, has been given over in marriage to Houri-like beauties, women as charming as angels.[11]

As for the councilors of state, the beloved spouse who sits with them on the throne of fulfillment is state power and their only close companion and confident who knows the secrets of their hearts, is the all-seeing sun. The present king and all the natives are Muslims of the Shāfiʿī sect.

The gold mines of the island

The island of Āchī is full of gold mines and even in the open fields you can find small particles of gold. There is a gold mine right near the king's residence but since he has no expenses, he does not see any reason to dig out the gold. A large river flows through the island and it is fed by several springs which are located in the mountains. The streams flow down and join one another before they reach the sea. After a flood when the water recedes, it is the custom for the natives to sift through the sand all along the river banks. They find many small gold particles and bits as large as a bean or a chick pea. The tiny particles which they find in or near the river are not taken into account but one-tenth of all the larger nuggets goes to the king's treasury. The other nine-tenths is the property of whoever has found it.

Gold in the interior

There are many mines a good distance away from the inhabited part of the island. No one exploits these rich mines because of their isolated position. To reach the interior of the island you must face wild animals and all the other hazards of the jungle. There are times, however, when a large number of natives join together and go into the jungle to work for a limited period of time. If they prove the worth of their life's coin in the melting pot of that jungle's hardship and toil, they reap great profits but if they have no luck or do not work hard enough, they return home bearing nothing but grief and affliction. Whatever is extracted from the distant mines is not taxed by the administration. The prospectors keep whatever they find.

Mining is more important than farming

A large part of the natives hunt for gold all year and consequently, except for a few gardens and orchards which the servants attend to, very little real agriculture is practiced. Rice and other basic foods are brought to Āchī from India and the other countries of Below the Winds. It must be added that the gold which is found on this island is of the finest purity and highest standard. The natives even find pieces of rock which are half stone and half gold, just as in Shahr Nāv they find logs which are half wood and half stone. The king's administration rents the rights to pan gold in one of the big rivers and charges ten bahārs of gold which is 350 royal mans. Other products of Āchī are tin, aloes wood, sapanwood, camphor, iron and elephants.

The king

It is the custom for the king to appear every day in public. He sits upon his throne, which has a peculiar curtain drawn all around it. The prime minister, the high judge, the princes and other dignitaries sit at a certain distance from the throne. Only the eunuchs are admitted behind the curtain and whenever a minister raises a question before the king, the reply comes through these eunuchs. When a matter is presented to the king for consideration, he passes on his command in simple terms and states exactly what must be done. The petitioner always agrees with the king's decision for better or for worse and merely adds 'May it be so'.

Ranks are based on swords

As is always the case in Below the Winds, the posts which exist in the island's administration are not based on any real power and authority. Everything is simply a show, like wearing a fancy dagger or a sword. However, those who wear gold swords do not have the highest rank. The sword made of savāsa, that is, an even mixture of gold and copper, denotes importance and high position. The men who hold positions of little importance are given the swords of gold whereas the Bārkān[12] of the state is issued a sword of savāsa.

The death sentence

When the courts issue an order for someone's death, a dagger is taken out of its sheath and in its naked state is transferred into the hands of one of the eunuchs. The eunuch is sent forth from the king's inner chambers to present the sword to the man who has been condemned. This sword is a sign that the eunuch has come to kill the person.

Foreign merchants

The merchants and captains of every race and nation come to Āchī for trade and present the island régime with gifts from whatever merchandise they have. These presents are taken before the king who orders that the foreign visitors be entertained and recompensed with gifts and honors in proportion to what they have sent him. If a rich Iranian with a large retinue comes to Āchī, the authorities tell him to send as much as possible of his deliciously cooked foods and sweets before the king, since his Majesty has acquired a taste for Iranian foods but he is not capable of having them properly prepared.

The local morals

The king and the people have a very strange sense of morals and proper behavior. If a foreigner who is just passing through stares at the wall of one of their houses and frequents a particular street a number of times, they become very suspicious of him and tell him 'That kind of behavior is considered a grave mistake in this country. If you do that again you are likely to bring about your own destruction.'

If in the future this man does the same thing and is caught in that neighborhood with no excuse, he is surely murdered or if there is some doubt as to whether he understood the first warning, the plaintiff takes him to the law court and presents the case before the authorities. After a few witnesses have testified and it has been proved that the foreigner committed this error several times, a naked sword is presented to the plaintiff and that is a death sentence for the defendant.

There are many slaves in Āchī

As in the rest of Below the Winds the natives reckon high rank and wealth by the quantity of slaves a person owns. It is their custom to rent slaves. They pay the slave a sum of money, which he gives to his master, and then they use the slave that day for whatever work they wish. This practice is especially common in Āchī where the natives and the king own many slaves. These slaves are drawn from every nation and race.

Every day a certain number of them is delivered to the king's administration and when the king has finished grinding each individual like so much grain in the dust of the year's turning mill and the expenses and mill tax have been extracted in the form of the slaves' services, the remainder is given back to the master and this whole procedure is not considered in any way base or unfair. The idea that they have so many slave girls and servants merely encourages them to think of themselves as all the more important.

Everyone on the island steals

Despite the many mines, the plentiful revenues and their general lack of expenses, the natives have blackened their face with shame. On the island of Āchī stealing is most common and this basic flaw of character has infected all the inhabitants, young and old. When the merchants are engaged in buying and selling, their body is all eyes. None the less the slippery customers prove to be such deft thieves, they manage to apply a soothing collyrium to the merchant's sharp sight and before the owner's tongue can pronounce 'I will sell it', the customer claims 'It is mine' and denies having stolen anything. Thus the price of much good merchandise is often lost.

Most of the natives of the island are afflicted with this chronic illness and even the high-born indulge in these dishonest practices. Since the police themselves are thieves and the judges let everything get by, it is very difficult to uproot and destroy this wicked preoccupation of the islanders. Even though every year they cut off the hands and feet of a certain number of thieves, the authorities have not been able to shorten the reach of crime and the natives have not yet set their feet on the path of honesty. The indelible stain of bad reputation has darkened the face of all the natives. Consequently, the merchants who go to Āchī are extremely cautious.

An example of local hospitality

As for their sense of hospitality, if a stranger arrives in this country late at night and approaches someone's house seeking a bed, the native will yell forth from inside 'Put out your lamp and go to sleep. It's the middle of the night.'

The booming mountain

There is a certain mountain in Āchī and whenever a ship is approaching the island a loud noise issues from the mountain's lofty peak as a signal for the inhabitants. If a single ship is coming, the noise occurs once. Otherwise a separate noise is heard for each ship. Whether this noise is made by the genii,[13] a native, a magic charm or some other device remains a mystery.

The buffalo cave

Another oddity is a peculiar cave on the side of a mountain. Every now and then many buffalo come out into the daylight and hunters pursue them. The buffalo that escape take refuge again in the cave and it seems that no one has ever penetrated to the end of that cave or really understands where these buffalo come from.

The musical spring and the genii king

Another strange sight is a beautiful clear-water spring located on an imposing mountain. There the climate is always cool and pleasant and every so often charming music and singing is heard coming from that lovely spot. Some nights the bright glow of lamps can be seen up there but no one is able to explain what it is. They say that in the most ancient times Ceylon and Āchī were both in the possession of the genii and once a week the king of the genii flew over to Āchī and would entertain himself with a banquet. Then he would fly back to Ceylon. Remains of the genii king's palace and throne are still to be seen on the peak of the musical mountain and it is obvious that those remains are not the work of the natives of Āchī.

Healing waters

Another wonder is a magic spring. If someone is afflicted with a particular disease and not simply dying of old age, the magic waters cure the sick person immediately. However, illness other than the burden of old age is very rare in that pleasant country.

The Franks tried to capture Āchī

In closing may we present this interesting anecdote about the island of Āchī. One of the well-known stories current in this region concerns a group of Franks who arrived a few years ago with well-outfitted ships and intended to conquer the island. The Frank commander boldly sailed into the harbor and began to wage war. When news of the fighting reached the palace, the king sent the following message to the commander: 'Tomorrow morning come ashore or send a trusted minister in your place that I may entertain you as my guest. You will have the opportunity to explain your purpose and I will be able to judge the situation.'

The king's banquet for the Franks

The Frank commander came ashore in person and when the banquet ceremonies began, a large uncut melon was brought out along with the other foods. The melon and a knife were placed before the commander and the servants announced, 'The king sends this melon especially for you. Cut it up and serve yourselves.'

As hard as the Frank tried he was not able to make a breach in the melon with a knife or even with a sword. Then slave girls came, cut the melon effortlessly and placed the portions before the astonished commander. When the Franks finished eating the melon, a declaration from the king was delivered.

The island of Āchī is like a large melon

'Since you do not have sufficient power to cut into this melon, how will you take possession of a slice of this flourishing island? Āchī is a closed, firm melon which God, the almighty Gardener, has half uncovered in the midst of the sea and with the hand of His mercy He has bound her to the trellis of water and wind and bestowed her upon these natives to enjoy as the fruit of His bounty. Turn back from such far-fetched desires, otherwise the inhabitants of this island will catch you offguard and destroy you. In the past they have destroyed other men like you whose hearts were yearning for the benefits of this fair climate.

The second attempt to take the island

The commander was embarrassed by the whole affair. He departed with his ships and reported what had happened to his superiors. The Frank authorities reproached the commander and criticized his decision to withdraw. Once again the Franks sent many ships against the island and they began to harass the merchants and travelers who came into the port.

The flaming river

News of these events was relayed to the king and he adopted the following tactic. There is a certain liquid substance peculiar to that region which the natives extract from the trees and it is rather like turpentine. The king's men threw huge quantities of this liquid into a river which is fed by the mountain springs and flows down through the island into the sea. At dawn they set fire to the whole river and since the light of morning was increasing over the horizon, the flashing flames were not so quickly distinguished. It was a while before the Franks realized that their ships were burning in a sea of fire and by the time they could get up their anchor chains, their whole fleet was destroyed. The departing soul barely had time to get clear of the body's sinking ship.

The Franks were permanently discouraged

From that time up until now the greed of the Franks has remained content with the harvest of that holocaust and as for capturing the island of Āchī they never again stirred up such a mad ambition in the head of their commanders. The heat of their desire was quenched by the scattered raindrops which fell from the cloud-like reports concerning that calamity. 'God alone knows all the fearsome details of these matters.'

The island of Andaman

One of the many strange islands which we passed on our voyage was the island of Andaman. This island is flourishing and extremely green and here lives a group of cannibals who have long teeth like dogs. The teeth of these savages are so long that they project from their mouth, but otherwise their bodies are like human beings. As for their dress they are content to wear nothing more than the leaves of trees to cover their loins. If anyone has the misfortune of falling into their hands, they carry off the poor man and eagerly devour him. For this reason people do not visit Andaman and not many details are known about the island or the inhabitants.

People who visited the island

It was heard from the councilors of the king of Shahr Nāv that quite a while ago a ship from the Siamese king's administration was caught in a storm and blown off its course. Then the winds died down completely and the helpless ship drifted in confusion for a good length of time. Finally, the breeze of Fate carried them near the island of Andaman. There was no more fresh water aboard and the pupils of the crew's eyes launched ships in the direction of dry land.

The crewmen are attacked

The only remedy was that the captain, who was from the nation of England, go ashore with a group of his men. All of them were armed with every weapon imaginable. They wandered up and down the island until they came to the source of their pursuits. There they gathered all the fresh water they could carry. But when the crewmen were about to return to their ship, a group of savages, who had hidden themselves along the path, jumped forth and set upon them in a fight. The savages were very fierce and carried off a few of the Englishmen.

The cannibals eat some Englishmen

At a short distance from the site of the battle the cannibals began eating their captives and no matter how much the other crewmen fired upon them they would not be interrupted.

The weapons of the savages

The bows and arrows of the natives are made of wood and their spears are made from fish bones. The way they use these arrows is very strange. When they want to hit a particular person they do not shoot directly at him but they aim straight up into the air. The arrow goes up as high as it can and then falls towards earth but it always hits the target just as they wish. The wounds inflicted are deadly and it is not clear whether the fish bone causes this or if they poison the arrows.

The crew gets back to the ship

In the end the captain was badly wounded but he managed to reach the shore with a certain number of his men. Once they were back to their rowboat they began firing a cannon which they had brought with them and only in that way were they able to frighten the natives and escape. Thus they reached their ship and set sail.

The evil influence of the captured weapons

During the fighting on shore a bow and some arrows fell into the hands of one of the crewmen. When they had left the island behind and were a certain distance out at sea, a violent lightning storm suddenly broke upon them and contrary winds blew up. The ship was almost battered to pieces and sent down. All the men aboard were so many pupils drowning in tears of fear. When their hope was almost gone it occurred to them that their misfortune might be due to the bow and arrows which were aboard. They knew well enough that those savage islanders were men involved with black magic and spells. Consequently someone threw the bow and arrows overboard and half an hour later the storm died down completely.

The unhappy crew and passengers only escaped from the sea's destruction after suffering much grief in the depths of their heart. The sailors explained that the men of that island are not powerful and strong in a physical sense but weapons have no effect upon them. Another strange point about these savages is that their feet are half a cubit wide.

The magic spring of Andaman

There is another story which is famous among the many stories told about the islands. We heard that there is a pool of water on the island of Andaman which God, the generous Bestower who forsees all man's needs, has caused to flow up from the alchemical springs of His bounty and the underground caverns of His power. Any metal that this water is poured over turns into pure gold and it is not necessary to pass through the various preliminary stages of the Alchemists such as dissolution, calcinification, recomposition and Qiṭmīr, the Dog of the Seven Sleepers.[14] Knowledge that this water does exist springs from the following story.

Shipwrecked on the island of the cannibals

They say that once a ship which was passing the island of Andaman was caught in a storm and began to sink. Some of the people aboard managed to save themselves and reached the shore by riding on a large piece of wood. However, when the survivors landed, the natives immediately captured them and cut them up into little pieces. These pieces the savages sent to each other as pleasant delicacies.

The clever barber

It so happened that among the prisoners there was a bath attendant who worked as a barber and a bleeder. When it was his turn to be eaten, he produced a mirror which he had kept with him and showed the savages the reflection of their fearsome faces. When they beheld their own countenances, they were stunned and they brought the man before their chief.

The chief spares the barber's life

Face to face with the chief they described the image and appearance of the prisoner's behavior. Since they had a bright, clear proof of what they reported the king's countenance lit up with interest. The chief spared the barber's life and after the local custom accorded a wife to the man and thus the man lived among those cannibals for a certain time.

Discovery of the magic water

One day when the barber was washing his razor in the above-mentioned spring, he beheld the steel suddenly transformed into gold. The glitter of this event lit up the mirror of his heart. As soon as he found the chance, he returned alone to the spring and filled several coconut shells with the miraculous water. This liquid treasure he carefully stored away. Every day thereafter he was disobedient. His thoughts and allegiance revolved about his store of magic water.

The escape

After a certain length of time he sighted a ship at sea and quickly built himself a raft to escape with. He put his trust in God, collected his coconut shells and with his raft managed to reach the ship. When he had been aboard for several days, he fell into a dark mood of melancholy.

The bleeder's melancholy

Now this barber and bleeder had always regulated the humors of his own constitution by bleeding regular customers and he was accustomed to make his profits when other men's blood began to flow.

He considered the vital blood of life and the act of drawing it out to be a noble livelihood and a profession directly involved with man's spirit.

The tongue of his scalpel went about its greedy work and opened the veins of men and his sharp-edged razor did not leave a single hair when it ranged over a client's head.

In his present state of ill-humor his head was not thinking clearly. How could the small coconut shell, which contained the fluids of his patience, not spring a leak and reveal the magic water?

Carelessness and impatience

While he was still aboard the ship he became possessed by the idea of testing his treasure and wished to see if the magic water had retained its original properties or not. He poured one drop of the precious water on a piece of iron and sure enough it changed into a lump of gold.

The bleeder is bled to death

However, the Franks of the ship took note of this miracle and without further fuss opened the vital artery of his life with the razor of destruction and thus they brought about his death. They proceeded to pour the remaining water over the ship's anchor and cannons and all the metal immediately turned into gold. When the ship reached its destination, the Franks told their superiors all of what had happened.

Andaman is impregnable

Other ships were sent out to capture the strange island but due to the wisdom of God, which is always most apt, there is no spot on the coast of that island where a ship can lie at anchor. The island is all sheer rock and mountains. Thus the Frank squadron returned home without making a dent in the island.

The Dutch were interested in the island

It was also heard that the Dutch were possessed with a passion to capture Andaman. They sent ships to the island several times but always remained thoroughly puzzled by the situation. Eventually they gave up and went home without achieving their aims. However, the Dutch Franks are not so hasty to set out on expeditions. If this report is true, it is strange that they were not able to think of a remedy for their predicament. Whether these events took place as described or have any basis of truth to them, 'Only God on high has knowledge of all the mysteries of this world.'

The island of Nākbārī

Another island is Nākbārī[15] which the author of 'Ajā' ibu 'l-Makhlūqāt describes in detail and refers to as Nīkābūs. It is actually very close to the island of Andaman. Nākbārī is inhabited and most of the fruits of India as well as wax, honey, ambergris and iron are to be found there. When a ship passes the island the inhabitants get in their boats and come out to meet it and they will trade whatever items the island produces for any old things. The natives are all very poor and if a ship comes to the island to take on supplies it is very easy to do business. No one is difficult to deal with.

Why the natives are sly traders

Not long ago an Iranian merchant from Māzandarān went to that island and settled there but he was in the habit of watering his milk and needling his silk and generally cheating the people. Now when the natives sell ambergris they have taken to adding wax and stones to the pure substance and have blackened their faces with dishonesty.

Nākbārī has a treaty with Andaman

The inhabitants of the island due to their being so close to Andaman used to suffer bitterly at the hands of the neighboring cannibals. Whenever the savages of that island saw a man from Nākbārī, they would catch him and eat him. Now an agreement has been made that as soon as someone dies in Nākbārī, the body is sent to the cannibals as tribute and in return the cannibals have promised to do no harm to anyone who is living.

The island of Manīla

Another island, which belongs to the islands of Ḥalīla, is called Manīla. From Shahr Nāv to that port takes twenty days if the winds are favorable. Manīla is now in the possession of the king of the Castillians and to reach his capital from that island is a journey of six months. Every few years the king changes the governor whom he has appointed. The usual practise among the Frank kings is to leave an officer in his post for three or four years and then when the term is up to see if the man has rendered service worthy of the throne.

If the official's behavior has been exemplary he is promoted to a higher post. Otherwise, if it is clear he was negligent in his duties, he is removed from office. This practise encourages officials to strive in the king's service and also stands as a constant warning to the wayward. Although the above-mentioned king does not derive much profit from this island, he finds it strategically valuable because it is six months' distance from his home kingdom.

The settlers on the island

Manīla has an extremely temperate climate and is exceptionally beautiful. It also possesses many fine houses. By now the Franks and men of other nations have built several thousand homes there. Every kind of product is found on the island especially sugar and white wax. The natives are always cheerful and are all rich. They are continually engaged in giving parties and enjoying themselves.

Gold mines and profits from trade

It may be added that there is a certain amount of gold to be found in the local mines. Manīla is actually not very far from China and Japan, thus every year ships from all over the world visit the island for trade and take away good profits. Recently, however, the king decreed that merchants may not stay in the port longer than the monsoon season.

The level of local crafts

A high level of gold work is practiced on the island and this craft is mostly in the hands of the Chinese who have settled there. Their crafts and manufactured goods, especially their work in gold and intricate lattice patterns, are so masterful they have inspired the verses:

> Whatever bright objects man can create,
> Beating or pouring silver and gold,
> Their hands can fashion as no man can fashion.
> Indeed they are masters of silver and gold.

In the arena of gold work and jewelry they have displayed such feats of skill that they have no rivals in the world market of Time and Place. Their jewelry is so fine and delicate it is a well-cut refutation of all the theories in favor of the indivisible atom.

The heavenly Sphere of Turquoise is so jealous beholding their filigree and turquoise enamel, he has adorned his night robes with the filigree of the stars and his daylight clothes with the bright blue of clear skies.

At night he has a thousand eyes, stars fixed with amazement at the genius of such intricate jewelry on earth.

The rare birds of those regions

A merchant in Shahr Nāv related that in the house of the local governor there is a bird similar in appearance to the cockatoo and this bird speaks the Frank tongue so well you would think a human being was speaking. In Manīla as well as all along the coast from Siam to China there live various wild birds, creatures of extraordinary color that are decorated with beautiful patterns. More strange than their bright colors is the fact that God's power has allowed them to acquire human speech after a certain amount of contact with men. It is a regular business to export these birds, especially to the kingdom of the Macassars who have recently lost a certain number of their ports to the Dutch Franks.

Capturing the exotic birds

The island of Manīla also produces nutmeg and cloves. The wild birds spend all their time in those spice trees, particularly when the trees are in bloom and the blossoms are wide open. At that time the birds over-indulge and eat so much that they faint. Then the hunters easily catch them and sell them. But these birds are very delicate and have such little strength, few of them remain alive in captivity. In all the surrounding islands as well there are birds that are very strange looking and have beautiful colors.

The author's gift to the Shāh

Recently an Arab who came from that distant country brought several specimens of these colored birds and he was planning to take them to India. Since these birds were worthy of coming before the blessed sight of our most noble king, the humble author contented the merchant and took them off his hands. It is the author's intention to present these birds as a gift in the hope of performing a small service for his Majesty. Along with the birds is a yellow and white monkey which was brought from the farthest islands of China for the Siamese king. The monkey was awarded to this worthless servant who accepted it and set out for the celestial threshold of Iran with the hope that God's infinite generosity would aid him to accomplish a pleasing gesture.

The great island of Japan

Of all the islands that exist in the various seas, Japan is by far the richest and the most magnificent. It is known throughout the world for its beauty and the extent of its flourishing population. Contrary to the rest of Below the Winds where spring is perpetual, the climate of Japan is perfectly balanced and has four distinct seasons.

In this respect it is said to be much the same as Iran, the pleasure spot of the world, and due to the changes of seasons the climate is very comfortable and healthy. The length of the island is about 1,000 farsakhs and everywhere there are flourishing settlements with fields under cultivation. Even the mountain sides have orchards which bear fruit both summer and winter. All year it is possible to obtain ice and snow and they have a large variety of wild animals and birds, falcons, the tarlān, hawks, the Shāhīn falcon and pheasants. The author has actually examined one of their pheasants which a merchant brought to Shahr Nāv. It was at least a cubit long. Consequently, the natives of the island all have a passion for hunting.

The location of Japan

During the monsoon the voyage from Shahr Nāv to Japan takes fifteen days but the return trip takes forty. One side of the island is near the coast of China but scholars believe that this island is the end of the inhabited world, that the sea in which it lies flows into the great ocean. The scholars who write on geography and have given details pertaining to Japan, mention that the local king is called Mahrāj or Yahvāj. There is this small degree of disagreement in their accounts.

The geographers who have written about the island

The author of the Rauẓatu'ṣ-Ṣafā refers to Japan as the island Ar-Rānij when he describes the islands in the sea of China. He also states that Japan is 1,000 farsakhs long and that the annual taxes which the treasury collects amounts to 6,000 mans of gold. The author of Ajā'ibu'l-Makhlūqāt, quoting Muḥammad ibn Zakarīya, writes that the king receives 200 mans of gold every day, and since gold is generally so plentiful the king has ordered that it be made into ingots and thrown in the sea. This is only one of the many marvels that same author mentions when he describes Japan. However, the humble author of this report, for fear of being prolix, has only made bold to include what he has ascertained from merchants who recently returned from the splendid island.

Precious metals

The merchants relate that there is a great abundance of precious metals on the island such as gold, silver and tin and there is also a large amount of gypsum. But so great is the extent of this mineral wealth, the pen's tongue is too thin and weak to undertake the full description. There is absolutely no limit, end or confine to the island's precious metals nor for that matter is there one restricted area where the metal can be obtained. Every mountain and field is a potential mine.

Prosperity but idolatry

It is also worth noting that the population of Japan is more dense than in any other part of the world but despite all these advantages the king and his subjects are engaged in a religion and creed of infidelity. They are all idolaters.

There are still a few corners of the island which are not under the king's direct control. None the less, every local governor is submissive to the royal authority and the greater part of the island is included in the kingdom, which is indeed a mighty and a splendid realm.

The capital and the king's palace

The journey up from the port to the king's capital takes fifty days but no foreigner has permission to visit the royal residence. It is said that the king's palace is located alongside a mountain where there are vast deposits of gold, and the palace consists of twelve levels. Each level has twelve steps leading up to it and on every level stands a separate palace built from bricks of solid gold and silver.

Mining

The author has heard several varying reports to the effect that every day the peasantry is kept busy digging up vast quantities of gold and silver and this work goes on in the remote mines. The precious metal is packed on animals and sent directly to the king's court. There an incredible treasure is continually being collected and stored away, but no one other than the king himself looks after the gold or enjoys this mass of wealth. The author of the Rauẓatu'ṣ-Ṣafā states that these huge amounts of gold and silver are always extracted from the far-off mines while no one works the mines which are near by.

The use of gold is restricted

It seems rather strange but despite this unusual abundance of gold the natives are forbidden to make use of it. The law is so strict on this point that if a person is caught possessing or is known to be hiding a single atom of the metal, he and his family will be destroyed down to the very last atom of their household.

The natives are cheerful and industrious

Contrary to the custom of Below the Winds every native in Japan is occupied with some particular job. As for the army, the king draws his troops from the peasantry, whereas the professional classes are separate from the rest of the people. In Japan all the natives regardless of their class wear real clothes and they are in the habit of shaving their heads. On the whole their daily life is happy and they spend much time in entertainments and festive gatherings.

The deceitful scheming of the Portuguese

Formerly there was a sizable group of Portuguese Franks living in the port and they carried off good profits from trade. They were held in high esteem and treated with the utmost dignity, at least up until a certain time, for it came to pass that their padres decided to dig a tunnel of deceit with the pickaxe of cunning and soon they had poked the head of their morbid schemes up through the ground of decency.

Tunnels and magnets

They began their digging from far off and burrowed their way underground until they reached the base of one of the larger idols. Then they hollowed out the inside of the idol from underneath so that it was possible for a man to raise his head up into the idol's stomach. When this work was finished, someone secretly entered the statue and began delivering wicked sermons from within. Besides this trick they contrived a system of magnets in the ceiling of one of the temples and were able to suspend an iron idol in mid air.

The talking idol converts the natives

With this kind of fraud and deception they had no difficulty in fooling the simple-minded Japanese. Once established by means of artificial miracles, they busied themselves converting the people, calling them to join their foreign faith. Thus they led those poor fools forth from one pit of error into another, the dilemma of the Frank religion. The pickaxe of their schemes was sharp and piercing, leaving its mark in the granite of the people's heart.

In no time at all thousands of misled Japanese joined the faith of these sly foreigners. The converts were so dazzled by this kind of trickery, they handed over all matters of government and trade to the Franks and were ready to follow any orders their new masters gave them. The situation continued like this until the Dutch discovered what manner of deception the Portuguese were practicing.

The superiority of the Dutch

It may be mentioned here that of all Christian nations the Dutch stand out as far superior. Their practical intelligence is known to all through the many tales and anecdotes which give a fair account of their exploits. It is clear that they possess a high degree of good sense and they are willing to apply themselves with energy to all their concerns. Stranger still, their particular faith displays a few true religious principles.

The Dutch uncover the tricks of the Portuguese

As it happened the Dutch were in the habit of visiting the port of Japan and carrying on trade and when they were confronted with the speaking statue and the airborne idol, they immediately recognized these tricks as sheer nonsense. They applied themselves to ascertaining the facts about what was really going on and it was not long before the spy of their thought brought forth his head from the tunnel of investigation. They quickly discovered the secret of the Portuguese and once that low scheme was uncovered the Dutch went straight to the capital.

The Dutch inform the king of Japan

They announced before the king: 'The Portuguese are playing certain cheap tricks to deceive the people and the population is beginning to turn towards them for leadership. If the Portuguese go on in this manner it will not be long before they increase their strength and attempt to take possession of the whole kingdom. If you doubt these words send a group of your men back to the port with us and we will show them exactly what the Portuguese are doing.' The king heard this report with great displeasure and quickly called out his army. The order was given to march on the port at once.

The king's army slaughters the heretics

When the army arrived it was clear that the Dutch statements were true and a great slaughter ensued. Young and old, natives and foreigners, everyone who was involved with the new religion was put to death.

Thus the heretics were completely exterminated and all their places of worship were destroyed, but from that time up until now no outsider has been given permission to visit the king's capital and even the merchants and travelers who come to the port are not allowed to remain longer than the monsoon season.

Only the Dutch have retained some favor

The interior of Japan remains a mystery, for it seems no foreigner has yet acquired any information concerning the roads and highways which run throughout the kingdom. Of all the outsiders, only the Dutch have maintained a certain degree of authority and esteem in that port. Consequently, every few years one of their men is placed in a kind of cage which is covered over with drapes and in that manner he is carried to the capital. Then the king commands the Dutch envoy to undertake certain tasks for the crown and sends him back to the port.

How the authorities treat the foreign merchants

When a merchant or traveler arrives in the port the ministers and port authorities send a group of men to the ship and whatever merchandise is aboard is carefully recorded. Then the officials depart but when they come out to the ship the second time they announce, 'We are willing to buy your goods for such and such a price. If that is satisfactory, well and good, if not, keep your merchandise and leave.'

The natives of that country will not dare buy and sell things themselves and so the foreign merchants are under a certain constraint. However, the price quoted by the officials is not usually a bad one, even though now prices are much lower than they used to be. Thus the merchants are still making good profits. Once the merchant agrees to sell, the merchandise is brought ashore and the merchant is assigned a house but before the affair is finally settled, there is one further detail.

When the officers escort the merchant from the ship to the shore, they make a point of passing by the same talking idol that the Portuguese Franks employed to perpetrate their hoax. The Japanese are keen to observe the foreigner's reaction and they expect him to place his foot on the idol's face without any hesitation. If the merchant is reluctant or hesitates, they kill him on the spot and confiscate his goods, assuming that they have caught one of their hated enemies. However, if all goes well the merchant is taken to his house and two boys are assigned to him as attendants.

Wicked houseboys

These boys behave like the wicked element of lust that is an ingrained part of man's imperfect nature. They apply themselves to inciting their guest to sins of the flesh and lascivious practices. If the merchant resists their suggestions other officials come and ask, 'What is wrong? Why do you not indulge in these little sins?'

Excuses

To avoid the issue the gentleman must answer, 'Indeed I have often engaged in these playful activities but at the moment I am suffering from a certain sickness which inhibits me. I am forced to give up this behavior until I am fully cured.' Thus installed in his house, the merchant is obliged to keep to his quarters.

Concluding business matters

Before the authorities go and leave him to himself, they record in detail the gold and other items the merchant wants in exchange for his merchandise. Once the monsoon has arrived again they procure everything he has requested and have it sent down to his ship. Finally, when the time is right they come to the merchant's house and abruptly announce, 'You are required to depart. All the goods you wished have been delivered and the set sums of money have been paid. Pack up and be off.'

Concessions for the Dutch

It is absolutely impossible for anyone to stay longer than the monsoon. Since the Dutch were very clever and proved themselves trustworthy, they have acquired the exclusive rights to import all the items that sell for a high price and they are continually making huge profits. From the point of view of the local authorities there is no lack of any particular commodity, so they feel free to co-operate with the Dutch alone. Thus the other visiting merchants are confined to their quarters and the natives are forbidden to trade directly with any foreigners.

The chief functions of the king of Japan

The king of Japan does not draw any revenues or profits from land and farming. A brief description of his daily routine is as follows. From the early morning until noon and again from the afternoon to the evening the king presides over the law court and he devotes all his attentions to the problems of his subjects. Like the rulers of the 'Abbāsid dynasty the king of Japan is always dressed in black. Thus he sits in the tribunal and metes out justice. One case which came up not long ago illustrates how the good king protects the nation.

A dishonest proposition

There was a particular troublemaker who flared up from among the embers of the lower classes and found a chance to forward an unjust proposal to the king through one of the higher courtiers. The gist of his scheme was: 'I have contrived a plan whereby both your Majesty and myself might greatly profit. Since your Excellency has absolute power in these matters, let it be decreed that no one but I may manufacture these simple goods which I now produce in competition with the other Japanese. If I am the only man who sells these goods, I will be able to raise the price as I please. For this privilege I would gladly pay the royal treasury a fine sum of money every year.'

The king's displeasure

The king was greatly displeased and replied: 'Indeed we have an evil proposal set here before us. From oldest times the subjects of our realm have been free to undertake the manufacture of these goods in question, for such goods are part of their everyday needs. This is not a matter of concern for the state, such as exports and imports, and a man who would interfere with the basic needs of the peasantry only intends evil. The fit course of action in this instance is to kill the despicable merchant along with all his family. A display of harsh punishment now will deter men from entertaining any such schemes in the future.'

It may also be added in passing that since gold is not considered very precious or rare, the king does not use dishes and utensils of that metal.

The brothels

The island of Japan supports many brothels which are stocked with very good-looking women and the custom is that each house posts a price list on the outside door. Even more strange than that is the fact that the males of the establishment bear names like Mūsh, Lūḥ, Zarbād, and the women have familiar Muslim names like Zainab and Fāṭima.[16] How the natives have acquired knowledge of these names is hard to explain and remains a mystery.

Japanese swords

The swords which are produced by the craftsmen of the island are beyond all powers of description. The tongue's blade grows sharp and cutting and refuses to submit to the author's will. Although it is true that the tempered blades of Japan cannot be compared with the generally high level of work throughout Iran, such as that of the craftsman Asad, and the shape of their swords is odd, rather like that of a large knife with a straight, wide blade, none the less the magnificent temper and lustre of their steel would make a diamond seem dim and worthless.

The amazing effects of a great sword

It would be no surprise if the mere thought of such a flaming blade set fire to the haystack of the enemy's life. Indeed imagining such a blade in the king's hand, the importunate petitioner trims and prunes the irksome tree of hopes and desires.

In the scales of competition only a hair's difference distinguishes the sharpness of this beautiful blade and the cutting edge of the beloved's arched eyebrows. But this strange blade is so perfectly straight, the eyebrows of the seductress curved in amazement.

Indeed, an odd wound has been inflicted. This sword is so sharp it has cut through the author's fantasy. The present description remains incomplete, as if beheaded. No matter what metaphors are matched with this sword such a blade emerges as the victor.

The swords of Japan are very rare outside the country

The natives look upon the marvelous weapon as one of their most prized possessions. It is therefore forbidden to remove this splendid sword from the sheath of that country and smuggling one out is almost impossible. Even if chance places the hilt of one of these swords in a merchant's hand, it is always difficult to market. It is really an unpopular novelty because of its irregular shape and its high price. Therefore the merchants have been reluctant to buy them.

One of these swords which was originally purchased for a large sum and transported to Shahr Nāv as a gift for the Siamese king did not bring much of a price at all on the open market, simply because of its proportions and the delicate construction.

How the Japanese make swords

There is a mysterious method which the craftsmen of Japan follow in order to make one of these swords. It is so time-consuming and difficult, it takes a hundred years to produce one blade. First they bury several quantities of their best steel in a spot which is very damp. There the steel remains for at least a few years before they dig it up and examine it. Whichever pieces do not show flaws are taken to the furnace and made into sword blades. But this is only one stage of the operation.

These blades are collected and buried in the damp earth again and when several years have gone by, they dig them up. The best of the group are sent back to the furnace for the second time where they are tempered once more. This tedious process is repeated several times until the sought after purity is attained.

Their calculations are so complicated and precise the very hour when they will put the finishing touch to their work is determined in advance. However, the last stage and exactly how they perfect the temper of the blade is not known.

The sword as a decoration

When the Japanese decide to get married it is the custom for the groom and the bride to present each other with swords, as if they were exchanging wedding gifts. The women of Japan consider the sword a piece of jewelry and it is customary for women to adorn themselves by wearing a sword at their side.

Chinese craftsmen in Japan

Since Japan is so close to China, a large number of Chinese have crossed over and settled on the island. Most of them are of the professional classes and they manufacture a variety of ingenious novelties of wood, gold, silver and porcelain. The porcelain in Japan is extremely fine and delicate, yet men of experience do not value it very highly. It is unfortunate but the potters do not take the pains to age their clay properly and the result is much the same as the old saying about a man who loses his head too easily in an argument, 'He is like a bowl that is hotter than the soup.' Thus the porcelain dishes of Japan do not resist heat well and are prone to cracking.

Paper and the value of money

The natives of Japan also manufacture a kind of Khān Bālighī paper[17] which takes its name from the world famous Khān Bālighī of Khiṭā. The money of Japan is a piece of gold beaten into a sheet as thin as paper. It weighs three mithqāls and four dāngs and since the merchants are continually extracting profits from Japan that peculiar money has been spread throughout all the countries which surround that region.

In Japan itself one mithqāl of that currency is bought and sold for one thousand dinars but in Shahr Nāv it will bring one thousand three hundred dinars. These are all the facts which this author ascertained concerning the prosperous island of Japan. Further knowledge rests with God, Who sees all and knows all.

Description of countries near Siam

It was stated earlier that there are many islands and important coasts in the distant seas of the east but the full tale's journey would indeed be long and most of the other foreign ports do not lie across the path to our goal. Thus the author continues his report on the sheets of clarity but at this stage the black horse of the author's pen admits its inability to traverse all quarters of those regions. The subject-depicting pen now points towards describing two of the many great lands which border on Shahr Nāv.

The land of Paigū

The first country of this part of our report is Paigū which is a flourishing land with well-populated provinces. To reach this country from Shahr Nāv takes ten days, or if you set out from Tanāsurī, only five or six days. There are those who believe that Paigū was once held and ruled over by the ancient hero Pīrān, the son of Vīsa, and that the well where Bīzhan[18] was imprisoned, is located in those regions. Yet it is clearly stated in the Nuzhatu'l-Qulūb that the famous well is in the city of Bābu'l-Abwāb, and since Paigū is quite far from Turkistan where all the above-mentioned heroes fought, it could not possibly have been the scene of their exploits. However the case may be, today the smaller coins used throughout Paigū are known as vīsas because Vīsa, the father of Pīrān, was the first man who used tin to make coins.

The origin of the natives

The inhabitants of that region, like the natives of Siam, are engaged in worshipping idols. And they spend all their wealth building temples and houses for the idols. Contrary to Shahr Nāv, most of the inhabitants of this country are Siamese but the king is an 'Abbāsid. In Shahr Nāv the king is Siamese and most of his peasantry is 'Abbāsid.

It is not improbable that the natives of Paigū are descendants of the line of Barmak. It is a well-known fact recorded in various texts how Hārūn destroyed the Barmakid family and scattered the few survivors.[19] A certain group of them escaped and seems to have found refuge in the vicinity of Khiṭā.

As was mentioned earlier, Shahr Nāv was once a province of Paigū and subject to the king of that country. Paigū is bordered on one side by the land of Rakhan,[20] where a separate king rules. Rakhan is generally considered part of Khiṭā and extends all the way to the frontier outposts of Bengal. On the eastern side Paigū joins with China. Copper, aloes-wood, sapan-wood, sandalwood, iron, elephants and wolves are found in Paigū. Shahr Ava is the king's capital.

A great ruby mine

In one of the border territories of Paigū there is a ruby mine located on the slopes of a mountain named Ghāplān. On the other side of this great mountain lies the Qipchāq Desert. It is a very long journey from the capital to the mine and the weather up on the mountain is extremely cold. The whole province is very isolated, being cut off by the jungle, and the king is not really able to maintain much control over the region. Hence, they are not able to work the mine all year long.

Originally the king of Paigū sent a few envoys to the territory where that rich mountain rises and they were able to conclude an agreement with the inhabitants on the slopes. The natives have a kind of measuring cup made out of reeds. The length and diameter of the cup indicates the amount of rubies it contains. Some of those rubies are as big as a pea or a bean and there are other rubies of all sizes. The natives present the king's administration with several cupfuls of every type. In exchange they accept basic provisions that are scarce in such a remote area.

If it happens that the natives have extracted even more rubies than the agreement called for, they bring them to the king's deputies and are willing to sell the extra jewels in accord with a fixed price. If the king's representatives are not interested, the natives are free to sell to whomever they wish. However, the very large rubies are always given to the king's administration.

The difference between the king of Paigū and the king of Siam

All the formal ceremonies and protocol of Paigū are the same as in Shahr Nāv. The only difference is that the king of Shahr Nāv has become accustomed to the manner and style of the Mughals. For a while now the Siamese king has been giving a certain amount of thought to proper form and procedure at the royal court. He has taken to riding and is concerned with his bearing and public appearance. Every day he leaves his palace and goes riding, hunting or sight-seeing.

However, the king of Paigū is just the opposite. No one besides the princes and the ministers of state ever sees him. Once a year when these pagans have a religious holiday, the king appears and grants a public audience. The merchants and foreigners who have come to Paigū to see the king for some specific purpose, must wait until that particular day. Then the king enters a special palace and sits himself upon a throne provided for the occasion. That palace has been built in a low-lying dell in order to encourage the cool breezes, which are bent over like old men, to enter without difficulty and circulate freely.

The merchants display their wares

The merchants who are visiting Paigū at that time, are called to these comfortable lodgings to have an audience with the king. They lay out their wares before the monarch just as the foreign merchants do in Iran. The translators state the prices of the various goods, while the merchants prostrate themselves, performing the uluk as in Shahr Nāv. The king receives what they have brought and thinks over the price for a while. Then he pays the foreigners with rubies of a somewhat higher value than they demanded.

The king's generosity

The ruby which is given in payment is wrapped up and sealed so that the merchant is not able to see exactly what he is getting. Thus the king dismisses the merchants without uncovering the value and price of the jewels. In fact the kings of Below the Winds, and the same is true for all the other infidels, have no part, portion or share in the gracious quality of generosity. Call to mind the saying, 'Generosity is a tree in the garden of Paradise.'

The heathen's lack of goods and character

Just as the infidel has no part in praising and worshipping God, the generous Gatherer of adoration, he is also excluded from savoring the honey of bestowing gifts, which quality of character is the fruit of the garden of Paradise. It is to the greater glory of God that the heathens have not acquired a portion of any of the finer material goods of this world. Thus they sit where they are, lost in the jungle of confusion.

The heathen is a foolish miser

When one of these infidels dies, no relative stands to inherit money nor is anyone the better off except the rūlīs, the religious men of that nation. As far as enjoying their money and wealth goes, whatever is not spent repairing temples and fashioning idols, they bury under the feet of their sacred statues. They also spend a certain amount of money when they cremate themselves. Otherwise, they do not use their wealth for anything constructive.

The king's clothing and general bearing

The king of Paigū does not have a professional army or even a distinct *corps* of servants and élite domestics nor does he possess regal clothes and bear himself with the dignity of a real king. The natives themselves are content to wear a simple loincloth and walk about with bare feet. They are not in the habit of wearing hats. Instead, they simply let their hair grow long.

The king's special hat

On the special day when the king gives his public audience, for an hour or so he wears a hat which resembles the kind of hat the puppeteers wear. It is made of wood and woven cane and the exterior surface is gilded with gold leaf. He places the hat upon his head but he seems to be afraid that it will fall off. To avoid such a mishap he has fastened the hat in place with a string that extends under his chin. This string is rather like the band of a turban cloth that keeps a turban firmly attached.

The king's robe

The king's robe has the same kind of sleeves as an overcoat but is shaped like an under tunic. The tunic which does go under his robe, resembles the breeches worn by a wrestler except that it is made of velvet stitched with brocade. The king wears all these fancy clothes on the holiday when he gives his public audience. The other days he is nude and only wears a loincloth like the rest of the natives of that country. He also lets his hair grow long.

The king's rubies

The king has selected certain huge rubies from his private collection, and this world, with all its experienced jewelers, has never before beheld such dazzling gems. It is his custom to have these rubies displayed in front of him on a tray.

The industrious Iranian and the fig tree

The following story is a testimonial of the king's lack of judgment and discrimination. A certain Iranian merchant came and settled in Paigū and for a long time he took great pains cultivating a fig tree. After much effort and trouble on the part of the merchant this seedling bore fruit and the fruit reached the perfection of ripeness. This was the noble fruit which God, the all-wise Gardener, concocted from opium and sugar cane, gave to the Prophet to swear by[21] and placed upon the table of life for the mortal guests of this world.

The king's ministers taste the figs

The merchant placed some figs upon a tray and had them delivered to one of the ministers, thus illustrating the famous saying 'The hyena always gets the best part.' The greedy minister, being a true jackal at heart, was used to eating roast snakes, lizards, dead birds and various other rotten foods even on festive occasions. Hence, his taste was especially delighted when he bit into one of the figs. He in turn sent a sample of the marvelous fruit to the other ministers.

The ministers inform the king

Being all united in speech and nature, they went before the king and described how delicious the new fruit was, that this fruit was undoubtedly straight from the garden of Paradise. They asked the king's approval to bring the fruit before his Majesty that he might incline to taste it himself. The king answered, 'How do you expect me to be inclined towards the trash which is in the house of a flea.' The king always refers to foreigners as despicable fleas.

The king agrees

But the ministers continued to beseech the king until he consented declaring, 'Good, I will taste this strange fruit, but go and fetch the whole tree. Dig it up by the roots and plant it in the royal garden.' The ministers carried out his decree.

A three-day period of caution

One of the customs of this king which deserves to be praised is that when he gives an important order, it does not go into effect until three days have elapsed. That way there is less chance the king will change his mind or regret the order. After three days if there is clearly an advantage in the standing order and all the councilors agree, the order is carried out. If the councilors do not think the command is wise, but there seems to be some error or negligence in the matter, they come before the king and present their advice until he changes his mind. The king generally listens to their view with attention and accepts their counsel.

The king profits from advice

In really difficult matters the king has recourse to his scholars and he orders them to enact whatever policies they think are best. This practise of deferring judgment is also the accepted procedure among the Christian kings who do not give an order concerning any affair without first obtaining the advice and consent of the ministers of state. For this reason the tree of their absolute power has not brought forth fruits of regret and sorrow in the field of monarchy.

China

The other important country which lies near Shahr Nāv and deserves to be included in this report is the powerful land of China. When the monsoon is blowing strong, a ship from Siam can reach the port of China in twenty days, but from there to the capital, which lies far inland, is still a journey of another forty days. The population of China is huge and it is reported that there are 1,029 different cities, every one of them rich and flourishing. The famous city Khān Bāligh, for example, is so large that it spreads for ten farsakhs.

Māchīn

For the sake of clarity it should be stated at this point that Māchīn is a separate country, which is located at the borders of China. As is recorded in the texts of scholars, the name Māchīn derives from Mahā Chīn, which once meant Greater China, but today these two countries are distinct and must not be confused.

14

China's renowned crafts

Above all else the natives of China are known for their skill in painting and the genius of their crafts. In all such fields the Chinese excel every nation past and present. Indeed the sight of the beholder is dazzled before their painted cloths and the brilliant work of their embroidery. However, on this subject scholars have employed pens more elegant and graceful than the brush of Mānī and the portrait of that country has been painted in all its colorful details.

Recent events

It is more appropriate if this author holds back his hand from a general description and instead undertakes an account of some recent occurrences in those regions. The humble author feels that these events are worthy of attention and are not wholly devoid of novelty. It is also hoped that this account may prove a cause of further understanding among men of insight and learning.

The Chinaman, Mūsh

The contents of this brief report are based on the statements of a certain minister's son from China. The gentleman's name was Mūsh and he was not without the ornamental necklace of education and good sense. Mūsh had just barely escaped the claw of destruction which the cat-like natives of China unleashed against him. In the end he took refuge in Shahr Nāv and has since been employed in the service of the Siamese king.

Pangūsī

As to the origins of China, the good gentleman Mūsh firmly believed that the first man to found a permanent settlement in that part of the world was someone called Pangūsī.[22] It would seem the Chinese have invented a large number of foolish tales concerning this fictitious founder and his deeds but worse than that they have no idea of the prophets and the apostles of God, neither Adam, the very first, nor Muḥammad, who was the glorious seal. They wander in error and by now have strayed so far afield from the truth, they consider their Pangūsī to be the lord of the universe. Up to this day these infidels tend images of their founder and render him worship in the temples. The extent of their ignorance is such that they are led to believe that Pangūsī never died. They speak of him as if he were alive even now.

The real founder of China

However, all their views are sheer nonsense. In the texts of history it is written that Yafūth ibn Nūḥ had a son named Chīn. It is perfectly clear that Chīn brought civilization to those empty regions and hence China derives its name from him. In fact, it was out of respect for his memory that the Chinese continued to bestow the kingship on the descendants of Chīn.

Changapchīn

Thus as the course of history advanced, one ruler after another ascended the royal throne and all along men from the noble line of Chīn held that high position. But the time came when Changapchīn rose to power, and his name means holder of the wonderous throne.

When a ruler gives himself to debauchery[23]

As fortune would have it, Changapchīn was a ruler who passed all his time in debauchery, cultivating every form of lewd amusement. He abandoned his body to uninterrupted pleasure and was lost in the negligence of wines.

His passions and lusts knew no bounds. From one hour to the next his intoxicated soul burned in the flames of wild music and whirling dancers.

The days of his frivolous life passed by in rapid succession like so many cups of undiluted wine, poured from the beaker of oblivion.

Fate, the expert musician, gave no warning but suddenly changed her key and the song of the king's destiny was shattered in disharmony and discord.

Out of stupidity the king dismissed his most valuable minister, Intelligence, the councilor of the state of existence and to fill the vacant post he chose the court favorites, Conceit and Self-esteem.

The king slowly turned his face away from worshipping God but in leaning too far to one side suddenly slipped and fell from the throne of justice. His hand let go the mighty cable of divine law and order and all his attentions deserted the helpless peasants, that fundamental charge which God bestows on kings.

Evil councilors exploit a weak king

For companions the king chose empty-headed men who mock and abuse the requirements of duty, who shun the burdens of responsibility, men totally devoid of the advantages of education, breeding and family honor. It was not long before the king began to consign important matters of state to that band of fools, not one of whom displayed the least sign of talent or personal worth.

Without taking the pains to melt the gold of their character in the crucible of wise scrutiny, he appointed them to positions of authority and trust and transferred the reins of government power into their weak and fallible hands.

Every detail of the king's affairs was coming to depend on the incompetence of those rogues. In accord with the saying, 'Whoever nurtures affection for a worthless fool, hopes to extract a smile from the weeping willow', the weak-minded king was destined to be sorely disappointed.

The councilors reveal their true nature

A black day was dawning over the empire. Now criminals were everywhere in office. Although they had restrained themselves while still striving to extend the grasp of their paw, once their claw had dug into high state power, they dropped all modesty and polite pretense like a useless veil. Before the eyes of the world at large they displayed their true character in all its poisonous vulgarity.

Little by little they increased their boldness and step by step they let their feet swerve from the outspread carpet of prudence and forethought. 'If at first the low-born appear reliable, soon enough they drop the veil and a treacherous nature stands revealed.' Once entrenched with confidence this herd of swine began its career oppressing the defenseless natives.

Rogues and cowards

The fearful gates of lawlessness and innovation were flung wide open and a multitude of injustices sallied forth against the peasants and the army. One man of rank and power was the same as the next, shivering cowards each and all, but here was a new breed of coward, a coward brave in displaying the filth of his impudence and immodesty.

In the annals of crime and cruelty such low natures have always been famous for their despicable wickedness. But what were practises so evil as to be previously only heard of in frightening tales suddenly became accepted behavior. Day by day the populace suffered further mistreatment and injury.

The good officials are persecuted

What happened next may appear beyond belief, but as a miser will flare up in rage if a fly steals from his drinking cup, so the low and worthless cannot bear the sight of honest men's success. In accord the newcomers struck out against the old officials and reduced everyone's fixed salaries throughout the whole country. Yes, whatever forms of foulness exist in the darkest realm of conception, these traitors brought to light in the theater of reality.

Men of experience and insight who had acquired their special skills through long years of service were trapped by new intrigues, and the outcome was inevitable. Conniving courtiers continually won the upper hand. Loyal and faithful councilors were set upon by a host of accusations and suddenly in the very presence of the king found themselves robbed of speech and condemned to death.

Thus in a short time the hands of all honest men were stung and broken and withdrew in pain from the affairs of the kingdom.

Famine and the metaphors of famine

But when tyranny and oppression reached a peak, it happened that the sprout of famine raised its ghastly head up through the soil of poverty. There was not a drop of rain in any province of the land. Mother cloud refused to let drip a single drop from the breasts of her mercy and thoughout the cradle of earth the thirsty-lipped raised their cries.

The drought spread and the fountains of China grew as dry as the eyes of cruel-hearted women who are not the least moved by the lover's supplications.

God, the almighty Avenger, hurled down the fire of his wrath into the harvest stacks of China's infidels. Smoke clouds of grief curled aloft, issuing from the very breasts of famine-stricken natives. Everywhere fumes of suffering rose into the air to pass away like the frail days of a Chinaman's insubstantial life.

The root of patience and endurance was torn out of the earth by the whirlwind of hunger and starvation. That year such brutal dryness fell that ears of corn once upright in the fields turned black as the beloved's ringlets and twisted into seductive curls.

Those days of drought were so oppressive to the throat, men of debauchery sought to wring out their wine-stained skirts.

Beside the moon's pale wafer is there anywhere a scrap of bread? The world is set abegging but bread is nowhere to be found. In the sky the white moon appears like a flat wafer of bread but longing sight has reduced her to a crescent. The eye of hungry men has devoured the moon's pale wafer. Dark Heaven is left to make its supper of an empty sky.

The wretched Chinese became so devoid of natural moisture, hairs no longer sprout on the farmland of Cathayan limbs.

The dryness reached the point that even soft down on the cheeks of blossoming boys changed into a black, rough beard for lack of freshness.

Heartbroken, the famous ruby of Badakhshān[24] pined for lost cool water and dripped the blood of unrequited love in his liver. Evermore he has borne a crimson face.

The seashell of 'Ummān wept, longing for beloved drops of rain and the eye of his heart brought forth the sparkling drop of a pearl.

As much as the guards of Heaven's dungeon whipped the clouds with lightning whips and the clouds bled red in the evening twilight, not once did the prisoners raise a thunderous cry or shed a single tear.

By now a rain cloud has not risen for so long in the sky, it was thought the wandering sign Aquarius had disappeared forever. Even if a wretched little cloud blew across the clear heavens, it was always as dry as a toy paper kite.

The palm tree of destruction

In that land of devastation and ruin nothing grew but a man's scant finger nail. Every seed scattered over that barren soil, fell in the same sad place and there a mighty palm tree grew. Praise be to God whose wrath creates such a vigorous, sturdy tree that can cast its shadow across a multitude of lands! What tree am I speaking of? The palm tree of dire famine, whose every leaf is a separate day of misery and ill-fortune.

There were no springs that flowed with cool, clear water. There were only men's tears mixed with the blood of grief.

It availed not then the pious beggar to display his bowl and staff in modest silence. For the shrill cries of ordinary men in desperation laid claims to the patron's generosity.

Men were forced to be content with the one food available, the kebab of hearts and livers scorched in the flames of starvation.

Everywhere men lay strewn upon the ground, their eyelids sealed with exhaustion. And just as well, for had they but glimpsed the naked poverty of their fellow creatures, their shamed sight would blink in blindness.

Taxation and oppression

Starvation had reached its final stage. By now the corrupt overseers of the human physique had eluded the sentry box of consciousness so often and absconded with so much nourishment from the body's vital food stores that the discontented farmers of the body were about to give up working the rice fields of life.

And yet it was that very moment that the despicable gang of state scribes chose to open the accounts of embezzlement and oppression. They appointed hordes of tax collectors whose job was to extract revenue from the non-existent harvest of that year's famine.

No matter how often the wretched peasants handed in debit sheets of poverty, their right to reductions and exemptions was suppressed. Only orders confirming the taxes or additional impositions were ever issued. All along the king remained in ignorance of what was taking place, just as he was unaware of the wise saying, 'When the king is lax with law and justice, the provinces one by one fall to the jackal and the locust.'

The peasants turn to a rich man for help

Finally conditions reached such a point that the peasants of one province could not bear the strain any longer. They assembled together and placed the humble coin of their lives in the common purse of friendship. But as there was nothing they could do by themselves, they went and stood before the palace door of a wealthy townsman. There they tuned up the shrill flutes of lamentation and played the Cathayan harp of complaint chanting in unison: 'Behold we are overwhelmed by poverty and have no tongue to reach the king. There is no hope unless a man of generous heart offers us his help and the generous do not wait for the beggar's tears of supplication.'

Help at last

The gentleman whom they approached with this tune was moved with compassion. In response he played upon the round tambourine formed by their assembly and tapped them with the merciful drumstick of his generosity. Before their sad, drawn faces he threw open the storehouse doors of gifts and prodigality. Without demanding pledges or any goods in exchange, he gave them whatever they needed, money for their land rents and city taxes, and supplies for farming and daily life.

The rich gentleman slandered

When news of this event reached the governor and the king's ministers, they were enraged with jealousy. Their sense of greed was offended that this gentleman had not stretched out his hands to exploit the oppressed peasants. To stir up trouble the governor sent a letter to the king stating 'A certain man is busy sniffing the winds of independence and seeks to establish his own rule. Already he has turned his head aside from rendering obedience to my authority.'

The peasants rally around their patron

The state authorities did not take the pains to investigate the truth of this report but straightaway imposed a huge fine on the maligned gentleman. An official was sent to collect the sum and the man of wealth could not refuse to pay, but from that time on the peasants of the province in accord with, 'Generosity will make a man your slave', offered the gentleman their soul on a platter and were prepared to follow his every command.

By now oppression had reached such a pitch everyone was in sore need of a drastic change. When the inhabitants of that province raised their heads and looked to the surrounding territories, they were shocked to see thousands of other souls caught and suffering in the same misery. In view of the general state of despair, the wealthy gentleman of insight sent out letters to all men of power throughout the land proposing that they join forces and take action together.

An alliance

An agreement was concluded among the several parties whereby each pledged a fixed number of men for the purpose of overthrowing and occupying all the provinces. The intention was that once the government was firmly in their hands, they would devise separate remedies for each of the many maladies of their land.

The provinces rebel

It happened that the arrow of their sound counsel hit the target of their desires. In no time they had effectively spread their bribes and gained full control of most parts of the country. The hands of their power grew sure and reached into every corner. One by one the various groups throughout the provinces notified each other of their independence and news of the widespread success was relayed to their chief, the gentleman of generous disposition. Indeed, by now he was considered the most important man in China.

The provinces are united

To celebrate the victory the above-mentioned overlord executed the local governor who had originally stirred up so much trouble. Next the wealthy gentleman turned his attention to uniting the independent provinces. He and his men swept across the country and every city they approached threw open the fortress gates in accord with the original agreement and when all the cities of the land were in his possession, his wandering eye settled on the capital.

Meanwhile back at the capital

Although news of these disquieting events had been constantly pouring into the royal court, the underhanded ministers concealed every detail from the king for fear of suffering his reproach. Thus everyone at the capital remained silent but lived from day to day in a state of terror. In the past the king's army was not needed for defense and consequently the troops had not been given their rightful pay. If a soldier was now ordered to take to the field of battle, straightaway he deserted and joined the enemy's ranks. The situation may be justly summed up by the verse:

> A rich land indeed of great length and great breadth
> But the innocent farmers were mistreated by their king

The rebel army grows as it approaches the capital

Thus the peasants were driven down the road of poverty and neglect and ended by joining the invaders. It was clearly a peasant's best course of action, for the oncoming army received him with kindness and handed him a sum of money. Day by day the number of deserters increased and soon the advancing rebel forces had grown to huge proportions. Nor was there resistance from any quarter offered on behalf of the ignorant king.

The king ignores all warnings

A few nobles tried to warn the king and inform him of the facts exclaiming, 'Alexander told the Chinese king, power is not based on idleness', but the king would not give any attention to their words and sought escape in feasting and pursuits of pleasure. There were times when the king rejected their sound reports as blatant lies. The situation could not go on like that for long. In the end a huge horde of men assembled and descended on the capital from all directions.

The king is abandoned to the rebels

News reached the court that over one hundred thousand men had forced their way into the city. The evil ministers were horrified and in accord with 'The traitor is the coward', chose flight, scattering down their separate paths. Meanwhile the invaders made their way through the city streets and were on the verge of penetrating into the royal palace. The king perceived his fatal situation. All his ministers were gone and he was abandoned to his own devices.

The king flees

There on the chessboard of events the king beheld himself checkmated by the knights of swift confusion. The queen of his reason decided he should flee on foot like a pawn and take refuge in a near-by fortress. One of the court eunuchs accompanied the king following him from behind like the black luck of that day.

The king is overcome with fear

Thus, two fugitives, they made their way up to the fortress which was built into the sides of a sheer mountain. But when the loud shouts and noise of the oncoming soldiers reached the king's ear his patience bent like an arch crushed under strain. The palm tree of his endurance was torn up from the roots. Now the rhythmic melody of their voices joined the frenzy of the circle dance of his escape and he was robbed of all his senses. The ecstatic song rang loud and clear, 'The man who seeks a life of ease should not put on the sash of government.'

The tree of broken endurance

This refrain prodded the king to undo his own royal cummerbund. He attached one end to a branch of the tree of broken endurance and eagerly made fast the other end to the neck of his submission. Thus he placed the head of acceptance under the heavy foot of revenge and handed over his sweet soul to that bitter end. What evil he committed in this world's house of retribution only worked against himself and no one else.

With the sturdy rope of pride and the firm-rooted tree of his honor he bore his pagan soul out of the house of this world into the realm of final reckoning. Like the evil sins which followed the king into the afterlife, the eunuch followed behind his master and in the very same manner consigned his spirit into the hands of the sacred Censor, the Collector of all souls.

The king's last will and testament

However, before the king gave up that final hold on life he bit the finger of regret so violently in the mouth of his grief that blood began to flow forth and with his finger for a pen he wrote a last will and testament on the bottom page of his robe.

One of his requests was: 'Do not ascribe the calamities of this kingdom to my name alone. Seek retribution from the men who counseled me. Neither is my family to blame for these unhappy events. Now that I am gone, treat them as you have always treated me, accord them respect and preserve their dignity.'

The soldiers arrive

The soldiers broke into the fortress and after conducting a short search found the dead king where he had hanged himself along with the eunuch. They read the postscript which was scrawled on the hem of his skirts and it was not long before they hunted out all the guilty ministers and executed them.

After the revolution

When the affairs of war were brought to a close, the conquerors gathered about themselves men of intelligence and experience, men distinguished among the people. All such persons were allocated posts in the new government and everyone was employed in accord with his special talents and training. Thus, matters of state being well in hand and order re-established, the leader of the victorious forces called for a general assembly and, feeling that the time was right, declared his wish to ascend the throne of absolute rule. There was no one on hand to oppose his will and the coronation ceremonies began then and there.

The voice of God

However, when the gentleman neared the throne and placed the royal crown upon his head, before he could actually seat himself in that lofty position, a secret voice sent by God, the invisible source of all inspiration, entered his ear: 'Stand back from the royal throne. Lions alone are fit to sit and look down from such heights. This is no place for a fool who struts about puffed up with vain conceits.' Next he heard the lines: 'You have cocked your hat and stand before the world in a daring pose but this heavy crown is made for a king and a mighty pair of shoulders.'[25]

A divine headache

With these warnings singing in his ears the gentleman was still intent on mounting the throne, but God, the all-wise Physician, hurled down upon him such a pounding headache, the governor of the man's existence was on the verge of abdicating from the throne of life. The pain was unbearable and caused him to fall from the steps of the throne. He lay sprawling on the ground in a daze but as soon as this pretender removed the crown from his head, the great Dispenser of secret cures lifted off the headache as if it were a cap that fitted too tightly.

The burden of kingship

The confused gentleman went on in this manner for a whole month, bending every effort to ascend the throne but each time his foot touched the first step, he was struck with the same illness, the headache of his headstrong ambitions. Thus, he could not sustain the painful burdens of kingship and it is written, 'If ruling over the world did not cause pain to a sovereign's head, his Lordship, the Sky, had not applied across his forehead the soothing ointment of the Milky Way.'

A good councilor is a doctor of the state

Wise councilors of state are the doctors who cure this very ailment, prescribing the salve of good management, the purgative of their clean thought, magnesia pills of mild influence and the smoothness of almond oil which relieves tension and constriction. These traditional health measures will always be the best.

The golden crown of sovereignty is not a helmet which affords the head protection. In fact, the man who wears a ruler's crown carries the burden of many heads upon the nape of his bare neck.

The advice of the physicians

Thus the physicians informed the would-be king: 'The only cure is to rid your head of the thoughts of government rule. Otherwise you are doomed to catch your foot in the snare of this disease and you will surely perish.'

The gentleman proved reasonable and accepted their advice declaring: 'The whim of wearing Jamshīd's crown no longer haunts my head. An everyday hat of decent felt is enough to shade me from the sun.'[26] The good man withdrew his foot from the royal throne and thereby freed his head from pain.

The Tatar prince

Back before the oppression and upheavals of war, a certain prince from the Tatars,[27] who was angered with his father, came to live in China and entered the service of the Chinese king. The king made him governor over one of the distant territories and there he had remained up until those recent days of confusion. When this prince was informed of the would-be king's difficulties in ascending the throne, he wrote to his father asking to be sent a great army from among the Tatar people.

The army assembled with haste and proceeded to penetrate into the lands of China. The gentleman who tried to sit on the throne but failed perceived the meaning of the old saying, 'Happiness and success do not depend on skill but only come with the support of Heaven.' He knew with certainty that it was not his lot to govern and it was clear that the army of China did not possess manliness sufficient to offer the Tatars resistance, therefore he decided it was best to ride out and welcome the Tatar prince with a show of friendship. He even escorted the prince and his troops into the capital and seated the prince on the throne of power.

Once established, the prince again sent to his father requesting several thousand more men. With these fresh recruits for his attendants, he set to work strengthening the foundations of his rule and began administering justice.

Alexander the Great in China

One of the problems facing the Tatar prince was a custom dating from ancient times. It is a well-known story how Alexander, the possessor of the two horns, thanks to his abounding fortune and his world-embracing power, conquered the whole of China. When he beheld the total lack of manliness in the men of the country, he decreed that there should be no distinctions observed between the males and females. Thus Chinese men adopted the habit of letting their hair grow to full length and just as nothing will bind them to keep their word, they gave up wearing a belt or binding their trousers at the waist. This is the outward sign of their inner deceits.

Native hair styles

From the time of Alexander the Chinese did not change as much as a single hair of their dress or bearing. They continued to braid their hair in a peculiar way and to top it off they would fix a large comb in it and pass a long gold pin through the middle, the kind of pin women use to part their hair.

Haircuts of the Chinese

By the time of these upheavals this manner of dressing and wearing their hair had become a time-honored tradition, but when the Tatar king's days of power began, he took the problem of dress and behavior by the hair and ordered that all the natives, high or low born, retain two braids and shave clean the rest of their head. This law was a heavy imposition and the cause of a great loss of face to those people. Many were reduced to utter despair and taking their head in the hands of sorrow, they fled to cities in other countries or to the islands off the coast.

Resistance failed

For a while thereafter the brother of the former king of China was taking refuge with the king of Paigū. When other discontent Chinese learned of his whereabouts, a large group of them assembled under his command. They tried their utmost to take back the kingdom of China but good fortune would not grant them assistance and in the end they were forced to flee and resume their exile.

When all these events took place

The unfolding of these events kept China in a state of turmoil for a long time and from the very beginning of the troubles up to the present day is a period of no less than forty-five years.[28] Now the Tatar king has died and his son sits upon the throne.

The astrologers

One of the more unusual aspects of this piece of history is that the astrologers are accredited with having predicted every detail of the great rebellion long before it began. The debauched king who came to be deposed everyday beheld the sea of destruction rising all about him but up to the very end he refused to believe the dire prophecies. 'The calamities which followed were the fruit of his own obstinancy.'

The embassy's return voyage

The author has restrained himself from presenting a detailed account of the lands of China for fear of becoming burdensome or appearing prolix and now he turns the reins of his light, cantering pen in the direction of describing countries and ports which we visited and investigated on our return voyage. May the narrative proceed with the help of God, for all men look to His bounty for assistance.

Date of departure from Siam

The pen of clarity continues its journey and writes that on the 15th of Ṣafar 1098[29] we set out from Shahr Nāv despite the fact that there was scarcely any monsoon left and all those who know the sea agreed that the monsoon season was finished.

The difficulty of hiring a ship

Besides the failing winds another problem faced our humble embassy. The Frank minister had inscribed the yak tail banner of his shameful luck with the order 'Capture every ship you meet.' He stationed so many of the administration's ships along the routes which travelers take, no foreign ship dared sail near Siam or even enter Siamese waters. The Frank minister's pirates were pillaging or confiscating all ships laden with goods and they clearly intended to kill all Muslims, who are the only true servants of God. This unstable situation made it impossible for us to hire a ship.

A decrepit ship from Sūrat

Only at a rather late date did the Siamese administration manage to procure a vessel, which belonged to a merchant from Sūrat. This poor man had the misfortune of coming to Siam for business and trade. The ship he owned was so old, it can only be compared to the ancient chests which the groom, Heaven, presented as the bride price for the old woman of the turning Spheres and the Pleiades.[30]

Sky was the first carpenter in existence and he took the planks from these old boxes after they had been exposed to thousands of celestial typhoons. With that useless old lumber he constructed the model for Noah's ark.

Before the old women, revolving Time, ever sat in front of the spinning wheel of the heavens to weave threads into her tapestry of days and nights, she had as a sample for her work the ropes and sails of this old ship.

We boarded the ship for fear of remaining in Siam

For lack of anything better the Siamese hired a ship in very bad condition. Fearing that, like our escort, we would be obliged to return from the port to the upper world of Siam, we humble servants handed over our bodies to Fate and we plunged down into that wreck of a ship which was the very collection basket of the angel Death.[31] Thus we escaped one sea of dangers and set out upon another.

The ship leaked and the drinking water ran low

After a few days of journeying along our watery path the ship suffered an awful mishap. In the middle of the sea she sprung a leak and so much water entered from every side that the head of hope went under and the heart began to drown. To add to this calamity the wind refused to give assistance and, like so many blasts of ill luck, continued to blow against us. By now the fresh water aboard was getting low and the dry, bitter taste of disappointment rose up in the palate of our souls.

Paṭānī, the first stop

Only after much suffering did we manage to arrive in Paṭānī, which is on one side of Shahr Nāv and is part of the countries of Below the Winds. That port is the very eye of beauty, happiness, abundance and prosperity. Most all the fruits of the surrounding countries are found there and they also have camphor, tin, aloes wood, sandalwood and sapan-wood. Small bits of gold are found there every year in the form of little stones, but this gold is not extracted from a regular mine. It is found on the ground's surface in the fields or even in the city itself.

Paṭānī is subject to Siam

There is no governor over Paṭānī and the peasants are Muslims who adhere to the Shāfiʿī sect. A while back the king of Siam, being encouraged by the good sense of Āqā Muḥammad and the lack of manliness displayed by the king of Paṭānī, without any warning sent a contingent of men to attack the kingdom. The king of Shahr Nāv was successful in this undertaking and a peace treaty favorable to Siam was concluded.

Flowers made of gold

Every year thereafter the natives of Paṭānī melted down several mithqāls of gold and worked the gold into the shape of a flower. For a certain length of time they continued to delight the nostrils of the Siamese king with the perfume of their tribute, but recently the flower drew its head in under the hood of disobedience. As soon as we replenished our store of fresh water, we departed from the port.

Malāqa

For the next three months we wandered across the sea in confusion, straying from our course and even managing to run aground in mud. During that time we stopped at the port of Malāqa and when we set out again it was in the direction of a group of deserted islands. These strange islands are located near Malāqa and are named Pal Dang Dang. But by then the force of the winds increased and our fresh water was running very low. Although the captain was eager to land somewhere along the coast, it was never possible.

The port of Kūchī[32]

Only after a series of mishaps and much hardship did we arrive in Kūchī, which is a port of the kingdom of Malīwār. That port is presently being held by the Dutch. Since by now the monsoon was over and our ship was badly damaged, we were forced to remain in that port for eight months in a state of collapse and ruin.

The rulers in the region of Kūchī

The kingdom of Kūchī with its extensive jungles and innumerable rivers is ruled over by many different rajahs and governors who are separated from each other by a distance of only two or three days journey. They sit in their office without any land, wealth or troops and beat a large drum yelling, 'Behold I am king!' and distinguish themselves among one another with noise and fanfare. The rajah of the locality where we landed is a Hindu and he does not wield any real power or maintain an impressive court. His army is composed of

15

the peasants. The custom in Kūchī is that when the rajah dies, his sister's son succeeds to the throne.

An anecdote about the royal succession

The natives explained that the origin of this practice goes back to those glorious days when the lofty presence of prophecy appeared on earth to fulfill his divine mission, indeed Muḥammad himself, God's prayers and peace be upon him and upon his family.

When the prophet was on earth

It is narrated in the texts and pages of the biographers and chroniclers when they describe that king of the domain of justice and religion, that heaven of the community's guidance, the sun of certain truth, the compass point of divine delegation, the prince of the true believers, peace be upon him, how a group of polytheists due to their dark fortune, the low position of their star of reason and their eye's blindness to the inner and the outer world, sought proof of the full moon's rising, proof of the divine revelation, by asking for a miracle from Muḥammad, the full moon of the skies of prophecy.

The miracle of splitting the moon

They stood like the three daughter stars of the Bear Constellation gathered about that axis of the heavens of religious guidance and they asked him, 'If your claims to prophetic powers be true, cause the moon in the sky to divide into two pieces.' When the mighty Prophet secured their promise to accept the faith if he performed this miracle, he pointed his moon-dividing finger at the sky and the moon was split in two.

The governor beholds the moon split in two

That very same night the governor of the kingdom of Malīwār beheld this miracle with his own eyes and the fixed star of his sense and reason was struck with amazement and transformed into a roving planet. His informants and men of counsel were assigned the task of explaining this phenomenon and upon studying the question like star gazers, they announced the joyful news that the Sun of prophecy had appeared in the highest spheres of revelation and was lighting and adorning the world with rays of guidance.

The rajah seeks the one, true prophet

The local rajah, along with all his family and relatives, immediately boarded a ship and set out to serve the Prophet. The rajah recognized that Muḥammad was the one true leader of men.

The rajah is sent a dream in time of danger

During the journey to Arabia their ship drifted into the waters of destruction and the frightened passengers, washing their hands of life, resigned their souls to Death. In the midst of this calamity sleep came upon the rajah and he was momentarily carried away from the hardships around him. In the realm of dreams he beheld an angelic figure who declared, 'If you wish to survive this hour of destruction cause blood to flow that it may soak into the deck.'

No volunteers for a human sacrifice

Despite the fact that the Hindus never kill anything, the rajah jumped up in a state of despair and sought the co-operation of his sons and relatives saying, 'I have been called to make a human sacrifice to God.' No matter how much he pressed the issue with his sons, no one of them would submit to being sacrificed, but each one of them turned his head away in disobedience.

The shrewdness of the rajah's sister

Finally one of the rajah's sisters who was accompanying him on the trip and was endowed with a good share of intelligence said, 'It is not necessary to kill anyone in order to save ourselves. If your dream calls for shedding blood, take my son and cut his arm or leg so a little blood will be sprinkled on the ship.'

They did just that and straightaway the wind of their desire rose. Thus they were able to sail on in safety and they succeeded in reaching their destination.

The king's will and testament

The rajah was made distinguished by attending on the Prophet's noble presence and was honored with the dignity of coming into the fold of Islam. Since the rajah was well aware of having profited by his sister's intelligence and good sense, in his last will and testament he wrote, 'May my own children not inherit a share in the kingdom but let my sister look after my sons and be my successor.' From that time up until now the natives of Kūchī have followed his last wish.

The apostasy of the natives

However, even though they believe in these events and tell this story themselves, it was only a short while before they lapsed back into their own religion and chose idolatry. To this day they have held to the path of error and they wander in perdition. Their only justification is, 'While the Prophet was alive we followed his religion. Afterwards differences appeared in that religion while our own has never admitted any flaws. And it is older. Thus we have returned to the faith of our forefathers.'

How the natives dislike the Muslims

Now the inhabitants of Kūchī avoid Muslims to such an extent and look upon them with such disdain, not one of these natives has ever met a Muslim face to face. The kingdom of Kūchī is extremely green and flourishing. One day when a certain Muslim was taking a walk to refresh himself he happened to pass by the rajah's palace. The palace grounds contain a pool which is about one hundred cubits long and is always kept full of water. Unfortunately one of the Muslim's servants stopped and washed his hand at the edge of the delightful pool.

The keepers were immediately aware of what he had done and descended upon him shouting and yelling, and a large number of angry men gathered about the wretched Muslim and his attendants. It seemed likely that the Hindus were intending to beat the Muslims and do them some real harm. In the end the affair was settled peacefully but the Hindus made it a point of explaining, 'This pool is for the rajah and the Hindus and twice a day they wash their bodies here. Meeting or having any contact whatsoever with Muslims is a cause of contamination for us. Therefore, keep away from this holy pool.'

The Muslim begged the rajah's pardon and made excuses for the servant's misbehavior. The whole matter seemed to be finished and done with but the rajah ordered the pool to be emptied, carefully cleaned out and refilled with fresh water. It was heard that if one of the Muslims who is a resident of Kūchī and understands these restrictions ever committed such a blunder, he would be arrested and severely punished.

The local form of punishment

The way the local authorities maintain justice is rather unusual. They will absolutely never execute a man neither do they hurt or torture thieves and evil-doers. Within the precincts of the palace estates stands a large building several storeys high. It is constructed so as to be very cool and comfortable. When someone commits a crime they take him into this building and expose him on one of the storeys.

Each storey is associated with a particular offense. The prisoner is confined to this building and carefully guarded over but they do not keep him in chains. It is not allowed to eat or sleep and if he is a Hindu, part of the punishment is that they do not allow him to wash his body. This penal system prescribes that if someone has spilt blood, he is to be exposed to the highest storey of the building.

Spices

In this kingdom there is a kind of cinnamon, which they call qirfa, and there is also quite a bit of pepper.

The Portuguese

Formerly the Portuguese Franks had possession of the port and held it for about four hundred years. They built a very handsome fortress which consists of well-layed-out, tall buildings. Thus they were able to maintain themselves and carry off good profits from trade.

The Dutch

Twenty-two years ago the Dutch declared war against the Portuguese and captured the fortress. They have since agreed to pay the rajah an even larger sum of money than the Portuguese were paying and now they take away the commercial profits. Kūchī is indeed a kingdom of abundance, beauty and fertility. It might be added that the Dutch are very strict and careful with the upkeep of the fortress.

Muslim pirates near Kūchī

Three days' journey from that kingdom there is another people also from the stock of Malīwār, but they are ruled by a separate king. They claim to adhere to Islam and the Shāfiʿī sect and most of them have learned the Quran by heart. Indeed the wise saying from the glorious Quran which is freighted with eloquence, was meant to refer to them, 'And behind him there was a king who seizes every ship by force.'

The pirates respect the Franks

They have many ships, small boats and dinghies which they have sent to sea and stationed in certain places for the sake of robbery and capturing helpless travelers. They will attack any vessel except one which belongs to the Franks. These pirates have already burned themselves several times in the crackling fire of the Franks.

Perseverance and self-justification

As soon as they catch sight of a ship, they pursue it and open fire once they are within range. They will struggle to capture a ship as long as their life's soul remains within them. The document which they bring forth to prove the legality of their actions is what the interceding ministers of the Shāfi'ī sect have published in their Quranic commentaries. 'It is lawful for man to hunt on land and sea.' But according to this group's interpretation hunting in the sea is taken to mean piracy and thus they have formally decreed that it is permissible to capture foreign ships.

Fellow Muslims or infidels

As further justification of their crimes they point out that as Muslims they are performing good works when they steal the property of non-believers. If, to begin with, the property in question belongs to Muslims, in accord with the saying, 'Indeed all believers of the faith are brothers', they claim their brothers' wealth by right of kinship.

When they capture a ship, they kill whatever race of people are aboard except Muslims. If a Muslim falls into their hands, they force him to admit that it is perfectly legal for them to take away his goods. Then the pirates reduce the poor man to utter nakedness and send him off with just enough provisions to reach the nearest shore.

Dīv island and the king's thrones

Not far from Kūchī is the island of Dīv which has its own king. He is a Muslim of the Shāfi'ī sect. Amber is found in large quantities on that island and they say the local king has even built a throne of this precious substance. However, the king himself does not sit upon this strange throne. He has his own ordinary seat where he sits facing the special throne with reverence, for he has set the Quran on top of the amber throne. The king sits in state before the Quran administering justice and examining legal disputes.

Trade in potsherds

In the port of Dīv island they do their trading with various kinds of broken sherds which they collect and send to different states in India. These sherds are sold on the mainland for money and the pieces which they carve and make into ornaments for the women are known as būq.

The island of Dīv is joined to the kingdom of Rānā which has its own rajah and land holder. The rajah has managed to gain full power over the island through marriage ties but his own kingdom is much more extensive. He also has a good-sized army. For a while now he has been paying tribute to the Mughal ruler of Hindustan.

The promiscuous Nayyār

There is another Hindu people called the Nayyār who inhabit the kingdom of Hindustan. The women of this tribe each have several husbands and each husband provides for a different need in the woman's household. When one of the husbands is present in the house, a piece of wood with a special shape is placed across the inside of the door so that no one can enter but as soon as the one man leaves, the wooden bar is lifted and another man has his turn. Because of this practice the male offspring do not have recognized fathers and inheritances are not passed on to the children. Everything is bequeathed to the wife.

The captain's trick

We were held up for repairs in Kūchī and spent six months of confusion in that port. When the monsoon finally arrived again we boarded our old ship and set out for Bandar 'Abbās. With favorable wind it only takes one month to travel from Kūchī to Iran, but the owner of our ship, having been forced in Siam to accept these humble travelers, had no intention of taking us to Bandar 'Abbās. He was secretly resolved on heading for his home port, Sūrat.

All along he was afraid to reveal his true plans to anyone, but when we raised the anchor to depart, he ordered the crew to steer a course for Sūrat. We humble servants were like blind men led on by the guidance of a stranger. For the moment we were happy entertaining thoughts of our homecoming, that we were about to reach our final halting place. Every day we expected to arrive at our destination. However, when a coast finally appeared in the distance, we were informed that it was the kingdom of Sīwā.

Sīwā, the rebel

Sīwā is a Hindu and one of the rajahs and landholders of Hindustan. His domain is very extensive and he has a large and powerful army. Recently he has turned his head from obedience and discarded his tameness before the Mughal government of Hindustan. He exhales enmity towards the all-powerful Mughal ruler and most of the time he is engaged in launching surprise attacks against the provinces and pillaging the king's lands. This unbridled rebel causes trouble on the high seas in the same manner and maintains many well-outfitted ships for piracy. Thus he is always robbing and capturing foreign ships and kills all the passengers who have the misfortune of falling into his hands.

We were attacked by pirates

Shortly after we sighted the shores of Sīwā's kingdom, a fleet of twenty-two boats approached our ship. The boats carried a total of about a thousand soldiers with muskets and cannons. The pirates were all the while pounding away on their kettle drums. Unfortunately, it happened that the wind died down and that enabled the pirates to get very close to us. From the moment the wind declined, they began to fight, firing off their muskets and cannons.

Caught in a helpless situation

Our ship was an Indian vessel and as we have already mentioned, very decrepit and disorderly, neither did it carry any military equipment, weapons or soldiers. There were two Franks aboard who were in charge of running the ship. Otherwise, there were no men fit to defend us with weapons.

The enemy's threats

The enemy became more bold, beating the kettle drums louder and firing their cannons and muskets. They realized that our ship was in very bad condition and they shouted at us saying, 'Keep your hands idle or once we board your ship, we will cut you up into small pieces.' Soon they were so close, we could see their faces and with the eye of our imagination we beheld ourselves defeated and the enemy victorious.

We took heart and invoked God's assistance

But despite the apparent futility of offering resistance, we loosened our voices into the air crying, 'Oh Lord I am overcome, send me Your merciful assistance.' We took comfort in the saying, 'How often have a few brave men defeated an army when God supported their cause.' Thus we nourished our hope and concluded that the right path was to fight and hold off the enemy. Our hearts turned to war and battle. We made firm the foot of our resistance in the face of their successive onslaughts which came from every direction.

Our bravery in face of their attacks

They fired their cannon at us 170 times and several of the passengers, servants and members of our humble party were martyred in the fray, but not one man showed signs of cowardice or fear. We calmed our hearts with the words, 'God will destroy your enemies.' And in accord with the saying, 'Never despair of God's abundant mercy', we kept our spirits high. Little by little we secured the day's victory and made firm the foot of our endurance. During that battle everyone aboard gave ample proof of his bravery and manliness.

The metaphor of victory

Finally the Sun, like a royal hawk with gold claws, dropped from the zenith of heaven and swerved towards the wide deserts of the west in pursuit of the black-winged raven, Night. The pirates fled like a flock of crows who fear the claws of a fast-falling falcon.

Blasts from the lightning-raining cannon and the Hell-blazing musket joined together with the diamond points of our swift arrows and destroyed two of their boats. Several of their men were drowned in the sea of God's mighty anger and the pirates were no longer able to withstand the heat of battle.

Their guiding star of fortune was as inauspicious as the planet Saturn and went into decline, setting in the western skies of distress. Thus, as befits the abject species of these pirates, they turned their backs and disappeared like a hollow bubble that breaks in the waves of the churning sea. Due to our never ending luck that always hits upon success, the pirates plunged back into the dark depths of non-being.

Certain outstanding qualities

Every young man aboard did his best in defending our ship and to recount the events is to inspire certain outstanding qualities, neither did anyone neglect serving our noble king in this whole affair but all gave a good account of their manliness. Praise be to God, for they have carried off the ball of virtue and fidelity in the field of rendering service to their patron. A strange event took place during the battle. Narrating these details will inspire outstanding qualities in the listener, I mean the qualities of devotion and faithfulness to our king.

The king's trunks

On deck there were two royal trunks which contained various items such as crowns, account books, an inlaid sword and other articles of formal dress. Twelve cannon shells landed in the immediate vicinity of these trunks. All the trunks which belonged to the other people on board were blown up and everything which they contained was destroyed. But the king's two trunks did not receive a single scratch. Every shell which flew towards them fell short and dropped at their feet and the shells were already cool and harmless.

The English were ill-treated

Thus we escaped, leaving the dangers of that encounter behind and we traveled on for a few more days until we reached the beginning of the Gulf of Sūrat. A while back, when the English complained of injustices which they were suffering at the hands of the Indian officials of Sūrat, no matter how often they presented their case before the Mughal court, they received no consideration. On some occasions they were even treated with insults and abuse.

They set up a blockade in the Gulf of Sūrat

The English then presented an account of the situation to their own king and the king turned the matter over to a gandarāl, which is

their word for commander of the army. Several warships were sent
to block the sea route of the merchants and travelers in that region.
The English ships would not, however, interfere with the Dutch and
the other Christians, since fighting with those nations in the past had
only caused many salty tears to be added to the water of the sea.

Thus the English were effectively cutting off the movement of
all travelers who were inhabitants of Sūrat or who wished to enter or
leave that port. The English were confiscating travelers' ships and
goods but made it a point to release the owners. It was hoped that
once the molested merchants were set free, they would complain
and advertise what had happened to them. This would draw attention
to England's power and position in the world. The gandarāl sent a
huge well-outfitted ship to anchor in that harbor and the ship had
three storeys, eighty cannons and carried two hundred soldiers
aboard. It sat there on the lookout to capture any other ship which
tried to enter or leave.

The English board our ship but behave with politeness

It so happened that the ship which we humble servants were being
transported in, belonged to the natives of Sūrat and we entered the
port and cast anchor during the English blockade. As soon as we
arrived, the English warship sighted us and came up alongside.
They sent a man to our ship to ascertain where we came from, what
we were carrying and who was aboard. When these questions were
properly answered, the English captain sent his delegate with a group
of soldiers to board our ship. The delegate and his men came before
the humble servants of this embassy and they displayed all the
formalities of friendship and hospitality. They did not attack and
pillage the ship but they did raise their king's flag above the mast
and then appointed several of their men to guard over the vessel.

The English offered us an escort

The next morning another messenger from the English arrived and
announced: 'We have standing orders to capture any ship belonging
to the natives of Sūrat as well as ships intending to visit that port.
Although this ship is the property of a man from Sūrat, because your
honorable embassy is aboard, we have refrained from attacking and
pillaging her. We are obliged to take this ship and the owner into
our custody. However, if you so wish, we will escort you into Sūrat
with all your possessions in one of our own ships. All the merchandise
now aboard, other than what is yours, will be sent to our gandarāl.'

We decided to go to Mumbāī with the English

Since it would not appear dignified to arrive in Sūrat without a ship of our own and since there was still some time before the monsoon, for our return voyage would be strong, the best choice seemed to go along in our same ship and follow the English to the island of Mumbāī. That island is in the vicinity of Sūrat and the headquarters of the English commander.

Thus the above-mentioned English captain appointed a group of his men and stationed them aboard our ship. They raised the anchor and steered a course for their island headquarters. When we arrived in Mumbāī, the gandarāl received us with a show of cordiality and politeness. Since our ship was in such a decrepit state and could not be trusted to arrive at Bandar 'Abbās, he begged us to wait for a certain number of days that he might procure a better ship for us and send us towards our goal in safety.

The English gain their demands

However, the earlier governor of Sūrat, who had caused trouble for the English, was removed from his post, and the great Mughal ruler appointed a new governor with the intention of bringing about a reconciliation and settling matters once and for all. As soon as the new governor arrived in Sūrat, he sent a messenger to the English declaring that in the future he would manage the affairs of state in accord with their interests.

We had no means of leaving Mumbāī

When this news reached the gandarāl, he set out for Sūrat along with all his ships and we humble servants, due to the fact that we had no ship, were not able to depart from that island for three and a half months. Mumbāī has a terrible climate and is extremely dirty and lacks almost everything, To keep from starving the natives are forced to sell their own children for two or three thousand dinars.

The island of Mumbāī

Formerly this island belonged to the king of Portugal but it was included in the dowry that his daughter brought with her when she married the son of the king of England. The island is empty and barren, extremely barren and devoid of anything that could be useful. Since they had no other place for their ships in the vicinity of Hindustan, the English settled this island and now keep it as a naval base. Mumbāī has nothing to export and is mostly a cause of additional expenses for the English. Hence, scarcely anyone visits or even passes near this island and it was not until the 5th of Jamīdu 'th-Thānī 1099,[33] after waiting and suffering all that time that we succeeded in renting a ship and setting sail for the royal court of Iran and indeed that glorious court is the refuge of all mankind.

Pirates

After traveling at sea for several days, we encountered two ships of the Sankālī and the Vārīl who are from among the Indian peoples. They live in the vicinity of Hindustan and are extremely bloodthirsty and fearless. They are continually practicing piracy on the high seas. When we crossed their path they had evidently been seeking some victims for a long time.

Drums and cannon fire

As soon as they spotted our ship, they beat the kettle drums of festivity and fired their cannons. But there was scarcely any wind and they were not able to get close enough to attack and board us. Thus these two pirate ships followed after us, one from each side. All that day they continued firing their cannons and kept up this semblance of fighting until night fell.

That night there was no wind

When Night placed his heavy hand over the delicate light of Day, the pirates withdrew their hand from battle. Then the wind died down completely so that none of the ships were moving at all. The star of their good fortune was not in ascendancy neither did they have a full moon to aid them. In that still darkness they were not able to stretch out their hand and grasp the skirts of their desire.

Without wind there was no escape

But we humble servants were caught in the same position. The light-stepping feet of our ship were bound by the absence of favorable winds. The space between us and the enemy was so short that voices from either side could be clearly heard. In this manner all three ships drifted in the dark sea, and since it was not possible to fight during the night, the enemy simply carried on shouting and yelling until dawn came.

The pirates' threats

The Indians were shouting: 'Our superior strength and power is clear to anyone with sense. Altogether we are four hundred strong. Therefore, do not seal your fate with a cruel death. Take down the sails now and hold back your hands from fighting. We will show you mercy. If we take your ship by force, there will be no quarter given. Everyone will be slaughtered.'

The following morning

As soon as the morning light returned, the pirates resumed beating the kettle drums and started firing their cannons. However, there was still not enough wind for them to get close to us or for us to make our escape. Everyone aboard our ship washed his hands of life and buckled up his waist for the struggle to come. We could only hope that divine favor might confer on us a victory befitting the auspicious aspirations of our noble king.

The Franks never surrender

The captain and the crew of our ship were English and among the Franks, especially the Dutch and the English, it is a standing order from their king never to give up the ship. Even if it is impossible to defeat the enemy, the Franks will not submit to the humiliation of being taken prisoner. Thus they are prepared to set fire to their own ships and perish in the flames before they will surrender and provide their enemies with booty. If they neglected that rule and acted in a cowardly manner, though they managed to escape from the pirates, they would be burned to death in the fires of their king's wrath.

We were all ready to die

Therefore, when the captain and the crewmen perceived how unsure their situation was, they brought out all the gunpowder and kerosene which was aboard and kept it ready on the deck. They calmly awaited that moment when the enemy might be on the verge of overtaking us and it would be necessary to set the ship on fire. We humble servants consigned our bodies to Fate. For the next three days and nights we were busy fighting in the manner already described. During that time the wind did not blow at all and neither side could gain an advantage.

God sent the winds

Finally, in accord with the saying, 'Indeed He answers those who call upon Him in their sufferings', we raised up our hands in prayer before God's tribunal, and He is the mighty judge of all mankind. Then a squad of violent winds rose up and blew so hard that the ships began to rock up and down in the waves. But no matter how hard the Indian pirates tried, they were not able to reach our ship.

We escaped with the wind of our desire

When night came, the winds grew even stronger. The enemy fell behind, abandoned to an inferior position. The sea currents flowed against the enemy whereas we humble servants caught the wind of our desire. Once again we eluded destruction in accord with our never fading luck.

> No matter what waters the scoundrel will cruise,
> He always fears the sea and hugs the shore.
> The irreligious master of a ship
> Refuses to launch out and put his trust in God.

The date of our arrival in Bandar 'Abbās

Finally, on the 24th of Rajab 1099[34] we entered the port of Bandar 'Abbās. Praise be to God, the days of suffering had passed, an age of grief and longing came to its end and we humble servants had survived.

THE CASE OF ABŪ'L-ḤASAN AND THE FALL OF ḤAIDARĀBĀD

The character of Abū'l-Ḥasan

The latest news from India concerns the fall of Ḥaidarābād[1] and the sad fate of Abū'l-Ḥasan. When Qutūb Shāh died, there were no sons to take his place as ruler. Abū'l-Ḥasan appeared. He was a distant relative of the late ruler but it was plain to see that this obtruder was without intelligence, learning or any sense of honor. He possessed no experience in affairs of state neither was he endowed with the benefits of natural wit and good sense.

Abū'l-Ḥasan's lack of good breeding

His childhood years were spent in unhampered freedom. All along as a youth he indulged his self-will and by the time he reached manhood, he brought forth his fully grown head from the robes of obstinacy and threw off the collar of proper respect.

How he was able to assume rule

It stands as one of the most despicable recent events that such an unqualified man was able to become the ruler of Ḥaidarābād and there is no doubt in this matter that Abū'l-Ḥasan only rose to the office due to the former ruler's lack of children and the fact that there was some remote connection between his and the late gentleman's family. Even so, Abū'l-Ḥasan owed much of his success to the unpredictable decrees of Heaven and the shrewd politicking of Sayyid Muẓaffar, who was once the secretary of the Iranian Mīr Jumla.[2]

Debauchery and vice

As strange as it may seem, Abū'l-Ḥasan did succeed in becoming ruler of Ḥaidarābād. But as is to be expected from an unrestrained animal nature, once Abū'l-Ḥasan was accorded the full power of his position, the pivot of his daily life became debauchery and vice. He lifted the veil of modesty and shame from his indiscriminating sight and proceeded deeper and deeper into the realm of licentious infamy.

234

It was not long before he completely withdrew his hand from the pursuit of legal justice and fostering the peasantry. But such behavior is the rule with evil men who show no gratitude before almighty God.

He dismisses the experienced men of state

Abū'l-Ḥasan immediately dismissed all the statesmen who had been employed by the late and venerable ruler, statesmen who were adorned with the precious qualities of intelligence, justice and gentlemanly generosity. In accord with the saying, 'If you give aid to an evil man, God turns that man against you', the former government officials witnessed Abū'l-Ḥasan cut short the hands of their power.

Infidels and rogues come to power

Being senseless and by nature a gullible fool, Abū'l-Ḥasan made a Hindu infidel[3] his favorite and gave him the post of prime minister and adviser. To fill the positions left empty by the loyal statesmen who were dismissed, Abū'l-Ḥasan raised up a group of rogues and base types from the low position of disrepute to high government posts.

Hindus favored

He lengthened the hands of Hindu power until those idolaters had sway over the heads of the Muslims. When a dispute arose between a Hindu and an ill-fated sayyid,[4] the new governor refused to mete out justice fairly but gave an order which destroyed the sayyid's upper hand in the case. In the end the Muslim had his hands cut off for punishment.

Pagan temples in a Shī'ite city

Ḥaidarābād is famous as a stronghold of the Shī'ites and honors the memory of 'Alī by taking its name from 'Alī's epithet, Ḥaidar, the Lion of God.[5] None the less, the Hindu minister decided to turn the city into a bulwark of disbelief and a refuge for heathendom. Thus he erected several pagan temples right alongside holy mosques.

Sīmājī, the heathen rebel

Abū'l-Ḥasan secretly tied the cords of friendship with Sīmājī, the son of Sīwā. Sīmājī is one of the landholders of Hindustan, a nonbeliever as was his father and all his forefathers and a confirmed enemy

16

of the Muslims. He has turned his head from rendering obedience to the Chosroes of the cities and lands of Hindustan and draws his breath in enmity against the great Mughal.

Most of the time he is on the lookout for a chance to attack and pillage the weaker provinces of Hindustan and he blocks the roads on land and sea for merchants and travelers. Previously a whiff of description of his situation and the calamities which he causes was presented in this narrative. He is indeed a shameless infidel and Abū'l-Ḥasan began cultivating his favor and affection. In secret Abū'l-Ḥasan was giving him aid and support and the empty-headed governor of Bījāpūr was giving him aid as well.

Bījāpūr

The governorship of Bījāpūr was a case similar to that of Ḥaidarābād. When the former governor died, a mere child came into office and due to his total lack of discrimination and good sense he began giving help to Sīmājī, who deserved the most severe punishment possible.

Both these wayward governors would not permit the army of Hindustan to pass through their territory and destroy that insufferable rebel. Such was the situation in Bījāpūr and Ḥaidarābād, thanks to the reckless incompetence of the two local governors. Both states were poorly organized and the posts of power and authority were consigned to unworthy and unscrupulous statesmen.

Abū'l-Ḥasan is warned by the Mughal king

Abū'l-Ḥasan withdrew his foot from the path which the governors of perfected intelligence travel along. He drew his daily breath in enmity against the established sovereignty of the Mughals. When this absurd governor had passed the limits of tolerance and several reports of his misbehavior had reached the mighty ruler of Hindustan, as is the duty and correct form for true sovereigns, the sultan sent the governor a letter which contained serious warnings and the royal command on how to govern in the future.

War is declared

However, there was no apparent improvement in Ḥaidarābād and Abū'l-Ḥasan's replies were mere nonsense. It was not long before the sultan became angered at the governor's indiscretions and assembled the learned doctors of the state. With a view to having the protection of their sanctity, he asked them for a religious decree.

They issued a decree demanding the immediate annihilation of Abū'l-Ḥasan. That very same day the sultan ordered the army to set out and the royal concerns focused on the conquest of Haidarābād and the extermination of the rebels.

The governor continues his debauchery in a near-by fortress

Still the ill-fated governor refused to bend his head in obedience, and despite the fact that he could not withstand the heat of the high-ranking sultan's army, he refused to surrender. After the fall of Baṣra[6] the governor deserted all his lands and barricaded himself in an impregnable fortress.[7]

Even when he was reduced to these circumstances, he did not have the sense to think of the necessary provisions and ammunition. Once inside his fortified palace he proceeded headlong with wild banqueting, although a funeral ceremony would have been more appropriate.

The councilors desert

He made the lowest and most vile men his councilors but they would not stay faithful to him for long. When they saw the siege closing in around them, as is the manner of men of their temperament, greed and ambition prompted them to desert. The ministers stained their faces with the indigo of infidelity, hoping to ward off an evil end.[8]

They join the Mughal camp

Thus their faces darkened in shame and their hearts disillusioned with the few days of love they had harbored for that unfortunate provincial state, they turned their backs on their patron and headed for the court of the Chosroes of Hindustan. Every day another group of Abū'l-Ḥasan's men turned their attention toward the noble sultan's army camp and abandoned the governor to his final reckoning.

Abū'l-Ḥasan's trusted general

Of all those who were then deserting Abū'l-Ḥasan, there was a man named Ḥusain Beg and he was originally from 'Alīābād in Māzandarān. Abū'l-Ḥasan had entertained the idea of raising this man to a high rank and though the fellow was only a poor rice farmer to begin with, the foolish governor made him general and gave him command over the whole fortress. The governor accorded this one general the highest authority and trusted in him above any other officer.

Ḥusain Beg writes to the Mughal prince

Thus, despite the fact that the enemy's army had surrounded the fortress, Abū'l-Ḥasan felt safe and his thoughts were completely engrossed in the pursuits of pleasure and festivity. However, Ḥusain Beg sent a messenger to the Mughal prince who was commanding the advance troops of the great sultan.

Ḥusain Beg's message was: 'If you promise to award me a high rank and important post, I will open a gate of the fortress and give you free entrance. Come at such and such a time on a certain night and you will be able to enter and take possession of the fortress.'

The prince captures the fortress

The prince sent back a formal letter of guarantee which granted the traitor's wishes and on the appointed night the prince entered through an open gate and brought a huge force of soldiers into the fortress, nor was there any fighting or other difficulties.

Abū 'l-Ḥasan is arrested

The troops proceeded to the house of the governor. There Abū'l-Ḥasan was in the habit of retiring after his feasts and wild parties. He would take a quantity of bhang and roll himself up in the quilt of negligence, lost in the embrace of imprudence. This day of rude awakening he was sleeping in a dead sleep devoid of dreams. The soldiers arrived, woke him up and took him by the arm to the prince.

The prince tries to intercede for the governor

The prince led Abū'l-Ḥasan forth from the fortress of neglect into the army camp of sudden awareness. The next morning the prince went before the lofty king of Hindustan, his father, and beseeched him to allow Abū'l-Ḥasan to come to the imperial court but the king declared, 'Anyone who is negligent of God and the final day of judgment, is not worthy of an audience.' The king ordered that Abū'l-Ḥasan be confined in prison.

The king turns against the prince

It also happened that the king's attitude towards the prince took a turn for the worse. The noble heir apparent seemed corrupted by his contact with Abū'l-Ḥasan and the governor of Bījāpūr and thus the king decided to arrest his own son[9] and put him in chains along with Abū'l-Ḥasan in the fortress of Daulatābād.

The child governor of Bījāpūr

The little governor of Bījāpūr[10] came before the king and the king received him with respect and honor. He kept the boy in his company and took him riding, hunting and sight-seeing and began a deep friendship with him. The king married the young boy's sister to one of the princes of the Mughal court and the boy himself was married to a young princess.

One of the deserters

One of the traitors who had turned his back on Abū'l-Ḥasan, came before the king and was awarded the title Mahābat Khān[11] and given a post that commands six thousand troops. Indeed a poet wrote an ode of satirical praise for the man, declaring:

> In this tricky game of life
> The Mahābat Khān threw two sixes.
> The world stood fixed in amazement.

The man who betrayed Abū'l-Ḥasan

The other fellow who had actually given over the fortress, was awarded a command of five thousand troops and thanks to his treachery and disloyalty, he won the title 'Khān among the men of 'Alī's rank'. Now his honorable person is stationed at Aḥmadnagar which is a central point between Hindustan, Bījāpūr and the Dekkan. There he is occupied repelling and destroying the enemies of the world and the true religion.

The effect of prince Akbar's seeking refuge in Iran

The very latest report had it that when the noble, high-ranking, prince Akbar, greatest of the princes of all India, firmamemt of excellence, that lucky planet of happiness, ornament of the throne of pomp and prosperity, jewel in the crown of imperial power, fruit-bearing tree in the orchard of Tīmūr's line,[12] ward of the star of providence, following the orthodox tradition of his famous fore-bears,[13] turned his hopeful face to Iran, the threshold and refuge of the world, this event greatly increased the tumult and confusion which prevails throughout the land of India. 'God knows best the truth of these rumors, for He has ears and eyes in every distant corner of the world.'

NOTES

Translator's Preface

1   Shāh Sulaimān reigned from 1666 to 1694.
2   The author uses 'Frank' to mean any European Christian.
3   See E. W. Hutchinson's *Adventures in Siam in the Seventeenth Century*, Royal Asiatic Society, London, 1940.

Introduction

1   All the quotations used in the author's introduction are from the Quran or the Ḥadīth, i.e. they have the authority of scripture.
2   Another name for the Prophet.
3   'Alī was a close relative of Muḥammad and became the Prophet's fourth successor, the last of the Orthodox Caliphs, i.e. the leaders of the Muslim community who had been close to the Prophet during his lifetime. When 'Alī was assassinated (A.D. 661) a great split took place in Islam, the split between the Sunnīs, or Orthodox, who accepted Mu'āwiya as the fifth Caliph, and the Shī'ites or Partisans, those who insisted that the Caliph be chosen from 'Alī's immediate family. The Safavids were Shī'ites and the religious propaganda of their regime put special emphasis on their family connections with 'Alī.
4   This title goes back to Khusrau, a Persian king of pre-Islamic times. His character and exploits have been embellished by legend, much as in the case of Alexander the Great. The title is loosely applied in praise of any later ruler.
5   The name Sulaimān is the Arabic form of Solomon, whose wisdom and proficiency in magic are the subject of many tales in Muslim literature. His signet ring bore the mystic hexagram which is familiar in the West as the Jewish star.
6   The fire steed or Burāq is the fabulous beast which bore Muḥammad up to Heaven. Riding on such an animal would imply a noble spirit prone to beatific visions.
7   This title was originally associated with rulers of Khiṭā and Tartary but eventually came to be loosely employed as lord or noble.
8   Sultan means potentate, sovereign, with the emphasis being on secular power as distinct, say, from the Caliph, whose power was in theory based on religious authority. Again this term is used loosely for ruler.
9   Imām generally means leader of the communal prayer, but for the Shī'ites it refers to the various descendants of 'Alī who were taken to be the leaders of Islam during their lifetime. The Safavid rulers traced their lineage back to the Prophet through 'Alī and the Imām, Mūsā al-Kāẓim.
10   Ḥusain and Ḥasan were the sons of 'Alī and contested the legality of Mu'āwiya becoming the fifth Caliph. They were slaughtered with a

group of their followers near Karbalā and are held in great reverence as martyrs by the Shī'ites.

11 A royal decree.

12 A common expression meaning everything in the world from the lowest to the highest.

13 Emperors of China or Chinese Tartary, but used loosely as a grand title for kings in general.

14 In legend the second dynasty of the ancient Persian kings.

15 Turkish designation of the year, 'Year of the Dog' 1682.

16 Joseph, who was sold into slavery in Egypt, resisted the advances of Potiphar's wife and forgave his brothers for their treachery.

17 Evidently some well-known stories noted for aptness and brevity.

Part I First Jewel

1 Port on the Persian Gulf.

2 27 June 1685.

3 A description of Hell.

4 Khiẓr is a legendary figure who guided Alexander on the quest for the Fountain of Youth. Later Khiẓr was especially noted for guiding sailors over water.

5 The maidān is a field's length.

6 Nāhīd, or the planet Venus, is personified as a young girl who is a very skilled musician.

7 The Gulf of 'Ummān, east of the Persian Gulf.

8 Ḥasan and Ḥusain, the Shī'ite martyrs, were slaughtered at Karbalā. First they were cut off from drinking-water, particularly the Euphrates, and when they would still not surrender they were attacked.

9 Kauthar is one of the fountains of Paradise, said to flow with milk, honey and wine over a bed of jewels. Its banks are made of pure gold.

10 When 'Alī was fighting to consolidate his position as fourth Caliph, he agreed to submit to arbitration with the enemy, but at that point 'Alī's more uncompromising followers deserted him and formed their own sect known as the Khārijites or the Dissenters.

11 The Portuguese of Muscat were attacked and defeated by the Arab Imām's army in 1649.

12 'Alī attacked the Khārijites when they would not remain faithful to his cause.

13 The extremist sect of the Khārijites who insisted on fighting to the end for their beliefs. They were mostly exterminated by A.D. 700.

14 'Uthmān was the third Caliph and he was assassinated. Mu'āwiya fought 'Alī supposedly to avenge 'Uthmān and both Mu'āwiya and 'Uthmān are held as enemies by the Shī'ites.

15 Commentary on the Quran.

16 An Arab tribe that God destroyed with a great wind. They had rejected a true prophet sent to reform them.

17 Jacob's patience is proverbial.

18 A fertile narrow province between the Elburz Mountains and the Caspian Sea.

19 The Sublime Assembly, the Court of Heaven.

20 The direction of Mecca from wherever one is standing. The direction the Muslims face when they pray.

21 The ruler.

22 Charles II died 6 February 1685 and was succeeded by James II.

23 The month when Muslims fast between dawn and sundown. 22 August 1685.

24 The passages which follow are good examples of a light, literary usage of images based on mystic contexts.

25 Fakhr Rāzī and Imām Ghazālī are both famous theologians. They are used here as literary examples of scholars who would normally not tolerate religious innovation.

26 The beautiful maidens who inhabit Paradise and entertain the faithful in the afterlife.

27 27 Ramaẓān, the night the Quran descended from Heaven. 'The night equal to a thousand months'.

28 The spelling of this word is not clear in the text.

Part II Second Jewel

1 This is the author's spelling for Tenasserim, the coastal region of Western Siam, now part of Burma.

2 16 September 1685.

3 A kingdom in Burma, located in the Delta of the Irawady.

4 Cathay, taken by Muslim geographers to be a kingdom separate from China.

5 An important port on the western coast of Siam where the French maintained a garrison for a short time. Now part of Burma.

6 The building is named after 'Alī's famous sword 'The Spine Splitter'.

7 Foods not prepared in accord with Muslim injunctions on cleanliness, or totally forbidden such as pork and certain sea life.

8 A school of fiqh or jurisprudence. The founder, Shāfi' (d. 820), based his juristic principles on deduction and conciliation of traditions. Fiqh in the wider sense covers all aspects of religion, politics and civic life.

9 This was the most popular school of fiqh, especially supported by the Sunnī Ottomans. It was also widely spread in India.

10 19 December 1685.

11 Rūm refers to Anatolia then under the Ottoman Turks, but the word derives from Rome as applied to the Byzantine Empire.

12 The chief of a hundred, a centurion, an officer's title. In accord with the military organization they may be of the left or right flank.

13 An ode with a particular form and content.

14 The Black Stone at Mecca around which Muslim pilgrims walk in order to perform their rites. The object of the pilgrimage.

15 The hudhud is the bird that bore Solomon's message to the Queen of Sheba which exhorted her to bow down to the one true God. The bird's

reward was a colorful crest which it wears as a sign of distinction and favor.
16 Iblīs is the Devil and there are various tales of how he tempted the pious Idrīs or Enoch. Idrīs is accredited with inventing clothing in ancient times before man knew how to sew.
17 David invented a kind of chainmail which was highly valued.
18 The great dome built by Nushīravān at Ctesiphon. Kasrā is a title like Chosroes, adapted from Caesar.
19 The famous seven-domed palace of Bahrām Gūr, the Sassanian king, constructed in harmony with the five planets and the sun and the moon.
20 A Muslim bathhouse.
21 Astarābād is a province between the Caspian and Khurasan.
22 The Nasnās is a mythical being halfway between a human and an animal, often sighted in the steppes of Central Asia.
23 Turcoman soldiers. Qizilbāsh means 'red head'. Sheikh Ḥaidar (d. 1488) gave his Sūfī partisans, who were all Shī'ite Turkomans, the famous scarlet cap with twelve scallops or gores (one for each of the twelve Imāms), which earned them the name Qizilbāsh. Shāh Ismā'īl, the founder of the Safavid dynasty, relied almost exclusively on the great Turkoman tribes for his support.
24 Hātim is an Arab famous in legend for his generosity. He would consume all his wealth to entertain a guest. Perhaps here a sash where one keeps money.
25 Jamshīd was an ancient Iranian king. In legends he is accredited with building Persepolis.
26 The dervishes. They sometimes play certain musical instruments.
27 A dish made of ground rice, milk and sugar, thicker than falūda.
28 A kind of sweet gelatinous drink. Flummery.
29 A mountain in the district of Hamadan.
30 The haqār is described in the Farhang-i-Niẓām as a bird that frequents the banks of rivers. Mostly referred to in Indian-Persian works.
31 The French embassy that came to Siam was also granted interviews during the elephant hunts.
32 The Garden of Purity, a universal history by Mīr Kwānd (d. 1498) in seven volumes.
33 Jamshīd, an ancient Iranian king, had a magic drinking cup which reflected, as if in a mirror, the whole universe. He could gaze into it like a crystal ball.
34 Mani, the founder of the Manichean religion, best remembered in Muslim literature as a great painter and penman.
35 Shāhrukh (1377–1427), the fourth son of Tīmūr. In the Maṭla'-i-Sa'dain 'Abdu'r-Razzāq describes the embassy to China. The embassy stayed in Khān Bāligh for five months between 1420 and 1421.
36 Mīrzā Bāysunghur was the son of Shāhrukh.
37 Hātim is an Arab referred to as a figure of generosity. See Part II, n. 24.
38 The ta'ziyat is the Shī'ite ceremony of mourning on behalf of Ḥasan and Ḥusain, who were martyred at Karbalā. The hardships of the siege

and the actual slaughter are re-enacted before a large audience. See part I, nn. 13, 27.

39   Lailā or Lailī, a beautiful woman described in Arabic and Persian romances. Majnūn was in love with her and was driven mad by his passion.

40   A famous spring in Paradise like Kauthar. See Part I, n.27.

41   Muḥarramu'l-Ḥarām is the first month of the Muslim year.

42   18 January 1687.

Part III   Third Jewel

1   Chīn, the son of Nuḥ or Noah. As Islam expanded and became conscious of distant lands such as China (Chīn), it was necessary to invent eponymous founders to include the new 'tribes' in the traditional genealogies. Noah is accredited with various sons who stand at the head of all such genealogies.

2   *Delicacies of the Arts and Sciences*, an encyclopaedic work of the fourteenth century by 'Āmilī.

3   The text is very corrupt in this passage as if the copyist is totally unfamiliar with the place names he is writing. Lāhūrī is probably a misspelling for Lāmūrī which was the name of one of the kingdoms of Sumatra. Havamāka is probably a mis-spelling for one of the forms of writing Malacca. The alternatives given in parentheses are other possible ways of reading the text.

4   *The Purity of Hearts*, an encyclopaedic work by Ḥamdu'llah Mustawfī 'l-Qazwīnī with a large section on geography. The author was born in 1281.

5   Abū Raiḥān, better known as Al-Bīrūnī, who wrote on mathematics and geography. Author of a famous work on India.

6   Muslim geographers divided the world into climes, a system which they inherited from the Greeks.

7   Another attempt at rationalizing genealogies. Part III, n. 1.

8   According to legend the first man to ever become a king, the founder of the ancient Iranian Peshdādian dynasty.

9   There are Portuguese sources from the late sixteenth century which describe this war and make mention of the hand to hand combat of the protagonists.

10   A famous quotation from Saʿdī's *Gulistān* (*The Rose Garden*).

11   A Turkish tribe in the Safavid regime.

12   In re-enacting the martyrdom of Ḥasan and Ḥusain it would be plausible to include weapons for the sake of realism.

13   17 October 1657. Phrai Narai actually came to the throne in 1659.

14   Gīlān is part of the Caspian coast, just west of Māzandarān. The chief city is Rasht.

15   From Ḥāfiẓ. Jamshīd used as a figure of a great ancient king.

16   This epithet goes back to the Quran where it probably refers to Cyrus the Great. Later it was transferred to Alexander in view of the extent of his conquests which ranged from pole to pole, or horn to horn, of the world.

17 The Arabs and Persians were very impressed with Greek philosophy, but like the Christian theologians they felt the strain of conciliating pagan logic with divine revelation.

18 This whole anecdote is full of very learned puns in the original. One level of the opening motifs is based on the parts of the psyche, such as reason, imagination, etc.

19 The *Book of Kings* by Firdawsī is the national epic of Iran.

20 An example of a literary reference to mystic terminology. The perfected heart recognizes poetry with a deeper meaning.

21 The hero Siāvakhsh was falsely accused of sleeping with his stepmother, who for her own part had attempted to seduce him.

22 Eponymous forefather of the Khazars. This passage is quoted from the *Rauẓatu'ṣ-Ṣafā* of Mīr Khwānd.

23 Prince of the New Year.

24 Nimrūd is an example of the worst of the idolaters but always felt that he was a true believer. If he calls certain people infidels, they are surely lost.

25 See Part II, nn. 18, 19.

26 Chief of 1,000, 100, 10. Ranks of officers in the Safavid army.

27 In the game of backgammon it is possible to block certain squares of your opponent.

28 It is a custom to brand oneself as a token of affection for a woman.

29 The druggist extracts opium from the poppy by slicing the flower in certain places.

30 The Heavens are divided into several spheres. The crystalline sphere is where God's throne is located, the empyrean.

31 Uncle of the Prophet and a hero of the earliest period of Islam. There were many tales about his daring in battle.

32 A warning in the Quran.

Part IV Fourth Jewel

1 *The Wonders of Creation* by Zakarīya ibn Muḥammadu'l-Qazwīnī (b. 1203), an encyclopaedic work. Short but rambling.

2 The *Wonders of Creation*, *Portraits of the Climes*, *Priceless Novelties* and *The Purity of Hearts*, all works containing geographical information.

3 Baḥrain was the major source of pearls in Iran. It still has a pearl industry today.

4 A legend about Buddha.

5 The author is confused because he expects all peoples to accept the Muslim genealogies which go back to Adam and Noah.

6 This metaphor is based on the belief that when a person sleeps his soul wanders outside the body.

7 The Muslim kingdom of Atjeh at the northern tip of Sumatra.

8 A male and female name. Characters from a story in *The Thousand and One Nights*, 'The Sword of the State and Beauty's Novelty'.

9 Fabulous gardens built by Shaddād ibn 'Ād to emulate the gardens of Paradise.

10 Zuhūrī is one of the poets associated with the Indian style in Persian. Jan Rypka in his *Iranische Literatur Geschichte* (Leipzig, 1959, p. 291) seems to believe this poet was almost completely unknown in Iran.

11 Four princesses ruled over Āchī from 1641 to 1699.

12 Prime minister. Term used in Siam as well.

13 The Jin, an order of spirits often spoken of in legend. Solomon commanded his own army of genii.

14 The Seven Sleepers were Christians who, according to legend, entered a cave to escape persecution by the Romans. They slept for a few generations and emerged from the cave when the persecution was over. Their dog, Qiṭmīr, was changed into a human due to his contact with such pious men. Base metals are changed into gold during the final stage of the alchemical process.

15 The author's spelling of Nicobar.

16 The three male names could be taken as words which mean mouse, tablet and gold wind or merely as strange sounds. The female names are actually common Muslim names for women.

17 Khān Bāligh, which gives its name to this paper, is the Cambaluc of Marco Polo or modern-day Peking. The name is of mongol origin.

18 All three heroes are from the Shāhnāma of Firdawsī.

19 The 'Abbāsid Caliphate which succeeded the Umayyids and reigned from 749 to 1258. Hārūnu'r-Rashīd's rule was one of the high points of the dynasty (786–808). He persecuted the Iranian house of Barmak, which had grown too powerful in the affairs of state.

20 Rakhan or Arakan was the name of the coastal strip of Burma north of the Irawady.

21 One of the suras of the Quran is called the Fig. The Prophet swears by the fig and the olive that his words are sent from God.

22 'P'an Ku is frequently described as separating the heavens and the earth, and as forming the sun, the moon and plants and animals.' *The Chinese, Their History and Culture*, K. S. Latourette, New York, Macmillan, 1947, p. 37.

23 The description which our author gives of the fall of Changapchīn is no doubt a re-telling of stories he heard in Siam about the fall of the Ming dynasty and the rise of the Manchus.

24 An area in Afghanistan noted for its fine rubies.

25 From Hāfiẓ.

26 Ibid.

27 The Manchus were a Mongolian race.

28 The Ming dynasty fell in 1644.

29 21 December 1686.

30 The groom, Heaven, is soliciting several wives at once—the turning wheel of the heavens who is personified as an old woman, and the Pleiades, a group of stars, each one considered a beautiful young girl.

31 The image is based on Siam appearing worse than death itself.

32 The port Cochin on the Malabar coast.

33   Jamīdu'th-Thānī is the same as the Muslim month Jumādā 'l-Ukhrā.
8 April 1688.
34   14 May 1688·

The case of Abū'l-Ḥasan

1   The prosperous kingdom of Ḥaidarābād was the last part of the subcontinent of India to resist the Mughal expansion. The Mughal emperor
referred to throughout the account is Aurangzīb.
2   Sayyid Muẓaffar was a general who gave support to Abu'l-Ḥasan.
Mīr Jumla was an Iranian and one of the ablest ministers of the Mughal
emperor, Aurangzīb.
3   Madanna, who was assassinated in 1686.
4   A sayyid is someone who claims descent from the Prophet's family.
5   The Mughals were Sunnīs, and Aurangzīb was especially zealous in
promoting orthodoxy.
6   This reference to Baṣra is not clear to me: ba'd az kharābī baṣra.
7   In 1687 Abū'l-Ḥasan flees the army of Aurangzīb and takes refuge in
the fortress of Golkonda which was near Ḥaidarābād.
8   A metaphor based on the practice of staining oneself with indigo as a
protective measure against the evil eye.
9   Shāh 'Ālam was arrested and kept in prison until 1695.
10   Bījāpūr fell on 12 September 1686, and that was all that stood between
Aurangzīb and Golkonda.
11   Muḥammad Ibrāhīm was the highest ranking noble to desert Abū
'l-Ḥasan and he was appointed Mahābat Khān by Aurangzīb.
12   Babur, the founder of the Mughal dynasty, traced his lineage back to
Tīmūr.
13   Muḥammad Akbar, Aurangzīb's fourth son, fled India and took
refuge in Iran in 1682. In the sixteenth century Humāyūn, the son of
Babur, fled India and took refuge at the court of Shāh Ṭahmāsp.

Weights and Measures

1 farsakh = 4 miles
1 tūmān = 10,000 dīnārs
1 tūmān = £3 6s. 8d., 1677 (*Hobson-Jobson*, Yule and Burnell)
1 catty (kātī) = generally 1⅓ lbs (*Webster's Unabridged Dictionary*)
1 royal man (man-i-shāhī) = 14 lbs (Hintze, *Islamische Gewichte*)
1 hūn = 630 grams weight or 577·5 grams pure silver (*Hobson-Jobson*,
Yule and Burnell)

Author's usage

10 bahārs = 350 royal mans, p. 171.
30 kātīs = 6 mans, p. 91.
1 tūmān = 5 kātīs

INDEX

'Abdu'r-Razzāq (former Iranian minister), 97
Abū'l-Ḥasan (governor of Ḥaidarābād), 234–40
Āchī, 174; gold, 175–6; king, 176; slaves, 177; attacks by Franks, 179–81
Adam, fall of, 170
Aloes wood, 151
Ambergris, 154–5
Andaman, 181–5
Āqā Muḥammad Astarābādī (former Iranian minister), 55, 98; punished, 100–1; sons, 59, 101–2; successors, 102
Authorship, 17

Bandar 'Abbās, 25, 233
Barber, shipwrecked, and magic spring, 183–5
Betel nut, 154
Bījāpūr, 236; fate of governor, 239

Camphor, 152–3
Cannibals, 182
Cat with the evil eye, 166
Ceylon, 168–73; elephants and pearls, 168; see also Dutch; Nahādān
Changapchīn, 205
Chelebī (governor of Sūhān), 50–1
Chīn and Māchīn, 87–8, 203
China, 203–17; debauchery and oppression, 205–7; famine, 207–8
Chinapatan, 33
Crocodiles, 164–5

Delegates, 20, 48, 85
Dīv, 224–5
Dutch: in Ceylon, 167; interested in Andaman, 185; take ports from Macassars, 188; expose Portuguese in Japan, 192; win favor in Japan, 193; concessions in Japan, 194; in Kūchī, 219; take Kūchī from Portuguese, 223

Elephants: ceremonies of the hunt, 65; king's retinue, 66; hunting site, 66; how the Siamese catch and tame elephants, 67; hunting with beaters, 78–9; elephants promised to Iran, 82–3; trade, 150

English: ship, 27; in India, 33–41; rent Chinapatan, 33; entertain embassy, 34; king dies, 36; elaborate party, 37; women, 37–9; religion, 40–1; war with Siam, 111; blockade Sūrat, 228–9; escort embassy to Mumbāī, 228–9

Fish, 163–4
Flying cat, 166
Frank minister, see Phaulkon
Frank religion, 40–1

Good rich man, 209, 213

Ḥaidarābād: fall of, 234–40; at war with Mughals, 236; fortress of Golkonda betrayed, 238; reward for the traitors, 239
Ḥājī Salīm (Siamese king's envoy to Iran), 20; exposed by Phaulkon, 104; arrested, 105; comes short in his accounts, 105
Ḥusain Beg (chosen ambassador), 20, 47–8
Ḥusain Beg (betrayer of Golkonda), 237–9
Hunting: elephants, 66–8; mountain cows, goats, 70; tiger, 72–3; birds, 73

Ibrāhīm Beg (Ḥusain Beg's replacement as ambassador), 58, 61–4
Iranian and fig tree, 202
Iranians: community in Siam meets embassy outside Sūhān, 51; loss of power, 58; lack of unity, 102; Siamese king's suspicion of them, 60; how they helped king to throne, 77, 94–7; Iranians in Siam before present king, 94; Iranian guard from India, 100; an Iranian and his lawsuit, 123–5; an Iranian with a title, 141–3; a second Iranian with a title, 143; Iranian minister's daily audience with Siamese king, 144; description of Iranian king's horses, 80–1
Islands, 159; fish, 163–4; tides, 161–3

Jalang, 49
Japan, 188–9; precious metals, 189–90; Portuguese deceits, 191–3; Dutch, 192–4; foreign merchants, 193; brothels, 195; swords, 196–7; Chinese craftsmen, 197; money, 197–8

249